The South China Sea Maritime Dispute

The South China Sea is a major strategic waterway for trade and oil shipments to Japan and Korea, as well as southern China. It has been the focus of a maritime dispute that has continued now for over six decades, with competing claims from China, Vietnam, the Philippines, Indonesia and Brunei. Recently, China has become more assertive in pressing its claims – harassing Vietnamese fishing vessels and seizing reefs in the Philippine claim zone. China has insisted that it has 'indisputable sovereignty' over the area and has threatened to enforce its claim. All of this is unsettling and draws in the United States, which is concerned about freedom of navigation in the area. The US has been supporting the Philippines and has been developing security ties with Vietnam as a check upon China. This book examines the conflict potential of the current dispute, discusses how the main claimants and the United States view the issue, and assesses the prospects for a resolution of the problem.

Leszek Buszynski is a Visiting Fellow at the National Security College, Australian National University, Canberra, Australia.

Christopher B. Roberts is Associate Professor and Director of Executive Education within the School of Humanities and Social Sciences at the University of New South Wales (Australian Defence Force Academy campus), Australia.

Routledge Security in Asia Pacific Series

Series Editors

Leszek Buszynski, Strategic and Defence Studies Centre, the Australian National University

William Tow, Australian National University

Security issues have become more prominent in the Asia Pacific region because of the presence of global players, rising great powers, and confident middle powers, which intersect in complicated ways. This series puts forward important new work on key security issues in the region. It embraces the roles of the major actors, their defense policies and postures, and their security interaction over the key issues of the region. It includes coverage of the United States, China, Japan, Russia and the Koreas, as well as the middle powers of ASEAN and South Asia. It also covers issues relating to environmental and economic security, as well as transnational actors and regional groupings.

The South China Sea Maritime Dispute

Political, legal and regional perspectives

**Edited by
Leszek Buszynski and
Christopher B. Roberts**

Routledge
Taylor & Francis Group

LONDON AND NEW YORK

First published 2015
by Routledge
2 Park Square, Milton Park, Abingdon, Oxfordshire OX14 4RN

and by Routledge
711 Third Avenue, New York, NY 10017

First issued in paperback 2016

Routledge is an imprint of the Taylor & Francis Group, an informa business

British Library Cataloguing in Publication Data
A catalogue record for this book is available from the British Library

Library of Congress Cataloging in Publication Data
The South China Sea maritime dispute: political, legal and regional
   perspectives/edited by Leszek Buszynski and Christopher B. Roberts.
   pages cm.– (Routledge security in Asia Pacific series; 28)
   Includes bibliographical references and index.
   1. South China Sea – International status. I. Buszynski, Leszek, editor
   of compilation. II. Roberts, Christopher B., editor of compilation.
   III. Buszynski, Leszek. Origins and development of the South China
   Sea maritime dispute. Contains (work):
   KZA1692.S68 2014
   341.4'480916472 – dc23
   2014012825

ISBN 13: 978-0-415-78760-4 (pbk)
ISBN 13: 978-0-415-72288-9 (hbk)

Typeset in Times New Roman
by Florence Production Ltd, Stoodleigh, Devon, UK

Contents

Illustrations

Figures

Maps

Notes on contributors

Leszek Buszynski is a Visiting Fellow at the National Security College, Australian National University. From 1997 to 2010, he was professor of International Relations, at the International University of Japan (IUJ). From 1997 to 2001, he was Dean of the Graduate School of International Relations at the IUJ and concurrently Director of the IUJ Research Institute. He has published widely on Asia Pacific security issues, including 'The South China Sea Maritime Dispute: Legality, Power, and Conflict Resolution', *Asian Journal of Peacekeeping*, 1(1), 2013, and 'The South China Sea: Oil, Maritime Claims, and U.S.–China Strategic Rivalry', *The Washington Quarterly* 35(2), March 2012.

Renato Cruz De Castro is a Professor in the International Studies Department, De La Salle University, Manila, and the holder of the Charles Lui Keung Professorial Chair in China Studies. He has a PhD from the University of South Carolina, where he was a Fulbright Scholar in 2001. His published work includes 'The Philippines in 2011: Muddling through a Year of Learning and Adjustment', *Asian Survey*, 52(1), January/February 2012, 'The Aquino Administration's 2011 Decision to Shift Philippine Defense Policy from Internal Security to Territorial Defense: The Impact of the South China Sea Dispute', *Korean Journal of Defense Analysis*, 24(1), March 2012, 'The Obama Administration's (Neo-Liberal) Engagement Policy in East Asia: Implications for U.S.–China Relations in the 21st Century', *Issues and Studies*, 47(2), June 2011, and 'Weakness and Gambits in Philippine Foreign Policy in the 21st Century', *Pacific Affairs*, 83(4), December 2010.

Do Thanh Hai is a doctoral candidate at the Strategic and Defence Studies Centre, Australian National University, before which he was a researcher with the Institute for Foreign Policy and Strategic Studies, Diplomatic Academy of Vietnam, a think tank affiliated to the Ministry for Foreign Affairs, Vietnam. He holds a Bachelor of Arts in International Relations from the Institute of International Relations in Vietnam and a Master of Arts from the European Master's Course 'Global Studies – A European Perspective' jointly offered by the University of Vienna and the University of Wroclaw. He was awarded an Erasmus Mundus Scholarship and the Award for Best Graduate of the Year 2008 by the Erasmus Mundus Global Studies Consortium.

Ralf Emmers is Associate Professor at the S. Rajaratnam School of International Studies (RSIS), Nanyang Technological University (NTU), Singapore. He is the author of *Resource Management and Contested Territories in East Asia*, Palgrave Macmillan, 2013, *Geopolitics and Maritime Territorial Disputes in East Asia*, Routledge, 2010, and *Cooperative Security and the Balance of Power in ASEAN and the ARF*, RoutledgeCurzon, 2003.

Jian Zhang is a Senior Lecturer in International and Political Studies in the School of Humanities and Social Sciences at the Australian Defence Force Academy, the University of New South Wales, Australia. He received his Bachelor's and Master's degrees from Zhejiang University in China and completed his PhD at Murdoch University, Western Australia. He has held teaching and research positions in the School of Economics at Zhejiang University and the Asia Research Centre of Murdoch University. His primary research interests are Chinese politics and foreign and security policy, Australia–China relations, international relations in Asia-Pacific, and Asia-Pacific regionalism. He is the author of *Government and Market in China: A Local Perspective*, Nova Science Press, 2004.

Christopher B. Roberts is Associate Professor and Director of Executive Education within the School of Humanities and Social Sciences at the University of New South Wales (Australian Defence Force Academy campus). Christopher specialises in Southeast Asian security, politics, and institutional developments. Notable publications include four sole authored and edited books – *Indonesia's Ascent: Power, Leadership, and the Regional Order* (Palgrave Macmillan, forthcoming), *ASEAN's Myanmar Crisis: Challenges to the Pursuit of a Security Community* (ISEAS, 2010), and *ASEAN Regionalism* (Routledge, 2012) – as well as an ASEAN commissioned (but AusAid funded) report on the East Asia Summit.

Donald R. Rothwell is Professor of International Law and Head of School at the ANU College of Law, Australian National University. His research has a specific focus on law of the sea, law of the polar regions and implementation of international law within Australia. His books include *Law of the Sea*, Edward Elgar, 2013, *Antarctic Security in the Twenty-First Century: Legal and Policy Perspectives*, with Alan Hemmings and Karen Scott, Routledge, 2012, *The International Law of the Sea*, with Tim Stephens, Hart, 2010, and *The Polar Regions and the Development of International Law*, Cambridge University Press, 1996. A co-edited book work with Alex Oude Elferink and Erik Molenaar, entitled The Law of the Sea and Polar Regions: Interactions between Global and Regional Regimes, is in press.

Clive H. Schofield is Director of Research and Professor at the Australian Centre for Ocean Resources and Security (ANCORS), University of Wollongong, Australia. He is presently an Australian Research Council Future Fellow and is Academic Leader of the University of Wollongong's Global Challenge research initiative on Sustaining Coastal and Marine Zones. He holds a PhD in Geography from the University of Durham, UK, and also holds an LLM in International Law from the University of British Columbia. He is one of the foremost authorities on maritime boundary delimitation and security in the Asia-Pacific region, including disputes over islands, and geotechnical and spatial analysis of claims to straight baselines around the world and their impact on maritime jurisdiction and ocean management. He is co-editor, with Bruce Elleman and Stephen Kotkin, of *Beijing's Power and Borders: Twenty Neighbors in Asia*, M. E. Sharpe, 2012, and is co-author, with Victor Prescott, of *The Maritime Political Boundaries of the World*, Brill, 2005.

Brendan Taylor is Head of the Strategic and Defence Studies Centre, Australian National University. He is a specialist on great power strategic relations in the Asia-Pacific, economic sanctions and Asian security architecture. His publications have featured in such leading academic journals as *International Affairs*, *Survival*, *Asian Security*, *Review of International Studies* and the *Australian Journal of International Affairs*. He is the author of *Sanctions as Grand Strategy*, which was published in the International Institute for Strategic Studies (IISS) Adelphi series, as well as *American Sanctions in the Asia Pacific*, Routledge, 2010. He is also the editor of *Australia as an Asia-Pacific Regional Power*, Routledge, 2007, *Insurgent Intellectual: Essays in Honour of Professor Desmond Ball*, ISEAS, 2012, and *Bilateralism, Multilateralism and Asia-Pacific Security*, Routledge, 2013.

Michael Wesley is Professor of National Security and Director of the School of International, Political and Strategic Studies at the Australian National University. He was Executive Director of the Lowy Institute for International Policy from June 2009 to August 2012 and Director of the Griffith Asia Institute at Griffith University, Brisbane, Australia. He completed his PhD at the University of St Andrews in Scotland. He is a Visiting Professor at the University of Hong Kong, and was a Lecturer at the University of New South Wales, Sydney, Australia. He was an official with the Australian government at the Office of National Assessments. He is the author of *There Goes the Neighbourhood: Australia and the Rise of Asia*, UNSW Press, 2011, and *The Howard Paradox: Australian Diplomacy in Asia 1996–2006*, ABC Books, 2007.

Acknowledgements

The editors would like to thank Michael L'Estrange, Director of the National Security College at the Australian National University, for approving the funding for the workshop on the South China Sea on 28 March 2013, upon which this book was based. Many thanks also to the staff of the college for their unstinting help and assistance in arranging the workshop and also for taking care of the many tasks and duties that followed. The college also funded the fieldwork undertaken by the editors in Kuala Lumpur, Phnom Penh, Hanoi and Beijing in April and June of the same year, for which we are most grateful. Many pertinent ideas, perceptive insights and percipient observations were gleaned from interviews, meetings and conservations that were conducted during the fieldwork, both on a strictly formal basis and in a more casual atmosphere. Most of the interviewees will remain nameless by their own choice, as required by their position and office, but some can be named and thanked for their time and contribution. A particular thank you to Prince Norodom Sirivudh for his explanation of Cambodia's position in ASEAN, Dr Tranh Troung Thuy of the Diplomatic Academy of Vietnam for his explanation of the Vietnamese position, and Dr Wang Hanling of Centre for Ocean Affairs and the Law of the Sea in Beijing for his views of China's policy towards the issue, and also for introducing us to Guangxi cuisine.

Abbreviations

ADMM	ASEAN Defence Ministerial Meeting
AMM	ASEAN Ministerial Meeting
ARF	ASEAN Regional Forum
ASEAN	Association of Southeast Asian Nations
CAFTA	China–ASEAN Free Trade Agreement
CCP	Chinese Communist Party
CLCS	Commission on the Limits of the Continental Shelf
CNOOC	China National Offshore Oil Corporation
CoC	Code of Conduct
CPV	Communist Party of Vietnam
DoC	Declaration on Conduct
EAS	East Asia Summit
EEZ	exclusive economic zone
ICJ	International Court of Justice
ITLOS	International Tribunal for the Law of the Sea
JMSU	Agreement on Joint Marine Seismic Undertaking
LCS	littoral combat ships
LNG	liquefied natural gas
LTE	low-tide elevation
nm	nautical mile
PAF	Philippine Armed forces
PLA	People's Liberation Army
PLA-N	People's Liberation Army Navy
PNOC	Philippine National Oil Company
PRC	People's Republic of China
PSC	Production-Sharing Contract
QDR	Quadrennial Defense Review
SEANWFZ	Southeast Asia Nuclear Weapons Free Zone
SIPRI	Stockholm Peace Research Institute
SOM	Senior Officials Meeting
TAC	Treaty of Amity and Cooperation
TPP	Trans-Pacific Partnership

UNCLOS	United Nations Convention on the Law of the Sea
USGS	United States Geological Survey
VFA	Visiting Forces Agreement
ZOPFAN	Zone of Peace, Freedom and Neutrality

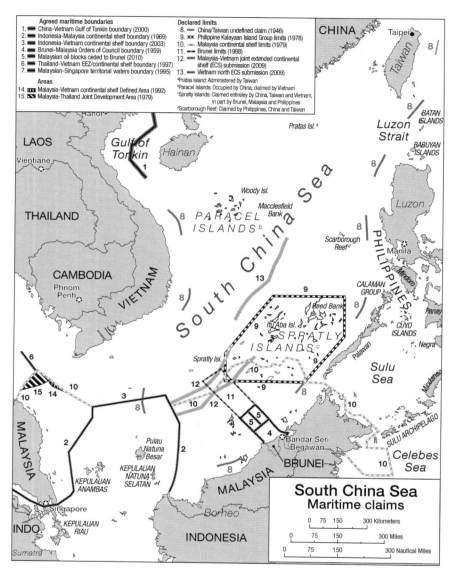

Agreed maritime boundaries
1. ▬ China-Vietnam Gulf of Tonkin boundary (2000)
2. ▬ Indonesia-Malaysia continental shelf boundary (1969)
3. ▬ Indonesia-Vietnam continental shelf boundary (2003)
4. ▬ Brunei-Malaysia Orders of Council boundary (1959)
5. ▬ Malaysian oil blocks ceded to Brunei (2010)
6. ▬ Thailand-Vietnam EEZ/continental shelf boundary (1997)
7. ▬ Malaysian-Singapore territorial waters boundary (1995)

Areas
14. ▥ Malaysia-Vietnam continental shelf Defined Area (1992)
15. ▧ Malaysia-Thailand Joint Development Area (1979)

Declared limits
8. ▬ China/Taiwan undefined claim (1946)
9. ✕✕ Philippine Kalayaan Island Group limits (1978)
10. ═ Malaysia continental shelf limits (1979)
11. ▬ Brunei limits (1988)
12. ▬ Malaysia-Vietnam joint extended continental shelf (ECS) submission (2009)
13. ▬ Vietnam north ECS submission (2009)

[a] Pratas Island: Administered by Taiwan
[b] Paracel Islands: Occupied by China, claimed by Vietnam
[c] Spratly Islands: Claimed entireley by China, Taiwan and Vietnam, in part by Brunei, Malaysia and Philippines
[d] Scarborough Reef: Claimed by Philippines, China and Taiwan

South China Sea
Maritime claims

0 75 150 300 Kilometers
0 75 150 300 Miles
0 75 150 300 Nautical Miles

Map 1 Maritime claims

Source: US Energy Information Administration

Map 2 Official Chinese map of the South China Sea with the nine-dash line

Source: Stein Tønnesson, 'China and the South China Sea: A Peace Proposal', Security Dialogue, September 2000, 31: 307–326

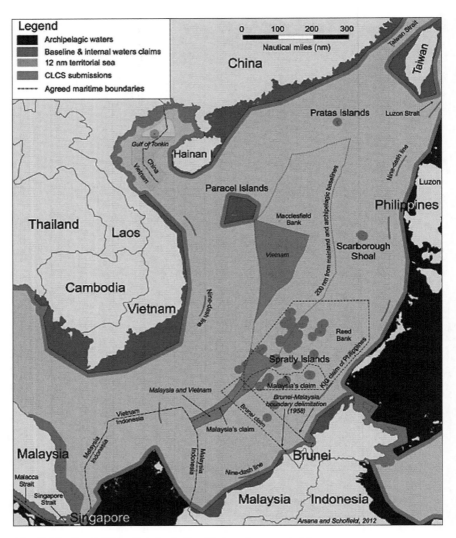

Map 3 The South China Sea, including Vietnam's current claim

Source: This map was prepared by Clive Schofield and Andi Arsana of the Australian National Centre for Ocean Resources and Security and is reproduced with permission from the *American Journal of International Law* © 2013 American Society of International Law. All rights reserved.

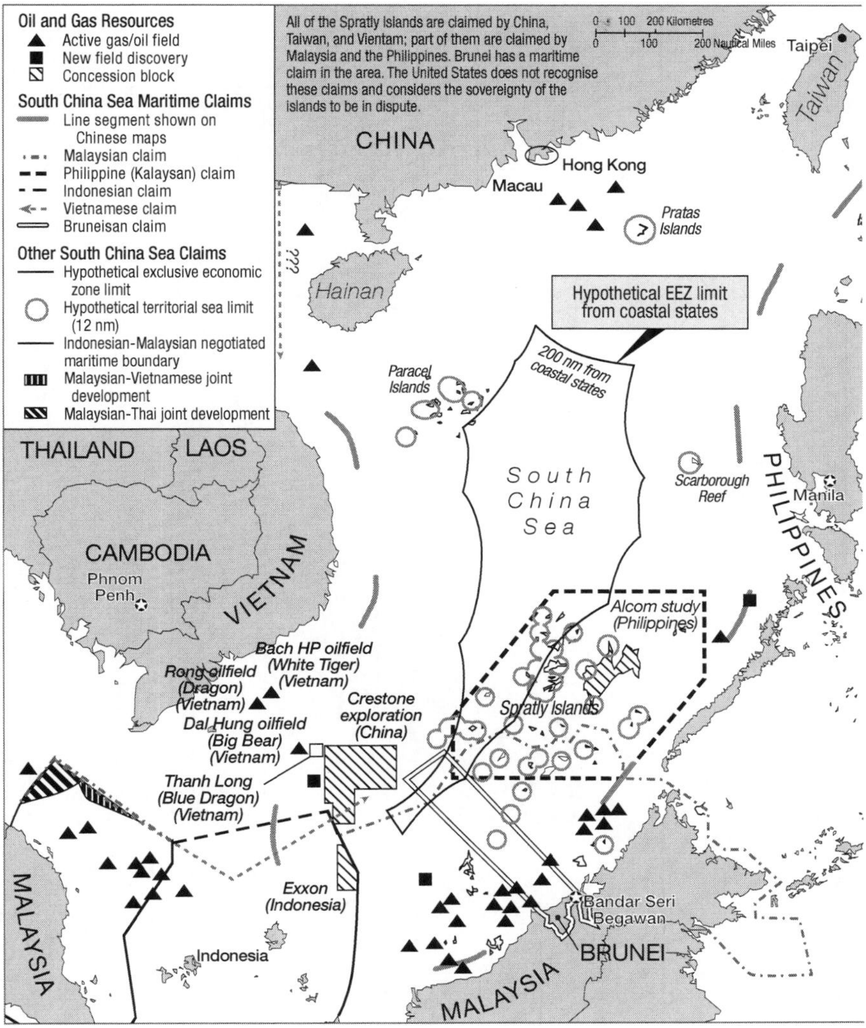

Oil and Gas Resources
▲ Active gas/oil field
■ New field discovery
◨ Concession block

South China Sea Maritime Claims
━━━ Line segment shown on Chinese maps
·━·━ Malaysian claim
━ ━ Philippine (Kalaysan) claim
─ ─ Indonesian claim
◄─·─ Vietnamese claim
═══ Bruneisan claim

Other South China Sea Claims
──── Hypothetical exclusive economic zone limit
◯ Hypothetical territorial sea limit (12 nm)
──── Indonesian-Malaysian negotiated maritime boundary
▥▥▥ Malaysian-Vietnamese joint development
▧▧▧ Malaysian-Thai joint development

All of the Spratly Islands are claimed by China, Taiwan, and Vientam; part of them are claimed by Malaysia and the Philippines. Brunei has a maritime claim in the area. The United States does not recognise these claims and considers the sovereignty of the islands to be in dispute.

0 100 200 Kilometres
0 100 200 Nautical Miles

CHINA
Hong Kong
Macau
Pratas Islands
Taipei
Taiwan

Hainan
???

Paracel Islands

South China Sea

Hypothetical EEZ limit from coastal states

200 nm from coastal states

Scarborough Reef
Manila
PHILIPPINES

THAILAND   LAOS

CAMBODIA
Phnom Penh

VIETNAM

Bach HP oilfield (White Tiger) (Vietnam)
Rong oilfield (Dragon) (Vietnam)
Dai Hung oilfield (Big Bear) (Vietnam)
Crestone exploration (China)
Thanh Long (Blue Dragon) (Vietnam)

Alcom study (Philippines)

Spratly Islands

Exxon (Indonesia)

Indonesia

Bandar Seri Begawan

MALAYSIA   BRUNEI

MALAYSIA

Map 4 South China Sea, showing EEZ claims
Source: CIA Maps

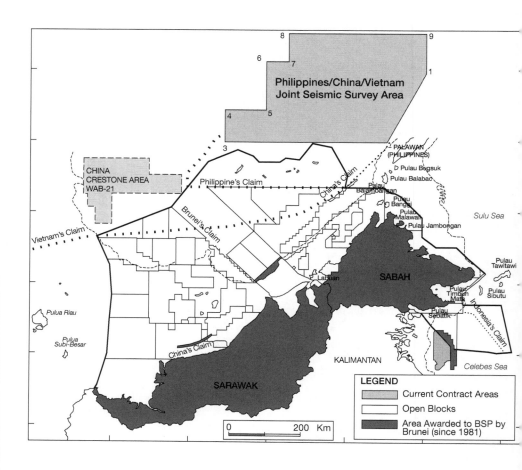

Map 5 The Joint Marine Seismic Undertaking 1
Source: www.southchinasea.org

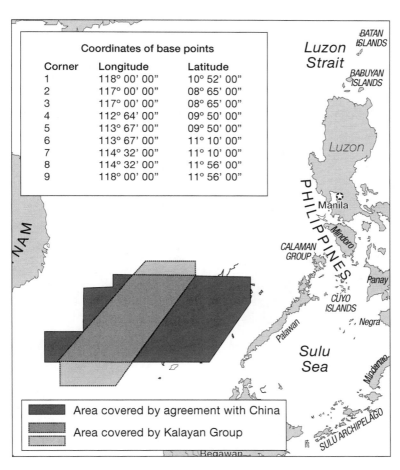

Coordinates of base points		
Corner	Longitude	Latitude
1	118° 00' 00"	10° 52' 00"
2	117° 00' 00"	08° 65' 00"
3	117° 00' 00"	08° 65' 00"
4	112° 64' 00"	09° 50' 00"
5	113° 67' 00"	09° 50' 00"
6	113° 67' 00"	11° 10' 00"
7	114° 32' 00"	11° 10' 00"
8	114° 32' 00"	11° 56' 00"
9	118° 00' 00"	11° 56' 00"

Area covered by agreement with China

Area covered by Kalayan Group

Map 6 The Joint Marine Seismic Undertaking 2

Source: Yvonne Chua of VERA Files (www.verafiles.org) and Ellen Tordesillas (www.ellentordesillas.com)

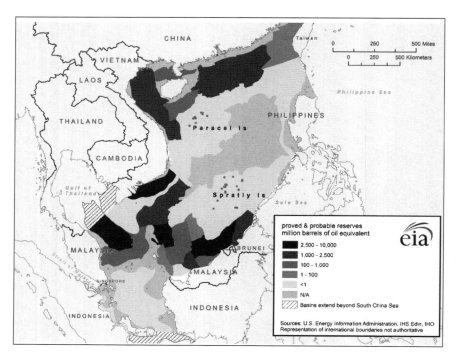

Map 7 Proven and probable oil reserves

Source: US Energy Information Administration

Introduction

The chapters in this volume are based on papers presented at a workshop on the South China Sea held on 28 March 2013, sponsored by the National Security College, the Australian National University, Canberra ACT. They have been revised according to feedback and comments received and suitably updated. The stimulus for the workshop was concern over the development of events there and the conviction, as expressed by some commentators, that the area was a potential 'flashpoint', which, under certain circumstances, could get out of control. Some see the issue as a case of Chinese pressure upon the Association of Southeast Asian Nations (ASEAN) claimants that are calling upon external support from the US and Australia. China, they say, is becoming expansionist and is pressing the ASEAN claimants to recognise its claim to the area by resorting to deliberately low-key pressure tactics against them. Others see the issue as a problem that could be resolved by negotiation and within the framework of international law. They argue that China is simply pressing for recognition of its rights to the area and will negotiate with the ASEAN claimants in good faith in time, or, to use a well-known expression often used by Chinese representatives, 'when conditions are ripe'. Some thought that the dispute should be looked at historically and that Southeast Asian cultures had traditionally deferred to China and would do so again over this issue. The ASEAN countries would learn to live with Chinese primacy, as they have always done. Still others are undecided and wait for events to play out before committing themselves to any particular view. Presenters at the workshop adopted various perspectives, which, one way or another, touched upon these views, depending on their professional background or their country affiliation.

Chapter 1, by Leszek Buszynski, examines the development of the dispute over the past few decades. It is necessary to remind ourselves that this was not always a major dispute in quite the same way that we see it now, and that it developed in stages. In the past, the South China Sea was China's southern maritime frontier, and not included within the borders of the empire. China is today engaged in an effort to transform what was a frontier zone outside the dynastic state into national territory, just like Taiwan or Tibet. Chapter 2 is by Clive Schofield, who analyses the conflicting and overlapping claims to the South China Sea from spatial, legal and geopolitical perspectives. He outlines the geographical context of the South China Sea to explain the factors that inform and underlie the South China Sea dispute. Chapter 3 is by Donald R. Rothwell, who examines the legal side of the dispute, specifically the capacity of the features in the South China Sea to generate maritime zones consistent with the 1982 United Nations Convention on the Law of the Sea (UNCLOS). One issue is whether these maritime features are Article 121 (1) islands, or Article 121 (3) rocks. A second issue is whether these features will be considered for the purposes of delimiting the exclusive economic zone (EEZ) or continental shelf maritime boundaries. Chapter 4 is by Jian Zhang, who explains China's perspective. He notes that China's assertive actions have been undertaken by civilian governmental and maritime law enforcement agencies, which could be described as 'administrative diplomacy'. Jian argues that within China, there is an increasing recognition of the importance and legitimacy of international law and UNCLOS, and that China may consider a diplomatic and even legal solution to the dispute in the future. In Chapter 5, Vietnam's perspective is explained by Do Thanh Hai, who argues that Hanoi has redefined its claims to maritime zones in the South China Sea to ensure consistency with international law and UNCLOS. Vietnam has clarified the limits of its EEZ and continental shelf claim, as measured from the baseline of the mainland, and may be willing to accept that the Spratly and Paracel features may not be entitled to full maritime zones. Vietnam has been pressed by China, which has made Vietnamese leaders aware of the importance of international law as a support for their own claims to the area. The Philippine position is outlined by Renato Cruz De Castro in Chapter 6. In this chapter, he examines China's challenge to the Philippine claim in the South China Sea, which led up to the two-month-long standoff between Philippine and Chinese civilian vessels in the Scarborough Shoal. He notes that the Philippines was the first to bring the South China Sea issue to adjudication when, in January 2013, it appealed to an Arbitral Tribunal under Annex VII of UNCLOS. In Chapter 7, Christopher B. Roberts analyses ASEAN's role in the dispute and the reasons for the divisions in ASEAN over the issue. ASEAN had been relatively unified during the 1990s, but since China has become more assertive over the South China Sea issue, it has become disturbingly divided between pro-Beijing members and claimants such as Vietnam and the Philippines, both of which seek ASEAN solidarity over the issue. In Chapter 8, Ralf Emmers adumbrates the US position over the South China Sea in the context of its rebalancing effort towards the Asia-Pacific. He notes that the US stresses the importance of freedom of navigation in the area and the need to uphold the key international rules for defining territorial claims in the South China Sea. In Chapter 9, Michael Wesley traces the implications for Australia and argues that Australia's disinterest in the issue is unsustainable, and that it has to become more ambitious. He stresses that Australia should promote a sustainable solution to the South China Sea dispute in recognition that its interests are affected. In Chapter 10, Brendan Taylor compares the South China Sea with other potential conflict zones in the region, such as the Korean Peninsula and the East Sea, and argues that despite the attention it receives, it should not be considered a crisis yet.

What kind of solution can there be that has not been discussed before? In Chapter 11, Leszek Buszynski and Christopher B. Roberts distinguish between stabilisation and resolution of the issue. Proposals to stabilise the issue to prevent conflict and escalation include Code of Conduct (CoC), which has been promoted by ASEAN, and an Incidents at Sea Agreement (INCSEA) of the kind that the two superpowers the US and the Soviet Union, concluded in 1972. Disturbing incidents have occurred in the South China Sea such as cutting the cables of Vietnamese vessels and the harassment of fishing vessels, which could result in accidental conflict. An INCSEA would detail procedures to avoid close contact between vessels in the area to prevent unintended clashes. Resolution of the dispute, however, is much more ambitious. Proposals to resolve the dispute include a legal resolution based on UNCLOS, joint development of the hydrocarbon resources, second-track diplomacy and a cooperative maritime regime. All had considerable appeal at the time they were raised, but none has been implemented. Despite the appeal of a legal resolution, China has not defined its claim in legal terms and shows no signs of doing so. This chapter calls for a UN conference on the South China Sea, which would deal with the legal situation of semi-enclosed areas where claims overlap. It would combine the benefits of a cooperative maritime regime with a legal resolution, and it argues that if there were to be a resolution of the issue, it would come about in no other way.

1 The origins and development of the South China Sea maritime dispute

Leszek Buszynski

Introduction

The South China Sea maritime dispute has evolved considerably over the past five decades. Once it was once a regional dispute over maritime claims left over from the past that did not trouble the main business of governments at the time. It escalated in importance for all governments concerned as maritime territory became coveted, not only for the resources found there, but for the purpose of state completion, as defined borders and the possession of territory have become symbols of statehood. The need to define maritime borders was an accompaniment to the task of state formation in the postcolonial era. Modern statehood is understood in terms of sovereignty, which is the right to rule over territory, as well as defined borders that mark the political and geographic boundaries of that territory. This created particular difficulties for the decolonised world, where frontiers were often vague and frequently overlapping. The legal principle of *uti possidetis* governed the formation of land borders and meant that decolonised states would inherit their borders from the colonial power at the time of independence. States were decolonised, however, without defined maritime borders, and the process of their definition was, for the most part, a postcolonial experience. The People's Republic of China (PRC) inherited the borders of the premodern Chinese state where they existed and claimed maritime borders as a similar inheritance. For the other claimants, Vietnam, the Philippines and Malaysia, the colonial powers had left them with no clear maritime borders, yet the completion of the process of state formation required that they declare them, particularly in the South China Sea. The result has been a scramble for occupation of islands and reefs among the claimants to demonstrate their claims.

The escalation of what is now known as the South China Sea maritime dispute has been the result of China's assertion of its claim to the area. Indeed, China's inveterate consistency over the issue has been remarkable over the past decades, and despite the predictions that China would negotiate the issue and compromise with the other claimants, it has persisted in its claim. China's assertiveness has been cyclical and comes in lurches, alternating with periods of quiescence and declarations of good neighbourliness, which others mistakenly understand as a willingness to negotiate and settle for the existing status quo. China has been motivated by various factors at different times; initially, it was the desire to exclude rival powers from the area, whether France, Japan and, much later, the Soviet Union. Then, when hydrocarbon resources were discovered in the area, it was oil and gas. Later, as the barely suppressed forces of nationalism were released by economic success, it became a matter of appropriating an outlying area within national borders as state completion. What was once a remote area of little inter-est to China became transformed into national territory that was under 'illegal' foreign occupation and had to be returned to the motherland. Accordingly, China has resorted to pressure tactics against the ASEAN claimants, Vietnam and the Philippines in particular, to recognise its claim. The dispute has become an arena of shadow great power rivalry as China's assertiveness draws in external powers, the US, Japan and also India.

The South China Sea as China's southern maritime frontier

Sovereignty and demarcated borders are modern notions. Premodern dynastic states had frontiers as protective spaces around their core territory from which threats would be excluded. Full control over the frontier was not required as long as rivals were kept at a distance. China's northern frontier with the Mongol tribes that continually threatened the empire was not a line, but a zone within which con-trol shifted according to the vicissitudes of military campaigns.[1] Frontiers were governed indirectly and local leaders served as buffer zones protecting the Han core of China against the threat posed by the nomadic tribes. There was no tradition of direct rule in the frontier zone, as many frontier states maintained relations with other states, as well as with the centre of empire.[2] On the other hand, a border in the Ming period was clearly defined and would have garrisons at regular intervals, sentry posts and border guards. At the border, officials would carry out the inspection of foreign embassies and tribute missions to Beijing, and would also prevent Chinese leaving without permission. China's sea border followed the Chinese coast, where local officials would inspect foreign ships and their cargoes. They would look for the *kanhe*, a document issued by the Ministry of Rites to show that the mission was genuine.[3]

The task for China since the late nineteenth century has been to recast an ancient empire system with outlying frontiers, including distant ethnic groups, into a modern state with sovereignty over territory and the establishment of clear and demarcated borders. This process has been called national territorialisation, and involves the absorption of ethnic groups into the dominant nationality, and the integration of frontier zones and borderlands into a modern nation state.[4] China has managed to negotiate defined land borders with most of its neighbours, but maritime borders are another story, as the outlying oceanic frontiers through which China's trade passed were distant from the centre and often shared with other states. The Chinese have reached to their ancient past to justify the conversion of maritime frontiers, over which they had little control, into maritime borders, over which they would be able exercise full sovereignty and control. One such area that has become a critical dispute because of the involvement of other claimants and external powers is the South China Sea. This was China's southern maritime frontier, an indeterminate area that was distant from the mainland and not part of the empire proper. Oceanic sovereignty, or the extension of state authority over distant sea space, made no sense to the Confucian literati of dynastic China when the sea border was understood as the coastline.[5] The Chinese habitually claim rights of first discovery over the South China Sea, but the difficulty is that while Chinese records mention the Paracels, there are no unambiguous ancient records for the Spratlys. China had little contact with the Spratly Islands, as Chinese trade routes in the South China Sea skirted the area.

Chinese interaction with this distant frontier in the South China Sea was weak. Two major trade routes connected southern China with Southeast Asia; the western route went along the along the Vietnamese coast; the eastern route connected Guangdong and southern China with Luzon and the Philippines; later, it linked up with the galleon trade, which operated between Acapulco, Manila and Southern China from the late sixteenth century until 1815. These two routes were well documented in Chinese sources, but neither traversed the Spratlys, which were known to be dangerous for navigation.[6] One of China's earliest sea maps is the Mao Kun map, dating from the early Ming period in the sixteenth century, which shows only the western sea route, which avoided the Spratlys. The Wang Dayuan text of 1349/50 AD was an early description of the South China Sea, the northern limit of which was the Paracel Islands, then a maritime zone beyong China.[7] There is little historical evidence of Chinese interest in the Spratlys.[8]

As a result of contact and rivalry with the Western colonial powers, the Chinese were compelled to define their maritime interests more clearly. The British were the first to navigate and survey the islands over 1762–1802, and in 1805 the Admiralty published a map of the South China Sea with many of the features named. It was Richard Spratly, the captain of the British Whaler *Cyrus* who visited the area in 1843, who gave his name to one island, as well as the archipelago.[9] At that time, the British interest was limited to surveying and charting, and there was no effort to claim sovereignty over the area. Most important in the definition of Chinese claims was the Sino-French war of 1884–1885 over the Tonkin Gulf, since France did have a specific interest in claiming the area. French intrusion into the Gulf of Tonkin alarmed the Chinese, and in 1902 Guangdong province dispatched three naval vessels to the Paracels under Vice Admiral Wu Ching-yung and Admiral Li Chun. They planted the imperial Chinese flag on several islands and erected a stone monument on North Island.[10] There were other reasons for the Chinese to be anxious, as the Japanese appeared on the scene when Japanese merchant Nishizawa Yoshiji settled on the Pratas Islands to mine the guano deposits of the area. In 1908, Guangdong despatched a second expedition to the Paracels under the same admirals, and in the same year the Pratas and Paracels appeared in maps published by Guangdong province for the first time.[11] A special provincial commission was established to manage and develop the islands, and it recommended that the Paracels be incorporated into Guangdong province. This was delayed by the collapse of the Qin dynasty in 1911, and only came into effect over 1921–1922.[12] Guangdong province sent a third expedition to the Paracels, which included members of a government commission headed by Shen P'eng-fei, which spent 17 days in the area. Shen's report was entitled 'Text of the Report on the Investigation of the Paracel Archipelago', and he wrote that 'the Paracel archipelago is our nation's southernmost territory. However, our people have paid it little attention'.[13] The Shen P'eng-fei report revealed little interest in the Spratlys, even though Hainanese fishermen had been visiting these islands for many years and named the largest island Itu Aba in their local dialect.[14]

China's interest in the Spratlys was awakened by French and Japanese intrusion into the area in the 1930s when it acted to exclude the presence of threatening foreign powers. A Japanese company had begun to fish in the area and to mine the guano deposits in 1917.[15] French action in the area was intended to exclude the Japanese, and in April 1930 France sent the gunboat 'Le Malicieuse' to the Paracels and Spratlys. The French championed the Vietnamese claim to both the Paracels and the Spratlys to give their own colonial rule over the area greater legitimacy. The governor of Indo-China, Pierre Pasquier, supported Vietnamese claims to the Paracels in 1931, and occupied the two main islands in the Spratlys, Itu Aba and Spratly Island. On 26 July 1933, France announced the occupation of nine islands and the annexation of the Spratlys. On 3 July 1938, the French announced the occupation of the Paracels to prevent the Japanese, who were becoming active in the area, from claiming the islands. Again, France declared that it was claiming these islands for the Vietnamese, whose claims to the area they supported. The Japanese, however, displaced the French, who by then were preoccupied with events in Europe. Japan occupied Hainan Island in February 1939, and by the following March occupied the major islands in the Spratlys, which were renamed 'Shinan'. A submarine base was constructed on Itu Aba to attack allied shipping and to support operations in the Philippines and Indo-China while a small garrison occupied Spratly Island.[16] Though the Japanese had claimed the South China Sea and occupied at least six islands, their defeat in the Pacific War resulted in their expulsion. After the end of the war on 9 December 1946, China sent a naval force to the Paracels and Spratlys. Two vessels went to the Paracels and Spratlys, where they removed Japanese markers and planted the Chinese flag over Itu Aba. On 7 April 1949, the Chinese Embassy in Manila declared that a garrison of 150 had been placed on Itu Aba to interdict the arms traffic through Hainan to communist forces.[17] As China fell to the communists, the KMT withdrew from the Paracels, where it had maintained a presence on Woody Island, which was subsequently occupied by the PRC in May 1950.[18] An unresolved issue was who had sovereignty after the Japanese occupation.

The San Francisco Conference was convened in September 1951 to decide the disposition of territories conquered by Japan, including the South China Sea. By this time, China had converted its southern maritime frontier into an area over which it claimed sovereignty according to modern international law. Before the Conference was convened on 15 August 1951, Chinese Foreign Minister Zhou Enlai declared Chinese sovereignty over the South China Sea, including the Spratlys, the Paracels, the Pratas islands and the Macclesfield Bank. Since the modern concept of sovereignty allowed for no half measures or ambiguity, China was obliged to declare full title over an area that was not properly part of the dynastic state, and had to provide a justification that would meet legal criteria. According to Article 2(f) of the treaty that resulted from the Conference, 'Japan renounces all right, title and claim to the Spratly Islands and to the Paracel Islands'. On 7 September, the South Vietnamese delegate to the Conference, Tran Van Huu, asserted Vietnam's claim to the same islands. The Soviet delegate, Deputy Foreign Minister Andre Gromyko, called for the transfer of all the islands of the South China Sea to the PRC, a proposal that was rejected by 46 votes to three.[19] The American delegate, John Foster Dulles, would not accept PRC representation at the conference, nor could he accept Gromyko's proposal. The conference stripped Japan of possession, but did not designate a successor. While the Americans could have transferred the area to the Republic of China as the successor state, that would have created problems with South Vietnam, which they wanted to keep on side against the communists. The inability of the conference to identify where sovereignty lay opened the door to competing claims that today remain unresolved. From then on, China developed and elaborated arguments to support its claim in various ways.[20]

Political declarations and legal claims distinguished

All claimants have made various political declarations of ownership, which, in many respects, fail to meet legal criteria as they have evolved over the years. According to international law, sovereignty over islands is decided by continuous, peaceful and effective occupation, or acts of state administration.[21] This principle was laid down in the Island of Palmas Case by the Permanent Court of Arbitration on 4 April 1928, which dealt with the issue of an island first discovered by Spain but later occupied intermittently by the Netherlands. As successor to Spain in the Philippines, the US claimed sovereignty, but the arbitrator, Max Huber, decided that rights of first discovery remain incomplete unless they are supported by acts of state authority. Whatever rights Spain may have had over the islands, they had lapsed after the failure to exercise those acts of state authority. Huber found in favour of the Netherlands, which could demonstrate peaceful and continuous display of state authority over the island.[22] Similarly, in the El Salvador/Honduras case of 1992, the International Court of Justice (ICJ) examined the evidence of possession, control, and the display and exercise of sovereignty to decide sovereignty. In the Eritrea/Yemen case of 1998, Yemen stressed the importance of 'ancient title' to the islands in dispute. While the court did not dismiss the notion, it referred to the Palmas precedent and used the test of the 'continuous display of governmental authority and presence' to decide ownership of the islands.[23] In the Malaysia/Indonesia dispute over Ligitan and Sipadan, the ICJ, in 2002, noted Malaysia's efforts to regulate and control the collection of turtle eggs and its maintenance of lighthouses constructed in the colonial era on both islands. It decided that these were acts of administration that revealed an 'intention to exercise state functions in respect of the two islands'.[24]

According to these principles, China's claim to the islands in the South China Sea cannot be supported by international law, though it may claim sovereignty over the Paracel Islands by occupation. China has occupied Woody Island in the Amphitrite group, or the Eastern Paracels, since May 1950, and over 19–20 January 1974 Chinese naval units ousted the South Vietnamese from the Western Paracels, giving China complete control of the archipelago. China, however, had occupied no part of the Spratlys until 1988, when, after a second naval clash with the Vietnamese near Johnson Reef, it was able to plant the flag on seven rocks and atolls. Occupation would give China certain incumbent rights over the Paracels and a foothold in the Spratlys, but little more. China's attempt to cite ancient records as a basis for sovereignty over all the South China Sea finds little support in international law. Justice Max Huber's tests in the Island of Palmas case noted that any rights obtained from history may be lost 'if not maintained in accordance with the changes brought about by the development of modern international law'.[25] UNCLOS recognises history or areas over which states may have traditional rights in the notion of 'historic bays' in Article 10 (6), subject to three criteria, including demonstrated authority over the area, continuity in that exercise of that authority and recognition by other states.[26] However, the extension of this concept into 'historic waters' to justify the Chinese position has no basis in law. In the El Salvador/Honduras case, the ICJ, in 1992, declared that 'historic waters as such did not and do not exist as an independent institution in the law of the sea'.[27]

China's U-shaped line

China's maritime borders have shifted south progressively as its maritime interests have expanded. China's first maritime border was drawn by cartographer Hu Jinjie in December 1914 in response to Japanese merchant Nishizawa Yohiji's activities in the Pratas Islands, which prompted the Chinese to negotiate a deal according to which the Japanese recognised the Pratas Islands as Chinese.[28] While Hu Jinjie's line included only the Pratas and Paracels, the expansion of this maritime border southward was to come later in response to French intrusion into the Spratys.[29] The Chinese government formed a Land and Water Maps Inspection Committee on 7 June 1933, which was intended to intended to identify the Chinese claim in the area. It gave Chinese names to 132 islands, reefs and other features in the area, but it did not include James Shoal as China's southernmost point. In April 1935, the committee drafted a map of the South China Sea, which included a U-shaped line with 11 dashes, with the southern border at James Shoal, which was just on 4° N latitude.[30] The U-shaped line was supposed to be the median line between China and the coastal states, but the baselines used were unclear. It was also unclear why 11 dashes were used. This map appeared in the committee's journal, and in February 1948 it was published by the Geography Department of the Ministry of Internal Affairs as 'The Administrative Division Map of the Republic of China'.[31] It was inherited by the People's Republic, becoming the basis of China's claim today, though two dashes were removed in 1953 as a concession to Vietnam in the Gulf of Tonkin area.

China has affirmed the U-shaped line as a basis for its claim but it has not explained whether it is a claim to islands or sea territory within the lines, or whether it represents the exact boundaries of China's claim. One Chinese interpretation is that it is a claim for islands and represents China's 'traditional maritime boundary' in the South China Sea.[32] Some Chinese have argued that the line represents China's claim over all the waters within it, including transportation, fishing and mineral extraction rights.[33] Others argue that it represents ownership of islands, and not a claim to the water within the line, and 'not a maritime boundary in the conventional sense'.[34] Another Chinese view suggests that it is 'not a boundary line of territorial waters and is non-exclusive', and that it does not prevent freedom of flight or navigation and does not conflict with EEZs or continental shelves.[35] The commonly accepted view is that the U-shaped line is a claim for islands and surrounding waters within the line, and if that is the case, how would those waters be defined? The Chinese have said that islands in the South China Sea should be entitled to territorial seas and economic zones, in which case the China entitlement could include much of the area within the U-shaped line.[36] However, under the legal principle of 'land dominates the sea', coastal length would be used to determine maritime rights, which would circumscribe Chinese claims to sea zone based on the islands there.[37] In May 2009, China attached a map that included the U-shaped line with its nine dashes to its diplomatic note to the UN Commission on the Limits of the Continental Shelf in protest against Vietnamese and Philippine claims. This was the first time that the line was used in an official communication.[38] Nonetheless, disputation remains because to have legal validity, maps should be incorporated in a treaty, and should conform to certain definitional requirements in terms of clarification of boundaries and the content of the claim.[39] The Chinese have recognised the legal weakness of the U-shaped line, and in 2012 convened a team of scholars from both Taiwan and the mainland to strengthen its legal validity. The President of the National Institute for South China Sea Studies in Hainan (NISCSS), Wu Shicun, has said that the intention is to give the international community a legal explanation of the U-shaped line.[40]

In any case, the U-shaped line is not the only basis of China's claim, and is simply representative of a historical sense of entitlement to the area, which, as Chinese officials say, gives China 'indisputable sovereignty' over the area. Nonetheless, China is obliged to seek a legal basis for that claim, and has attempted to apply its own interpretation of UNCLOS in support. On 15 May 1996, China declared strait baselines around the Paracel Islands and adjacent waters, which turned them into 'internal waters', for which freedom of navigation is restricted.[41] According to Article 46 of UNCLOS, only an archipelagic state can draw baselines around islands, which China is not. Moreover, the sea area enclosed by China's baselines exceeds the ratio of water to land enjoined by Article 47, which is 9:1; in China's baselines, the ratio is 26.1:1, which is well beyond the limit.[42] Chinese scholars have been seeking an archipelagic justification for its claim, claiming that as UNCLOS recognises archipelagic states such as Indonesia and the Philippines, so it should recognise states with archipelagos.[43] The issue was discussed during the negotiations for UNCLOS and supported by a number of states, including China, but maritime states such as the US, the UK, the USSR and Japan opposed what they regarded as an attempt to restrict freedom of navigation.[44]

ASEAN claimants

Vietnam's claim to the South China Sea was raised initially by the Bao Dai government in South Vietnam, and while the country was divided the North said little about the issue. South Vietnam insisted on Vietnam's rights as a 'colonial successor state', claiming that it inherited sovereignty from France and was the legitimate heir after the San Francisco Conference divested Japan of sovereignty. Vietnam has argued that its representative at the Conference Tran Van Huu had declared Vietnam's sovereignty over the two archipelagos without any protest.[45] France, however, protested the Vietnamese claim, insisting that only the Paracels were ceded to Vietnam as a result of decolonisation enforced by the Geneva Conference of 1954, and not the Spratly Islands. The French Charge d'Affaires in Saigon declared, on 9 June 1956, that France had retained sovereignty over the Spratlys.[46] Nonetheless, the Vietnamese argued that the international community had recognised Vietnam's historical and legal sovereignty over the Paracel and Spratly Islands.[47] Vietnam has also argued on historical grounds, claiming that the Hoang Sa and Truong Sa were *res nullius* in the seventeenth century when the Nguyen clan opened contact with these two archipelagos and had their activities recorded in Vietnamese documents.[48] Vietnam's historical arguments face the same hurdles as the Chinese, as its historical documents are inconclusive, and there is little historical evidence of contact with the Spratlys. Its claims have not yet been defined according to legal criteria.

Vietnam's claim, however, was weakened somewhat by the statement by North Vietnam's Prime Minister Pham Van Dong of 14 September 1958, which declared support for Chinese Premier Zhou Enlai's declaration of a territorial sea of 12 nautical miles, which included the Paracel and Spratly archipelagos.[49] It was published in the Vietnamese party newspaper *Nhan Dan* on 22 September and has been cited as evidence by the Chinese that it indicated acceptance of the Chinese claim to the South China Sea. It also prevented the Vietnamese from pursuing their own claim according to the legal principle of estoppel. The Vietnamese have countered that Pham Van Dong's statement was made in 'urgent' circumstances when Vietnam needed Chinese support, and in any case it was recognition of the Chinese 12 nautical mile limit from the mainland and did not constitute acceptance of China's claim to the South China Sea.[50] Physical occupation of islands is a stronger basis for Vietnam's claims. It may have lost the Paracels to China, but it occupies some 21–27 islands, rocks and atolls in the Spratly Islands, which was accomplished in two phases – after reunification in 1975 and after the naval clash with China in March 1988. Vietnam initially claimed full maritime zones, EEZs and continental zones for both the Paracels and Spratlys in the expectation that this would bring great benefits, but it now accepts the prevailing legal view that the islands there may only have limited zones, and in some cases only a 12 mile territorial sea.[51] The Vietnamese understood that adherence to legality and UNCLOS would strengthen its claim and may weaken the Chinese position.

Philippine interest in the Spratlys dates back to 17 May 1950, when President Quirino, in response to the Nationalist Chinese garrisoning of Itu Aba, declared that area belonged to the Philippines.[52] Philippine adventurer Tomas Cloma visited the islands in March 1956, and claimed rights of first discovery, calling the area Kalayaan, or 'freedomland', which included 53 islands, rocks or atolls. On 21 May, he sent a letter to Vice President Garcia, hoping that the Philippines would support his claim, and on 22 May sent another letter to the Chinese Embassy. South Vietnam, China and the Republic of China (ROC) protested, which prevented the Philippines government from supporting the claim at that time.[53] After Philippine forces failed to wrest Itu Aba from the ROC, President Ferdinand Marcos claimed the area in a diplomatic note sent to the ROC on 10 July 1971.[54] In it, he declared support for Tomas Cloma's claim area, described as *res nullius*, and raised a second argument to the effect that a de facto trusteeship had been created over the islands, since the San Francisco conference had not identified a successor to Japan. A third argument mentioned in the note was that the Spratly Islands were within the archipelagic territory of the Philippines.[55] Accordingly, the Philippines was the successor state to Japan, and since the issue had been left unresolved by the San Francisco Conference it could claim the Spratlys on the basis of *res nullius*. As a fourth argument, the Philippine Foreign Ministry also insisted, unconvincingly, that Kalayaan was separate from the Spratly Island group to avoid controversy with China and Vietnam.[56] A fifth argument was that Kalayaan is part of the continental shelf of the Philippine archipelago, and subsequently justified by Article 76 of UNCLOS.[57] In April 1972, Manila incorporated Kalayaan into the province of Palawan to be administered as a municipality, with Tomas Cloma as chairman of the board. On 11 June 1978, President Marcos issued Presidential Decree 1596, which formally claimed the Kalaayan Island Group (KIG) for the Philippines, and on 17 July Marcos issued another presidential decree, which declared that the KIG was within the Philippine EEZ.[58] The Philippine claim, as based on *res nullius*, is contestable, and the political declarations of sovereignty can be challenged legally. The invocation of the continental shelf may be a claim for resources, but not for the features within it, and, moreover, there is no natural prolongation of the continental shelf from the mainland since the Palawan trough separates the Spratlys from the Philippine archipelago.[59] Nonetheless, the Philippines occupied seven islands in the Kalayaan zone over 1970–1980 and has garrisoned Pag-Asa, or Thitu Island, which is the second largest in the Spratlys. The Philippine claim has not always received domestic support, and National Security Advisor Rafael Ileto once told the press that he had recommended that President Cory Aquino give up the Spratly claim, in view of the inability of the Philippines to defend it.[60] Ileto's advice, needless to say, was ignored.

The Malaysian claim to the surrounding sea zones of Sarawak and Sabah was stimulated by the Philippine claims and by Manila's occupation of islands in its claimed area. In 1978, Malaysia undertook a survey of this maritime area, and in the following year published a map including boundary lines, but no coordinates, for its claim. Malaysia's claim to the sea area is based on the continental shelf, which will not sustain a claim for the islands. In 1984, Malaysia proclaimed an EEZ, but without specifying coordinates or baselines to give it effect.[61] Malaysia occupied Terumbu Layang Layang in September 1983 and turned it into a tourist attraction with a small hotel. It occupied five features in its claim area and has claimed eleven.[62] Indonesia was not a claimant in the South China Sea, but became involved when, in April 1995, a Chinese map revealed that the Chinese claim line cut through the Natuna Islands gas field, which was being exploited by a Pertamina-Exxon consortium. While Foreign Minister Ali Alatas played down the issue, saying that the map was illustrative and not a formal claim, the Indonesian military was disturbed and increased regular patrols around the area. In June 1995 and September 1996, military exercises were conducted in the area, which, as Armed Forces Chief Feisal Tanjung declared, were intended to demonstrate that Indonesia would defend its territorial waters around the islands.[63] Brunei claims a continental shelf and its resources, but not Louisa Reef, which lies within it.[64] Finally, though Taiwan is not an ASEAN claimant, it claims the area according to the original 11-dash line, which it has not defined, and continues to occupy the largest island, Itu Aba, with a small garrison. Taiwan shares the claim with Beijing, but resists its call for a common position against the ASEAN claimants.[65]

Oil exploration and exploitation

The oil reserves of the South China Sea attracted attention in the late 1960s and early 1970s. Geophysical surveys were conducted in the Visayas in the Philippines in the 1950s until the early 1960s, but the data were kept confidential by the oil companies.[66] Offshore drilling took place in shallow areas of the coasts of the claimants and surveys indicated a number of basins in the South China Sea that could be exploited. Brunei's offshore fields were developed from 1972 while Malaysia began drilling around the same time. Surveys undertaken in 1969 indicated reserves of oil and gas, but in the early 1970s deep water drilling was limited to 200 metres. The 1973–1974 oil shocks were a stimulus to exploration in the area, and in March 1976 the first commercial field began operation off the Philippine island of Palawan at Reed Bank, involving a consortium of three Swedish and seven Philippine companies. The Philippine claim to Kalayaan, as formalised in the Marcos Presidential Decree of June 1978, may have been motivated by oil, as increases in the price of oil stimulated the search for offshore alternatives. By 1979, there were nine offshore wells in the Philippine claim area producing 9.1 million barrels daily or 1.3 million tons, or about 15 per cent of the petroleum consumed in that country.[67] China's interest in the oil reserves of the South China Sea was stimulated by the exploitation conducted by the Philippines, and also by a 1976 ECAFE geologic survey of the area, which indicated sizable reserves in the area.[68]

China's move into the Spratlys was a result of what the Chinese regarded as their exclusion from the area, which had become more important not only in terms of its oil reserves, but also its strategic value. A reunited Vietnam tilted towards the Soviet Union, concluding an alliance with it in November 1978 and allowing the Soviet navy the use of Cam Ranh Bay, while China sought to exclude Soviet naval vessels from the area. Various minor clashes were reported between China and Vietnam over 1979 and 1982 as China increased the size of its South Sea fleet to five destroyers, while over 1980–1983 Chinese air patrols over the Spratlys were also reported. In May 1983, Peoples Liberation Army Navy (PLA-N) vessels surveyed these islands, and in 1984 the first comprehensive survey of the area was produced. In 1987, China decided upon a physical presence on Fiery Cross Reef, where construction of facilities began on 3 February 1988. Observation towers were placed on other reefs such as Subi Reef, Johnston Reef, Cuarton Reef, Gaven Reef, and Dongment Jiao.[69] A naval clash with Vietnam on 14 March 1988, in which three Vietnamese vessels were sunk and 73 sailors were lost, was a result of Chinese efforts to establish a presence on the Spratly Islands. Eventually, China occupied seven features and placed markers on another two.

Over 1992–1995, two events occurred that clarified Chinese intentions in the South China Sea. One was the Law on the Territorial Sea and the Contiguous Zone, which was passed by the National People's Congress and announced on 25 February 1992. The law basically restated the 1958 Declaration on the Territorial Sea.[70] Article 2 of the 1992 law stated that China's 'territorial land' included the mainland and 'various affiliated islands', including the Paracel and Spratly Islands.[71] It added that the 'territorial sea refers to waters adjacent to its territorial land'. The law made these islands part of China's 'territorial land', while the surrounding sea up to a 12 mile limit was China's territorial sea. This law determined that the mainland, Taiwan and the Paracel and Spratly Islands were all part of one China. At the time, the declaration had a shock effect upon the other claimants, which was mitigated somewhat by its idiosyncratic nature, seemingly unrelated to UNCLOS. China had defined these islands as part of the mainland, but had not identified which were included, nor had it specified the borders of the territorial sea it had claimed. Such omissions rendered the declaration more political than legal. Second, China's interest in the oil reserves of the Spratlys was revealed when, in May 1992, China National Offshore Oil Corporation (CNOOC) concluded an exploration contract with the American Crestone Energy Corporation. This was the first time that China had involved an international oil company in the Spratlys. The two companies planned to gather seismic data and conduct drilling tests in an area also claimed by Vietnam, provoking furious Vietnamese protests. Crestone President Randall C. Thompson told the press that China offered the American drilling crews naval protection. The US State Department admitted that an American official was present at the contract signing ceremony in Beijing, although it was quick to point out that the US did not support Chinese territorial claims in the area.[72] Vietnam reacted by signing an exploration contract with Mobil in April 1992 to exploit the Blue

Dragon field, and in April 1996 an agreement was signed with the Texas-based oil company Conoco (now ConocoPhillips) for exploration in blocks that overlapped with China's Crestone concession.[73] Tensions increased between Vietnam and China, and several near clashes were reported.

ASEAN's efforts to maintain the status quo

Throughout the 1980s and 1990s, it was widely assumed in ASEAN circles that the South China Sea dispute was an extension of the Sino–Vietnamese conflict and the six ASEAN members were spectators in their dispute. It was believed that as Vietnam's relationship with China normalised, the situation in south China would improve. In this scenario, China would be engaged by regional institutions in regular dialogue, which would constrain its behaviour and encourage it to accept the status quo in the area. To this end, ASEAN was obliged to avoid any issue that would offend China, and would not get involved in bilateral disputes between any of its members and China.[74] This distinction between bilateral and collective relationships with China was critical for ASEAN's engagement policy, as it meant no matter what disputes members may have with China, the collective ASEAN position would not waver. While China at that time seemed to reciprocate ASEAN overtures, the gap between these bilateral and collective relationships was not exposed. In the 1990s, some observers thought that 'a significant turning point' had been reached as a result of Deng Xiaoping's Open Door Policy, as China was perceived to be stabilising the boundaries of its territorial sovereignty.[75] In this hopeful context, ASEAN resorted to recurring efforts to obtain China's commitment to the status quo, each heralded as a step forward at the time and justified by what was regarded as positive interest on the part of the Chinese. The status quo, however, kept changing as China expanded into the area, which meant that there was no fixed position that would serve as a basis for ASEAN negotiations. The first such effort was the 'ASEAN Declaration on the South China Sea', which was concluded with China on 22 July 1992. The declaration stressed the 'necessity to resolve all sovereignty and jurisdictional issues pertaining to the South China Sea by peaceful means, without resort to force'.[76] There was also the hope that the series of annual track-two workshops on the South China Sea called 'Managing Potential Conflicts in the South China Sea', devised by Ambassador Hasjim Djalal of Indonesia and strongly supported by Foreign Minister Ali Alatas, would engage China and contribute to a resolution of the issue.[77]

It came as a surprise when the Philippines discovered that China had, in late 1994, occupied Mischief Reef in its claim zone, an action that was regarded as a violation of the 1992 ASEAN Declaration on the South China Sea. In this case, China had built four raised octagonal structures on steel pylons with a small pier, a helipad and radar antenna.[78] While Chinese Foreign Minister Qian Qichen declared the structures were built for local fishermen as living quarters, Philippine President Fidel Ramos reported that the Chinese had told him that the structures were built by lower-level functionaries who had acted without the knowledge and consent of the central government.[79] Subsequent extensions of these structures and the construction of new structures on other reefs, however, suggested central direction and protection. This action triggered uproar within the Philippines, which reached for ASEAN support, but to no avail. On 18 March, ASEAN foreign ministers called upon the parties to 'refrain from taking actions that destabilize the region and further threaten the peace and security of the South China Sea'.[80] A few months later, at the 28th ASEAN Foreign Ministers Meeting in July 1995, ministers expressed their 'concern' over the issue, but were restrained by their interest in the ASEAN-China Senior Officials Consultation (ACSOC), which first began in April.[81] The Philippines also attempted to raise the issue with the newly created ASEAN Regional Forum (ARF) in the same month, but senior officials kept the issue off the agenda to avoid offending the Chinese.[82] In July 1996, the third ARF noted the issue, but while the Philippines was eager for the forum's support, it only 'welcomed efforts by countries concerned to seek solutions by peaceful means'.[83] The Philippines was disillusioned with ASEAN, as its hopes that the regional organisation would support its position in relation to China were dashed. For the Philippines, it meant a reassessment of the US after the Philippine Senate had ejected the US from the naval base in Subic Bay in 1992. Manila could not invoke the 1951 Mutual Defense Treaty with the US, since the Americans had made it clear that the treaty would not apply to the disputed area, which was not part of the archipelago when the treaty was signed.[84] With a changed view of the US, the Philippines concluded a Visiting Forces Agreement (VFA) with it in 1998, which was ratified by the Philippine Senate in May 1999, indicating a strengthening of Philippine security links with the US.[85] ASEAN, however, went ahead with its effort to obtain Chinese endorsement of the post-Mischief Reef status quo in the Declaration of Conduct (DoC), which was concluded with China in November 2002. The Parties declared in Article 4 to 'resolve their territorial and jurisdictional disputes by peaceful means, without resorting to the threat or use of force'. In Article 5, they agreed to exercise 'self-restraint in the conduct of activities that could complicate or escalate tensions'.[86] ASEAN observers were elated that China had signed a multilateral agreement with ASEAN, and hoped that it would lead to a code of conduct that would bind the parties to an avoidance of conflict and the peaceful resolution of disputes. The status quo that it referred to was post-Mischief Reef, which meant that the Philippines was obliged to concede the issue to China in the hope that China would be deterred from taking further steps. Moreover, in the Chinese view, the DoC was supposed to restrain the ASEAN claimants from fishing activities and engaging international oil companies in exploration and drilling in an area China had claimed. Their failure to do so was a justification for further Chinese pressure and tensions.[87]

The national territorialisation of the South China Sea

In the past, while the Chinese may have insisted on sovereignty over the area, they stopped short of pressing for control or for the exclusion of the other claimants, which buoyed ASEAN hopes that a negotiated resolution would be possible. China's interest in excluding rival powers from the area or its interest in hydrocarbon resources did not result in a demand for exclusive possession or control, which would accompany the claim to sovereignty – that came much later. Since 2009, China has became more assertive as it proceeds with its national territorialisation of the South China Sea, or in other words, the absorption of what was historically a maritime frontier into national territory. The Chinese were no doubt motivated by a heightened sense of confidence when the global financial crisis weakened the United States and perceived an opportunity to advance Chinese interests in these areas. Some have argued that the increased assertiveness is the result of a greater role for the military in Chinese foreign and security policy, whose intention is to counter the US military presence in the Western Pacific and the alliances with Japan and South Korea.[88] The Chinese began to identify the South China Sea as a 'core interest', and as a *Xinhua* commentary noted, 'by adding the South China Sea to its core interests, China has shown its determination to secure its maritime resources and strategic waters'.[89] Chinese authorities have been creating the conviction in the public mind that the South China Sea has always been part of China, as much as Taiwan or any other territory of China. When China classified the South China Sea islands as part of its 'territorial land' in the 1992 law, ASEAN leaders interpreted this declaration as a reiteration of existing policy, but they failed to anticipate its effects. In April 2012, the U-shaped line appeared on new Chinese passports as part of a map of China to buttress this conviction among Chinese.[90] In January 2013, China published maps that included the South China Sea and Taiwan in a 10-dash line with the mainland and made them indistinguishable to the Chinese public.[91] A strong stance over the South China Sea is, no doubt, a way of demonstrating the leadership's nationalist credentials and to strengthen the regime's domestic position as it faces various new challenges.[92] Ratcheting up the rhetoric and invoking nationalism over the issue places real constraints upon the Chinese leadership, making compromise and negotiated solutions to the issue much more difficult, if not impossible. Once cast as Chinese territory in the public mind, there can be no going back, as no Chinese leader would want to appear as a Li Hongzhang by compromising the South China Sea claim with the other claimants.[93]

   In support of this nationalist posture, the Chinese have argued that their historical rights to the South China Sea predated UNCLOS and should be recognised by international law. According to this Chinese view, UNCLOS does not exclude, but complements, the customary rules of international law, which uphold historical rights based on fishing, navigation and other marine activities conducted by the Chinese in the past. The Chinese people, it is claimed, 'have, without a challenge, enjoyed and exercised certain rights in the South China Sea throughout recorded history. Those rights do not derive from UNCLOS'.[94] This strong feeling that China's 'rights' in the area are not recognised by international law has become more widespread in China and has animated populist views on the subject. The problem from the legal perspective is that fishing and navigation activities that may have been conducted by local Hainanese people in the area do not immediately translate into a claim for title, as historical rights and historical title are two different things. Unless the Chinese can demonstrate that these activities were accompanied by a claim to the area on the part of dynastic authorities in Beijing at the time, their position will be unconvincing. Dupuy and Dupuy have argued that long use of a territory alone will not meet the legal requirement to demonstrate effective and continuous occupation, and that China's assertiveness over this issue does not, from a legal perspective, constitute a position 'that is even minimally persuasive'.[95]

Harassment and power

China intends to compensate for its dubious legal position by resorting to harassment tactics against the ASEAN claimants and by repetitive and apodictic declarations of sovereignty. The claim of 'indisputable sovereignty' is strongly asserted, and not based on rational argument for the most part, in the hope that if made often and long enough, it would be accepted by the international community. The concern is that without a sufficient legal basis for its claim, the Chinese leadership will be pushed by nationalist forces that it cannot control and will increasingly resort to power to obtain what it cannot get legally. China has deployed new maritime capabilities, called 'fishery patrol' vessels, to the South China Sea and resorted to harassment tactics against ASEAN claimants. These vessels include the 4,500-ton *Yuzheng 311, 202* and *302*, as well as the modern *Haixun 21* and *Haixun 31*. China also has announced plans to increase its maritime surveillance forces to 16 aircraft and 350 vessels by 2015. Vessels such as the 3,000-ton *Haixun 11* and *Haixun 31* will support the smaller *Haijian 84* and *Haijian 72* maritime surveillance vessels, boosting China's presence and capability in the area. In 2012, China's State Oceanic Administration reported that 58 patrol missions were conducted in the South China Sea, and these missions are expected to increase. Their purpose will be to monitor shipping and carry out surveying duties to 'protect maritime security', and to inspect foreign vessels operating in 'Chinese waters'.[96] In July 2013, China announced the integration of maritime surveillance, the coastguard and customs into an expanded State Oceanic Administration with the capacity to conduct more frequent patrols in the North, East and South China Seas.[97]

China's harassment tactics in the South China Sea have targeted Vietnam and the Philippines. So far, Malaysia has been avoided, as the Malaysian claim is further removed from both Vietnamese and Philippine claims and is not an immediate target. Moreover, the Malaysian leadership has adopted a policy of bandwagoning with China, hoping that protestations of friendship would offer protection against China. However, in their claim to the South China Sea, the Chinese have made no exceptions for Malaysia so far. In March 2013, Chinese naval vessels conducted a patrol and training mission around James Shoal, which is at the southern limit of the U-shaped line and 80 kilometres off the coast of Sarawak, well inside the Malaysian claim. The Malaysians, indeed, have become concerned.[98] Chinese maritime surveillance vessels have been discouraging major oil companies whose oil exploration vessels have been contracted by ASEAN claimants from operating in the area, obliging them to seek permission from China. Vietnam has complained of regular incidents when Chinese maritime surveillance vessels severed the exploration cables of Vietnamese survey ships; such incidents were reported on 26 May and 9 June 2011, and 30 November 2012. China has also imposed an annual fishing ban around the Paracels from 16 May to 1 August. Vietnam has vociferously protested, claiming that its fishermen are regularly arrested by Chinese patrol vessels, their vessels confiscated and an exorbitant fine demanded for their release. Additionally, China seized Scarborough Shoal from the Philippines when two Chinese maritime surveillance vessels prevented a Philippine coastguard vessel from arresting Chinese fishermen poaching in the Philippine claim zone. China's Ambassador to ASEAN, Tong Xiaoling, insisted that the reef had been Chinese since 'ancient times', and waters around the island were traditional fishing grounds for Chinese fishermen.[99] Chinese attention has moved to Second Thomas Shoal, some 240 kilometres off Palawan, where Chinese maritime surveillance vessels have appeared regularly in 2013.[100]

External powers

The national territorialisation of the South China Sea cannot be isolated, as it has implications for external powers. The South China Sea embraces some of the world's busiest sea lanes, which link Northeast Asia to the Indian Ocean and the Middle East, and it has been estimated that over half of the world's annual merchant-fleet tonnage passes through the area. Oil imported by Japan, South Korea, Taiwan and southern China is shipped through the Malacca Straits and the South China Sea, which gives it a special strategic significance.[101] US interest in the issue was largely distant until China began applying pressure upon the ASEAN claimants to extend control over the area. In strategic terms, Chinese control of the South China Sea would allow it to threaten the sea lanes of the Western Pacific, and the oil lifelines of Japan and South Korea. China would also gain strategic advantages in naval rivalry with the US by increasing the operational reach of its growing navy and using the South China Sea as a protective bastion for its strategic missile-carrying submarines, particularly the Jin class submarine with the JL-2 missile that can target the US homeland.[102] The US defends its right of innocent naval passage and is concerned that China would exclude American energy companies from exploration and drilling from an area it regards as domestic waters.[103] Moreover, Chinese control over the South China Sea could trigger the fragmentation of ASEAN, whose unity has supported a favourable regional order conducive to the American presence. Indeed, ASEAN unity has been challenged as the pro-China Cambodia and the pro-US Philippines line up on different sides, while non claimants such as Thailand want to avoid the issue altogether.[104] China's assertiveness in the South China Sea was an important factor behind the Obama administration's *rebalancing* policy, also called the *pivot* strategy, of rearranging military forces in the Asia region, which was announced in November 2011.[105]

Under pressure from the Chinese in the Senkaku/Diaoyu Islands dispute, where China is adopting similar harassment tactics, Japan also is becoming involved. The Japanese fear that Chinese control over the South China Sea would threaten their oil supplies and trade with the Middle East and Europe. Japan has moved to strengthen security cooperation with both Vietnam and the Philippines, and has offered Manila 10 patrol boats to strengthen its maritime capability.[106] The Japanese coastguard intends to train Philippine and Vietnamese personnel to boost security cooperation. India also wants to protect its oil companies that have contracted with the Vietnamese for exploration and survey work in the area. The Indian oil company Oil and Natural Gas Corporation is involved in a gas and oil exploration block off the coast of Vietnam, and has been warned by China to desist.[107] Should it require protection against Chinese harassment, India may send its own naval vessels, further complicating the situation. The concern is that Chinese pressure against the ASEAN claimants would increase and there would be more incidents of harassment, involving greater risks. As the Chinese assert their 'indisputable sovereignty' over the area and engage domestic nationalism, the Chinese leadership is pushed into positions from which they cannot easily back down, which then creates the conditions for conflict and escalation.

Conclusion

China has been engaged in an effort to appropriate a maritime frontier, which was shared with others, and include it within national borders, over which it seeks to exercise sovereignty. This effort at national territorialisation, however, lacks a clear legal foundation beyond the Paracels, and Chinese claims to the Spratlys, insofar as they are based on history, remain contestable. Despite the Chinese insistence on ancient title, China's claim to the area is relatively new. Historically, the South China Sea was China's southern maritime frontier, and not considered part of the dynastic state. In the late nineteenth century, China's southern maritime border was presumed to follow the coast and it was as a result of Japanese and French intrusion that its interest was extended to the Paracel and Spratly Islands. China's moves to appropriate the South China Sea conflicts with the positions of the ASEAN claimants, who have acquired legal rights in the Spratlys, though not necessarily through their political claims, but as a result of their occupation of features. How China would deal with the ASEAN claimants is a critical issue. Some Vietnamese fear that China will clear the South China Sea of all other claimants by force, with disastrous results for all concerned, China included. More likely, China will continue with a prolonged campaign of harassment against the ASEAN claimants to get them to accept a regional resolution of the issue that would leave it in a dominant position. A resolution of this kind would demand that the ASEAN claimants surrender their legal rights under UNCLOS and international law and recognise the superiority of China's historical claim. The result would then be declared legal as a regional solution, in conformity with the Chinese understanding of law, which would have considerable repercussions for UNCLOS and international law. The difficulty for China is that external powers, particularly the US and Japan, have become concerned about Chinese moves in the area, and doubt that China would respect freedom of navigation for foreign oil exploration, as well as for maritime surveillance vessels. For them, Chinese domination of the area would undermine their own positions in the wider region, Japan over the Senkaku/Diaoyu Islands and the US in the Western Pacific. For this reason, they have been encouraging the ASEAN claimants, Vietnam and the Philippines, to resist Chinese pressure, which could create the conditions for escalation of the dispute.

Notes

1 For a discussion of China's northern frontier, see Owen Lattimore, *Studies in Frontier History: Collected Papers 1928–1958*, Oxford University Press, London, 1962, pp. 127, 469–472.

2 M. Taylor Fravel, *Strong Borders, Secure Nation: Cooperation and Conflict in China's Territorial Disputes*, Princeton University Press, Princeton, NJ, 2008, pp. 47–50.

3 Csaba Oláh, 'Border Defence, Border Inspection and Foreign Embassies in the Ming Period', in Zsombor Rajkai and Ildikó Béller-Hann (eds), *Frontiers and Boundaries: Encounters on China's Margins*, Harrassowitz Verlag, Wiesbaden, 2012, p. 126.

4 Noboru Ishikawa, *Between Frontiers: Nation and Identity in a Southeast Asian Borderland*, Ohio University Press, Athens, OH, 2010, p. 4.

5 Marwyn S. Samuels, *Contest for the South China Sea*, Methuen, New York, 1982, pp. 47, 51.

6 Roderich Ptak, *China, the Portuguese, and the Nanyang: Oceans and Routes, Regions and Trade (c. 1000–1600)*, Ashgate, Farnham, 2004, pp. 107–124.

7 Roderich Ptak, *China, the Portuguese, and the Nanyang*, pp. 416–419.

8 Marwyn S. Samuels, *Contest for the South China Sea*, pp. 47, 51.

9 Geoffrey C. Gunn, 'Anglo-French Rivalry over the Spratlys (1930–1937): An Aspect of World Historical Incorporation', in R. D. Hill, Norman G. Owen and E. V. Roberts (eds), *Fishing in Troubled Waters: Proceedings of an Academic Conference on Territorial Claims in the South China Sea*, Centre of Asian Studies, University of Hong Kong, Hong Kong, 1991.

10 Dieter Heinzig, *Disputed Islands in the South China Sea: Paracels-Spratlys-Pratas-Macclesfield Bank*, Otto Harrassowitz, Wiesbaden, 1976, pp. 26–27.

11 Dieter Heinzig, *Disputed Islands in the South China Sea*, p. 27.

12 Marwyn S. Samuels, *Contest for the South China Sea*, pp. 53, 54, 56, 57.

13 Marwyn S. Samuels, *Contest for the South China Sea*, pp. 53, 54, 56, 57.

14 Dieter Heinzig, *Disputed Islands in the South China Sea*, pp. 26–27.

15 Dieter Heinzig, *Disputed Islands in the South China Sea*, pp. 26–27.

16 Dieter Heinzig, *Disputed Islands in the South China Sea*, p. 27.

17 J. K. T. Chao, 'South China Sea: Boundary Problems Relating to the Nansha and Hsisha Islands', in R. D. Hill, Norman G. Owen, and E. V. Roberts (eds), *Fishing in Troubled Waters: Proceedings of an Academic Conference on Territorial Claims in the South China Sea*, Centre for Asian Studies, Hong Kong, 1991.

18 Dieter Heinzig, *Disputed Islands in the South China Sea*, p. 33.

19 Gromyko declared at the conference that 'As regards the American-British draft peace treaty with Japan in the part pertaining to territorial questions, the Delegation of the USSR considers it necessary to state that this draft grossly violates the indisputable rights of China to the return of integral parts of Chinese territory:

Taiwan, the Pescadores, the Paracel and other islands severed from it by the Japanese militarists'. 'Statement of the First Deputy Minister of Foreign Affairs of the USSR, A. A. Gromyko, at the Conference in San Francisco (1951)', *Ministry of Foreign Affairs of Japan*, www.mofa.go.jp/region/europe/russia/territory/edition92/period4.html (accessed 2 June 2014); Chao, 'South China Sea'.

20 Chinese claims were reiterated on 15 August 1951, 29 May 1956, 4 September 1958, 27 February 1959, 5 April 1959, 13 May 1960; Taiwanese claims, 12 July 1971, 25 January, 9 August, 27 August, 26 October 1973. Dieter Heinzig, *Disputed Islands in the South China Sea*, p. 42.

21 Jon M. Van Dyke, 'Disputes over Islands and Maritime Boundaries in East Asia', in Seoung-Yong Hong and Jon M. Van Dyke (eds), *Maritime Boundary Disputes, Settlement Processes, and the Law of the Sea*, Martinus Nijhoff, Leiden, 2009.

22 Permanent Court of Arbitration, the island of Palmas case (or Miangas), United States of America v. the Netherlands, The Hague, 4 April 1928, www.pca-cpa.org/showfile. asp?fil_id=168 (accessed 2 June 2014).

23 'Territorial Sovereignty and Scope of the Dispute (Eritrea and Yemen)', *Reports of International Arbitral Awards* XXII: Permanent Court of Arbitration 1998.

24 'International Court Finds that Sovereignty over Islands of Ligitan and Sipadan Belongs to Malaysia', ICJ/605 17 December. The Hague: International Court of Justice, 2002, www.un.org/News/Press/docs/2002/ICJ605.doc.htm (accessed 2 June 2014). Other cases that illustrate the need to demonstrate formal acts of state authority to support claims to title include the Clipperton case between France and Mexico in 1931, Minquiers and Ecrebos between France and the UK in 1953, and the Gulf of Fonseca case involving El Salvador and Honduras, with Nicaragua intervening in 1992. See Van Dyke, 'Disputes over Islands and Maritime Boundaries in East Asia', pp. 62–75.

25 Permanent Court of Arbitration, the island of Palmas case.

26 ICJ study in 1962, Juridical Regime of Historic waters includes Historic Bays.

27 See Land, Island and Maritime Frontier Dispute (El Salvador/Honduras: Nicaragua intervening), Judgment of September 11, 1992, I.C.J. Reports 1992, p. 351 [pp. 588–589] 383. Max Planck Institute for Comparative Public Law and International Law, www.mpil.de/ww/en/pub/research/details/publications/institute/wcd.cfm?fuse action_wcd=aktdat&aktdat=202030000200.cfm (accessed 2 June 2014).

28 In 1907/08, the Japanese merchant Nishizawa Yoshiji settled on the Pratas Islands, prompting the governers of Kuangsi and Kuangtung provinces to negotiate a deal, according to which Nishizawa received 130,000 silver dollars, in exchange for which he recognised the Pratas as Chinese territory. Dieter Heinzig, *Disputed Islands in the South China Sea*, p. 26.

29 Zou Keyuan, 'The Chinese Traditional Maritime Boundary Line in the South China Sea and its Legal Consequences for the Resolution of the Dispute over the Spratly Islands', *The International Journal of Marine and Coastal Law*, 14(1), March 1999.

30 Zou Keyuan, 'The Chinese Traditional Maritime Boundary Line in the South China Sea'.

31 Li Jinming Li Dexia, 'The Dotted Line on the Chinese Map of the South China Sea: A Note', *Ocean Development & International Law*, 34, 2003.

32 Li Jinming and Dexia Li, 'The Dotted Line on the Chinese Map of the South China Sea'.

33 Deputy Director of the National Institute of South China Sea Studies in Hainan Liu Feng reportedly made such comments. Jane Perlez, 'China Asserts Sea Claim with Politics and Ships', *New York Times*, 11 August 2012.

34 Zhiguo Gao, 'The South China Sea: From Conflict to Cooperation?', *Ocean Development & International Law*, 25(3), July–September 1994.

35 Tang Ifang, 'On the dotted line', *Beijing Review*, 21 February 2013.
36 PRC working paper entitled 'Sea Area within the Limits of National Jurisdiction' submitted to Subcommittee 2 on 16 July 1973, suggested that China regarded the islands as serving as a basis for claiming territorial sea and economic zones, but it is silent on the issue of a continental shelf. Hungdah Chui, 'South China Sea Islands: Implications for Delimiting the Seabed and Future Shipping Routes', *The China Quarterly*, 72, December 1977.
37 Maritime Delimitation and Territorial Questions between Qatar and Bahrain, (Qatar *v.* Bahrain) Summary of the Judgment of 16 March 2001, International Court of Justice, www.icj-cij.org/docket/index.php?sum=443&code=qb&p1=3&p2=3&case=87&k=61&p3=5 (accessed 2 June 2014).
38 Zou Keyuan, 'China's U-shaped Line in the South China Sea Revisited', *Ocean Development & International Law*, 43(1): 18–34, 2012.
39 Masahiro Miyoshi, 'China's "U-Shaped Line" Claim in the South China Sea: Any Validity Under International Law?', *Ocean Development & International Law*, 43(1): 1–17, 2012. Florian and Pierre-Marie Dupuy, 'Legal Analysis of China's Historic Rights Claim in the South China Sea', *The American Journal of International Law*, 107(1): 124–141, January 2013.
40 'Chinese Scholars to Study South China Sea Borderline, Says Expert', *Xinhuanet*, 24 October 2012.
41 Zou Keyuan, 'The Chinese Traditional Maritime Boundary Line in the South China Sea'.
42 Daniel J. Dzurek, 'Maritime Briefing – The Spratly Islands Dispute: Who's on First?', *International Boundaries Research Unit*, 2(1), 1996. Sophia Kopela, *Dependent Archipelagos in the Law of the Sea*, Martinus Nijhoff, Leiden, 2013, pp. 138–139.
43 Hungdah Chui, 'South China Sea Islands: Implications for Delimiting the Seabed and Future Shipping Routes'.
44 States supporting the concept of archipelagos as part of a continental state in UNCLOS include China, India, Australia, Ecuador, Greece, Spain, Argentina, Portugal, France, Canada and Honduras, but they did not present a common draft proposal and did not cooperate. Sophia Kopela, *Dependent Archipelagos in the Law of the Sea*, p. 31.
45 *White Paper on the Hoang Sa (Paracel) and Truong Sa (Spratly) Islands*, Republic of Vietnam Ministry of Foreign Affairs Saigon, 1975.
46 Chao, 'South China Sea'.
47 'Diplomatic Note 1958 with Vietnam's Sovereignty over Paracel, Spratly Islands', *Vietnam.net*, 21 July 2011, http://english.vietnamnet.vn/en/special-report/10961/diplomatic-note-1958-with-vietnam-s-sovereignty-over-paracel—spratly-islands.html (accessed 2 June 2014).
48 'Vietnam and the East Sea', *Vietnam Peace and Development Foundation*, Hanoi, 2012, www.vpdf.org.vn/index.php?option=com_content&task=view&id=295&Item id=61 (accessed 2 June 2014).
49 'Diplomatic Note 1958 with Vietnam's Sovereignty over Paracel, Spratly Islands'.
50 'Diplomatic Note 1958 with Vietnam's Sovereignty over Paracel, Spratly Islands'.
51 Stein Tønnesson, 'Vietnam's Objective in the South China Sea: National or Regional Security', *Contemporary Southeast Asia*, 22(1), August 2000.
52 Chao, 'South China Sea'.
53 Hsiao Shiching, *The Nanshas (Spratys) Disputes*, 2nd edn, Color Lithographic Press, Quezon City, 1999, pp. 38, 39.
54 Daniel J. Dzurek, 'Maritime Briefing – The Spratly Islands Dispute'.
55 Henry Rhoel R. Aguda and Jesusa Loreto A. Arellano-Aguda, 'The Philippine Claim over the Spratly Group of Islands: An Application of Article 76 of the UNCLOS', *The Philippine Law Journal*, 83(3), January 2009. Also Haydee B. Yorac, 'The Philippine Claim to the Spratly Islands Group', in Theresa C. Cariño (ed.), *China–*

ASEAN Relations: Regional Security and Cooperation, Philippine-China Development Resource Centre, Quezon City, 1998, pp. 67–87.

56 Wilfrido Villacorta, 'The Philippine Territorial Claim in the South China Sea', in R. D. Hill, Norman G. Owen and E. V. Roberts (eds) *Fishing in Troubled Waters: Proceedings of an Academic Conference on Territorial Claims in the South China Sea*.

57 Henry Rhoel R. Aguda and Jesusa Loreto A. Arellano-Aguda, 'The Philippine Claim over the Spratly Group of Islands: An Application of Article 76 of the UNCLOS', *The Philippine Law Journal*, 83(3), January 2009.

58 Lowell Bautista and Clive Schofield, 'Philippine-China Border Relations: Cautious Engagement Amid Tensions', in Bruce A. Ellman, Stephen Kotkin and Clive Schofield (eds), *Beijing's Power and China's Borders: Twenty Neighbors in Asia*, M. E. Sharpe, Armonk, NY, 2013.

59 Mark J. Valencia, Jon M. Van Dyke and Noel A. Ludwig, *Sharing the Resources of the South China Sea*, Martinus Nijoff, The Hague, 1997, p. 30.

60 *Straits Times*, 20 February 1995.

61 R. Haller-Trost, 'Limitations of International Law: The Case of Malaysia's Territorial Claims in the South China Sea'. In R. D. Hill *et al.*, *Fishing in Troubled Waters, University of Hong Kong, Hong Kong*, pp. 216–236.

62 Forbes, 'Malaysia and China'

63 John McBeth, 'Oil Rich Diet', *Far Eastern Economic Review*, 27 April 1995; *Sunday Times*, 9 April 1995; *Straits Times*, 27 June 1995; John McBeth, 'Deep Background', *Far Eastern Economic Review*, 12 September 1996.

64 Daniel J. Dzurek, 'Maritime Briefing – The Spratly Islands Dispute'.

65 'Taiwan Sticking to Extensive S. China Sea Claims that Mirror China's: Ma', *Kyodo News International*, 22 November 2013, www.globalpost.com/dispatch/news/kyodo-news-international/131122/taiwan-sticking-extensive-s-china-sea-claims-mirror-ch (accessed 2 June 2014).

66 Roderick O'Brien, *South China Sea Oil: Two Problems of Ownership and Development*, ISEAS, occasional paper no. 47, 1977.

67 Marwyn S. Samuels, *Contest for the South China Sea*, pp. 157–158.

68 Marwyn S. Samuels, *Contest for the South China Sea*, pp. 160–161.

69 John W. Garver, 'China's Push through the South China Sea: The Interaction of Bureaucratic and National Interests', *China Quarterly*, 132, December 1992.

70 Daniel J. Dzurek, 'Maritime Briefing – The Spratly Islands Dispute'.

71 Law on the Territorial Sea and the Contiguous Zone of 25 February 1992, www.un.org/depts/los/LEGISLATIONANDTREATIES/PDFFILES/CHN_1992_Law.pdf (accessed 2 June 2014).

72 Michael Richardson, 'Oil Hunt in South China Sea: Some See Flash Point', I, 30 June 1002. 'Territorial Disputes Simmer in Areas of South China Sea', *Oil and Gas Journal*, 13, July 1992, www.ogj.com/articles/print/volume-90/issue-28/in-this-issue/exploration/territorial-disputes-simmer-in-areas-of-south-china-sea.html (accessed 2 June 2014).

73 Daniel J. Dzurek, 'Maritime Briefing – The Spratly Islands Dispute'.

74 Mohamed Jawhar bin Hassan, 'Disputes in the South China Sea: Approaches for Conflict Management', in Derek da Cunha (ed.), *Southeast Asian Perspectives on Security*, ISEAS, Singapore, 2000, pp. 103–107.

75 Allen Carlson, *Unifying China, Integrating with the World: Securing Chinese Sovereignty in the Reform Era*, Stanford University Press, Palo Alto, CA, 2005, p. 61.

76 '1992 ASEAN Declaration on the South China Sea, Adopted by the Foreign Ministers at the 25th ASEAN Ministerial Meeting in Manila, Philippines, on 22 July 1992', www.aseansec.org/1196.htm (accessed 2 June 2014).

77 Lee Lai to, *China and the South China Sea Dialogues*, Praeger, Westport, CT, 1999, Chapter 4.
78 Ian James Storey, 'Creeping Assertiveness: China, the Philippines and the South China Sea Dispute', *Contemporary Southeast Asia*, 21(1), April 1999.
79 *Straits Times*, 10 February 1995; *Straits Times*, 11 March 1995; *South China Morning Post*, 16 February 1995.
80 *Straits Times*, 19 March 1995.
81 Joint Communiqué of the Twenty-Eighth ASEAN Ministerial Meeting Held at Bandar Seri Begawan, Brunei Darussalam, on 29 and 30 July 1995, United Nations, 4 August 1995, http://unispal.un.org/UNISPAL.NSF/0/E9B54D392329EAB185256223004C55 A5 (accessed 2 June 2014); Rodolfo C. Severino, 'ASEAN and the South China Sea', *Security Challenges*, 6(2), Winter 2010.
82 *Straits Times*, 24 May 1995.
83 Chairman's Statement, Third ASEAN Regional Forum Jakarta, 23 July 1996, ASEAN Regional Forum, http://aseanregionalforum.asean.org/library/arf-chairmans-statements-and-reports/181.html (accessed 2 June 2014).
84 The US position was that the 1951 treaty applied to the borders of the Philippine archipelago as they were defined by the Treaty of Paris of 1898 and the 1935 constitution. Rodolfo C. Severino, 'The Philippines' National Territory', *Southeast Asian Affairs*, 2012. See also *Straits Times*, 13 December 1996.
85 Renato Cruz de Castro, 'The US-Philippine Alliance: An Evolving Hedge against an Emerging China Challenge', *Contemporary Southeast Asia*, 31(3), December 2009.
86 'Declaration on the Conduct of Parties in the South China Sea', *Association of Southeast Asian Nations*, www.asean.org/asean/external-relations/china/item/declaration-on-the-conduct-of-parties-in-the-south-china-sea (accessed 2 June 2014).
87 Interview sources, Beijing 2013.
88 Michael D. Swaine and Fravel M. Taylor, *China's Assertive Behavior Part Two: The Maritime Periphery*, China Leadership Monitor no. 35, Carnegie Endowment for International Peace, 2000, http://carnegieendowment.org/files/CLM35MS.pdf (accessed 2 June 2014).
89 'Modernizing Navy for Self-Defense', *Xinhuanet.com*, 13 July 2010, http://news.xinhuanet.com/english2010/indepth/2010-07/13/c_13397060.htm (accessed 2 June 2014).
90 Mark McDonald, 'A New Map in Chinese Passports Stirs Anger across the Region', *New York Times*, 25 November 2012.
91 'China Publishes New Maps: South China Sea Islands Highlighted', *Xinhua*, 17 January 2013.
92 Jane Perlez, 'China Asserts Sea Claim with Politics and Ships', *New York Times*, 11 August 2012.
93 Li Hongzhang (1823–1901) was a Qing dynasty official who signed the Treaty of Shimonoseki with Japan in April 1895, and has since been reviled as a traitor in China.
94 Zhiguo Gao and Bing Bing Jia, 'The Nine Dash Line in the South China Sea: History. Status and Implications', *The American Journal of International Law*, 107(1): 98–124, January 2013.
95 Florian and Pierre-Marie Dupuy, 'Legal Analysis of China's Historic Rights Claim in the South China Sea'.
96 Wang Qian, 'Maritime Forces to be Beefed up Amid Disputes', *China Daily*, 17 June 2011, www.chinadaily.com.cn/china/2011-06/17/content_12718632.htm (accessed 2 June 2014).
97 'China's Restructured SOA Goes into Official Operation', *Xinhua*, 22 July 2013; 'New China Coast Guard Expected to Do More Patrolling', *Taipei Times*, 24 July 2013.
98 Interview with Malaysian official, Kuala Lumpur, 4 June 2013.

99 Xu Tianran, 'Manila Moves to Quell Spat', *Global Times*, 15 May 2012.
100 Bonnie S. Glaser and Alison Szalwinski, 'Second Thomas Shoal Likely the Next Flashpoint in the South China Sea', *China Brief*, 13, 21 June 2013.
101 'South China Sea', *US Energy Information Administration*, 7 February 2013.
102 'China to Deploy New Strategic Missile Class of Submarines Next Year', *Washington Times*, 23 July 2013.
103 'China Again Warns Foreign Oil Firms on South China Sea Exploration', *Reuters*, 1 November 2011, www.abs-cbnnews.com/business/10/31/11/china-again-warns-foreign-oil-firms-south-china-sea-exploration (accessed 2 June 2014).
104 Interview with former member of Thai Parliament, Bangkok, 4 December 2013.
105 Justin Logan, 'China, America, and the Pivot to Asia', *Policy Analysis No 717*, Cato institute, 8 January 2013, www.cato.org/sites/cato.org/files/pubs/pdf/pa717.pdf (accessed 2 June 2014).
106 'Loan Plan for new Philippine Patrol Ships Unveiled', *Japan Times*, 28 July 2013.
107 'China Cautions India against Oil Exploration in South China Sea', *Times of India*, 5 December 2012.

2 Adrift on complex waters

Geographical, geopolitical and legal dimensions to the South China Sea disputes

Clive Schofield

Introduction

The South China Sea is often characterised as a complex and highly contested maritime space. This large, semi-enclosed sea is host to convoluted coastal geography, complicated in particular by the presence of numerous island groups and other insular features of diverse types. Problematically, many of these offshore features are subject to assertions of sovereignty by multiple states. Moreover, the fact that the South China Sea is bordered and largely encircled by claimants with often competing national interests gives rise to pressing concerns of a geopolitical nature. Adding to the complexity of this scenario are international legal uncertainties, especially with respect to key law of the sea issues, such as the definition of baselines, the regime of islands, historic rights, and concerning potential extended continental shelf rights. As a consequence of contested sovereignty over South China Sea islands, coupled with the above-mentioned geographical and legal complexities, together with competing geopolitical interests, broad, though ill-defined, areas of overlapping maritime claims exist in the South China Sea. These multifaceted and interrelated factors contribute to the seemingly intractable nature of the territorial and maritime disputes that exist among the South China Sea littoral states. The objective of this chapter, therefore, is to explore geographical, geopolitical and legal dimensions of the South China Sea disputes with a view to highlighting and, to the extent possible, clarifying issues arising. The chapter concludes that the the resolution of these long-standing and arguably increasingly contentious disputes is unlikely in the near term, suggesting that the South China Sea states are indeed likely 'adrift on complex waters' for the foreseeable future, as the title to the contribution suggests.

Geographical context

A number of geographical issues inform understanding of the South China Sea disputes. The South China Sea is a broad but semi-enclosed maritime space located between the southern coast of China and Taiwan to the north, the mainland and peninsular coasts of Southeast Asia to the west and the archipelagic island groups of the Philippines, Borneo and Indonesia to the east and south. The limits of the South China Sea have been defined as extending southwards from the Strait of Taiwan to around the 3° south parallel of latitude.[1] It has, however, been suggested that the 1° north parallel of latitude may be a more appropriate southern limit.[2] If the latter definition is taken, the total surface area of the South China Sea (including the Gulf of Thailand) has been calculated at approximately 3 million square kilometres (equivalent to around 874,660 square nautical miles).[3]

The South China Sea is bordered by multiple political entities, namely, clockwise from the north, the People's Republic of China (PRC), Republic of China (Taiwan), the Philippines, Malaysia, Brunei Darussalam (Brunei), Indonesia, Singapore and Vietnam (together with Cambodia and Thailand on the South China Sea's Gulf of Thailand extension). This necessarily has significant consequences in terms of maritime jurisdiction. The number and proximity of the South China Sea coastal states to one another means that multiple overlapping maritime claims are inevitable, thus creating the requirement for numerous maritime boundaries to be delimited. The potential for coincident claims to the same maritime space is accentuated by the semi-enclosed nature of the South China Sea, which dictates that the maritime claims of the littoral states tend to converge and overlap with one another. That said, the dimensions of the South China Sea suggest that there is in excess of 400 nautical miles between opposing shores, meaning that a large potential high seas pocket, or 'donut hole', may exist in the central South China Sea.

The coastal geography of the South China Sea is, however, complicated by the presence of a profusion of generally small islands, islets, rocks, shoals and reefs. Sovereignty over many of these features is contested among the littoral states. Further, the coastal fronts of the islands of the South China Sea are potentially of great significance to the maritime claims of the littoral States, and, indeed, the maritime jurisdictional scenario in the South China Sea is considerably complicated by their presence. The principle island groups of the South China Sea are as follows (clockwise from the north-west):

- *The Paracel Islands*, which comprise around 130 islands, predominantly divided between the Crescent and Amphritite groups (disputed between China/Taiwan and Vietnam).[4]
- *The Pratas Islands*, the principle feature of which is Pratas Reef, which is a circular coral reef 11 miles across, enclosing a substantial lagoon (under the administration of Taiwan, claimed by China).[5]
- *Scarborough Reef (or Shoal)*, a feature consisting of a large coral atoll, submerged at high tide, save for several small outcrops, and associated lagoon (disputed between China/Taiwan and the Philippines),[6] and *Macclesfield Bank*, which is an entirely and permanently submerged feature.[7]
- *The Spratly Islands*, consisting of around 150–180 generally small[8] islands, islets, rocks and reefs, as well as numerous low-tide elevations and submerged features (claimed in whole or in part by Brunei, China/Taiwan, Malaysia, the Philippines and Vietnam).[9]

- *The Natuna Islands*, which comprise an extensive (over 200) group of islands in the south-western South China Sea.[10]

As indicated above, with the exception of the Natuna Islands, which are under the uncontested sovereignty of Indonesia, sovereignty over all of these island groups is subject to dispute.

With respect to issues of maritime jurisdiction, the South China Sea islands are potentially highly significant, but also, surprisingly, not especially well understood. In part, this stems from a long-standing perception of these insular features of being of little importance other than as potential hazards to navigation. For example, the Spratly Islands were described in 1889 as a 'labyrinth of detached shoals'.[11] Moreover, the term 'dangerous ground' has traditionally featured on British Admiralty navigational charts of the area occupied by these features.[12] While contemporary understanding of the coastal geography and hydrography of the South China Sea has improved considerably, it remains the case that definitive information regarding the nature and status of the predominantly disputed insular features of the South China Sea remains hard to come by. This is in large part because classifying types of insular features, especially what constitutes an 'island' that is above high water, versus a low-tide elevation that is submerged at high tide but exposed at low tide, and also features that are permanently below the surface of the sea even at low water, is an especially difficult proposition in the South China Sea context (see below). This is the case primarily because the South China Sea possesses a tidal regime that has been described as 'among the most complex in the world'.[13] This, in turn, renders the definition of both high and low water levels technically problematic, as these reference levels vary both spatially and temporally in the South China Sea. This is an important consideration for three key reasons. First, only features above high tide can be considered to be land that is capable of being subject to a claim to sovereignty. Second, defining the low-water line is essential to differentiating between land and sea, and therefore the starting point for measuring maritime claims. Third, the distinct types of insular feature referred to above have different capacities to serve as basepoints for the generation of claims to maritime space. These legal and technical conundrums are addressed in further detail below.

Geopolitical drivers

The intrinsic value of the disputed islands of the South China Sea can be considered to be negligible.[14] Underscoring this seemingly rather dismissive evaluation is the fact that the overall land area of the infamously disputed Spratly Islands has been estimated to be of the order of only 8 square kilometres.[15] Indeed, the largest islet among the Spratlys, Itu Aba (Taiping Island), is reportedly only 1.4 kilometres in length and 370 metres across.[16] That said, the disputed islands and associated overlapping maritime claims have important underlying geopolitical dimensions that go far beyond the apparent insignificance of the disputed features themselves.

Sovereignty and geostrategic issues

Sovereignty remains a key consideration in the South China Sea disputes. At their core, these disputes involve sovereignty over territory (i.e. over the territory of the disputed islands, albeit limited in scope). Despite deepening globalisation, the Westphalian territorial states have by no means withered away. Territorial states are, as the name suggests, dependent, at least in part, on the possession of a 'defined territory'.[17] These concepts remain alive and well in East and Southeast Asia, as witnessed by numerous territorial disputes within these regions. Moreover, domestic political considerations, including those associated with nationalism and regime legitimacy, and often coupled with long-standing historical rivalries and animosity, also come into play in this context.[18] Further, although, as noted above, the physical dimensions of the territory that is in dispute can be regarded as near-insignificant, the settlement of these sovereignty disputes is an essential precondition to the resolution of the multiple overlapping maritime claims occurring in the South China Sea. This is because of the long-standing and generally accepted legal dictum that 'the land dominates the sea'. This fundamental understanding was confirmed by the International Court of Justice (ICJ) in 1969, and has been repeatedly re-emphasised since that time.[19] Consequently, claims to maritime jurisdiction depend on sovereignty over land territory.

A related point here is that the UN Convention on the Law of the Sea (UNCLOS) gives states a primary role, which is perhaps unsurprising since UNCLOS was the creation of states.[20] Crucially, only coastal states may advance claims to maritime jurisdiction. This can be concluded from the terms and language of the Convention, which emphasise the role of states. For example, in the preamble to UNCLOS, reference is made to the desirability of establishing 'a legal order for the seas and oceans' through the Convention 'with due regard to the sovereignty of all States'. Similarly, UNCLOS repeatedly mentions coastal states in relation to the prescribed limits to maritime jurisdiction laid out under the Convention. For example, Article 3 of UNCLOS provides that 'Every *State* has the right to establish the breadth of its territorial sea up to a limit not exceeding 12 nautical miles, measured from baselines' (emphasis added).

The presence of multiple states concerned with the South China Sea arena, both claimant states and interested extra-regional players, also tends to complicate matters, as there are numerous competing and frequently incompatible national interests to take into consideration. There remains a general desire on the part of coastal states to not only espouse inflexible, non-negotiable positions, particularly regarding territorial disputes (i.e. concerning the disputed islands of the South China Sea), but also to assert sweeping unilateral maritime claims in order maximise the maritime spaces of the South China Sea subject to their own national jurisdiction. The latter trend, it should be noted, is entirely in keeping with long-standing trends towards 'creeping coastal state jurisdiction' and the national self-interest of states. The competition for sovereignty over the disputed South China Sea islands and their associated maritime spaces also needs to be set against regional developments in terms of the changing balance of power in the South

China Sea, as well as the broader backdrop of geostrategic rivalry between China and the United States. It is abundantly clear that China's armed forces are undergoing a rapid process of modernisation efforts. While it is also the case that other South China Sea claimant states are also actively pursuing force modernisation initiatives, the pace and scope of the transformation of the People's Liberation Army Navy clearly outstrips their combined efforts. This shift in the regional balance of power, and particularly the growing asymmetry in military terms between China, on the one hand, and the other South China Sea claimant States, on the other, affects the strategic and geopolitical context of the South China Sea disputes.[21] Here it is worth noting that the South China Sea disputes themselves are put forward as a justification for such military modernisation efforts.

The interests of extra-regional players, such as the United States, in the South China Sea add another dimension to the scenario. These interests, predominantly centred around conflict prevention and ensuring that navigational freedoms are maintained as they are, are generally compatible with those of the claimant states themselves. Nonetheless, tensions have emerged, especially regarding military activities on the part of non-South China Sea coastal states. These concerns have been given impetus by the US strategic reorientation, or 'pivot', to Asia. In particular, distinct differences between China and the United States have emerged regarding the interpretation of UNCLOS provisions regarding survey activities or intelligence gathering and other military activities in the EEZ of other states – something that has led to multiple incidents and friction between these states.

Access and sea lines of communication

Seaborne trade has been described as the 'backbone' of global trade, with the order of 90 per cent of global trade by volume being carried by sea.[22] This is certainly the case for states and economies located in East and Southeast Asia, broadly, and the South China Sea littoral states, in particular. Arguably, the key underlying and long-standing use to which the coastal states put the waters of the South China Sea and beyond is as a link to other states, and particularly as a conduit for maritime trade. Indeed, it is difficult to overestimate the importance of freedom of navigation to the coastal states of the South China Sea region, as seaborne trade is critical to the economies of the region. Many of the states and economies within the South China Sea region are natural resource-poor, yet feature economies and industries that are highly dependent on access to such resources. This demand for resources and raw materials can only be met through imports, the vast majority of which are carried by sea. The South China Sea is therefore host to a series of Sea Lines of Communication (SLOCs) of regional and global significance.[23] There is also a strong, and increasing, energy security dimension to sea lane security in the region. For example, it has been estimated that around one-third of oil carried by sea globally, equivalent to 15 million barrels per day, transits the Straits of Malacca, the southern gateway to the South China Sea.[24] The South China Sea also serves as the key route for the delivery of liquefied natural gas (LNG), carrying an estimated 6 trillion cubic feet or more than half of the global LNG trade in 2011.[25]

These SLOCs connect constricting 'chokepoints' that provide entry to and egress from the South China Sea. Of particular note in the southern part of the South China Sea are the Straits of Malacca and Singapore, at the south-western entrance to the South China Sea, and the Karimata Strait, providing access to the Java Sea and Indonesia's archipelagic waters, and thus the Straits of Sunda. In the northern South China Sea, the Taiwan Strait, between Taiwan and mainland China, and the Bashi and Balintang Channels, located between Taiwan and the Philippines main island of Luzon, are significant. The South China Sea can also be accessed to the east via the Mindoro Strait and Cape Verde Passage (connecting to the Sulu Sea within the archipelagic waters of the Philippines). Moreover, the South China Sea can be entered via the Straits of Lombok and Makassar, and then the Balabac Strait between the Philippines archipelago and Borneo.[26] The SLOCs connecting these key chokepoints do not represent a single sea lane, but rather a network of routes used for navigation. What is worth noting, however, is that despite the fact that the disputed islands of the South China Sea are often referred to as being located on or straddling these SLOCs, in fact the island groups in question have long been regarded primarily as hazards to navigation. Consequently, much maritime traffic, for instance travelling between the Malacca and Singapore Straits and ports in East and Northeast Asia, tends to sail well to the west of the disputed Spratly Islands. Similarly, the Palawan Passage route skirts the east of the Spratlys archipelago.[27]

Marine spaces and resources

As observed above, in line with the maxim that 'the land dominates the sea', claims to maritime areas are necessarily secondary to questions of territorial sovereignty. Nonetheless, sovereignty and sovereign rights over maritime spaces and the resources contained, or thought to be contained, therein have proved to be important factors underlying and arguably driving the South China Sea disputes. Of particular note here are long-standing, though arguably not especially well-founded, perceptions that the South China Sea hosts substantial reserves of seabed energy resources. Recent incidents involving oil and gas surveying and exploration activities also tend to reinforce the view that access to valuable oil and gas resources underlying contested waters is an important contributing factor to the South China Sea disputes (see below). Certainly, the potential presence of substantial and, critically, close-to-hand reserves of, particularly, oil, would be extremely attractive to the South China Sea claimants in light of their predominantly energy intensive economies and in the face of their generally increasing energy security concerns.[28]

However, it can be contended that such perceptions regarding the oil and gas resource potential of the South China Sea and particularly the disputed waters of the South China Sea are potentially highly likely to be misleading. In the first place, the existence of broad areas of overlapping maritime claims and active jurisdictional disputes over these spaces tends to forestall concerted exploration efforts – including seismic surveys, let alone exploratory drilling. Consequently, estimates regarding resource potential of disputed areas are predominantly speculative, and therefore highly unreliable. In this context, it is worth noting that three key geological factors, or 'play elements', are required for hydrocarbons to potentially be present. These are a highly porous and permeable sedimentary reservoir, organic rich source rock and a low permeability seal or capping rock.[29] Where these elements are absent, the presence of hydrocarbons is extremely unlikely. In fact, this situation applies for much of the central part of the South China Sea, which comprises oceanic crust.[30] However, even where surveys suggest that the key geological play elements are present, this does not guarantee the presence of hydrocarbon resources – exploratory drilling is required for discoveries to be made, something that is nigh on impossible in the context of highly contested waters such as those of the South China Sea.

Further, there is persistent confusion in both the media and academic literature with respect to oil reporting terminology. In particular, resource and reserve estimates are often used interchangeably. The former term refers to oil resources in situ, while the latter relates to that fraction of the resources that may be recovered at current market price and present technical capabilities.[31] While it is well to recognise that the reserve estimate is likely to change over time, particularly as the price of oil fluctuates – generally termed the price-reserve relationship – as well as with progress in oil exploration and extraction technologies, the fact remains that only a fraction of oil in the ground is recoverable due to price and technological constraints. For example, for an under-explored 'frontier' province such as the South China Sea, the oil field recovery factor may be as low as 10 per cent of the resource volume (though recovery factors of the order of 35 per cent may be anticipated for better-explored provinces). Such recovery factors stand in distinct contrast to those for gas fields, which are generally around 75 per cent.[32]

The frequent confusion between resource and reserve estimates, whether from misunderstanding, a degree of journalistic licence or an overt desire to inflate figures with a view to emphasising the potential importance of the disputed maritime spaces, leads to highly misleading statements regarding the seabed energy resource potential of disputed waters. To a large extent, the lack of use of best practice oil reporting in the literature on the potential resources contained in (or under) disputed maritime spaces helps to explain the often wild variations in estimates as to the resource potential of these spaces. For example, in the South China Sea, resource estimates regarding hydrocarbons vary hugely. In 1993/94, a report published by the United States Geological Survey (USGS) provided a figure of 28,000 million barrels (Mb) of oil, which, once reserves already included in national inventories are subtracted, leads to an estimate of undiscovered South China Sea resources of 21,500 Mb.[33] In stark contrast, characteristically optimistic Chinese resource estimates for the region range between 105,000 and 213,000 Mb.[34] In light of the above suggestions that the South China Sea represents 'China's Persian Gulf'[35] can be regarded as highly unlikely.

While the potential seabed energy resources of the South China Sea have tended to excite significant attention and excitement, this focus on largely unproven hydrocarbon resources, to a large extent, has tended to obscure the importance of and distract attention from the region's well-proven marine living resources. The semi-enclosed, tropical environment of the South China Sea and Gulf of Thailand hosts marine environments of exceptional richness in biodiversity terms. These environments support fisheries of significance in global, and certainly regional, terms. It has been estimated that the South China Sea alone accounts for as much as one-tenth of global fish catches.[36] These marine living resources are fundamental to the food security of coastal populations numbered in the hundreds of millions. Access to the waters of the South China Sea and Gulf of Thailand in order to exploit these abundant living resources therefore represents an enduring maritime concern of the littoral states and Taiwan. It follows that the preservation and protection of the marine environment supporting living resources that are so crucial from a food security perspective should be top policy priority for the South China Sea coastal states. Unfortunately, however, the marine environment, biological diversity and living resources in question are widely acknowledged to be under serious threat as a result of a combination of unregulated, and often competitive and destructive, fishing practices, together with rapid coastal development and related marine pollution and habitat destruction. Over 80 per cent of reefs are at great risk and will collapse within 20 years unless unsustainable practices are abated; 70 per cent of mangrove cover has been lost in the last 70 years, and at current rates of habitat loss the remainder will be lost by 2030; and 20–60 per cent of seagrass beds have similarly disappeared over the last 50 years, with the remainder also threatened with destruction.[37]

Legal uncertainties

The international legal framework against which to assess the maritime claims of the South China Sea States is provided by UNCLOS in particular, to which almost all of the South China Sea States are parties.[38] UNCLOS outlines provisions relating to the definition of baselines along the coast, the spatial dimensions of claims to maritime jurisdiction, coastal and other state rights and responsibilities within such zones and concerning the delimitation of maritime boundaries where overlapping maritime claims occur. It should be noted that the Convention is not of direct relevance where disputes concerning sovereignty over land territory, such as the South China Sea islands, arise. Instead, international law concerning the acquisition of sovereignty over territory applies. As a number of these issues are dealt with by Donald Rothwell in this volume, this section deals with two problematic legal issues directly related to the geographical and geopolitical uncertainties outlined above (i.e. concerning the definition of baselines and the interrelated issue of the definition and categorisation of different types of insular feature).

Baselines

As noted above, maritime claims are dependent on sovereignty over land territory possessing a coast. Baselines along the coasts are, therefore, fundamental to
claims to maritime jurisdiction both because they define the extent of land territory from which maritime jurisdictional rights arise and because they define the
'starting line' for the measurement of such maritime claims. Additionally, the
definition of baselines is a vital precursor to the delimitation of maritime boundaries, given the near overwhelming weight of state practice in favour of the use
of equidistance lines, at least as the starting point for the delimitation of maritime
boundaries, especially between opposite coastlines.[39] Similarly, the two-stage and,
more recently, three-stage approach to maritime boundary delimitation, which has
emerged from recent cases before international courts and tribunals, also starts
with the construction of a provisional boundary line based on the equidistance
method. Equidistance lines can only be constructed from the baselines, or, more
specifically, critical basepoints, of the coastal states involved. UNCLOS provides
for multiple types of baselines. However, in the absence of any other claims,
'normal' baselines coincident with the low-water line as shown on large-scale
charts recognised by the coastal state concerned will prevail.[40] In the context of
the South China Sea, normal baselines, as well as the Convention's provisions on
the baselines of reefs,[41] are particularly relevant to the baselines of the generally
disputed South China Sea islands. The difficulty, as noted above, however, is that
discerning the location of the low-water line is especially problematic in the South
China Sea. This not only means that it is difficult to define the land/sea interface,
and thus the extent of the area of land involved, but problems also arise in terms
of the classification of different types of insular feature (see below).

With regard to the mainland coasts of the states surrounding the South China
Sea, several of the states concerned have taken the view that their coasts are
sufficiently deeply indented and cut into or fringed with islands in their immediate
vicinity to justify the definition of systems of straight baselines as provided for
under Article 7 of UNCLOS.[42] Such claims to straight baselines have been made
by Cambodia, China (and Taiwan), Thailand and Vietnam.[43] Additionally, while
Malaysia has yet to officially publicise the location of its straight baselines, it
is evident that such claims have been made.[44] These claimed straight baselines
are predominantly extensive and often front generally smooth coastlines or serve
to link small, widely separated and distant from shore islands. Consequently, these
claims have attracted international protests.[45] Additionally, two of the South
China Sea littoral states, Indonesia[46] and the Philippines,[47] are archipelagic
states and have defined archipelagic baselines in accordance with Article 47 of
UNCLOS.[48]

Definition of types of insular feature

UNCLOS provides for several types of insular feature. An island is defined under
Article 121 (1) as 'a naturally formed area of land, surrounded by water, which

is above water at high tide'. The use of the term 'naturally formed' eliminates man-made islands from consideration. This is reinforced by Article 60 (8) of the Convention, which states in explicit terms that artificial islands, installations and structures 'do not possess the status of islands', that they 'have no territorial sea of their own' and further that they have no impact on the delimitation of maritime boundaries.[49] It is also made explicit that an island also needs to be 'above water at high tide' – something that, as noted above, may be difficult to discern in the complex tidal environment of the South China Sea. Article 5 of the Convention, dealing with normal baselines, will apply to islands unless other types of baselines, such as straight baselines, have been claimed. Even then, there is a need to link, or 'tie back', systems of straight baselines to anchor or turning points located on the normal baseline. Similarly, Article 6, dealing with reefs, requires the location of the low-water line to be determined, as this provision relates to islands located on reefs and the location of 'the seaward low-water line of the reef'.[50] Article 13 of the Convention defines another type of insular formation, the low-tide elevation (LTE). LTEs comprise 'a naturally formed area of land which is surrounded by and above water at low tide but submerged at high tide'.[51] LTEs may be employed as basepoints for the measurement of maritime claims, but only if they are 'situated wholly or partly at a distance not exceeding the breadth of the territorial sea from the mainland or an island'.[52] Where a feature rising from the sea floor does not emerge above even the low-tide level, it has no special status or capacity to be used as a basepoint for the measurement of maritime claims.

From the foregoing, it is clear that the definition of both low- and high-water lines is crucial to determining whether a particular feature can be classified as an island (above high tide), low-tide elevation (above low tide but submerged at high tide) or as a non-insular, submerged feature (submerged at low tide).[53] Such definition requires, first, that a vertical datum be chosen and, second, that hydrographic surveys be undertaken in order to define low and high water levels according to the vertical datum selected. The term 'vertical datum' refers to the level of reference for vertical measurements such as depths and heights of tide. It is worth noting here that neither the Geneva Conventions of 1958 nor UNCLOS specify a particular vertical datum. This choice of vertical datum is thus left up to the individual coastal state. There is therefore no inherently 'wrong' low-water line choice. However, if two states opt for differing vertical datums, insular features may, for example, be represented as an island or rock on the chart of one state, but as a mere low-tide elevation on the other state's chart.

While the judgment in one recent case, *Territorial and Maritime Dispute Case* between Colombia and Nicaragua before the ICJ, has shed some additional light on the issue of defining insular features, key questions remain unanswered.[54] On the positive side, the ICJ provided a more detailed reading of Article 121 of UNCLOS than on any previous occasion in its deliberations over a broad shallow-water bank called Quitasueño and the insular features arguably present upon it. From this ruling, it has become clear that the composition of an island and its size are irrelevant to its status as an island under Article 121, so long as the feature concerned is naturally formed and above high tide.[55] The ICJ encountered difficulties regarding disagreements between the parties over the proper low- and high-water levels to apply in the particularly shallow waters under consideration. Ultimately, the Court relied on the fact that under either of the tidal levels preferred by the parties, one feature in particular was above high tide and so qualified as an island, but other features whose insular status was contested were not conclusively proven to be islands.[56] This aspect of the Court's ruling is therefore not necessarily readily applicable to other potentially analogous scenarios.

These distinctions are significant in the South China Sea context because what type of insular formation is involved has potentially dramatic implications for the capacity of the features concerned to generate maritime claims on behalf of whichever State is ultimately deemed to hold sovereignty over them. In particular, Article 121 (2) provides that such islands are to generate claims to maritime zones in the same manner as 'other land territory'. However, Article 121 (3), however, creates a disadvantaged sub-category of island, the 'rock' that 'cannot sustain human habitation or economic life of their own', and in consequence have no exclusive economic zone (EEZ) or continental shelf rights. Where there remains significant uncertainty, despite voluminous academic commentary and analysis, is precisely how to distinguish between an island capable of generating entitlements to EEZ and continental shelf rights, and a mere 'rock', which cannot.[57] Should the disputed South China Sea islands be capable of generating EEZs, for example, the potential high-seas pocket located in the central part of the South China Sea disappears. That said, care should be taken not to over-emphasise the importance of the generally very small, isolated and sparsely or uninhabited disputed islands of the South China Sea in terms of their capacity to generate maritime claims. There exists a long history of such small, remote insular features, such as those present in the South China Sea, being awarded only limited (or no) weight or effect in the context of the delimitation of maritime boundaries, especially those related to EEZ and continental shelf rights.[58]

Incremental progress? Maritime claims and agreements

In keeping with the relevant provisions of UNCLOS, the South China Sea coastal states have generally claimed 12 nautical mile territorial seas, and EEZs to 200 nautical miles from baselines, together with continental shelf rights.[59] While most of these claims have tended to be 'ambit' ones in accordance with the maximum allowable breadth of the maritime zone in question, some more specific unilateral claims have been advanced, notably within the Gulf of Thailand,[60] by Malaysia in 1979,[61] by Brunei in 1988[62] and Indonesia in 2010.[63] The South China Sea is also host to claims to maritime space apparently based on historic arguments. Within the Gulf of Thailand, Thailand has, since 1959, claimed the northernmost extension of that body of water, the Bight of Bangkok, as a historic bay.[64] Additionally, Cambodia and Vietnam have, since 1982, claimed an oblong area of 'joint historic waters' projecting from their coasts (but within their claimed straight baselines, in the Gulf of Thailand).[65] The Philippines has also long claimed rights within its Treaty Limits (i.e. the 'box' formed by several late nineteenth- and early twentieth-century treaties).[66] The Philippines' claim to territorial sea rights within the Treaty Limits box, and thus out to 285 nautical miles at its furthest extent from the Philippine baselines,[67] are incompatible with UNCLOS, and have led to international protests.[68]

China's controversial 'nine-dash line', or 'U-shaped line' claim (see Map 2) may also signify a historic claim to large portions of the South China Sea, although it remains unclear precisely what this broken line actually signifies. This line derives from a map issued in 1947 by the Republic of China. This claim was subsequently adopted by the PRC in 1949, albeit with two dashes removed, and the dashes shown being made shorter and somewhat differently located, from the early 1950s.[69] It remains uncertain whether the nine-dash line represents a claim to sovereignty over the territory (i.e. the disputed islands) within it, is indicative of a unilateral claim to a maritime boundary, or represents a claim to the maritime spaces within the dashes, whether as historic waters or another type of maritime zone. The status of the nine-dash line has been challenged as part of the arbitration case initiated by the Philippines in 2013.[70] Specifically, the Notification and Statement of Claims of the Philippines states that 'China's maritime claims in the South China Sea based on its so-called "nine-dash line" are contrary to UNCLOS and invalid'.[71] While this suggests that an authoritative legal interpretation of its meaning may in due course be forthcoming, this depends on the Arbitration Tribunal concluding that it has jurisdiction to rule on this issue.[72]

Further, submissions relating to the outer limits of the continental shelf where it extends beyond 200 nautical miles from baselines, made in 2009 by Vietnam alone, and Malaysia and Vietnam jointly to the United Nations Commission on the Limits of the Continental Shelf (CLCS), have led to some clarification in the maritime claims of at least some of the South China Sea states.[73] The implication of these submissions is that, as far as Malaysia and Vietnam at least are concerned, the disputed islands of the South China Sea should not be awarded full 200 nautical mile EEZ and continental shelf rights.[74] These submissions prompted China to issue protest notes that, importantly, included maps showing China's nine-dash line.[75] These notes led to responses and counter-protests from other interested South China Sea states – notably, Indonesia, Malaysia, the Philippines and Vietnam – which, in turn, led to further diplomatic correspondence.[76] These diplomatic (and not so diplomatic) exchanges are revealing, in that they serve to, at least partially, clarify the positions of these states. What is also clear, however, is that China not only regards the disputed South China Sea islands as being 'indisputably' subject to Chinese sovereignty, but that these islands are capable of generating the full suite of claims to maritime jurisdiction.[77]

Maritime boundary and joint development agreements

As noted, the South China Sea is therefore a semi-enclosed sea, albeit a large one, within the meaning of Article 123 of UNCLOS. This is significant, in that this article provides that such states bordering enclosed and semi-enclosed seas 'should cooperate with each other in the exercise of their rights and in the performance of their duties' under the Convention is therefore applicable. Thus, although the South China Sea tends to be portrayed as being a host to numerous contentious territorial and maritime disputes and as a potential arena for conflict, several encouraging maritime agreements have been achieved, albeit generally at the periphery of the South China Sea. Notable examples include Thailand and Malaysia's territorial sea delimitation in 1979[78] and partial continental shelf delimitation of the same date,[79] the Thailand-Vietnam EEZ agreement of 1997,[80] China and Vietnam's 2000 agreements on maritime boundary delimitation through the Gulf of Tonkin/Beibu Gulf,[81] the Indonesia-Vietnam continental shelf boundary of 2003,[82] and Indonesia and Singapore's territorial sea boundary agreements of 1973 and 2009.[83] Brunei-Darussalam and Malaysia inherited territorial sea boundaries from the United Kingdom,[84] and also appear to have clarified their maritime boundary issues through a 16 March 2009 Exchange of Letters.[85] Additionally, the South China Sea hosts multiple maritime joint development agreements and cooperative arrangements of a practical nature. These include those between Malaysia and Thailand (agreed in principle in 1979[86] and implemented from 1990),[87] concerning seabed energy resources, between Malaysia and Vietnam, also related to seabed hydrocarbons exploration and development in 1992,[88] and between China and Vietnam in 2000, concerning joint fishing activities as part of their above-mentioned maritime boundary treaty.[89] Cambodia and Thailand also agreed, in principle, to pursue an accord on maritime joint development for part of their overlapping claim areas in 2001, although little progress has subsequently been achieved to date.[90] Further, through their 2009 Exchange of Letters, Brunei and Malaysia reportedly reached an accommodation with respect to formerly disputed seabed areas now confirmed as under Brunei's jurisdiction, but with the participation of Malaysia's national oil company, Petronas, in their exploration.[91]

Further joint development is often posited as the ideal way to overcome the long-standing and apparently intractable disputes evident in the South China Sea. On the face of it, this option appears to offer many advantages. However, numerous impediments to realising a joint development solution to the South China Sea disputes swiftly arise. It is notable, for example, that past practice in relation to maritime joint development has been exclusively on a bilateral basis. The multilateral nature of the South China Sea disputes would therefore seem to make the realisation of a joint arrangement involving up to six parties highly challenging. A further key issue that swiftly arises is a spatial one – precisely where would joint development apply to geographically? This is an especially problematic issue in light of lack of clarity concerning the maritime claims of many of the claimant states, as well as significant disagreement between them as to the legitimacy of each other's claims. Further, even if a joint zone arrangement was somehow defined, how resource benefits would be shared would likely be a particularly contentious issue to address.

Adrift on complex and increasingly contested waters?

The title of this contribution suggests that the South China Sea states, in particular, are seemingly 'adrift' on complex waters. It seems clear from the foregoing that complexity, whether viewed from geographical, geopolitical or legal perspectives, is an enduring theme in the South China Sea. Further, incremental progress around the periphery of the South China Sea notwithstanding, it can be argued that the South China Sea is becoming an increasingly contested maritime space. The sovereignty disputes over islands that are at the root of the problem remain unresolved, and there appears little prospect of their being addressed in the foreseeable future. Further, while the submissions on the outer limits to the continental shelf made to the CLCS, and the diplomatic notes that they prompted, have provided some welcome clarification regarding at least some of the previously ambiguous claims of the South China Sea coastal states, the stark differences between the opposing positions of the claimant states have also been highlighted.

What does appear to have changed in recent years is that there has been a significant escalation in tensions in the South China Sea. In particular, in recent years a series of incidents have occurred involving Chinese maritime surveillance and enforcement agencies, and Chinese flagged fishing vessels in waters closer to the proximate mainland and main island coastlines than to the nearest disputed islands. Such actions appear to be based on the nine-dash line 'claim' rather than maritime claims in line with the terms of UNCLOS advanced from the disputed islands. Incidents have included enforcement activities related to fisheries jurisdiction, for example with respect to waters that Indonesia considers to form part of its EEZ,[92] as well as interventions to disrupt oil and gas survey and exploration activities conducted by Malaysia, the Philippines and Vietnam in their respective coastal waters. Moreover, in June 2012, the China National Offshore Oil Corporation (CNOOC) issued tenders for oil concessions in close proximity to the Vietnamese coastline and within its claimed EEZ, yet just within the nine-dash line[93] and in 2014 deployed a deep-water oil rig to disputed waters off the Paracel Islands, leading to a confrontation between China and Vietnam.[94] These incidents appear to have, in part, arisen as certain South China Sea coastal states, notably Indonesia, Malaysia, the Philippines and Vietnam, have sought to undertake activities in what they consider to be 'their' waters proximate to their mainland and main island coasts. These states appear to have taken the view that those parts of the South China Sea closer to their undisputed territories than to any disputed feature in the South China Sea are undisputed. It is increasingly apparent that China disagrees. Worryingly, China not only appears resistant to such efforts to restrict or minimise the area of the South China Sea subject to dispute in principle, but is apparently increasingly willing to back up its assertions with enforcement actions on the water, apparently up to the (uncertain) limits of the nine-dash line, and thus to the vast majority of the South China Sea as a whole. In this context, the extremely limited progress towards realising conflict avoidance and management mechanisms beyond the non-binding 2002 Declaration on the Conduct of Parties in the South China Sea (DoC) is telling.[95] It also remains open to question whether recent efforts on the part of the Philippines to initiate arbitral proceedings with China under Annex VII of UNCLOS on a number of uncertainties in the Chinese position, including the status of the nine-dash line and the status and role of certain South China Sea insular features, will bear fruit.[96] In the absence of an unanticipated breakthrough, therefore, the South China Sea coastal and claimant states do appear set to remain adrift on increasingly complex and contested waters for the foreseeable future.

Notes

1 According to the International Hydrographic Organization, the southernmost defining point of the South China Sea is Lucipara Point on the east coast of Sumatra. See *Limits of Oceans and Seas*, the International Hydrographic Organization (IHO) Special Publication No. 23, 3rd edn, Monte Carlo, 1953.
2 Hasjim Djalal, 'South China Sea Island Disputes', in M. H. Nordquist and J. N. Moore (eds), *Security Flashpoints: Oil, Islands, Sea Access and Military Confrontation*, Martinus Nijhoff, The Hague, 1998, pp. 109–133, at p. 109.
3 Djalal, 'South China Sea Island Disputes', p. 109. Technically, the correct abbreviation for a nautical mile is 'M', while 'nm' denotes nanometres. However, 'nm' is widely used by many authorities (e.g. the UN Office of Ocean Affairs and the Law of the Sea) and appears to cause less confusion than 'M', which is often assumed to be an abbreviation for metres.
4 See UKHO, *China Sea Pilot*, Vol. 1, 8th edn, United Kingdom Hydrographic Office, Admiralty Sailing Directions, Taunton, 2010, pp. 75–78.
5 UKHO, *China Sea Pilot*, Vol. 1, p. 78.
6 The relevant British Admiralty Sailing Directions (Pilot) describe Scarborough Reef as being 'steep-to on all sides and consists of a narrow belt of coral enclosing a lagoon of clear blue water'. South Rock, at 3 metres high, is the 'tallest rock' located at the southeast extremity of the reef. See UKHO, *China Sea Pilot*, United Kingdom Hydrographic Office, Vol. 2, 9th edn, Admiralty Sailing Directions, Taunton, 2010, p. 74.
7 Termed a 'below-water atoll' in the relevant British Admiralty Pilot with a least depth of water of 9.1 metres over it. See UKHO *China Sea Pilot*, Vol. 1, pp. 68–69.
8 The feature among the Spratly Islands group is Itu Aba (Taiping Island), which is approximately 1.4 kilometres long and 370 metres wide, with an area of around 50 hectares.
9 Estimates regarding the number of features comprising the Spratly Islands vary considerably. The range of 150–180 is provided by D. J. Dzurek, 'The Spratly Islands: Who's on First?', *Maritime Briefing*, 2(1), International Boundaries Research Unit, Durham, 1996, p. 1. See also C. H. Schofield, 'Dangerous Ground – a Geopolitical Overview of the South China Sea', in Sam Bateman and Ralph Emmers (eds), *The South China Sea: Towards a Cooperative Management Regime*, Routledge, London, 2009, pp. 7–25, at pp. 9–10.
10 See UKHO, *China Sea Pilot*, Vol. 2, pp. 78–86.
11 A. G. Findlay, *Indian Archipelago and China Directory*, 3rd edn, Richard Holmes Laurie, London, 1889, p. vi. Quoted in D. Hancox and J. R. V. Prescott, *Secret Hydrographic Surveys in the Spratly Islands*, The Maritime Institute of Malaysia, Kuala Lumpur, 1997, p. 1.
12 Schofield, 'Dangerous Ground – a Geopolitical Overview of the South China Sea', p. 10.
13 Y. Lyons, 'Prospects for Satellite Imagery of Insular Features and Surrounding Marine Habitats in the South China Sea', *Marine Policy*, 45, 2014, pp. 146–155, at p. 150.
14 Schofield, 'Dangerous Ground – a Geopolitical Overview of the South China Sea', p. 12.

15 Schofield, 'Dangerous Ground – a Geopolitical Overview of the South China Sea', p. 9. Similarly, it has been suggested that the total land area of the 13 largest disputed islands in the Spratly Islands group amount to an area of a mere 1.7 square kilometres. See D. Hancox and J. R. V. Prescott, *A Geographical Description of the Spratly Islands and An Account of Hydrographic Surveys amongst Those Islands*, Maritime Briefing, 1(6), International Boundaries Research Unit, Durham, 1995. See also R. Beckman, 'The UN Convention on the Law of the Sea and the Maritime Disputes in the South China Sea', *American Journal of International Law*, 107, 2013, pp. 142–163, at p. 143.

16 Hancox and Prescott, *A Geographical Description of the Spratly Islands*, p. 8. See also Schofield, 'Dangerous Ground – a Geopolitical Overview of the South China Sea', p. 9.

17 Article 1 of the Montevideo Convention on the Rights and Duties of States provides that states should possess a 'defined territory', a permanent population, a government and the capacity to enter into international relations with other states. See *the Montevideo Convention on the Rights and Duties of States opened for signature 26 December 1933*, 165 LNTS 19 (entered into force 26 December 1934).

18 See Schofield, 'Dangerous Ground – a Geopolitical Overview of the South China Sea', p. 19. See also C. H. Schofield, I. Townsend-Gault, H. Djalal, I. Storey, M. Miller and T. Cook, *From Disputed Waters to Seas of Opportunity: Overcoming Barriers to Maritime Cooperation in East and Southeast Asia*, National Bureau of Asian Research Special Report No. 30, July 2011, at p. 19. See also I. Storey, *Southeast Asia and the Rise of China: The Search for Security*, Routledge, London and New York, 2011.

19 This point was emphasised by the International Court of Justice in its first case concerning jurisdiction beyond the territorial sea, the *North Sea Continental Shelf Cases (Germany v Netherlands, Germany v Denmark)*, 1969, ICJ Reports, 3, especially paragraph 19. The Court made specific reference to Article 2 of the *Convention on the Continental Shelf*, 1958, 9, *Convention on the Continental Shelf*, Geneva, 29 April 1958, in force 10 June 1964, in UN Doc. A/CONF.13/L.55.

20 *United Nations Convention on the Law of the Sea*, Montego Bay, 10 December 1982, in force 16 November 1994, in UNTS, vol. 1833, p. 3, www.un.org/Depts/los/convention_agreements/convention_overview_convention.htm (accessed 2 June 2014), hereinafter 'Law of the Sea Convention' or 'UNCLOS'. At the time of writing, UNCLOS had 166 parties comprising 165 states, plus the European Union. See United Nations, Division for Ocean Affairs and the Law of the Sea, Office of Legal Affairs, *Chronological List of Ratifications of, Accessions and Successions to the Convention and the Related Agreements as at 18 September 2013*, United Nations, Division for Ocean Affairs and the Law of the Sea, Office of Legal Affairs, 2013, www.un.org/Depts/los/reference_files/chronological_lists_of_ratifications.htm#The United Nations Convention on the Law of the Sea (accessed 2 June 2014).

21 See C. H. Schofield and I. Storey, *The South China Sea Dispute: Increasing Stakes, Rising Tensions*, Occasional Paper, The Jamestown Foundation, Washington, DC, October 2009, pp. 23–24.

22 United Nations Conference on Trade and Development, *Review of Maritime Transport 2008*, Geneva, 2008, p. 8.

23 See, for example, Schofield and Storey, *The South China Sea Dispute*.

24 'The South China Sea is an Important World Energy Trade Route', *United States Energy Information Administration (EIA)*, 4 April 2013, www.eia.gov/todayinenergy/detail.cfm?id=10671 (accessed 2 June 2014).

25 'The South China Sea is an Important World Energy Trade Route'.

26 See *Admiralty Ocean Passages of the World*, 5th edn, UKHO, Taunton, 2004.

27   C. Rahman and M. Tsamenyi, 'A Strategic Perspective on Security and Naval Issues in the South China Sea', *Ocean Development & International Law*, 41, 2010, pp. 316–318.

28   N. Owen and C. H. Schofield, 'Disputed South China Sea Hydrocarbons in Perspective', *Marine Policy*, 36(3), 2012, pp. 809–822, at pp. 811–812.

29   Owen and Schofield, 'Disputed South China Sea Hydrocarbons in Perspective', p. 813.

30   Owen and Schofield, 'Disputed South China Sea Hydrocarbons in Perspective', p. 813.

31   Owen and Schofield, 'Disputed South China Sea Hydrocarbons in Perspective', p. 813.

32   Owen and Schofield, 'Disputed South China Sea Hydrocarbons in Perspective', p. 813.

33   Owen and Schofield, 'Disputed South China Sea Hydrocarbons in Perspective', p. 815. See also *Energy Profile of the South China Sea, United States Energy Information Administration (EIA)*, Washington, DC, 2008, www.eia. doe.gov/emeu/cabs/schina.html (accessed 2 June 2014).

34   Owen and Schofield, 'Disputed South China Sea Hydrocarbons in Perspective', p. 815.

35   See, for example, Chen, Xiao, 'Naihai de ziyuan shijie' [The world of resources in the South China Sea], *Sanlian shenghuo zhoukan* [Sanlian Life Weekly], 46, 15 November 2010, pp. 62–67, at p. 64.

36   See UNEP/GEF, *Reversing Environmental Degradation Trends in the South China Sea and Gulf of Thailand*, www.unepscs.org (accessed 2 June 2014). See also Schofield, 'Dangerous Ground – a Geopolitical Overview of the South China Sea', pp. 17–18.

37   UNEP/GEF, *Reversing Environmental Degradation Trends in the South China Sea and Gulf of Thailand*, www.unepscs.org (accessed 2 June 2014).

38   This statement applies to the coastal states and entities that border the South China Sea 'proper' (i.e. China/Taiwan, the Philippines, Brunei Darussalam (hereinafter, 'Brunei'), Malaysia, Indonesia and Vietnam). Among the states bordering the Gulf of Thailand extension of the South China Sea, only Cambodia is not yet a party to UNCLOS. See United Nations, Division for Ocean Affairs and the Law of the Sea, Office of Legal Affairs, *Chronological List of Ratifications of, Accessions and Successions to the Convention and the Related Agreements as at 18 September 2013*.

39   J. R. V. Prescott and C. H. Schofield, *The Maritime Political Boundaries of the World*, Martinus Nijhoff, Leiden, 2005, pp. 239–240.

40   UNCLOS, Article 5.

41   UNCLOS, Article 6.

42   Article 7 of UNCLOS allows coastal states to depart from normal, low-water line, baselines along selected parts of their coastlines 'where the coastline is deeply indented and cut into', or if there is a 'fringe of islands' along the coast in its 'immediate vicinity'.

43   See S. Bateman and C. H. Schofield, 'State Practice Regarding Straight Baselines in East Asia – Legal, Technical and Political Issues in a Changing Environment', Advisory Board on the Law of the Sea (ABLOS) on *Difficulties in Implementing the Provisions of UNCLOS*, International Hydrographic Bureau Monaco, October 2008, pp. 16–17, www.gmat.unsw.edu.au/ablos/ABLOS08Folder/ablos08_papers.htm (accessed 2 June 2014).

44   That Malaysia claimed straight baselines can be inferred from its 1979 *Peta Baru* (New Map), which shows straight line limits to portions of Malaysia's claimed territorial sea limit. Malaysia enacted a Baselines of Maritime Zones Act in 2006, but has yet to publish coordinates for its claimed straight baselines, although some of the straight baselines concerned are illustrated on maps contained in Malaysia's joint submission on outer continental shelf limits with Vietnam. The *Peta Menunjukkan Sempadan Perairan dan Pelantar Benua Malaysia* (Map Showing the Territorial Waters and Continental Shelf Boundaries of Malaysia), often referred to as the *Peta Baru* (New Map), was published by the Malaysian Directorate of National Mapping in two sheets, 21 December 1979. See also *Joint Submission to the Commission on the Limits of the Continental Shelf pursuant to Article 76, paragraph 8 of the United*

Nations Convention on the Law of the Sea 1982 in respect of the southern part of the South China Sea, Executive Summary, 6 May 2009, www.un.org/Depts/los/clcs_new/submissions_files/submission_mysvnm_33_2009.htm (accessed 2 June 2014); Vivian L. Forbes, 'The Territorial Sea Datum of Malaysia', *MIMA Bulletin*, 14(4), 2007, pp. 7–8.

45 See, in particular, J. Ashley Roach and Robert Smith, *United States Responses to Excessive Maritime Claims*, 3rd edn, Martinus Nijhoff, Leiden, 2012, pp. 57–133.

46 See Indonesia's 1960 Act No. 4/Prp/1960 concerning Indonesian Waters and Act no. 6/1996 on Indonesian Waters, together with *Peraturan Pemerintah* (PP), Government Regulations No. 38 of June 2002 and No. 61 of 1998. See also Clive H. Schofield and Andi Arsana, 'Closing the Loop: Indonesia's Revised Archipelagic Baselines System', *Australian Journal of Marine and Ocean Affairs*, 1(2), 2009, pp. 57–62.

47 See, in particular, Republic Act No. 9522, An Act to Amend Certain Provisions of Republic Act No. 3046, As Amended by Republic Act No. 5446, To Define the Archipelagic Baselines of the Philippines, and for Other Purposes, 10 March 2009. See Law of the Sea Bulletin, No. 70, 2000, p. 32.

48 See M. Tsamenyi, C. H. Schofield and B. Milligan, 'Navigation through Archipelagos: Current State Practice', in Myron H. Nordquist, Tommy B. Koh and John Norton Moore (eds), *Freedom of the Seas, Passage Rights and the 1982 Law of the Sea Convention*, Martinus Nijhoff, The Hague, 2008, pp. 134–138.

49 UNCLOS, Article 60 (5) does, however, provide that safety zones of not more than 500 metres may be declared around such artificial islands or installations.

50 See UNCLOS, Article 6.

51 See UNCLOS, Article 13 (1).

52 See UNCLOS, Article 13 (2).

53 See C. M. Carleton and C. H. Schofield, 'Developments in the Technical Determination of Maritime Space: Charts, Datums, Baselines, Maritime Zones and Limits', *Maritime Briefing*, 3(3), International Boundaries Research Unit, Durham, 2001. See also *A Manual on Technical Aspects of the United Nations Convention on the Law of the Sea, 1982*, International Hydrographic Organization (with the International Oceanographic Commission and the International Association of Geodesy), Special Publication no. 51, 4th edn, Monaco, 2006, Chapter 2, pp. 16–20, www.iho.shom.fr/ (accessed 2 June 2014).

54 *Territorial and Maritime Dispute (Nicaragua v Colombia)*, Judgment, 19 November 2012, pp. 191–193, www.icj-cij.org/docket/files/124/17164.pdf (accessed 2 June 2014).

55 *Territorial and Maritime Dispute (Nicaragua v Colombia)*, Judgment, 19 November 2012, para. 37.

56 *Territorial and Maritime Dispute (Nicaragua v Colombia)*, Judgment, 19 November 2012, paras 35–36.

57 See UNCLOS, Article 121.

58 See, for example, C. H. Schofield, 'Islands or Rocks – is that the Real Question? The Treatment of Islands in the Delimitation of Maritime Boundaries', in M. H. Nordquist, J. N. Moore, A. H. A. Soons and H.-S. Kim (eds), *The Law of the Sea Convention: US Accession and Globalization*, Martinus Nijhoff, Leiden, 2012, pp. 322–340.

59 See, for example, *Annual Admiralty Notice to Mariners No. 12*, United Kingdom Hydrographic Office (UKHO), 2013, www.ukho.gov.uk/ProductsandServices/Maritime Safety/AnnualNm/12.pdf (accessed 2 June 2014).

60 See C. H. Schofield and M. Tan-Mullins, 'Claims, Conflicts and Cooperation in the Gulf of Thailand', *Ocean Yearbook*, 22, Martinus Nijhoff, Leiden, 2008, pp. 75–116.

61 Through Malaysia's *Peta Baru* (New Map).

62 Maps Showing Continental Shelf of Brunei Darussalam (1988) and Maps Showing Fishery Limits of Brunei Darussalam (1988). Also of note is the Map Showing Territorial Waters of Brunei Darussalam (1987). See I. Storey, 'Brunei's Contested

Sea Border with China', in B. Elleman, S. Kotkin and C. H. Schofield (eds), *Beijing's Power and China's Borders: Twenty Neighbors in Asia*, M. E. Sharpe, Armonk, NY, 2012, pp. 36–45. See also R. Haller-Trost, 'The Brunei-Malaysia Dispute over Territorial and Maritime Claims in International Law', *Maritime Briefing*, 1(3), International Boundaries Research Unit, Durham, 1994, pp. 4–5.

63 Bakosurtanal, *Map of the Republic of Indonesia*, Bakosurtanal, Cibinong, 2010.

64 See Schofield and Tan-Mullins, 'Maritime Claims, Conflicts and Cooperation in the Gulf of Thailand', pp. 90–91.

65 *Agreement on Historic Waters of Vietnam and Kampuchea*, 7 July 1982. See J. I. Charney and L. M. Alexander, *International Maritime Boundaries*, Vol. III, Martinus Nijhoff, Dordrecht, 1998, pp. 2364–2365.

66 Specifically, the Treaty of Peace between the United States and Spain, signed at Paris, 10 December 1898, T.S. No. 343 (Treaty of Paris); the Treaty between Spain and the United States for the Cession of Outlying Islands for the Philippines, signed at Washington, 7 November 1900, T.S. No. 345 (Cessation Treaty); and the Convention between the United States and Great Britain Delimiting the Philippine Archipelago and the State of Borneo, signed at Washington, 2 January 1930, T.S. No. 856 (Treaty of Washington). See, for example, L. Bautista and C. H. Schofield, 'Philippine-China Border Relations: Cautious Engagement Amid Tensions', in B. Elleman, S. Kotkin and C. H. Schofield (eds), *Beijing's Power and China's Borders: Twenty Neighbors in Asia*, M. E. Sharpe, Armonk, NY, 2012, pp. 234–249.

67 See Prescott and Schofield, *The Maritime Political Boundaries of the World*, p. 452.

68 See Tsamenyi, Schofield and Milligan, 'Navigation through Archipelagos'.

69 The PRC's nine-dash line is located generally closer to the mainland and main island coasts of the other South China Sea littoral states than its counterpart defined earlier by the Republic of China. See, for example, Li Jinming and Li Dexia, 'The Dotted Line on the Chinese Map of the South China Sea: A Note', *Ocean Development & International Law*, 34, 2003, p. 287; Zou Keyuan, 'The Chinese Traditional Maritime Boundary Line in the South China Sea and its Legal Consequences for the Resolution of the Dispute over the Spratly Islands', *International Journal of Marine and Coastal Law*, 14, 1997, p. 52; Kuan-Hsiung Wang, 'The ROC's Maritime Claims and Practices with Special Reference to the South China Sea', *Ocean Development & International Law*, 41, 2010, pp. 237–252.

70 The arbitration was instituted on 22 January 2013, when the Philippines served China with a 'Notification and Statement of Claims'. This is available from the Department of Foreign Affairs of the Republic of the Philippines at www.dfa.gov.ph (accessed 2 June 2014).

71 'Notification and Statement of Claims', p. 13.

72 The arbitration was instituted under Annex VII of UNCLOS. China responded to the Philippines Notification and Statement of Claims by indicated that it does not accept the arbitration and has opted not to participate in its proceedings. Nonetheless, the Arbitration Tribunal has been established, and Rules of Procedure adopted with the Permanent Court of Arbitration acting as Registry for the case. See the website of the Permanent Court of Arbitration at www.pca-cpa.org/showpage.asp?pag_id=1529 (accessed 2 June 2014).

73 Joint Submission to the Commission on the Limits of the Continental Shelf pursuant to Article 76, paragraph 8 of the United Nations Convention on the Law of the Sea 1982 in respect of the southern part of the South China Sea, Executive Summary, 6 May 2009, www.un.org/Depts/los/clcs_new/submissions_files/submission_mysvnm_33_2009.htm (accessed 2 June 2014); Submission to the Commission on the Limits of the Continental Shelf pursuant to Article 76, paragraph 8 of the United Nations Convention on the Law of the Sea 1982, Partial Submission in Respect of Vietnam's

Extended Continental Shelf: North Area (VNM-N), Executive Summary, 7 May 2009, www.un.org/Depts/los/clcs_new/submissions_files/mysvnm33_09/chn_2009re_mys_v nm_e.pdf (accessed 2 June 2014). See also I. M. A. Arsana and C. H. Schofield, 'Adding Further Complexity? Extended Continental Shelf Submissions in East and Southeast Asia', Maritime Energy Resources in Asia: Legal Regimes and Cooperation, National Bureau of Asian Research Special Report No. 37, Seattle, February 2012, pp. 35–39.

74 Arsana and Schofield, 'Adding Further Complexity?', pp. 57–58.

75 See 'Note from the Permanent Mission of the People's Republic of China addressed to the Secretary General of the United Nations', CML/17/2009, 7 May 2009, www.un. org/Depts/los/clcs_new/submissions_files/submission_mysvnm_33_2009.htm (accessed 2 June 2014). See also an English language translation of China's reaction to Vietnam's submission at www.un.org/depts/los/clcs_new/submissions_files/vnm37_ 09/chn_2009re_vnm.pdf (accessed 2 June 2014).

76 See the website of the CLCS at www.un.org/Depts/los/clcs_new/submissions_files/ submission_mysvnm_33_2009.htm (accessed 2 June 2014) and www.un.org/Depts/ los/clcs_new/submissions_files/submission_vnm_37_2009.htm (accessed 2 June 2014).

77 China responded to a protest on the part of the Philippines vigorously, in the course of which it was stated that 'China's Nansha (Spratly) Islands is [*sic*] fully entitled to Territorial Sea, EEZ, and Continental Shelf'. See the website of the CLCS at www. un.org/Depts/los/clcs_new/submissions_files/submission_vnm_37_2009.htm (accessed 2 June 2014).

78 Treaty between the Kingdom of Thailand and [the Republic of] Malaysia Relating to the Delimitation of the Territorial Seas of the Two Countries of 24 October 1979. See J. I. Charney and L. M. Alexander, *International Maritime Boundaries*, Vol. I, Martinus Nijhoff, Dordrecht, 1993, pp. 1096–1098.

79 Memorandum of Understanding between Malaysia and the Kingdom of Thailand on the Delimitation of the Continental Shelf Boundary between the Two Countries in the Gulf of Thailand was signed on 24 October 1979. See *International Maritime Boundaries*, Vol, I, pp. 1105–1107.

80 Agreement between the Government of the Kingdom of Thailand and the Government of the Socialist Republic of Vietnam on the Delimitation of the Maritime Boundaries between the Two Countries in the Gulf of Thailand. See J. I. Charney and R. W. Smith, *International Maritime Boundaries*, Vol. IV, Martinus Nijhoff, Dordrecht, 2002, pp. 2692–2694.

81 D. A. Colson and R. W. Smith (eds), Agreement between the Socialist Republic of Viet Nam and the People's Republic of China on the Delimitation of the Territorial Sea, Exclusive Economic Zone and Continental Shelf between the Two Countries in the Tonkin Gulf, 25 December 2000 (entry into force 30 June 2004). See 'People's Republic of China-Vietnam', *International Maritime Boundaries*, Vol. V, Martinus Nijhoff, Leiden, 2005, pp. 3745–3758. See also, Nguyen Hong Thao, 'Maritime Delimitation and Fishery Cooperation in the Tonkin Gulf', *Ocean Development & International Law*, 36, 2005, pp. 25–44.

82 Agreement between the Government of the Socialist Republic of Vietnam and the Government of the Republic of Indonesia concerning the delimitation of the continental shelf boundary, 26 June 2003 (entry into force 29 May 2007). See 'Agreement between the Government of the Socialist Republic of Vietnam and the Republic of Indonesia concerning the Delimitation of the Continental Shelf Boundary', *International Maritime Boundaries*, Vol. VI, Martinus Nijhoff, Leiden, 2011, pp. 4301–4315.

83 Agreement Stipulating the Territorial Sea Boundary Lines between Indonesia and the Republic of Singapore in the Strait of Singapore, 25 March 1973 (entry into force 29 August 1974). See 'Territorial Sea Boundary: Indonesia-Singapore', *Limits in the Seas*, 60, The Geographer, US Department of State, Washington, DC, 11 November 1974.

See also 'The Signing of The Treaty between the Republic of Indonesia and the Republic of Singapore Relating to the Delimitation of the Territorial Seas in the Western Part of the Strait of Singapore', Press Release Ministry of Foreign Affairs, Indonesia, Jakarta, 10 March 2009, www.deplu.go.id/_layouts/mobile/PortalDetail-PressReleaseLike.aspx?l=en&ItemId=c148acb8-88c6-4e24-9dd3-352ec9cd90c2 (accessed 2 June 2014).

84 The territorial sea boundaries between Brunei and Malaysia were defined in 1958 out to the 100 fathom isobath through two British Orders in Council. See *International Maritime Boundaries*, Vol. I, pp. 924–928.

85 See I. Storey, 'Brunei's Contested Sea Border with China', pp. 39–41. It is also notable that Brunei's submission of preliminary information to the United Nations Commission on the Limits of the Continental Shelf further states that maritime boundaries between Brunei and Malaysia have been delimited by virtue of the 1958 Orders in Council and 'an Exchange of Letters dated 16 March 2009', which served to delimit territorial sea, EEZ and continental shelf rights 'to a distance of 200 nautical miles'. See 'Brunei-Darussalam's Preliminary Submission Concerning the Outer Limits of its Continental Shelf', 12 May 2009, www.un.org/Depts/los/clcs_new/commission_preliminary.htm (accessed 2 June 2014).

86 Memorandum of Understanding between the Kingdom of Thailand and [the Republic of] Malaysia on the Establishment of a Joint Authority for the Exploitation of the Resources of the Sea-Bed in a Defined Area of the Continental Shelf of the Two Countries in the Gulf of Thailand, done on 21 February 1979. See *International Maritime Boundaries*, Vol. I, pp. 1107–1123.

87 Memorandum of Understanding between the Kingdom of Thailand and [the Republic of] Malaysia on the Establishment of a Joint Authority for the Exploitation of the Resources of the Sea-Bed in a Defined Area of the Continental Shelf of the Two Countries in the Gulf of Thailand, done on 21 February 1979. See, *International Maritime Boundaries*, Vol. I, pp. 1107–1123.

88 Memorandum of Understanding between Malaysia and the Socialist Republic of Vietnam for the Exploration and Exploitation of Petroleum in a Defined Area of the Continental Shelf Involving the Two Countries was signed on 5 June 1992, and entered into force on 4 June 1993. See *International Maritime Boundaries*, Vol. III, pp. 2335–2344.

89 Agreement on Fishery Co-Operation in the Tonkin Gulf between the Government of the People's Republic of China and the Government of the Socialist Republic of Vietnam, 25 December 2000. See Nguyen Hong Thao, 'Maritime Delimitation and Fishery Cooperation'.

90 Although it was suggested in 2009 that in the context of deteriorating bilateral relations, including clashes along their land boundary in the vicinity of the Temple of Preah Vihear, as well as Cambodia's appointment of ousted Thai Prime Minister Thaksin Shinawatra as an economic adviser, Thailand intended to unilaterally abrogate the 2001 Memorandum of Understanding, in fact this does not appear to have formally taken place. See 'Thai Cabinet Approves Ending Maritime Talks with Cambodia', Kyodo News Agency, 10 November 2009, www.thefreelibrary.com/Thai+Cabinet+approves+ending+maritime+talks+with+Cambodia.-a0212122709 (accessed 2 June 2014); 'Details Sought on "Secret" Meetings', *The Nation*, 3 September 2011, www.nationmultimedia.com/2011/09/03/national/Details-sought-on-secret-meetings-30164385.html (accessed 2 June 2014).

91 See Storey, 'Brunei's Contested Sea Border with China'.

92 Arsana and Schofield, 'Indonesia's "Invisible" Border with China', pp. 60–79.

93 See China National Offshore Oil Corporation (CNOOC), 'Notification of Part of Open Blocks in Waters under Jurisdiction of the People's Republic of China Available for Foreign Cooperation in the Year of 2012', 23 June 2012, http://en.cnooc.com.cn/data/html/news/2012-06-23/english/322127.html (accessed 2 June 2014).

94 See, for example, B. Spegele, V. Trong Khanh and J. Cuneta, 'Vietnam, Philippines Incidents Raise Sea Tensions', *The Wall Street Journal*, 7 May 2014, http://online.wsj. com/news/articles/SB10001424052702304431104579547241211054588 (accessed 10 March 2013).

95 For the text of the Declaration on the Conduct of Parties in the South China Sea, see the ASEAN website at www.asean.org/asean/external-relations/china/item/declaration-on-the-conduct-of-parties-in-the-south-china-sea (accessed 2 June 2014).

96 See the website of the Permanent Court of Arbitration at www.pca-cpa.org/show page.asp?pag_id=1529 (accessed 2 June 2014).

3 The 1982 Convention on the Law of the Sea and its relevance to maritime disputes in the South China Sea

Donald R. Rothwell

Introduction

International law has a significant role to play in the multiple disputes that exist throughout the South China Sea. The first relevant area of international law is that dealing with territoriality and the basis under international law that states are able to assert, and have recognised, territorial claims. This area of international law is well developed, and notwithstanding the passing of an era when new lands were being discovered and territorial claims were asserted, international courts are still being called upon to settle a number of contemporary territorial disputes.[1] Some of these disputes concern the direction of a territorial boundary, while others go directly to title over land territory such as islands.[2] The second body of international law of relevance is that associated with the law of the sea. The law of the sea has steadily developed over 400 years, first through customary international law based upon the practice of states and then post-World War II, increasingly through the development of new treaties.[3] The First United Nations Conference on the Law of the Sea took place in 1958, which resulted in the conclusion of four separate treaties dealing with a range of law of the sea issues, including the recognition of some maritime zones, including the territorial sea and continental shelf, and rights and freedoms over the high seas.[4] The Third United Nations Conference on the Law of the Sea ran from 1973 to 1982, and resulted in agreement being reached upon the 1982 United Nations Convention on the Law of the Sea (UNCLOS), which entered into force in 1994. UNCLOS remains the dominant international law of the sea instrument that identifies the scope and extent of various maritime zones, and also provides mechanisms for the delimitation of maritime boundaries.

The adoption of UNCLOS, which is sometimes referred to as a 'constitution of the oceans',[5] was a significant confidence-building measure with respect to the management of the world's oceans, in that it confirmed the rights and entitlements of coastal states to assert a range of maritime zones that extended as far as 200 nautical miles offshore, and in certain cases could extend as far as 350 nautical miles. However, it also confirmed the entitlements of all states to enjoy certain basic freedoms in the world's oceans, the most significant of which is the freedom of navigation, which extends not only over the high seas, but also extends over the coastal states' maritime zones, albeit limited through very precise navigational regimes such as the right of innocent passage in the 12 nautical mile territorial sea.[6]

While international law recognises that 'the land dominates the sea', and accordingly coastal states need to be able to demonstrate their territorial sovereignty in order to be able to assert maritime claims, once territoriality is confirmed then a coastal state enjoys significant entitlements of sovereign rights and jurisdiction over its adjacent maritime domain. In this respect, the capacity of relatively small areas of territory, such as an island, to generate a significant maritime claim needs to be appreciated.[7] While overlapping maritime claims will be subject to an obligation on the part of the coastal states concerned to agree upon maritime boundaries (see UNCLOS, Articles 15, 74, 83), nevertheless the potential entitlements of a coastal state to be able to enjoy access to living and non-living resources such as fish stocks, and oil and gas, make the confirmation of territoriality and the assertion of appropriate maritime claims a significant sovereign right.

Noting that there remain throughout the South China Sea a number of significant territorial disputes over islands, especially in the Spratly Islands, this chapter will give particular attention to the law of the sea and the role of UNCLOS in the South China Sea maritime disputes. All of the key Southeast Asian states with interests in the South China Sea are parties to UNCLOS, which is helpful in bringing certainty to the legal framework that applies throughout the region. The chapter will first begin with a review of maritime entitlements under the law of the sea, followed by a discussion of how those entitlements are resolved, maritime boundary delimitation, and the efforts by the Philippines to settle some of its South China Sea disputes with China via UNCLOS mechanisms.

The law of the sea and maritime entitlements

UNCLOS has resulted in greater certainty with respect to the number of maritime zones that coastal states are able to assert, and the extent of coastal state rights and jurisdiction that can be exercised within those zones. Of particular relevance for this discussion are the following:

- Territorial sea, which extends 12 nautical miles offshore and is a zone within which the coastal state exercises sovereignty over the seabed and subsoil, water column and the airspace above (UNCLOS, Article 2). The only major limitation on coastal state sovereignty is the obligation to respect the right of foreign ships to exercise the freedom of navigation via the right of innocent passage (UNCLOS, Article 17).
- Exclusive economic zone (EEZ), which extends 200 nautical miles offshore (UNCLOS, Article 57), and within which the coastal state enjoys sovereign rights over the living and non-living resources found in the seabed, subsoil and water column, and also exercise jurisdiction with respect to marine

environmental protection and management, and marine scientific research (UNCLOS, Article 56).

- Continental shelf, which extends to a minimum of 200 nautical miles, and in certain cases may extend as far as approximately 350 nautical miles (UNCLOS, Article 76), over which the coastal state enjoys sovereign rights over the living and non-living resources found on the seabed and the non-living resources of the subsoil and associated jurisdiction, with respect to artificial islands and installations that have been built for the purpose of enjoying these sovereign rights (UNCLOS, Article 77).

In addition to the entitlements generated by these maritime zones, certain states are able to assert their status as 'archipelagic states', consistent with Part IV of UNCLOS. In the South China Sea, the Philippines has asserted this status through the declaration of archipelagic baselines that have enclosed the waters of the Philippine archipelago.[8] Within these 'archipelagic waters', the Philippines enjoys virtually complete sovereignty, subject to certain navigational freedoms for foreign ships. Indonesia has also asserted its status as an archipelagic state.[9] However, given its geographic location, this has not had significant legal implications for the South China Sea.

All of the maritime zones noted above are asserted offshore a coastal state with a presumption in favour of the use of the low water mark along the coast being the 'normal baseline' (UNCLOS, Article 5). However, depending on the configuration of the coastline and its associated maritime features, a coastal state may seek to draw 'straight baselines', which are permissible in the case of deeply indented and cut-into coastlines, or where there is a fringe of islands along the coast in its immediate vicinity (UNCLOS, Article 7). Subject to some associated technical rules, including that straight baselines must not depart from the general direction of the coastline of the coastal state, maritime zones are capable of being proclaimed from a combination of the normal baseline and also straight baselines. However, the practice of some coastal states in this respect has proven controversial, with Vietnam's baselines having been the subject of diplomatic protest by China, Thailand and the United States due to them not conforming with UNCLOS's provisions.[10] A related matter of controversy in the South China Sea is the status of China's 'nine-dash line', which is a line that appears on official Chinese maps of the South China Sea that encompasses very large portions of the sea, apparently within a form of baseline-type claim.[11] Considerable ambiguity surrounds the status of China's 'nine-dash line'. It would appear that the line cannot be properly characterised as a Chinese assertion of a straight baseline consistent with UNCLOS, but rather that it takes the form of a territorial and maritime line that encompasses areas within which China asserts territorial sovereignty, and also maritime sovereignty and/or maritime sovereign rights and jurisdiction.

Once the extent of a coastal state's territorial entitlements are confirmed, and its maritime claims asserted from relevant baselines, the asserted maritime claims of a coastal state will begin to take shape. Nevertheless, a distinction needs to be made in the law of the sea between the delineation of maritime claims, which goes to the basis in international law for such a claim to be asserted and the outer limits of that claim, and the delimitation of maritime boundaries between neighbouring states. The South China Sea's congested maritime domain means that it will rarely be the case that a maritime zone will be capable of claim without overlapping an equivalent entitlement of another state. This will trigger the need for the resolution of a maritime boundary between the two states.

The delineation of a maritime claim and the ability of a coastal state to be able to justify the outer limits of that claim based upon UNCLOS raise different issues from the delimitation of maritime boundaries between two or more neighbouring states. In the South China Sea, this is an important consideration, as in most instances the assertion of a maritime claim and the delineation of that claim is the first-order issue that will need resolution. This includes whether, under existing international law, that maritime feature enjoys a capacity to generate a maritime zone, and if so what zones in particular that maritime feature has a capacity to generate. In this respect, the South China Sea is a unique maritime region in which maritime claims are predominantly generated from offshore islands and associated maritime features such as rocks and atolls. While there are significant maritime claims generated offshore along the coastline of continental Southeast Asia, especially in the case of Brunei, Malaysia and Vietnam, it is the islands that make up the Paracel and Spratly Island groups, and archipelagos such as the Philippines, that dominate. In this respect, the UNCLOS distinction between Article 121 (1) islands generating the complete suite of maritime zones, while Article 121 (3) rocks generate only a territorial sea and contiguous zone, is crucial. As noted below, this raises significant threshold issues with respect to the legal characterisation of certain maritime features. Once that matter is resolved, then a very extensive body of international law and practice concerning the delimitation of maritime boundaries between neighbouring states comes into play, within which well-settled principles can be applied.[12]

Disputes concerning the legal status of maritime features

A central aspect of UNCLOS is that it confers entitlements to assert a claim over a maritime zone to a 'coastal State' (UNCLOS, Articles 2, 33, 56, 76). While the term 'coastal State' is not defined in UNCLOS, it is taken to encompass any state that has a territorial entitlement that encompasses a sea coast. This extends not only to continental states, but also to island states, including those that are properly characterised as archipelagos, such as Indonesia and the Philippines. Problematic issues arise with respect to maritime features claimed by coastal states, including those that have been subject to territorial claim or are encompassed within territorial claims, and the capacity of those features to generate maritime zones. These features will range in size from islands, as properly defined, through the whole gamut of associated maritime features, including atolls, cays, islets, rocks, banks, shoals and reefs. The status of these features, and their ability to be subject to territorial claim and their ultimate capacity to generate maritime zones, can be contentious. This is certainly the case with respect to such features in the South China Sea that are at the centre of land and maritime disputes. As observed by Beckman:

> None of the claimants in the South China Sea have clarified which features they consider to be islands, rocks, low-tide elevations, artificial islands, and so on. The resulting uncertainty is noteworthy since the majority of features are not above water at high tide.[13]

In the case of islands, Part VIII of UNCLOS details the 'Regime of Islands', which contains provisions of considerable significance for the South China Sea. Article 121 (1) defines an island as 'a naturally formed area of land, surrounded by water, which is above water at high tide', which can be referred to as an Article 121 (1) island. An artificial island does not therefore meet the criteria,[14] nor does an area of land not above water at high tide, which may, in other respects, meet the criteria of a low-tide elevation (UNCLOS, Article 13 (1)). Rocks, shoals or reefs that may be visible at low tide are therefore not islands for the purposes of UNCLOS. The importance of Article 121 (1) islands under UNCLOS is that they generate the complete range of maritime zones, including the resource-significant EEZ and continental shelf. A small island can therefore generate a continental shelf or EEZ that may be many times the size of the island's land dimensions and considerably more economically valuable in terms of living and non-living natural resources.[15] Rocks that 'cannot sustain human habitation or an economic life of their own' do not enjoy an entitlement to a continental shelf or an EEZ (UNCLOS, Article 121 (3)), but will still nonetheless enjoy a territorial sea and contiguous zone. These maritime features can be referred to as Article 121 (3) rocks. Perhaps the most prominent of these features is Rockall, which is a UK-claimed rock in the Atlantic Ocean to the west of Scotland, which the UK has conceded does not generate a continental shelf or EEZ.[16] Importantly for present purposes, given the multiplicity of maritime features scattered throughout the South China Sea from Article 121 (1) islands, to Article 121 (3) rocks, to features of lesser status such as reefs and shoals, UNCLOS is silent on how these features are to be identified. As such, there is no authoritative list of these maritime features in the South China Sea.

Unsurprisingly, Article 121 has generated some analysis and consideration by international courts as to the distinction between islands and rocks, and the differential entitlements they enjoy to maritime zones. For example, in the *Monte Confurco* and *Volga* cases before the International Tribunal for the Law of the Sea (ITLOS), Judge Vukas expressed a view that the sub-Antarctic Kerguelan Islands (France) and the Heard and McDonald Islands (Australia) in the Southern Ocean were not islands from which the coastal states were entitled to claim EEZs consistently with UNCLOS.[17] In the case of the two Australian islands, Judge Vukas gave particular importance to the fact that the islands were uninhabited. However, such a view regarding sub-Antarctic islands, which considers the distinction between an Article 121 (1) island and an Article 121 (3) rock turns on whether the maritime feature is inhabited or is capable of habitation, has not found wider support in ITLOS or other international courts.[18] It can therefore be observed that naturally formed islands, which are juridically recognised as such under Article 121, do generate an entitlement to all UNCLOS maritime zones. It would appear that whether such islands are inhabited or not would not be determinative as to their capacity to generate an EEZ or continental shelf, though it may highlight issues associated with the island's size and whether it is capable of sustaining human habitation, including the presence of fresh water.

A further category of maritime feature referred to in UNCLOS is a 'low-tide elevation', which is defined as 'a naturally formed area of land which is surrounded by and above water at low tide but submerged at high tide' (UNCLOS, Article 13 (1)). Low-tide elevations can be distinguished from Article 121 (3) rocks, in that they are not subject to appropriation other than when they fall within the territorial sea limits of the coastal state, and are otherwise not to be equated with land territory. Therefore, low-tide elevations do not generate a territorial sea when located beyond the breadth of the territorial sea from the mainland or an island. Otherwise, low-tide elevations may be used as a base point for a straight baseline when delineating the outer limits of maritime zones, and may be relied upon during maritime boundary delimitation between neighbouring states.

In the South China Sea, distinguishing between Article 121 (1) islands, Article 121 (3) rocks and low-tide elevations is of considerable significance. This is because of the number of maritime features that are in dispute, and the efforts made by some of the disputing states to build structures such as platforms, light-houses and small dwellings on these features in an effort to sustain their territorial claims.[19] One of the most prominent of these features in the South China Sea is Mischief Reef, which has been the subject of construction works.[20] When it is considered that in sum, the total land area of the 13 largest islands in the Spratly Islands group is 1.7 square kilometres, a further appreciation is gained of the significance that is attached to determining whether those features are Article 121 (1) islands because of the EEZ and continental shelves those very small maritime features may potentially generate.[21]

Recent jurisprudence of the International Court and its significance for the South China Sea

Even since the seminal decision of the International Court of Justice (ICJ) in the 1969 *North Sea Continental Shelf* case,[22] the ICJ and other international tribunals have been engaged in a project of developing the jurisprudence of maritime boundary delimitation, which, in recent decades, has begun to reflect the key principles found within UNCLOS.[23] This jurisprudence is a key indicator to the rights and entitlements of coastal states in the South China Sea, and especially as to how an international court would view a request to delimit a maritime boundary. In 2012, the ICJ handed down its most recent judgment in a maritime boundary dispute, which has consequences for how maritime disputes in the South China

Sea may eventually be settled. In the *Territorial and Maritime Dispute (Nicaragua v Colombia)* case,[24] the ICJ was called upon to determine sovereignty over a number of islands and maritime features in the Caribbean Sea claimed by Nicaragua and Colombia, the maritime entitlements of those features, and the EEZ/continental shelf boundary. The judgment of the court explored a range of issues that not only bear similarities to aspects of the land and maritime disputes in the South China Sea, but set a precedent for the interpretation of the relevant international law. The judgment will be influential in how states asserting sovereignty and maritime claims in the South China Sea view their positions, and may influence some states in their views as to whether a negotiated settlement of their maritime claims would be beneficial or whether they would favour adjudication. In particular, the ICJ considered the definition in international law of islands and associated maritime features, their entitlements to maritime zones, and the impact of these features upon maritime boundary delimitation between two states with joint claims over a maritime area. Of particular significance to the situation in the South China Sea is how the court dealt with Colombia's maritime entitlements in the Southwestern Caribbean Sea immediately adjacent to the Nicaraguan coast and at some distance from the Colombian metropolitan coast.

The status of some of the maritime features in the Caribbean Sea was a major feature of the *Nicaragua v Colombia* case. The eastern Nicaraguan coastline that fronted the Caribbean Sea generally runs north/south, with some minor bays, indentations and peninsulas. However, it was offshore features, comprising a mix of islands, reefs, cays, banks, shoals and atolls, over which Colombia and Nicaragua claimed sovereignty that created a particular dynamic for the ICJ when it came to assessing the law of the sea dimensions of the dispute. In this respect, the court took the step of actually seeking to characterise the various maritime features in the contested area, including the Alburquerque Cays, East-Southeast Cays, Roncador, Serrana, Quitasueño, Serranilla and Bajo Nuevo.[25] The court also sought to define certain maritime features, including cays, atolls, banks and shoals (*Nicaragua v Colombia* 2012: [20]). A key threshold issue for the ICJ was the capacity of these features to be subject to appropriation, and the court reaffirmed established principles in this respect by distinguishing between the capacity of islands, even very small islands, to be subject to appropriation, while low-tide elevations cannot be appropriated other than if they fall within the territorial sea.[26]

An issue that particularly confronted the court was its capacity to be able to distinguish between maritime features that were properly islands, and those that were properly low-tide elevations, and in that respect the ICJ was mindful of the need for appropriate evidence to demonstrate that a feature was above water at high tide.[27] This was an issue that was particularly significant in the case of Quitasueño, which was described by the court as a 'large bank approximately 57 km long and 20 km wide'.[28] The parties differed as to their characterisation of the features associated with Quitasueño. Nicaragua was of the view that it was a shoal in which all of the features were permanently submerged at high tide, while Colombia relied upon two surveys of the area, one of which had argued that there were 34 individual features that qualified as islands, and 20 low-tide elevations that were located within 12 nautical miles of the identified islands.[29] In addressing this question, the court restated the requirement under Article 121 (1) of UNCLOS that an island was 'naturally formed' and that international law focuses on whether the feature is above water at high tide rather than its geological composition.[30] That one of the disputed features on Quitasueño was small and composed of coral was considered irrelevant to a finding that it was an island, with the ICJ observing that 'international law does not prescribe any minimum size which a feature must possess in order to be considered an island'.[31] The court then concluded this analysis by observing that 'the legal regime of islands set out in UNCLOS Article 121 forms an indivisible regime'.[32]

The consequence of this finding by the ICJ, which is its most comprehensive statement as to the legal effect of Article 121, makes clear that the three paragraphs that make up that Article are to be considered as a whole. The consequences are that when consideration is given to the maritime entitlements of an island, there will be a need for characterisation of that feature as to not only whether it meets the criteria for recognition as an island for the purposes of international law, but additionally whether it is properly an Article 121 (1) island or an Article 121 (3) rock. Such a determination will then become critical with respect to what the Court has termed the 'maritime entitlements' of that feature, which would not only extend to the delineation of maritime claims generated from that island, but also how the island would be factored into any delimitation of a maritime boundary with other states.

Maritime boundary delimitation practice and the South China Sea

A significant law of the sea issue for the South China Sea relates to how maritime boundaries may be determined following confirmation of territorial sovereignty over islands and associated maritime features and whether they are capable of generating the full suite of maritime zones. It can first be observed that the law of maritime boundary delimitation is very well developed. Articles 73 and 84 of UNCLOS provide a legal framework, within which coastal states can seek to delimit their overlapping EEZ and continental shelf boundaries by negotiation, or international courts and tribunals can apply developed legal principles to bring about their resolution.[33] The second observation is that, as noted above, the majority of the South China Sea islands that are currently contentious are generally small in size, are either uninhabited or have very small permanent or itinerant populations, and are at some distance either from continental Asia or major island systems such as the Philippines archipelago. Beckman has highlighted these issues by observing that within the Spratly Islands grouping, there are more than 140 identifiable islets, rocks, reefs, shoals and sandbanks, of which less than 40 are islands for the purposes of Article 121 (1).[34] A total of 60 of these maritime features have been the subject of occupation by the competing claimants.[35]

International courts and tribunals have traditionally been conscious of the potential distorting effects that islands have on maritime boundaries, especially if those islands are granted their full entitlement to extensive maritime zones, such as a continental shelf or EEZ, and a number of judicial techniques have been applied to address this problem.[36] There are also examples in state practice where small, sparsely inhabited islands that are located very close to the mainland of another state have been given minimal effect in negotiated maritime boundaries settled by way of treaty.[37] This significance of ensuring that small islands do not have a distorting impact upon a maritime boundary is further reinforced in UNCLOS, which makes clear that the delimitation of these maritime zones is to achieve an 'equitable outcome' (UNCLOS, Articles 74 (1), 83 (1)), and this is also reflected in recent ICJ decisions.[38] When these issues were recently confronted by the ICJ in the *Nicaragua v Colombia* case, the court sought to apply the delimitation methodology that it had endorsed in the 2009 *Black Sea* case.[39] That approach first required the idetification of a provisional delimitation line, consideration of whether there are relevant circumstances that justify adjustment of that line to achieve an equitable result, and finally the application of a disproportionality test.[40] Importantly in the context of the relevant maritime area, the court emphasised that in applying this methodology the provisional delimitation line would take into account the territories of the parties, including the island territories, using methods that were 'geometrically objective and appropriate for the geography of the area'.[41] This is suggestive of the fact that the ICJ would not seek to adopt a narrow approach in identifying the relevant maritime area, but would be prepared to take into account differing circumstances, which would be relevant in any assessment of the South China Sea.

Following construction of the provisional median line, the ICJ in *Nicaragua v Colombia* proceeded to take into account relevant circumstances. In this respect, consideration had been given to whether, if the Colombian islands were granted their full entitlements to an EEZ and continental shelf, Nicragua's EEZ and continental shelf rights, as generated to the east offshore its mainland coast and those of its islands, would be 'cut off' by as much as three-quarters of the area into which the coast projects. Referring to this 'cut-off' effect, the ICJ concluded that islands should not be treated as though they were a continuous mainland coast stretching for over 100 nautical miles. As such, this was a factor for consideration in determining whether a provisional boundary line should be adjusted to produce an equitable result.[42] The ICJ also observed that Colombia's entitlements should also be maintained, and that likewise there was no consequential cut-off applied in the case of the Colombian islands.[43]

Taking all of these factors into account, the ICJ then came to a deliberation as to the course of the maritime boundary. The court proceeded to draw a line that connected up the western limits of the maritime entitlements of the principal Colombian islands, from which straight lines were then drawn so as to connect the EEZ and continental shelves of these islands east into the Caribbean Sea, thereby ensuring respect for the maritime entitlements of these islands.[44] With respect to the other two Colombian maritime features that were to the north of this line – Quitasueño and Serrana – the court concluded that both were entitled to only generate a 12 nautical mile territorial sea, with the effect that both were enclaved within an area of Nicaraguan EEZ and continental shelf.[45] In the case of Quitasueño, the court concluded that the feature referred to as QS32 was a rock from which only a 12 nautical mile territorial sea could be generated.[46] With respect to Serrana, the determinative factor for the purposes of boundary delimitation was its small size and remoteness, which meant that to achieve an equitable result, it was necessary to limit the island to only a 12 nautical mile territorial sea.[47]

In drawing conclusions as to the significance of this decision for the South China Sea, great care needs to be exercised due to the very distinctive maritime geography of the Caribbean Sea that was under review and the similarly distinctive maritime features of the South China Sea. Nevertheless, the following general conclusions would seem to be supportable. The first is that the ICJ demonstrated that it was prepared to undertake a forensic analysis in order to determine whether certain maritime features are Article 121 (1) islands, Article 121 (3) rocks or are properly characterised as low-tide elevations. The ICJ also confirmed that it would take a holistic approach to its interpretation of Article 121, and the court is well aware of the implications that arise from the characterisation of different maritime features. The second is that the ICJ, albeit in the context of the delimitation methodology that is being applied in the interpretation of Articles 74 and 83 of UNCLOS, considered a range of issues as they relate to islands in its assessment of what are the relevant circumstances following the drawing of a provisional equidistance or median line. To that end, clearly the size of the island and its potential distorting effect upon a maritime boundary are factors to be considered. In the context of the South China Sea, this decision suggests that even if territorial sovereignty was conclusively settled over islands and associated maritime features, there is every likelihood that the ability of these features to generate vast maritime claims would be compromised. This would be the case either because these features are not Article 121 (1) islands, or because they would have a distorting impact upon the maritime boundaries based upon competing maritime claims from continent or island land masses whose status is not in dispute.

Philippines Annex VII arbitration application

A distinctive feature of UNCLOS is that Part XV of the Convention contains compulsory dispute resolution procedures. A separate International Tribunal for the Law of the Sea is created with jurisdiction to determine disputes that arise under UNCLOS, while there are complementary processes for states to also refer their disputes to ad hoc arbitral tribunals.[48] This creates a series of mechanisms for the peaceful settlement of law of the sea disputes, though there do exist some exceptions that are found in Article 298. One of the most significant recent developments with respect to South China Sea maritime disputes occurred in January 2013, when the Philippines commenced Annex VII arbitral proceedings against China under UNCLOS.[49] The Philippines' notification to China, dated 22 January 2013, activated procedures under Article 287 and Annex VII of UNCLOS. The Philippines' notification and statement of claim states:

> The Republic of the Philippines brings this arbitration against the People's Republic of China to challenge China's claims to areas of the South China Sea and the underlying seabed as far as 870 nautical miles from the nearest Chinese coast, to which China has no entitlement under the [UNCLOS] . . . and which, under the Convention, constitute the Philippines' exclusive economic zone and continental shelf.[50]

The Philippines' claim gives particular attention to the asserted invalidity under UNCLOS of China's 'nine-dash line'. The Philippines contests the validity of this line and any attempts by China to assert sovereignty or sovereign rights over islands and other maritime features found within this area.[51] The Philippines' application seeks an award from the Arbitral Tribunal that:

1   the respective rights and obligations of the parties are governed by UNCLOS and that China's claims based on the 'nine-dash line' are invalid;
2   determines whether certain maritime features claimed by China and the Philippines are under Article 121 of UNCLOS islands, low-tide elevations or submerged banks, and whether they are capable of generating maritime zones greater than 12 nautical miles; and
3   enables the Philippines to exercise and enjoy rights within its EEZ and continental shelf.[52]

The Philippines' application raises a number of procedural issues that will need to be addressed prior to the Annex VII Arbitral Tribunal determining the claim on the merits. The first relates to China's acceptance of the jurisdiction of the Tribunal to hear and determine the Philippines' claim. In 2006, China made a Declaration after its ratification of UNCLOS in which it declared under Article 298 that it did not accept certain compulsory dispute resolution procedures under Part XV, including disputes with respect to 'historic bays or titles'.[53] This raises issues as to whether elements of China's disputes with the Philippines in the South China Sea would fall within this exception, including what precisely are the historic titles that China asserts in the South China Sea.[54] The second is that on 19 February 2013, China rejected the Philippines' application for Annex VII arbitration and indicated that it would not participate in the proceedings.[55] This position would appear to be based upon China's view that, consistent with its Article 298 Declaration, the Annex VII Tribunal lacks jurisdiction. On 1 August 2013, China submitted a *note verbale* to the Permanent Court of Arbitration, which is the registry for the proceedings, indicating that 'it does not accept the arbitration initiated by the Philippines', and that it will not be participating in the proceedings. Nevertheless, Annex VII of UNCLOS contains procedures whereby if one of the parties chooses to not participate in the proceedings, an Arbitral Tribunal can be constituted and proceed to a hearing of the application even in the case of a default appearance (UNCLOS, Annex VII, Articles 3, 9). The Tribunal, in the case of default of appearance, will need to make a determination that it does possess jurisdiction over the dispute, but also that the claim is 'well founded' in both fact and law (UNCLOS, Annex VII, Article 9).

While the Philippines' application raises a number of issues with respect to China's claim to both land and maritime features in the South China Sea, it has been drafted in order to avoid questions of territorial sovereignty and also historic title. Ultimately, however, this will be a threshold issue for the Arbitral Tribunal to determine. If the Tribunal does come to the view that it has jurisdiction, then its determination of the Philippines' claim would be the first by an international court or tribunal of the disputed law of the sea issues that exist in the South China Sea. In that respect, the judgment would have implications for a number of the other disputes that exist in the region where China's claims are at the centre of many of the controversies, and has the potential to bring clarity to some of the legal issues, especially with respect to the ability of certain maritime features to generate maritime zones under UNCLOS. Such an outcome would be of great benefit in terms of bringing some ongoing certainty to the interpretation and application of UNCLOS in the South China Sea.

Conclusion

The law of the sea, and especially UNCLOS, dominates any appreciation of how the South China Sea claimants have sought to assert their maritime claims and entitlements, how those claims are viewed within the framework of UNCLOS, and how both a political and legal resolution could be brought about with respect to those claims. The Philippines' 2013 commencement of arbitration proceedings against China highlights just how significant the law of the sea is to the resolution of some disputes that exist in the South China Sea. In this context, there are three dimensions as to how the legal framework of the law of the sea can be considered. The first is through UNCLOS itself and how it can be interpreted consistently with treaty law. The second is through state practice and how that practice may have evolved since UNCLOS was concluded, especially as it relates to the inter-pretation of some ambiguous provisions of the Convention. The third is the weight to be accorded to the jurisprudence of international courts and tribunals in interpreting UNCLOS and related provisions. When particular consideration is given to this latter dimension, especially in the light of recent ICJ decisions, such as that of *Nicaragua v Colombia*, an appreciation is gained of the implications of the decisions of international courts and how some of the South China Sea claimants view their territorial and maritime assertions. This is especially the case if there is an appreciation of the very limited capacity of some South China Sea maritime features to generate either an EEZ or continental shelf under the Article 121 regime of islands; or even if those features did generate a maritime entitlement, their capacity to significantly influence the direction of a maritime boundary

between continental or mainland states. Such an objective determination as to the
status of these features may ultimately have an impact on the current geopolitics
within the region, and may act as a catalyst for other means of dispute resolution,
including the reaching of negotiated political agreements on maritime claims.

Notes

1 H. Nasu and D. R. Rothwell, 'Re-Evaluating the Role of International Law in Territorial
   and Maritime Disputes in East Asia', *Asian Journal of International Law*, 4, 2014,
   pp. 55–79.
2 'Case Concerning Sovereignty over Pulau Ligitan and Pulau Sipadan (Indonesia/
   Malaysia) (2002)', *International Court of Justice Reports*, p. 625.
3 D. R. Rothwell and T. Stephens, *The International Law of the Sea*, Hart, Oxford, 2010,
   pp. 1–24.
4 R. R. Churchill and A. V. Lowe, *The Law of the Sea*, 3rd edn, Manchester University
   Press, Manchester, 1999, p. 15.
5 T. T. B. Koh, 'A Constitution for the Oceans', in United Nations, *The Law of the Sea:
   United Nations Convention on the Law of the Sea*, United Nations, New York, 1983,
   pp. xxxiii–xxxvii.
6 See Article 17, United Nations Convention on the Law of the Sea (1982) 1833 United
   Nations Treaty Series, p. 397.
7 V. Prescott and C. Schofield, *The Maritime Political Boundaries of the World*,
   2nd edn, Martinus Nijhoff, Leiden, 2005, p. 57.
8 Rothwell and Stephens, *The International Law of the Sea*, p. 187.
9 Rothwell and Stephens, *The International Law of the Sea*, p. 187.
10 J. A. Roach and R. W. Smith, *Excessive Maritime Claims*, 3rd edn, Martinus Nijhoff,
   Leiden, 2012, pp. 99–100.
11 Z. Gao and B. B. Jia, 'The Nine-Dash Line in the South China Sea: History, Status,
   and Implications', *American Journal of International Law*, 107, 2013, pp. 98–124.
12 Rothwell and Stephens, *The International Law of the Sea*, pp. 383–410.
13 R. Beckman, 'The UN Convention on the Law of the Sea and the Maritime Disputes
   in the South China Sea', *American Journal of International Law*, 107, 2013,
   pp. 142–163.
14 Prescott and Schofield, *The Maritime Political Boundaries of the World*, p. 58.
15 'Nauru Country Study Guide', *International Business Publications*, Washington, DC,
   1, 2011, p. 49.
16 C. R. Symmons, 'Ireland and the Rockall Dispute: An Analysis of Recent Developments', *IBRU Boundary and Security Bulletin*, Spring 1998, pp. 78–93; Prescott and
   Schofield, *The Maritime Political Boundaries of the World*, p. 83.
17 *Monte Confurco (Seychelles v France)* (Prompt Release) (2000), Judgment of 18
   December 2000, [2000] ITLOS Reports; *Volga (Russian Federation v Australia)*
   (Prompt Release) (2002), Judgment of 23 December 2002, [2002] ITLOS Reports.
18 Prescott and Schofield, *The Maritime Political Boundaries of the World*, pp. 75–81.
19 Beckman, 'The UN Convention on the Law of the Sea and the Maritime Disputes in
   the South China Sea', p. 151.
20 D. J. Dzurek, 'China Occupies Mischief Reef in Latest Spratly Gambit', *IBRU Boundary
   and Security Bulletin*, April 1995, pp. 65–71.
21 Beckman, 'The UN Convention on the Law of the Sea and the Maritime Disputes in
   the South China Sea', p. 151.
22 *North Sea Continental Shelf (Federal Republic of Germany v Denmark; Federal
   Republic of Germany v The Netherlands)*, Judgement of 20 February 1969, [1969]
   International Court of Justice Reports, p. 3.

23 Rothwell and Stephens, *The International Law of the Sea*, pp. 393–397.
24 *Nicaragua v Colombia*, Judgment of 19 November 2012, International Court of Justice Reports.
25 *Nicaragua v Colombia*, 2012, p. 24.
26 *Nicaragua v Colombia*, 2012, p. 26.
27 *Nicaragua v Colombia*, 2012, p. 36.
28 *Nicaragua v Colombia*, 2012, p. 24.
29 *Nicaragua v Colombia*, 2012, pp. 28–29.
30 *Nicaragua v Colombia*, 2012, p. 37.
31 *Nicaragua v Colombia*, 2012, p. 37.
32 *Nicaragua v Colombia*, 2012, p. 38.
33 Rothwell and Stephens, *The International Law of the Sea*, pp. 397–407.
34 Beckman, 'The UN Convention on the Law of the Sea and the Maritime Disputes in the South China Sea', p. 143.
35 Beckman, 'The UN Convention on the Law of the Sea and the Maritime Disputes in the South China Sea', p. 144.
36 Rothwell and Stephens, *The International Law of the Sea*, pp. 404–406.
37 Treaty between Australia and the Independent State of Papua New Guinea concerning Sovereignty and Maritime Boundaries in an area between the two Countries, including the area known as the Torres Strait, and Related Matters (1978) Australian Treaty Series 1985: No. 4.
38 *Maritime Delimitation in the Black Sea (Romania v Ukraine)*, Judgment of 3 February 2009, International Court of Justice Reports, pp. 187–188.
39 *Maritime Delimitation in the Black Sea*, 2009, pp. 115–116.
40 *Nicaragua v Colombia*, 2012, pp. 190–193.
41 *Nicaragua v Colombia*, 2012, p. 191
42 *Nicaragua v Colombia*, 2012, p. 215.
43 *Nicaragua v Colombia*, 2012, p. 216.
44 *Nicaragua v Colombia*, 2012, p. 237.
45 *Nicaragua v Colombia*, 2012, p. 238.
46 *Nicaragua v Colombia*, 2012, p. 238.
47 *Nicaragua v Colombia*, 2012, p. 238.
48 J. G. Merrills, *International Dispute Settlement*, 5th edn, Cambridge University Press, Cambridge, 2001, pp. 167–193.
49 Republic of the Philippines, *Notification and Statement of Claim*, Department of Foreign Affairs, Manila, 22 January 2013.
50 Republic of the Philippines, *Notification and Statement of Claim*, p. 1.
51 Republic of the Philippines, *Notification and Statement of Claim*, p. 2.
52 Republic of the Philippines, *Notification and Statement of Claim*, p. 6.
53 See 'China, Declaration Made after Ratification, 25 August 2006', Division for Ocean Affairs and the Law of the Sea, Office of Legal Affairs, United Nations, www.un.org/Depts/los/convention_agreements/convention_declarations.htm (accessed 11 October 2013).
54 Z. Gao and B. B. Jia, 'The Nine-Dash Line in the South China Sea', pp. 98–124; F. Dupuy and P. M. Dupuy, 'A Legal Analysis of China's Historic Rights Claim in the South China Sea', *American Journal of International Law*, 107, 2013, pp. 124–141.
55 *The Republic of the Philippines v The People's Republic of China*, Permanent Court of Arbitration, The Hague, 2013.

4 China's South China Sea policy

Evolution, claims and challenges

Jian Zhang

Introduction

The renewed tension between China and some other claimant states over the disputed islands and waters in the South China Sea in the late 2000s has generated widespread concerns about growing Chinese assertiveness in bolstering its claims. In contrast to its relatively conciliatory approach to the South China Sea dispute in the early to mid-2000s, Beijing has appeared to become increasingly uncompromising when handling the dispute. Moreover, its constant reluctance to clarify its expansive but ambiguous claims that are represented by the controversial 'U-shaped line' constitutes a major obstacle to the resolution of the dispute and raises concerns over China's ultimate ambitions over the strategically important South China Sea. Does recent Chinese assertiveness represent a decisive shift of China's South China Sea policy driven by the country's rapidly growing economic and military clout?

A number of explanations have been made for China's recent assertive and tougher stance. One influential explanation seeks to locate the growing Chinese assertiveness in the country's fragmented policymaking structure and diffuse maritime administrative system. According to this view, recent Chinese actions have been largely a product of lack of policy coordination within the Chinese governmental system, wherein different bureaucratic agencies compete to advance their own interests.[1] While such a view is certainly valid, what remains unclear is why Beijing has become increasingly assertive in recent years, but not earlier, given that fragmentation has been an integral and long-standing problem in the Chinese polity.[2] Some others argue that recent Chinese assertiveness has largely been driven by China's new naval strategy seeking to control the South China Sea due to its intention to compete with the United States for regional primacy.[3] Moreover, it is widely perceived that intense domestic nationalism has been a key driving force behind China's tougher posture. While these two factors have undoubtedly influenced Beijing's policy, they cannot fully explain the specific manners in which China has more forcefully asserted its claims in recent years. Particularly, it should be noted that instead of using naval assets, for the most part China's assertive actions have been undertaken by civilian governmental and maritime law enforcement agencies, and more often than not in the form of 'administrative diplomacy' through diplomatic and administrative measures.[4]

This chapter seeks to provide additional insights into the causes and nature of China's recent actions in the South China Sea. It makes three major arguments. First, the chapter argues that recent Chinese assertiveness represents a major and arguably long-term strategic shift in China's policy regarding the South China Sea, featured by the emergence of an increasingly proactive and purposeful approach to solidify Chinese claims. Second, it argues that instead of being motivated by a growing ambition of seeking regional dominance and control of the South China Sea, China's new assertive approach has been driven more by a deep and increasing sense of anxiety. It reflects a growing concern within China that Beijing's past moderate policy has failed to effectively protect the perceived Chinese sovereignty and maritime interests against the increasingly intensified 'encroachments' by other claimant states. Third, despite Beijing's constant refusal to settle the dispute through international legal mechanisms, this chapter argues that China's changing approach is also partly driven by an increasing recognition of the importance and legitimacy of international law, including the United Nations Convention on the Law of the Sea (UNCLOS), and by serious considerations of seeking a future diplomatic, and even legal, solution to the dispute. Ironically, the growing importance Beijing has placed on international law, and its subsequent intentions to build a stronger legal basis through various administrative and jurisdictional measures to consolidate its claims, have led to a more proactive and assertive approach, raising further tensions in the South China Sea and challenging the status quo.

Before going into details, a few caveats are in order. First, China's increasing toughness in the South China Sea does not mean that Beijing intends to settle the dispute anytime soon, nor does it indicate a more militaristic approach to the South China Sea dispute. Instead, Beijing's new approach reflects its recognition that the dispute will remain a protracted and challenging issue that is difficult to be resolved by the use of force, but rather requires a long-term strategy consisting of proactive diplomatic, administrative and legal measures to consolidate its claims. Beijing's continuing reluctance to clarify the nature and scope of its claims in the South China Sea further indicates its lack of intentions to resolve the dispute in the near future. Second, while being more forceful to defend its claims, Beijing is keenly aware of the negative impacts of its assertiveness on China's broader strategic interests in Southeast Asia. It has thus also made efforts to minimise regional apprehensions and tensions caused by its recent tough actions in the South China Sea. In this context, maintaining a proactive stance to defend China's sovereignty and maritime rights and interests (*weiquan*) in the South China Sea while simultaneously maintaining a stable regional environment (*weiwen*) remains a tough balancing act for the Chinese leadership for the decades to come.

This chapter will proceed in the following three sections. The first section examines China's evolving approaches to the South China Sea dispute, focusing on the causes behind China's recent assertiveness. The second section discusses the ambiguous nature of China's claims to the South China Sea and the evolving Chinese perspectives of the legality of the U-shaped line that is central to China's claims. The third section discusses the policy dilemma faced by Beijing in bolstering China's claims in the South China Sea and its renewed charm offensive in 2013 to maintain a positive relationship with Southeast Asian countries. The paper concludes with some observations of the implications of China's evolving approaches for the future of the South China Sea dispute.

Beijing's evolving approaches towards the South China Sea dispute: towards growing assertiveness?[5]

Despite China's claim of 'indisputable sovereignty' of the islands in the South China Sea, its approach to the long-running dispute has varied at different periods of time. The People's Republic of China (PRC) first made its official claims to the islands in the South China Sea in August 1951 through an announcement made by the then Chinese Premier and Foreign Minister Zhou Enlai. The announcement claimed that, among others, all the Nansha Islands (Spratlys), Zhongsha Islands (Macclesfield Bank), Dongsha Islands (Pratas) and Xisha Islands (Paracels) 'have always been China's territory'.[6] The announcement was made in response to the signing of the San Francisco Treaty, which required that Japan renounce its rights to the islands it occupied in the South China Sea. Between the 1950s and early 1970s, however, the South China Sea issue received relatively low priority on Beijing's overall national development and foreign policy agenda. China paid greater attentions to the South China Sea in the 1970s in response to the actions undertaken by other countries to claim and occupy various islands in areas claimed by China, and took control of the Paracels after a military clash with South Vietnam in 1974.[7]

The signing of UNCLOS in 1982 has substantially affected China's attitudes to the South China Sea. Beijing has increasingly recognised the economic and strategic significance of the maritime domain. As a state party to UNCLOS, since the early 1990s Beijing has developed a body of domestic laws stipulating China's maritime sovereignty and rights largely within the framework of UNCLOS. These laws include the 1992 'Law of the People's Republic of China on the Territorial Sea and the Contiguous Zone', which asserted China's sovereignty claims over various maritime territories, including the areas listed in the above-mentioned 1951 announcement. Following its ratification of UNCLOS in 1996, Beijing promulgated a 'Law of the People's Republic of China on the Exclusive Economic Zone and Continental Shelf'[8] in June 1998 to state its maritime rights in the relevant waters. In the 1980s and 1990s, Beijing undertook a number of aggressive actions to enforce its claims. In 1988, China's military clashed with Vietnamese forces over the Johnson (Chigua) Reef in the Spratlys. China's occupation of Mischief (Meiji) Reef in 1995 and subsequent expansion of the structure it built on the reef in 1998 elicited vehement protests from the Philippines and raised regional concerns about Chinese 'creeping assertiveness'.[9]

Since the late 1990s, Beijing has adopted a more moderate approach, largely due to the need to improve relationships with ASEAN countries. In November 2002, China signed the 'Declaration on the Conduct of Parties in the South China Sea' (DOC) with ASEAN countries, and in October 2003 it signed the ASEAN

Treaty of Amity and Cooperation in Southeast Asia, becoming the first non-ASEAN country to do so. Beijing has also actively promoted the idea of 'shelving the dispute and seeking joint developments' (*Gezhi zhengyi, gongtong kaifa*)[10] with other claimant states to manage the dispute. In 2005, China, Vietnam and the Philippines signed an agreement to undertake joint seismic surveys in the South China Sea.

The late 2000s, however, have seen growing concern among the Chinese analysts that such a moderate policy has failed to protect China's sovereignty and maritime rights and interests. This concern has been particularly acute with regard to other disputant states' exploitation of energy resources in the disputed areas. Ever since the discovery of hydrocarbon resources in the South China Sea in the 1960s and 1970s, competition over accessing the oil and gas has become one of the most important sources of tension between China and other Southeast Asian claimants. While estimates of the scale of the oil and gas reserves in the South China Sea vary, Chinese analysts generally believe that the maritime domain is a critically important source of energy for China's long-term economic development. The area was also officially listed as one of the ten national strategic oil and gas fields in China.[11] Some have estimated that the total oil and gas reserves in the South China Sea could account for one-third of the total energy reserves of China.[12] Others have even referred to the South China Sea as 'China's Persian Gulf'.[13]

However, many Chinese analysts increasingly hold the view that the DOC has not been effective in preventing other claimant states from undertaking actions that advance their claims and exploit the energy resources in the South China Sea at the expense of China's interests. For example, some Chinese scholars have observed warily that 'currently the oil and gas resources in the South China Sea are being exploited at an alarming rate and scale by other claimant states', claiming that 'the annual oil production of the other claimant states in the South China Sea is as high as 50 million tons, equivalent to the peak annual production of China's largest onshore oil field: The Daqing Oil Field'.[14] Another analyst warned that 'given the current rate of exploration, the energy resources of the South China Sea will be exhausted within the next 20 years'.[15] Chinese concerns were further reinforced by the growing involvements of foreign oil companies in oil and gas exploration in the disputed areas. An official report noted that in recent years, in addition to the Western oil companies, energy firms from India and Russia also signed various contracts with the Southeast Asian claimants, making the South China Sea dispute even more sensitive and complicated for China to deal with.[16]

Not surprisingly, some Chinese analysts began to argue that Beijing should reconsider the proposal of pursuing joint development, arguing that such a proposal is largely unrealistic and should not be the core of China's South China Sea policy.[17] An article published in the popular *International Herald Leader*, a newspaper run by the official Xinhua News Agency, bluntly referred to the period since the signing of the DOC as a 'lost decade' for China.[18] At the official level, Chinese frustration was perhaps most clearly expressed by a recent article in the *People's Daily*. The article stated that while China proposed and adhered to the principle of 'shelving the dispute and seeking joint development', other countries should not take advantage of this to make frequent 'encroachments' on Chinese territories by taking unilateral actions, warning that countries who made 'strategic misjudgments on this issue will pay the deserved price'.[19]

Growing disputes over fishing between China and other Southeast Asian claimants has become another major source of Chinese frustration over the current situation in the South China Sea. Accounting for around 10 per cent of the world's fishing catch per year, the South China Sea has been a historical fishing ground for Chinese fishermen from coastal provinces such as Hainan, Guangdong and Guangxi. In recent years, China's conflicts with other claimant states over fishing in the disputed area have occurred more frequently, causing periodical diplomatic tensions and sometimes heightened mutual public hostility. For example, according to a Chinese report, the number of Vietnamese boats that engaged in illegal fishing in areas surrounding the Paracel Islands increased from 21 in 2000 to more than 900 in 2007.[20] Moreover, it is reported that between 1989 and 2010, there were more than 380 reported incidents involving foreign countries 'attacking, robbing, detaining and killing' Chinese fishing boats and fishermen. These incidents affected 750 Chinese fishing boats and 11,300 fishermen, with 25 Chinese fishermen killed, 24 injured and some 800 detained and sentenced by foreign countries.[21] In a recent media interview, a leading Chinese maritime strategist stated that 'in recent years, other claimant states have taken increasingly frequent actions violating China's maritime rights and interests, leading to an unprecedented grim situation in the South China Sea'.[22] Chinese commentators have angrily labelled the situation in the South China Sea one of 'small countries bullying the big power' (*Xiaoguo qifu daguo*).

Apart from the increasing concern of losing valuable economic resources, a more significant and deepening worry among Chinese analysts is that the actions of other claimant states, such as exercising jurisdictional controls and exploiting resources, will strengthen these states' claims over the sovereignty and the maritime interests of the disputed areas. Such anxiety is further reinforced by growing recognition among Chinese scholars that China's claims over the South China Sea based on historical grounds will be unlikely to carry much weight in the contemporary international legal environment.[23] A number of Chinese legal experts have recognised that current international law and legal practice prioritise continuous and effective occupation and administration over that of historical discovery, warning that the current actions of other claimant states to reinforce their effective control over the dispute areas may place them in a favourable legal position in future dispute settlements.[24] Some commentators even argue that if the South China Sea islands that currently are being occupied by other countries stay under other countries' control for more than 50 years, China will have legally lost its sovereignty for these islands forever. By this calculation, it is suggested that given that some island features in the South China Sea were occupied by other countries in the 1970s, China might lose those Islands in 2020 if it does not take more effective measures to defend its sovereignty over these islands.[25]

Moreover, despite China's growing naval capability and the occasional tough statements made by some People's Liberation Army (PLA) commentators, most of the Chinese analysts and policymakers recognise that the use of force does not constitute a viable solution to the South China Sea dispute. Given China's multilayered strategic, political, economic and diplomatic interests in Southeast Asia, Chinese analysts generally believe that a military solution is neither feasible nor desirable for the foreseeable future. Some Chinese scholars thus warily argue that China is currently caught in a difficult situation featured by three 'cannots': it cannot reach an agreement with other claimants to resolve the dispute through diplomatic negotiations, it cannot afford to resort to force, and it cannot afford to allow the current situation to last indefinitely (*Tan bu long, Da bu de, Tuo bu qi*).[26]

In this context, many Chinese analysts argue that China needs to take a more proactive, rather than reactive, approach to strengthen its claims through administrative, diplomatic and legal means. For example, the Chinese maritime legal expert Qu Bo argues that China should take concerted measures to reinforce its control over the disputed areas in the South China Sea. According to him, China should: adopt a zero-tolerance approach to the presence of other nationals in the area surrounding the Paracels; take greater efforts to strengthen its controls over the seven features occupied by China in the Spratlys and the surrounding maritime areas; establish and enforce relevant maritime laws and regulations; make greater use of jurisdictional measures to demonstrate China's sovereignty; strengthen the capability of the city of Sansha in defending China's maritime rights in the disputed areas; increase Chinese military presence; and respond promptly to any actions by other countries that violate China's sovereignty.[27] After China's stand-off with the Philippines over the Scarborough Shoal in April 2012, Chinese legal analyst Zhang Lei warned that while China has indisputable historically based sovereignty of the shoal, it also needs to take strategic and proactive measures to demonstrate and strengthen its continuous and effective administrations of the shoal on the basis of international law.[28] The growing attention paid to the current international legal norms was also reflected in official government documents. For example, in the 2012 Ocean Development Report released by the State Oceanic Administration (SOA), it is explicitly stated that China's claims to sovereignty of the South China Sea islands are based on 'historical discovery, occupation and longstanding, continuous and effective administration'.[29]

It is not surprising that the late 2000s have seen the emergence of a more assertive and purposeful approach on the part of Beijing to bolster its claims through increasingly proactive and systematic measures. In 2008, the Chinese State Council authorised China Marine Surveillance (CMS) under the State Oceanic Administration to commence regular patrols (*Xun hang*) over all the maritime areas claimed by China, including the South China Sea. In 2009, CMS claimed for the first time that it undertook regular patrols over the entire claimed areas in the South China Sea, reaching as far as Zengmu Ansha (James Shoal).[30] In 2010, the CMS ship established a sovereignty marker on the Zengmu Ansha

(James Shoal) during its patrol.[31] Moreover, in 2011, the CMS undertook a series of 'special rights protection operations' (*zhuanxiang weiquan xingdong*) in the South China Sea, particularly targeting the 'illegal activities' of foreign countries undertaking 'oil and gas explorations and exploitations, maritime survey and military surveillance'.[32] It is thus not an isolated incident that in May 2011, a CMS ship cut off the cable of the Vietnamese seismic survey vessel, Binh Minh 2, in a disputed area in the South China Sea. In addition to the CMS, China's Fisheries Administration Bureau (FAB) under the Ministry of Agriculture has also taken more proactive measures against what it regards as illegal fishing in the disputed areas, and to protect the operations of Chinese fishermen against what it considers harassment by foreign countries. In February 2013, the director of the South China Sea Division of the FAB said that the key missions of his division was to undertake regular escort missions (*huyu*) to Chinese fishing vessels in the Spratly Islands, to exercise effective control over the areas surrounding Scarborough Shoal, Mischief Reef and the Paracel Islands.[33]

Recent external developments provided further impetus for China to take a more assertive approach to counter other countries' claims over the disputed areas in the South China Sea. In May 2009, a joint submission had been made by Vietnam and Malaysia to the Commission on the Limits of the Continental Shelf (CLCS) regarding their claims for continental shelves beyond their EEZ in the South China Sea. To protest against this, China subsequently submitted a *note verbale* on 7 May 2009 restating China's indisputable sovereignty over the islands of the South China Sea and adjacent waters. What is notable, however, is that China also attached to its diplomatic note a map indicating the controversial U-shaped line, the first time China officially used such a map to support its claims over the South China Sea.[34] Moreover, in response to Vietnam's promulgation of a national law of the sea that stipulates its claims over the Paracels and Spratlys, in July 2012 China declared the establishment of a new city, Sansha, which will have jurisdiction over the Paracels, Spratlys and Macclesfield Bank. While the idea of establishing Sansha was considered by Beijing as early as 2007, it was not formally approved due to various considerations.[35] This announcement thus clearly signified Beijing's new assertive approach to reinforcing its claims by establishing a prefecture-level formal government that can exercise full administrative and jurisdictional functions over the disputed areas.[36] According to Wu Shicun, Director of China's National Institute for South China Sea Studies, the establishment of Sansha has been an important step in China's effort to solidify its sovereignty claims through administrative and jurisdictional measures (*fali weiquan*).

In China's twelfth five-year plan, announced in March 2011, it was stipulated that China was to strengthen law enforcement efforts to protect its maritime rights and interests. In 2012, amid China's growing conflict with other countries over the disputed maritime territories, Beijing established 'the Central Maritime Affairs Leadership Small Group Office' (*Zhonggong zhongyang haiyang quanyi gongzuo lingdao xiaozu bangongshi*) to coordinate policies regarding China's maritime rights and interests, highlighting the importance placed by the Chinese leadership on maritime affairs. Members of the Leadership Small Group include, among others, the Foreign Ministry, the State Oceanic Administration and the military. In his report to the 18th Party congress in December 2012, Chinese President Hu Jintao stated that China was to build a strong maritime power, and resolutely protect its maritime rights and interests.

China's proactive stance to assert its claims is further demonstrated by the issuance of a new version of the Chinese passport in November 2012. The passport contains a map of China that includes its claimed South China Sea area within the U-shaped line. According to one analysis, 'By printing the passports, and inviting other states to stamp their visas in them, Beijing is attempting to gain recognition for its claims to sovereignty [of the South China Sea]'.[37] In March 2013, China further announced its plan to reorganise the SOA to enhance China's maritime law enforcement capability. In addition to the CMS, the new SOA will take control of the FAB, the Coast Guard Forces of the Public Security Ministry and the Maritime Anti-Smuggling Police of the General Administration of Customs. The SOA will undertake law enforcement activities in the name of China Maritime Police Bureau. In the meantime, a National Maritime Commission was to set up to coordinate China's maritime strategy.

China's claims in the South China Sea, the U-shaped line and its controversies

China's territorial and maritime claims

Ironically, despite China's growing assertiveness, its claims in the South China Sea are ambiguous. Among all the claimant countries in the South China Sea, China has the most expansive claims. Essentially, China's claims fall into two categories. The first is territorial claims. China has long made explicit claims to the sovereignty of all four islands groups in the South China Sea, namely the Pratas (Dongsha) Islands, the Paracel (Xisha) Islands, the Spratly (Nansha) Islands and the Macclesfield Bank (Zhongsha) Islands. China also includes the Scarborough Shoal (Huangyan Dao) as part of the Macclesfield bank. The second type of China's claims is related to the maritime rights to the relevant waters in the South China Sea. Unlike its territorial claims, however, China's claims in this regard are more ambiguous, as both the nature and geographical scope of the maritime rights claimed by China are yet to be sufficiently clarified. As a result of its expansive territorial and maritime claims, Beijing is currently in disputes over the Spratlys and its surrounding waters with Vietnam, the Philippines, Malaysia and Brunei, over the Paracels and its surrounding waters with the Vietnam, and over the Scarborough Shoals and the surrounding waters with the Philippines. China's maritime claims also overlap with portions of Indonesia's claimed EEZs near the Natuna Islands.

The territorial claims made by China to the island groups of the South China Sea are essentially based on historical grounds. Since 1949, the Chinese government has stated on numerous occasions that the island groups in the South

China Sea have been part of the Chinese territories for centuries. At the official level, such historically based claims have been most comprehensively presented in two substantial documents released by the Foreign Ministry of the PRC in 1980 and 2000. The first document, entitled 'China's Indisputable Sovereignty over the Xisha and Nansha Islands', was issued on 30 January 1980 in response to Vietnam's 1979 White Paper on the Paracel and Spratly Islands.[38] The second document, 'The Issue of South China Sea', was released in June 2000, focusing exclusively on China's claims to the Spratly Islands amid rising regional concerns of China's growing presence in the area after the 1995–1998 Mischief incident. The document contains five sections, entitled 'Its Origin (of the Issue of the South China Sea)', 'Historical Evidence to Support China's Sovereignty over Nansha Islands', 'Jurisprudential Evidence to Support China's Sovereignty over the Nansha Islands', 'Basic Stance and Policy of the Chinese Government in Solving the South China Sea Issue' and 'International Recognition of China's Sovereignty over the Nansha Islands'.[39]

According to these documents, the Paracels and Spratlys have been parts of the Chinese territory since ancient times because 'China was the first to discover, develop and administer'[40] these island groups. Citing historical data, the documents described that the Chinese people began sailing in the South China Sea as early as the second century BC during China's Han Dynasty, and were the first to discover and name the Paracels and Spratlys. Those islands were recorded in Chinese historical books as early as in the Three Kingdoms period (AD 220–265). From the Tang (AD 785–805) and Song (AD 960–1279) Dynasties at the latest, Chinese people have lived on the Paracels and Spratlys and engaged in various economic activities such as fishing and planting. Successive Chinese governments, according to the documents, have exercised continuous jurisdictions over the islands for more than 1,000 years since as early as in the Northern Song Dynasty (AD 960–1127).[41]

The documents also went to considerable length to demonstrate how the Chinese governments before and after 1949 have forcefully defended China's sovereignty against foreign invasions of the South China Sea islands. For example, according to the documents, when France tried to assert claims to the Paracel Islands in 1931 and later further occupied nine islands of the Spratlys in 1933, the then Republic of China's (ROC's) Kuomingtang (KMT) government staged its protests through various diplomatic and administrative measures. Apart from lodging diplomatic protests to the French government, the KMT government also established a 'Committee for the Examination of Land and Sea Maps' to check and approve the names of the islands in the South China Sea. The committee also compiled and published the *Map of the South China Sea Islands*, which marked all four island groups as part of China's territory. Also, at the end of World War II, when Japan renounced all the rights to its occupied islands in the Paracels and the Spratlys, the KMT government recovered the islands in 1946, erected sovereignty marks and set up military garrisons on various islands, including the Taiping (Itu Aba) Island, which is the largest island of the Spratlys.[42] In 1947, the government also renamed 159 islands, reefs, islets and shoals in the South China Sea, including the Nansha Islands, for administrative purposes. As the successor of the Republic of China government, the People's Republic of China government, which came to power in 1949, has continued to exercise China's sovereignty over the islands.

While the accuracy and legal significances of the historical and jurisdictional evidence presented by China to support its claims are subject to debate, the idea that the four island groups in the South China Sea have always been China's 'sacred territory' has been deeply immersed in the mind of the Chinese public before and after 1949. It should also be noted that the Republic of China government, which was relocated to Taiwan in 1949, still maintains the same historically based claims to the South China Sea islands as the PRC government.

If China's claims over the sovereignty of the islands in the South China Sea have been explicitly made, its claims to the maritime rights over the water areas are more ambiguous and are based on a complicated mix of legal and historical grounds. Some of China's claims of maritime rights are made, in accordance with evolving international law of the sea, on the basis of China's territorial claims to the islands. China first made official claims to the water areas in the South China Sea on 4 September 1958, when Beijing issued a Declaration on China's Territorial Sea.[43] The Declaration stipulated that the breadth of the territorial sea of the People's Republic of China will be 12 nautical miles, and declared that:

This provision applies to all territories of the People's Republic of China including the Chinese mainland and its coastal islands, as well as Taiwan and its surrounding islands, the Penghu Islands, the Dongsha Islands, the Xisha Islands, the Zhongsha Islands, the Nasha Islands and all other Islands belonging to China which are separated from the mainland and its coastal islands by the high seas.[44]

Such a declaration was made, in part, as an effort to assert China's title to the territorial sea of its mainland and offshore islands in the context of the international negotiations for the Law of the Sea in Geneva in 1958. It was also intended to defend the PRC's sovereignty of the South China Sea islands and the adjacent waters against the hostile US military activities in the context of the 1958 Taiwan Strait crisis.[45]

After signing UNCLOS in 1982, China, like all other littoral states, has made further claims to various maritime zones based on its claimed land features in the South China Sea. In 1992, China promulgated its Law on the Territorial Sea and Contiguous Zone. Article 2 of the Law asserted that all four island groups in the South China Sea are part of China's land territories, and thus entitled to territorial seas and contiguous zones. In 1996, China published the baselines for the Paracel Islands, which served to delineate the islands' territorial seas and contiguous zones. China's 1998 Law on the Exclusive Economic Zone (EEZ) and the Continental Shelf further established the legal basis for claiming EEZs and continental shelves from eligible island features.

China's claims of maritime jurisdictions in the South China Sea, however, are not solely limited to the above-mentioned maritime zones that it could claim under

UNCLOS. Instead, it appears that Beijing also believes that it possesses some 'historic rights' to the broader maritime spaces in the South China Sea. Such a view is clearly reflected by Article 14 of China's 1998 Law on EEZ and Continental Shelf, which states specifically that 'No provisions of this Law can prejudice historical rights of the People's Republic of China'.[46] While the substance or geographical coverage of the 'historic rights' has never been clearly defined by the Chinese government, it is generally acknowledged by Chinese analysts that such a clause was made primarily with reference to the South China Sea.[47] As discussed in the following, the ambiguity of China's historically based maritime claims has been further compounded by the controversial 'U-shaped line' in the Chinese maps of the South China Sea.

The U-shaped line and China's claims in the South China Sea

China's claim of 'historic rights' to the South China Sea have been closely linked to the 'U-shaped line' in the Chinese map (see Map 2). The line first appeared in Chinese maps drafted by private Chinese cartographers as early as 1914, and was originally a continuous line covering some areas of the South China Sea.[48] Later, partly as a response to French occupation of the Spratly Islands, on the maps published in the 1930s the line was extended to include the Spratlys as part of the Chinese territory. In 1947, as part of its efforts to recover the South China Sea islands from Japan post-WWII, the Ministry of Internal Affairs of the KMT government compiled a *Map of the Location of the South China Sea Islands* for internal use. On this map, a 'U-shaped line' consisting of 11 dashes was drawn to replace the previous continuous line. The map was subsequently published in an official atlas of national administrative districts released by the KMT government in February 1948.[49] The then government provided no explanations of nature of the line, however. It is not clear whether the line represents China's national territorial boundary in the South China Sea or simply delineates China's ownership of the island groups within the line. Nevertheless, the line has remained in all Chinese government maps published in the mainland since 1949, though two dashes in the Gulf of Tonkin were dropped by Beijing in 1953. In early 2013, in the new map of China published by China's state mapping authority Sinomap press, a new dash was added alongside Taiwan to demonstrate China's sovereignty claims of the island.[50]

As mentioned in the previous section, China's use of the 'U-shaped line' map in its 2009 *note verbale* to the CLCS, in response to the joint submission by Vietnam and Malaysia regarding their continental shelf, reinforced the uncertainties regarding China's claims. The diplomatic note not only stated that 'China has indisputable sovereignty over the islands in the South China Sea and the adjacent waters, and enjoys sovereign rights and jurisdiction over the relevant waters as well as the seabed and subsoil thereof',[51] but also attached the 'U-shaped line' map to the document. This caused widespread concerns about whether the term 'the relevant waters' refers to only the EEZs and continental shelf of the islands claimed by China, or covers all water areas within the 'U-shaped line'. There are external suspicions that China might seek to claim all the islands and water areas within the line as its historical waters, or even territory.[52] Not surprisingly, the use of the 'U-shaped line' map caused protests from other claimant states, which strongly questioned the legal basis of the U-shaped line.[53]

Ironically, in contrast to external commentators who have largely been dismissive of the legality of the 'U-shaped line', Chinese analysts have generally attached great importance to the line, seeing it as an important legal pillar supporting China's territorial and maritime claims in the South China Sea. There are, however, divergent views within China about the legal meaning of the 'U-shaped line' and the nature and scope of China's claims.[54] One view is to see the 'U-shaped line' as a national territorial boundary line. According to this view, all areas within the line are either China's internal waters or historic waters over which China has enjoyed full sovereignties. Such a view, however, is increasingly losing currency among China's South China Sea scholars, partly due to its contradictions with China's own practices and law. As many scholars pointed out, since 1949, China has never treated the areas as internal waters, given its declaration of maintaining freedom of navigations for foreign vessels in the area. Moreover, if the whole area within the line is China's territorial waters, then it would have been legally redundant or incompatible for China to publish the baselines for the Paracels in 1996.[55]

Another view is that the 'U-shaped line' only represents China's ownership of the four island groups within the line, and the associated sovereignty rights over the EEZs and continental shelves that are claimable from these insular features. It is reported that some Chinese Foreign Ministry officials expressed such a view to ASEAN diplomats in Beijing.[56] Moreover, it was reported that the former Chinese President, Jiang Zemin, articulated a similar position to Indonesian President Suharto during a visiting to Jakarta in 1994.[57] However, China's recent practice in the South China Sea appeared to contradict such a view. As mentioned in the previous section, since 2008, the CMS has expanded its law enforcement operations in all water areas within the line. Moreover, such a view was strongly opposed by many Chinese legal and maritime scholars. It is argued that such an interpretation of the 'U-shaped line' ignored the historic rights China has acquired over the maritime domain within the line through Chinese people's historical usage of the areas.[58]

In recent years, it appears that the view that the 'U-shaped line' should be interpreted as China's 'historic rights line' (*lishi xing quanli xian*) has become increasingly influential. According to this view, the 'U-shaped line' embodies China's multilayered claims of sovereignty and maritime rights. It first and foremost represents China's sovereignty over the island groups in the South China Sea and its territorial waters, as well as UNCLOS-based maritime rights associated with the islands. It also represents China's historic rights to all the water areas within the line. Such historic rights, while not clearly specified, would include mainly the rights to resources and navigation in the areas.[59]

Such an interpretation of the 'U-shaped line' was most clearly presented in a recent article jointly written by Professor Zhiguo Gao, the Executive Director of the official China Institute of Marine Affairs under the SOA, and a judge of the International Tribunal for the Law of the Sea (ITLOS), and Professor Bingbing Jia in the School of Law at China's Tsinghua University. According to Guo and Jia, the 'U-shaped line' has three legal meanings. First, it represents China's title to the island groups within the line, including sovereignty over the islands and other insular features, and China's UNCLOS-based entitlements to 'the waters and seabed and subsoil adjacent to those Islands and insular features'. Second, the line 'preserves Chinese historic rights in fishing, navigation, and such other marine activities as oil and gas development in the waters and on the continental shelf' in the entire areas within the line. Third, the line can potentially serve as 'maritime delimitation lines' between China and other claimant states.[60]

It is worth noting that in a 1994 article published by Gao in *Ocean Development & International Law*, he argued that the 'U-shaped line' on the Chinese map 'is merely a line that delineates ownership of islands rather than a maritime boundary in the conventional sense'.[61] Gao's changing position is thus significant. In particular, it should be noted that in July 2013, shortly after President Xi Jinping came to power, the CCP's Poliburo organised a special study session on the theme of building China into a great maritime power (*jianshe haiyang qiangguo*). Gao was one of the two experts giving presentations to the Chinese leadership in the study session on maritime affairs. Given this, and considering Gao's position in China's State Oceanic Administration, his changing view might have significant influence on China's future legal position over the 'U-shaped line'.

The importance placed by China on the 'U-shaped line' is also caused by a widely held view among Chinese scholars and policymakers that China's historic rights to the South China Sea existed long before the enactment of UNCLOS. Thus, they insist that UNCLOS should not be the only legal framework for delineating the maritime boundary. As one leading Chinese scholar of maritime affairs argues, 'both the U-shaped line and UNCLOS constitute the legal basis of China's maritime rights and interests in the South China Sea and the two are complementary'.[62] Thus, China appears to take what some scholars regard as a UNCLOS-plus approach to its claims in the South China Sea.[63] That is, on the one hand, China makes claims to the sovereignty rights to the EEZs and continental shelves that can be generated from the islands in the South China Sea in accordance with UNCLOS. On the other hand, it seeks recognitions of additional 'historic rights' to the waters within the 'U-shaped line'.

While many Chinese scholars understand that the concept of 'historic rights' is a highly contested issue in the current international laws, they hold the view that international law is dynamic, and to a great extent influenced by state practice and shifting power relationships. Thus, they hold the view that the nature of the South China Sea dispute is a 'legal warfare', depending on who can influence the international legal discourses. They argue that China should more actively involve and participate in international legal debate to shape and influence the evolution of international law in its favour.[64] For example, according to Wu Shicun, Director of China's National Institute for South China Sea Studies, the South China Sea dispute is taking place in four different battlegrounds, including:

> the first line battleground in the real maritime domain (*yixian zhanchang*), the legal battleground regarding the applicability and interpretation of the International Law (*falue zhanchang*), the battleground of making code of conduct (*guize zhanchang*) and the battleground of public opinion (*yulun zhanchang*).[65]

In this context, it is reasonable to expect that China will not only be unlikely to give up its claims based on the 'U-shaped line', but rather it will make greater efforts to defend the legality of the line.

China's South China Sea dilemma: between sovereignty and stability

China's emerging proactive and purposeful strategy to strengthen its claims in the South China Sea is, however, not without challenges. Indeed, China faces an acute policy dilemma. On the one hand, Beijing feels hard pressed to be more assertive to protect China's sovereignty and maritime rights and interests in the face of intensified competitions over resources in the South China Sea, complicated legal challenges arising from the actions of other claimant states, and strong domestic nationalistic sentiments. On the other hand, Beijing is keenly aware of the adverse impacts of its tough stance on China's broader strategic interests and positions in the region. Thus, balancing the dual needs of more forcefully bolstering China's claims while maintaining regional stability that serves China's broader strategic interests constitutes a tough foreign policy task for the Chinese leadership.

Beijing's awareness of such a dilemma is clearly reflected in a recent speech made by Chinese President Xi Jinping in the above-mentioned July 2013 Politburo study session on building China into a great maritime power. In his speech, while Xi stated that 'in no way will the country [China] abandon its legitimate rights and interests, nor will it give up its core national interests',[66] he also stated that China should 'coordinate the two overall strategic issues of maintaining stability [in the region] and safeguarding rights' (*tongchou weiwen he weiquan liangge da ju*). As noted by a commentator, such a statement highlighted the equal importance given by the Chinese leadership to the issues of maintaining a stable region (*weiwen*) and safeguarding China's 'maritime rights and interests' (*weiquan*).[67] It is thus not surprising to find that in the same speech, Xi urged that China should endeavour to promote mutually beneficial friendly cooperation, and seek and expand common interests with other countries, while at the same time calling for greater efforts to strengthen China's 'capability in safeguarding maritime rights and interests'.[68] In this context, according to Xi, China will adhere to its long-standing policy of 'shelving disputes and carrying out joint-development'.[69] This section will thus discuss some of China's recent balancing acts to mitigate regional concerns about its actions in the South China Sea while continuing to bolster its claims.

China, ASEAN and the Code of Conduct

China's balancing act has perhaps been most clearly manifested in its dealing with ASEAN over the South China Sea dispute. In China's external relations, ASEAN has occupied a particularly important place. Since the early 1990s, China has actively engaged with the ASEAN on multiple fronts as part of its regional strategy to create a stable and favourite external environment that serves to facilitate China's economic growth. Essentially, the strategy has two key elements. The first is to pacify regional countries' concerns about the potentially disruptive impact of a rising China on regional stability. The second is to prevent regional countries from siding with other external great powers in any containing-China efforts.[70] In this context, over the last two decades, engagement with ASEAN has been a top priority of Chinese foreign policy.

China's attitudes towards ASEAN's role in the South China Sea dispute have been decidedly ambivalent, however. On the one hand, China's long-standing position is that the dispute should only be settled through bilateral negotiations between claimant countries themselves. Thus, it has been resisting any suggestions that ASEAN be involved as a party in the settlement of the South China Sea dispute. This is because, from Beijing's point of view, the dispute is not a matter between China and ASEAN, since China has disputes with only four ASEAN countries in the South China Sea. In China's view, there is neither the need nor the use for other non-claimant countries to be involved in the dispute settlement. China has thus particularly been sensitive, if not hostile, to any ASEAN attempts of forming a unified stance over the South China Sea issue. This is clearly reflected by the widely speculated Chinese intervention in the July 2012 ASEAN Ministerial Meeting (AMM) in Phnom Penh, which, for the first time in its 45-year history, failed to issue a joint communiqué due to the disagreement among ASEAN member states over whether the South China Sea dispute should be included in the communiqué. It was reported that Cambodia, which was then Chair of ASEAN, and a close ally of China, adamantly refused to include the Philippines' proposals to mention recent tensions in the South China Sea in the communiqué. It was widely perceived that China's heavy-hand closely door activities had been the key factor for Cambodia's actions and the eventual failure of issuing a joint communiqué.[71]

On the other hand, China also sees ASEAN as a useful vehicle to manage tensions in the South China Sea, given that Beijing's preferred bilateral negotiations for settlement, which have been strongly resisted by some other claimants, are difficult, if not impossible, to occur. In this context, for China, engaging with ASEAN to manage conflicts in the contested maritime area, though not desirable, will at least help prevent some claimant states from seeking the direct involvement of external powers, especially the United States, into the dispute. In this context, in 2002, China and the 10 ASEAN member states signed the DOC. In the document, all parties made pledges to make efforts to reduce tensions in the area through confidence-building measures and agreed to exercise self-restraint by not undertaking activities that might complicate and escalate disputes. The DOC, however, is not a legally binding document, and subsequent negotiation over the implementation of the DOC proved to be difficult, partly due to disagreement between China and ASEAN over whether ASEAN would meet as a group first before negotiating with China. In July 2011, China and ASEAN finally reached agreement on an eight-point guideline for implementing the DOC, which dropped ASEAN's initial insistence on meeting separately as a group.[72] While the guideline still lacks substance, it creates the opportunity for China and ASEAN to put the issue of developing a legally binding Code of Conduct (COC) in the South China Sea – the ultimate goal of the DOC – on the agenda.

China's recent engagement with ASEAN over the guideline for implementing the DOC shows its growing recognition of ASEAN as an unavoidable key interlocutor in the South China Sea dispute. In a recent article written by a researcher of China's influential Shanghai Institute for International Studies, the author argues that despite China's resistance, the South China Sea dispute has become increasingly 'ASEANISED' (*Dongmeng hua*), with ASEAN playing an increasingly direct and active role in the management of the dispute. According to him, the 'ASEANISATION' of the dispute thus represents a third way of managing the South China Sea issue in addition to China's own preferred bilateralism and its long-resisted 'internationalisation' (*guoji hua*) of the dispute. He argues that while ASEAN's greater role in the dispute poses challenges for China, it is also useful to prevent the issue from being further internationalised with the greater involvement of other external great powers. According to the author, ASEAN's own interests in maintaining its leadership role in regional affairs and its concerns about the likely great power rivalry in the region make the organisation reluctant to draw in other external powers into the dispute management and settlement. The author thus argues that China should accept the reality of the growing 'ASEANISATION' of the South China Sea dispute and change its approaches to ASEAN accordingly. He suggests that China should be more accommodative to ASEAN's role in managing conflicts among disputant states, while at the same time taking a more active approach to prevent ASEAN dominating the negotiation of the COC process.[73]

Such a view has been visibly evident in China's changing approach to the negotiation of the COC. For a long time, China has been reluctant to negotiate with ASEAN on a legally binding COC. Instead, China has insisted that priority should be given to the implementation of the DOC, and that negotiation of the COC should only take place when 'time is ripe'. More recently, however, there have been some changes in China's attitudes. In April 2013, Chinese Foreign Minister Wang Yi reportedly indicated that China agreed to hold an ASEAN-China working group meeting on the COC in the near future. In August 2013, he further revealed that China and ASEAN have agreed to hold consultations on the 'Code of Conduct in the South China'.[74] On 14–15 September, China and ASEAN held their first round of official consultation on the COC at the 6th Senior Official Meeting on the implementation of the DOC, in the city of Suzhou at China's Jiangsu province.[75] This is the first time that China discussed with ASEAN countries officially about the COC. As a result of the meeting, China made commitments to continue the consultation process in future.[76]

China's changing attitude to the COC is driven by several considerations. First and the foremost, as widely perceived, China's more positive attitude to the COC is largely driven by the need to improve its relationship with ASEAN countries in the face of greater pressures from a more unified ASEAN. China, however, also has two other more sophisticated considerations. The first is to play a more proactive role in shaping the content of the COC to ensure it is compatible with China's interests. The second is to prevent other external powers from being involved in the COC negotiation. Immediately after the September 2013 SOM meeting in Suzhou on the COC, an article published in the *People's Daily* stated that the consultation of the COC represented China's proactive initiative to guide the rule-making process in the South China Sea. The consultation between China and ASEAN, according to the article, shows that the process of making the COC should be firmly controlled only by countries in the region. Moreover, the article argues that as a regional great power, China has an unquestionable responsibility to not only participate in, but also guide, the design of the COC.[77]

There are some key disagreements between China and some other claimant states over the nature and scope of the COC, however. China insists that the COC should only be a conflict-prevention and conflict-management instrument, not an arrangement for dispute settlement. Thus, the COC should be about regulating countries' conduct in the South China Sea, with the aims to reduce tensions and promote cooperation. Any resolution of the disputes should, however, only be made through bilateral negotiation between China and other claimant countries. It was noted that some other clamant states, however, want the COC to address the issue of sovereignty claims, especially China's 'U-shaped line' claims.[78] It is thus not surprising that the above-mentioned *People's Daily* article warned that 'other countries should not expect that China will sacrifice its sovereignty and maritime rights for making a deal' in the South China Sea dispute.[79]

Moreover, China insists that the negotiation of the COC should be a step-by-step process and should not be rushed. According to Chinese Foreign Minister Wang Yi, negotiation of the COC should be based on four principles: realistic expectation, consensus through negotiations, elimination of interference and step-by-step approach. He warned that some ASEAN countries should not expect to have a 'quick fix' on the COC and/or to impose their wills on other countries.[80] Given the considerable differences between China and some ASEAN claimant countries, the process of negotiation of COC will be clearly a protracted one.

China's new charm offensive in South East Asia

Apart from engaging with ASEAN on the COC, since early 2013 China has also made a range of new initiatives to improve its broader relationships with ASEAN countries and to separate the South China Sea issue from its overall relationship with Southeast Asian countries. During 2–8 October 2013, Chinese President Xi Jinping made a seven-day visit to Southeast Asia, including state visits to Indonesia and Malaysia, and attending the 21st APEC informal leadership meeting in Bali. While the main purpose of Xi's visit was to attend the APEC meeting, his visits to the two founding members of the ASEAN were perhaps more important. In Indonesia, Xi gave a speech to the Indonesian parliament – the first foreign leader given the honour to do so. In his speech, Xi announced China's intention to further improve its relationship with ASEAN. Describing that China's relationship with ASEAN now 'stands at a new historical starting point', he stated that China wishes to build a more closely knit 'China–ASEAN community of common destiny'.[81] He also pledged that China will be committed to resolve the territorial disputes with some Southeast Asian nations peacefully through dialogue and friendly consultation on an equal basis. During the visits, Xi also announced, with Indonesian President Susilo Bambang Yudhoyono and Malaysian Prime Minister Najib Razak, to upgrade China's bilateral relations with the two countries to a 'comprehensive strategic partnership'. A range of agreements was also signed between China and the two countries covering cooperation in the areas of trade and investment, energy cooperation and high-level dialogue, and defence engagement and joint combating against transnational crime.

Immediately following Xi's visit, Chinese Premier Li Keqiang also visited the region on 9–15 October 2013, to both attend the East Asia Summit and visit Brunei, Thailand and Vietnam. Like Xi, in his speech to the East Asia Summit, Li restated China's commitments to cooperate with ASEAN countries to promote the implementation of the DOC and consultation of the COC to maintain peace and stability in the South China Sea. At the China–ASEAN Summit, he also proposed a new treaty of friendship and good neighbourliness between China and ASEAN. During an interview given to ASEAN press in Beijing prior to his visit, he also announced seven proposals to develop closer China–ASEAN relations, including upgrading the China–ASEAN Free Trade Zone, defence exchange and cooperation, cooperation in financial areas, maritime cooperation, and people-to-people exchange, in addition to the proposed new treaty.[82]

During his visit to Vietnam on 13–15 October, Premier Li reached agreements with Vietnamese Prime Minister Nguyen Tan Dung to enhance bilateral cooperation in all fields. More importantly, they also agreed to manage their maritime disputes in the South China Sea and resolve the dispute peacefully. Specifically, the two sides agreed to establish a working group to explore joint development maritime projects in the areas beyond the Gulf of Tonkin Bay, though the location of the possible joint development remains unclear. According to the Chinese Foreign Ministry Spokeswoman, Hua Chunying, the agreement to explore the possibility of joint development represents 'an important breakthrough'.[83] It is worth noting that in his visit to Brunei a few days earlier, Li and Brunei Sultan Hassanal Bolkiah also agreed to seek closer cooperation in joint exploration and exploitation of maritime oil and gas resources.[84]

Conclusion

China's new assertive approach to the South China Sea dispute will have far-reaching consequences for regional stability and future resolution of the dispute. Instead of reflecting a short-term, reactive policy stance, Beijing's recent actions represent a long-term, proactive and purposeful approach to bolster Chinese claims. China's new assertiveness, however, does not signify an increasing inclination to resort to force to settle the dispute. Rather, it reflects a growing intention to employ legal, diplomatic and administrative measures to augment the basis of its claims to gain leverage in future diplomatic and legal negotiations. It should also be noted that despite its assertive approach, Beijing does not want to let the South China Sea issue dominate its relationship with ASEAN and the other claimant states. Instead, Beijing has taken efforts to reduce the damage caused by its increasingly assertive actions to its regional status by continually promoting closer economic, political and cultural relationships with Southeast Asian countries. Nonetheless, China's new assertive approach will certainly add new uncertainties to the already tension-ridden South China Sea.

Notes

1 International Crisis Group, 'Stirring Up the South China Sea (I)', *Asia Report*, 223, 23 April 2012.
2 K. G. Lieberthal and D. Lampton, *Bureaucracy, Politics, and Decision Making in Post-Mao China*, University of California Press, Berkeley, CA, 1992.
3 L. Buszynski, 'China's Naval Strategy, the United States, ASEAN and the South China Sea', *Security Challenges*, 8(2), 2012, pp. 19–32; C. Thayer, 'China's Naval Modernisation and US Rebalancing: Implications for Stability in the South China Sea', Paper presented at the 4th International Workshop on the South China Sea, Ho Chi Minh City, 18–21 November 2012.
4 For example, see 'China's Passport Move Stokes South China Sea Dispute', *Strategic Comments*, 18(10), 2012; see also M. T. Fravel, 'China's Strategy in the South China Sea', *Contemporary Southeast Asia*, 33(3), 2011, pp. 292–319.
5 A portion of this section is adapted from Jian Zhang, 'China's Growing Assertiveness in the South China Sea: A Strategic Shift?', in L. Buszynski and C. Roberts (eds), *The South China Sea and Australia's Regional Security Environment*, National Security College Occasional Paper, no. 5, Australian National University, September 2013.
6 Chi-kin Lo, *China's Policy Towards Territorial Disputes: The Case of the South China Sea Islands*, Routledge, London, 1989, p. 28.
7 Guo J., 'Nanhai diyuan xingshi yu zhongguo zhengfu dui nanhai quanyi de weihu' (The geostrategic situation in the South China Sea and the Chinese government's efforts to protect its rights and interests in the South China Sea), *Taipingyang Xuebao* (Pacific Journal) 19(5), 2011, 83–91.
8 Both laws can be found at the official website of China's State Oceanic Administration at www.soa.gov.cn/zwgk/fwjgwywj/shfl/; the English version of the law documents can be found at www.asianlii.org/cn/legis/cen/laws/ (accessed 2 June 2014).
9 I. Storey, 'Creeping Assertiveness: China, the Philippines and the South China Sea Dispute', *Contemporary Southeast Asia*, 21(1), 1999, pp. 95–118.
10 Luo G., 'Lijie nanhai gongtong kaifa yu hangxing ziyou wenti de xin silu: jiyu guojifa shijiao kan nanhai zhengduan de jiejue lujing' (New thinking on joint development

and freedom of navigation in the South China Sea: Paths for resolving the South China Sea dispute based on international law), *Dangdai yatai* (Contemporary Asia-Pacific Studies), 3, 2012, pp. 65–77.

11 Du Debin, Fan Fie and Ma Yahua, 'Nanhai zhuquan Zhengduan de zhanlue taishi ji zhongguo de yingdui fanglue' (The strategic situation in the South China Sea dispute and China's policy responses), *Shijie dili yanjiu* (World Regional Studies), 21(2), 2012, pp. 1–17.

12 Yang G., 'Lun Zhongguo zai nanhai wenti shang de guojia liyi' (On China's national interests in the South China Sea dispute), *Xin dongfang* (The New Orient), 6, 2012, pp. 10–16.

13 Chen X., 'Nanhai de ziyuan shijie' (The world of resources in the South China Sea), *Sanlian shenghuo zhoukan* (Sanlian Life Weekly), 46, November 2010, p. 64.

14 Du *et al.* 'Nanhai zhuquan Zhengduan de zhanlue taishi ji zhongguo de yingdui fanglue', p. 9.

15 An Y., *Nanhai anquan zhanlue yu qianghua haiyang xingzheng guanli* (Security strategy in the South China Sea and strengthening maritime administration), Zhongguo jingji chubanshe, Beijing, 2011, p. 179.

16 *China's Ocean Development Report 2010*, Haiyang chubanshe, Beijing, 2010, p. 43.

17 Luo G., 'Lijie nanhai gongtong kaifa yu hangxing ziyou wenti de xin silu: jiyu guojifa shijiao kan nanhai zhengduan de jiejue lujing'.

18 Liang J. and Li X., *Zhongguo zai nanhai shi qu de shi nian* (China's lost decade in the South China Sea), 2011, http://news.china.com/focus/nhctsj/11101498/20110628/16618928.html (accessed 13 March 2013).

19 'Yanzhong de zhanlue wupan' (Serious strategic misjudgments), *People's Daily*, 2 August 2011.

20 Liang and Li, *Zhongguo zai nanhai shi qu de shi nian.*

21 *China's Ocean Development Report 2012*, Haiyang chubanshe, Beijing, 2012, p. 71.

22 Ma H. and Chen L., 'Haiyang fagui di yi ren' (No. 1 expert in maritime law), *Caijing*, www.caijing.com.cn/ajax/print.html (accessed 2 June 2014).

23 International Crisis Group, 'Stirring Up the South China Sea (I)', p. 17.

24 Zhang L., 'Jiaqiang dui huangyan dao youxiao kongzhi de guoji fa yiju' (Enhancing effective control of the Scarborough Shoal on the basis of international law), *Faxue* (Legal Science), 8, 2012, pp. 67–75.

25 For example, see Shao L., 'Zai bu xingdong, zhongguo jiang yongjiu shiqu nansha' (If China does not take actions, it will lose the Spratlys forever), *Xin Jishi* (New Documentary), 1, 2009, pp. 7–8.

26 For example, see Zhang S., *Zhongguo Haiquan* (*Chinese sea power*). Renmin ribao chubanshe, Beijing, 2009, p. 21.

27 Qu B, 'Nanhai zhoubian youguan guojia zai nansha qundao de celue ji woguo de duice jianyi' (The Spratlys strategy of the relevant countries in the South China Sea and advice for China's policy responses), *Zhongguo faxue* (China Legal Science), 6, 2012, pp. 58–67.

28 Zhang L., 'Jiaqiang dui huangyan dao youxiao kongzhi de guoji fa yiju', p. 73.

29 *China's Ocean Development Report 2012*, p. 51.

30 *China's Ocean Development Report 2012*, pp. 341–342.

31 *China's Ocean Development Report 2012*, p. 351.

32 *China's Ocean Development Report 2012*, p. 352.

33 Liang G., 'Nanhai yuzheng guanyuan: Zhongguo jiang zai nansha haiyu kaizhan changtai hua huyu' (South Sea Fishery Official: China will undertake regular escort operation for Chinese fishermen in the maritime areas of the Spratlys), http://world.huanqiu.com/regions/2013-02/3671208.html (accessed 25 February 2013).

34 For the significance and controversy surrounding the 'U-shaped line', see the discussion in the next section on China's claims in the South China Sea.

35 J. Dreyer, 'Sansha: New City in the South China Sea', *China Brief*, XII(16), 17 August 2012, Jamestown Foundation, pp. 6–9.
36 Prior to this, China only had an ad hoc county-level working committee 'Xi, Nan, Zhong Sha (Sansha) Working Committee'as its administrative arm in the South China Sea. The working committee, however, is not a formal level of government, and lacks relevant administrative and jurisdictional authority. Li J., 'Sansha shi cheng li shi mo' (The Establishment of the Sansha City), *Liaowang dongfang zhoukan* (Oriental Outlook Weekly), 6 August 2012.
37 'China's Passport Move Stokes South China Sea Dispute'.
38 FMPRC (Foreign Ministry of the People's Republic of China), 'China's Indisputable Sovereignty over the Xisha and Nasha Islands', *Beijing Review*, 7, 18 February 1980, pp. 15–24.
39 FMPRC (Foreign Ministry of the People's Republic of China), *The Issue of South China Sea*, June 2000, www.fas.org/news/china/2000/china-000600.htm (accessed 11 October 2013).
40 FMPRC, 'China's Indisputable Sovereignty over the Xisha and Nasha Islands', p. 18.
41 FMPRC, 'China's Indisputable Sovereignty over the Xisha and Nasha Islands', pp. 15–18.
42 FMPRC, 'China's Indisputable Sovereignty over the Xisha and Nasha Islands', pp. 18–19.
43 Fravel, 'China's Strategy in the South China Sea', p. 293.
44 'Declaration of the Government of the People's Republic of China on China's Territorial Sea', 4 September 1958. The English version of the Declaration can be accessed at www.asianlii.org/cn/legis/cen/laws/rotscotnpcotaotdotgocts1338/ (accessed 2 June 2014).
45 Guo Y., 'Guanyu linghai de shengming de fabu ji dui nanhai quanyi de weihu' (The promulgation of 'the Declaration on the Territorial Sea' and the protection of China's maritime rights and interests in the South China Sea), *Journal of Zhejiang Ocean University*, 27(3), 2010, pp. 10–14; Zhou G., 'Wo zhengfu guanyu linghai de shengming de zhongda yiyi' (The great significance of our government's declaration on the territorial sea), *Shijie zhishi* (World Affairs), 18, 1958, pp. 16–17.
46 'The Law of the People's Republic of China on the Exclusive Economic Zone and Continental Shelf', www.asianlii.org/cn/legis/cen/laws/lotprocoteezatcs790/ (accessed 2 June 2014).
47 For example, see Jia Y., 'Nanhai "duanxuxian" de falu diwei' (The legal status of the 'dashed line' in the South China Sea), *Zhongguo bianjiang shidi yanjiu* (China's Borderland History and Geography Studies), 15(2), June 2005, pp. 112–120.
48 Jia Y., 'Nanhai wenti de guoji fali' (The International Law Theory of South China Sea Issues', *Zhongguo faxue* (China legal science), 6, 2012, pp. 31–32; Z. Gao and B. Jia, 'The Nine-Dash Line in the South China Sea: History, Status, and Implications', *The American Journal of International Law*, 107(1), 2013, pp. 98–124.
49 Jia Y., 'Nanhai wenti de guoji fali'; Gao and Jia, 'The Nine-Dash Line in the South China Sea'.
50 'China's New "10-dash line map" Eats into Philippine Territory', www.gmanetwork.com/news/story/319303/news/nation/china-s-new-10-dash-line-map-eats-into-philippine-territory (accessed 2 June 2014). See also Gao and Jia, 'The Nine-Dash Line in the South China Sea', p. 110.
51 Gao and Jia, 'The Nine-Dash Line in the South China Sea', p. 106.
52 International Crisis Group, 'Stirring Up the South China Sea (I)', p. 3; J. deLisle, 'Troubled Waters: China's Claims and the South China Sea', *Orbis*, Fall 2012, pp. 613–620.
53 Gao and Jia, 'The Nine-Dash Line in the South China Sea', pp. 106–108.

54 For useful discussions of these various views, see Jia Y., 'Nanhai "duanxuxian" de falu diwei'; Li Jinming, 'Guoneiwai youguan nanhai duanxuxian falu diwei de yanjiu shuping' (A review of the foreign and domestic studies of the legal status of the 'dotted line' in the South China Sea), *Nanhai wenti yanjiu* (Southeast Asian Affairs), 2, 2011, pp. 54–62.

55 Jia Y., 'Nanhai "duanxuxian" de falu diwei'; Li Jinming, 'Guoneiwai youguan nanhai duanxuxian falue diwei de yanjiu shuping'.

56 International Crisis Group, 'Stirring Up the South China Sea (I)', p. 3.

57 You J., 'Deciphering Beijing's Maritime Security Policy and Strategy in Managing Sovereignty Disputes in the China Seas', *Policy Brief*, October, S. Rajaratnam School of International Studies, Nanyang Technological University, Singapore, 2013, p. 9.

58 For example, see Jia Y., 'Nanhai "duanxuxian" de falu diwei'.

59 Jia Y., 'Nanhai "duanxuxian" de falu diwei'; Gao and Jia, 'The Nine-Dash Line in the South China Sea'; Jin Yongming, 'Zhongguo nanhai duanxuxian de xingzhi ji xiannei shuiyu de falu diwei' (The nature of China's 'dotted line' in the South China Sea and the legal status of the waters within the line), *Zhongguo faxue* (China Legal Science), 6, 2012, pp. 36–48.

60 Gao and Jia, 'The Nine-Dash Line in the South China Sea', pp. 123–124.

61 Z. Gao, 'The South China Sea: From Conflict to Cooperation?', *Ocean Development & International Law*, 25(3), 1994, p. 346.

62 Jia Y., 'Nanhai "duanxuxian" de falu diwei', p. 120.

63 P. Dutton, 'The Sino-Philippine Maritime Row: International Arbitration and the South China Sea', *East and South East China Seas Bulletin*, 10, 15 March 2013, Center for a New American Security, Washington, DC.

64 Wei L., '"Sida zhanchang" sheng wen nanhai yanjiu' ('Four major balttleground' drive South China Sea Studies), *Huanqiu shibao* (Global Times), 12 September 2013, http://world.huanqiu.com/interview/2013-09/4349758.html (accessed 24 October 2013); Jin Y., 'Lun nanhai wenti tezhi yu haiyang fa zhidu' (On the unique feature of the South China sea Issue and the legal system of the law of sea), *Dongfang faxue* (Oriental Law Journal), 4, 2011, p. 78.

65 Wei L., '"Sida zhanchang" sheng wen nanhai yanjiu'.

66 'Xi Advocates Efforts to Boost China's Maritime Power', *Xinhuanet*, 31 July 2013, http://news.xinhuanet.com/english/china/2013-07/31/c_132591246.htm (accessed 2 November 2013).

67 M. T. Fravel, 'Xi Jinping's Overlooked Revelation on China's Maritime Disputes', *The Diplomat*, 15 August 2013.

68 'Xi Advocates Efforts to Boost China's Maritime Power'.

69 'Xi Advocates Efforts to Boost China's Maritime Power'.

70 E. Medeiros, 'Is Beijing Ready for Global Leadership?', *Current History*, 108(719), 2009, pp. 250–256.

71 C. Thayer, 'Code of Conduct in the South China Sea Undermined by ASEAN Disarray', USNI News, 18 July 2012, http://news.usni.org/2012/07/18/code-conduct-south-china-sea-undermined-asean-disarray (accessed 2 June 2014).

72 C. Thayer, 'Sovereignty Disputes in the South China Sea: Diplomacy, Legal Regimes and Realpolik', Paper presented to the International Conference on Topical Regional Security Issues in East Asia, St Petersburg State University, Russian Federation, 6–7 April 2012.

73 Zhao G., 'Lun nanhai wenti "dongmenghua"de fazhuan: dongmen zhengce yanbian yu zhongguo yingdui' ('Aseanisation' of South China Sea Issue: ASEAN Policy Shift and China's Resposne), *guoji zhanwang* (Global Review), 2, March–April 2013, pp. 85–100.

74 C. Thayer, 'ASEAN and China Consultations on a Code of Conduct in the South China Sea: Prospects and Obstacles', Paper presented to the International Conference on

Security and Cooperation in the South China Sea, Institute of Oriental Studies, Russian Academy of Sciences, Moscow, Russian Federation, 18 October 2013, p. 12.

75   'China, ASEAN to Ignore "Distractions"', *China Daily*, 16 September 2013.

76   'Asean, China to Speed up Code of Conduct', *Bankok Post*, 16 September 2013.

77   Zhong S., 'Zhongguo dui nanhai xingwei zhunze cuoshang you zhujian, bu qucong waibu yali' (China has its own opinion on the consultation of the code of conduct in the South China Sea and will not bow to external pressures), *People's Daily*, 16 September 2012.

78   You J., 'Deciphering Beijing's Maritime Security Policy and Strategy in Managing Sovereignty Disputes in the China Seas', p. 9.

79   Zhong S., 'Zhongguo dui nanhai xingwei zhunze cuoshang you zhujian, bu qucong waibu yali'.

80   Thayer, 'ASEAN and China Consultations on a Code of Conduct in the South China Sea'.

81   'President Xi to Give Speech to Indonesia's Parliament', *China Daily*, 3 October 2013, www.chinadailyasia.com/news/2013-10/03/content_15090901.html (accessed 3 November 2013).

82   'Li Keqing jieshou dongmeng meiti caifang' (Li Keqiang Receives Interviews from the ASEAN Media Groups), http://news.sina.com.cn/c/2013-10-09/121828385068.shtml (accessed 2 June 2014).

83   'Vietnam Vows to Boost Political Ties with China in Visit', *Bloomberg News*, 15 October 2013, www.bloomberg.com/news/2013-10-14/vietnam-seeks-to-boost-political-trust-with-china-during-li-trip.html (accessed 2 June 2014).

84   'China, Brunei Agree to Seek Closer Maritime Energy Cooperation', *Xinhua News Agency*, 11 October 2013, http://news.xinhuanet.com/english/china/2013-10/11/c_132788933.htm (accessed 2 June 2014).

5   Vietnam's evolving claims

Do Thanh Hai

Vietnam is one of the claimants in the South China Sea disputes. Its claims for sovereignty of islands and maritime regions of the sea overlap either wholly or partly with those of Brunei, China, Taiwan, Malaysia and the Philippines. This chapter examines the evolution of the claims of unified Vietnam to maritime territories in the South China Sea since 1975, and compares them with the provisions of the United Nations Convention on the Law of the Sea (UNCLOS). To this end, the chapter will look into Hanoi's policy statements, its responses to major incidents at sea, and the outcomes of the negotiations between Vietnam and its neighbours. It also examines the legal actions of Vietnam to trace continuity and adjustments in its maritime regulations. The chapter maps out the main determinants behind these shifts.

Claimed maritime zones as security buffers before *Doi Moi*, 1986

After unification in April 1975, Vietnam claimed the East Sea, internationally referred to as the South China Sea. Unified Vietnam inherited from South Vietnam the longstanding claim to sovereignty over the entire Paracel and Spratly clusters of islets – referred to in Vietnamese as Hoang Sa and Truong Sa, respectively – on a historical and legal basis. It published three White Papers in 1979, 1981 and 1988, and presented a wide range of historical and legal data to prove its peaceful acquisition of – and continuous, effective administration over – the island groups by different Vietnamese state authorities since the feudal reign of the seventeenth century when these islands were *terra nullius*. Additionally, Hanoi contested the legitimacy of China's use of force to expel the Vietnamese from the Paracel archipelago in January 1974 and some Spratly reefs in March 1988.[1] To support its claim and pre-empt other claimants' assertive moves, Vietnam vigorously expanded its presence in the Spratlys throughout the 1980s.[2] In the early 1990s, Vietnam occupied between 21 and 24 Spratly features.[3]

Hanoi also relied on the developing maritime legal order to claim a range of rights and jurisdictions over a large expanse of maritime areas. Vietnam's oceanic position was overall consistent with the rules established by UNCLOS, except for four areas. First, in the Statement on the Territorial Sea, Contiguous Zone,

Exclusive Economic Zone and Continental Shelf of the Socialist Republic of Vietnam, published on 12 May 1977, Hanoi claimed a full suite of maritime zones as recommended by the Revised Single Negotiating Text not only for its mainland coast, but also for its offshore 'islands and archipelagos' (Article 5).[4] Though no specific names of islands and archipelagos were mentioned, it is a reasonable assessment that Hanoi sought to establish exclusive economic zones (EEZs) and continental shelf entitlements for the Spratly and Paracel features. UNCLOS, concluded in November 1982, stipulates that islands are entitled to EEZs and continental shelves, while rocks, which are unable to sustain human habitation or economic life of their own, are not (Article 121). It was a controversial issue as to whether these insular features could be considered as fully fledged islands that could generate EEZs and continental shelves of their own, or just rocks. Almost all these insular formations in the Paracels and Spratlys are inherently remote, small, barren and largely unable to host permanent human habitation without regular supplies.[5]

Second, Hanoi proposed the status of 'historic waters' to the entire area of the Gulf of Tonkin. This position was first articulated in the Vietnam-China negotiations on the Gulf of Tonkin from August to November 1974. It was restated in the Declaration on the Baseline of Territorial Waters by the Vietnamese government in November 1982 (Article 3).[6] It should be noted that the 1958 Geneva Convention on Territorial Sea and Contiguous Zone and UNCLOS have no provisions for historic waters, but references to historic bays. From the Vietnamese perspective, there were no differences between 'historic waters' and 'historic bays', and these terms could be used interchangeably.[7] Though the notion of 'historic bays' was part of international customary law, there has been no consensus on the definition. Vietnamese legal experts held that historic waters must meet three conditions, namely deeply indented geographical configuration, economic, security and defense significance, and prolonged usage of the waters by the coastal states.[8] In this connection, they rationalised Vietnam's position by referring to longstanding usage and control of the Tonkin Gulf on the part of France/Vietnam and China, and by recalling that invasion forces had used the area as a staging ground in the past.[9] Its argument of 'historic waters' indicated that Hanoi had a strong interest in exercising full jurisdiction over its part of the gulf as 'internal waters'.

Third, Vietnam followed the practices of some countries in the region to delineate straight baselines deriving from the central and southern parts of its coastline (see Map 8). UNCLOS established two sorts of baseline. The normal baseline is determined by 'the low-water line along the coast as marked on large-scale charts officially recognized by the coastal State' (Article 5). The straight baselines are defined as 'joining appropriate points' in localities that satisfy such geographical conditions as 'deeply indented and cut-into coast', or 'a fringe of islands along the coast in its *immediate* vicinity', or unstable coastlines because of the presence of deltas and other natural conditions (emphasis added).[10] Hanoi controversially drew a 10-segment straight baseline system, connecting 11 base points, all of which but two are on near-shore islands along its coast. A number of islands are rather distant from the mainland. This baseline system ran for a total of 846 nautical miles and subsumed an area of roughly 27,000 square nautical miles as internal waters.[11] In defence of this position, the spokesperson of the Foreign Ministry of Vietnam stated:

> although some base points are about 50–70 nautical miles from shore and more than 100 nautical miles from each other, our stipulations on the baseline of [the] territorial waters do not conflict with the stipulations of international law and custom.[12]

A Vietnamese legal specialist argued that several far-shore islands were selected because they played an important part in the defence system of South Vietnam.[13] Some international legal experts were of the conviction that some parts of the baseline systems of Vietnam did not closely follow the related provisions of UNCLOS. Victor Prescott, an Australian Law of the Sea expert, held that the inappropriate application of straight baselines enabled Vietnam to incorporate significant sea area into its internal waters, more than if low waterline and closing lines were used across the many mouths of the Mekong River.[14] The application of straight baselines would significantly expand the limits of Vietnam's maritime zones as measured from the baseline seaward, at the expanse of high seas or maritime zones of coastal countries on the opposite side. If this baseline was used as a point of departure in negotiations on maritime boundaries with other South China Sea coastal states, it could perceivably give Vietnam a more advantageous starting position at the bargaining table.

Lastly, Hanoi also applied restrictions on foreign vessels' navigation through its territorial waters and contiguous zones. UNCLOS defends innocent passage, which is defined as traversing territorial seas or proceeding to or from internal waters that is not prejudicial to the peace, good order or security of the coastal state (Articles 18 and 19). However, Vietnam adopted a number of rules that denied the right of innocent passage for warships not only in the territorial sea, but also in many circumstances in the contiguous zone. Vietnam's Decree No. 30-CP, dated 29 January 1980, on Regulations for Foreign Ships Operating in Vietnamese Maritime Zones ruled that all foreign military vessels were required to apply for authorisation from Vietnamese competent authorities 30 days before traversing its territorial sea and contiguous zones. Once the permission was granted, the ships were to inform the Vietnamese Ministry of Communication and Transportation 48 hours before passing in the contiguous zone (Article 3). The regulation also inhibited the simultaneous presence of three or more warships of the same flag state in its territorial waters (Article 5). Besides, military exercises and other military-related activities were forbidden in the contiguous zone (Article 13).[15] It was also stipulated that foreign ships traversing through Vietnam's territorial seas must follow fixed routes and lanes defined by the Vietnamese authorities (Article 9). These stipulations were no doubt indicative of Vietnam's anxiety at the presence of foreign warships in the waters near its coast.

Though Vietnam did not clarify the limits of its claimed maritime territory, these positions suggested that Vietnam aimed to use international law to establish maximum exclusive or partial jurisdiction over a vast span of maritime area beyond its coast. The most illustrative example of Vietnam's maritime ambition was the controversial Vietnam Petroleum Concession Block Map, which was published and circulated in the late 1980s. In the map, the Gulf of Tonkin was divided by the extension of the historic red line and the concessional area encompassed most of the south-central South China Sea (see Map 9). The map reinforced the interpretation that Vietnam claimed exclusive economic zones and continental shelves for the Spratly features.[16] In 2001, in his book titled *Conflict and Cooperation in Managing Space in Semi-Enclosed Sea*, Vivian L. Forbes published an important map of South China Sea claims, which depicted Vietnam's claim by a single-line boundary. The line encompassed both Paracel and Spratly areas and subsumed more than half of the South China Sea area (see Map 10).[17] The map was out of date by the time of its publication, because it failed to reflect Vietnam's changing position on the status of the Paracel and Spratly features and the agreement on the maritime delimitation of the Tonkin Gulf signed by Vietnam and China in December 2000. Nonetheless, it was reproduced in several important works on the South China Sea dispute in the aftermath.[18]

Though these claims were made prior to the signing of UNCLOS in November 1982, the Vietnamese were obviously aware of the consensus reached at UNCLOS negotiations at related points of time. It should be noted that assertions of expansive claims by regional countries were common before the conclusion of the UNCLOS negotiations. In 1958, China claimed to apply the straight baseline principle to its mainland, its coastal islands and the South China Sea island groups, including the Tungsha (Pratas), Hsisha Islands (Paracels), the Chungsha (Macclesfield Bank) and the Nansha (Spratly Islands). Besides, Beijing also considered the Gulf of Bo Hai (Pohai) and the Hainan Strait (Chiungchow Strait) as internal waters.[19] Southeast Asian states such as Burma, Malaysia, Thailand, Indonesia and the Philippines also delineated controversial straight baseline systems around their coasts.[20] In this backdrop, not to do so would have created serious disadvantages to Vietnam in countering contending claims to the South China Sea islands and waters. As a matter of fact, Vietnamese legal commentators referred to the specific practices of other countries to legitimise Hanoi's position.[21]

Perhaps, Hanoi's interpretations of the law of the sea may have reflected its distrust of the utility of international law at that time. It should be noted that Hanoi was seriously engaged in the negotiations on the Law of the Sea only after it won a protracted war with the United States forces and South Vietnam to unify the country. The communist government was short of expertise in modern international law, in general, and the law of the sea, in particular. Its legal experts were heavily influenced by socialist ideology and Soviet scholarship, which highlighted socialist and capitalist confrontation. Besides, Vietnamese strategists, who were moulded in wars and conflicts, were no doubt suspicious of the function of international law as a means to control aggression. Thus, from Hanoi's viewpoint, international law was a tool to further national interests rather than a means of regulating relations among states.[22]

Besides, Vietnam's national security concerns in the post-war period figured significantly behind its maritime positions. No doubt, these radical claims were a manifestation of Vietnam's great interest in controlling the immediate sea areas that were important to its national defence. It was sensible because since the mid-nineteenth century, Vietnam was confronted with many more overwhelming seaborne attacks than ever before. This long-standing history of struggle against bigger naval powers clearly shaped its self-defensive apprehension of international affairs. Geopolitically speaking, given the country's elongated and fragmented mainland territory, the maritime corridor provides a fluid platform from which to maintain the cohesion of north and south, thereby helping to retain national unity. The lack of a hinterland created a critical consciousness of its coastal vulnerabilities. Additionally, its limited naval capabilities vis-à-vis major adversaries drove Vietnam to rely on additional measures to protect its territorial integrity. Under these circumstances, Vietnamese leaders saw new opportunities in the emerging oceanic order to promote national unity and to create a buffer zone around its coast. A *Nhan Dan* article on the fifth anniversary of the 1977 statement proclaimed: 'since the founding of the State of Van Lang, our country has gone through many stages of development; but this marked a *turning point* in our national history: Our country expanded eastward vigorously on the basis of international law' (emphasis added).[23]

Shifts in Vietnam's maritime interests after *Doi Moi*

Since the mid-1980s, economic development had become the highest priority for the Vietnamese leadership. Amid a severe socio-economic crisis, the Communist Party of Vietnam (CPV) initiated a package of reforms, known as *Doi Moi*, intended to transform the crippled, centrally planned economy into a market economy in December 1986. Economic reform was followed by a foreign policy reorientation. Departing from traditional advocacy of socialist internationalism and the deliberate use of force, Hanoi asserted its new foreign policy of diversification and multilateralisation in order to create a peaceful and stable external environment favourable to economic development. Consequently, Vietnam decisively moved to improve its relations with neighbouring countries and major powers of the world.[24] These changes delineated the contours of Vietnam's maritime interests.

In the first place, as peace and stability in all the frontiers became a pressing need, Hanoi grew increasingly interested in maintaining the status quo over the island chains, and in promoting proper settlement and management of the territorial disputes. Though convinced that its claims had a better historical and legal basis than those of others, Hanoi was not in the position to press its territorial claims forcefully because of its modest naval and air capabilities as compared with China, and the absence of a counterbalancing ally. Also, overt competitive strategies – such as the aggressive pursuit of territorial integrity or offensive military capacity – could undermine its focus on economic development and its efforts to expand cooperation with its neighbours. Therefore, the Vietnamese framed the disputes over the island groups and the Tonkin Gulf either as 'historical differences' that should be resolved peacefully or 'destabilising factors' that should be managed in a way that would not disturb the overall relations with its neighbours.[25]

As a result, Hanoi became more proactive and cooperative in handling existing territorial disputes. Since 1991, Hanoi has keenly engaged with its neighbours, bilaterally and multilaterally, to find settlements for or to better manage the existing border and territorial disputes. Vietnam sought to develop a dense web of bilateral dialogues with China, from high-level talks to grass-root exchanges, to expand cooperative activities and defuse territorial tensions. Three specialised technical-level working groups between the two sides were established to discuss the land border, the maritime boundary in the Tonkin Gulf and the 'maritime issues' in the South China Sea proper between 1992 and 1995.[26] At the same time, Hanoi also initiated negotiations with Laos and Cambodia on the land borders, with the Philippines on a bilateral code of conduct at sea, and with Malaysia, Thailand and Indonesia about the delimitation of the overlapping maritime zones in the Gulf of Thailand and in the South China Sea.[27] These efforts yielded a number of concrete achievements. In June 1992, Vietnam signed an agreement with Malaysia on the joint development of the area of overlapping continental shelf claims to the south-west of Vietnam. In August 1997, Vietnam and Thailand concluded an agreement to settle the disputes over the boundaries of their continental shelves and EEZs in the Gulf of Thailand. In December 1999, Vietnam and China signed a treaty on the demarcation of the land border. One year later, they reached an agreement on the maritime boundaries and an agreement on fishery cooperation in the Gulf of Tonkin. In June 2003, Vietnam and Indonesia inked a deal on delimiting the continental shelf boundary in the area to the north of the Natuna Islands.[28] In the multilateral arena, Vietnam was active behind ASEAN efforts to develop a regional code of conduct in the South China Sea.[29]

Besides, during the *Doi Moi* period, the Vietnamese leadership placed more emphasis on the development of maritime areas under its jurisdiction. It was widely believed in Vietnam that the country is entitled, as stipulated by UNCLOS, to 1 million square kilometers of sea area that is three times larger than the size of Vietnam's land territory. It was estimated that the seas around Vietnam hold a reserve of 1.2 billion barrels of oil equivalent, a fish stock of 2,744,900 tons (allowable catch of 1,372,400 tons) and a great deal of other resources.[30] Besides, Vietnam's 3,000 kilometre coastline and thousands of islands create natural advantages for aquaculture, shipbuilding, shipping and sea tourism. The 8th National Party Congress of the Communist Party of Vietnam in June 1996 stated:

> The maritime and coastal areas, which are strategically important in terms of economy, security and defense. These areas have advantages for economic development and serve as the gate for the country to connect with the world and main attraction for foreign investments.[31]

Vietnam's greater interest in the commercial aspects of the sea was manifest in key documents regarding maritime development. On 6 May 1993, the Politburo of the Communist Party of Vietnam adopted Resolution 03-NQ/TW on key tasks to develop 'maritime economy' in the foreseeable future.[32] The resolution set the goal of developing Vietnam into a major 'maritime power' for exploiting marine resources, defending the country's maritime domain and protecting the marine environment. The resolution saw the goals as interrelated, and indicated that the Vietnamese leadership regarded the expansion of sea-related activities as an important means to defend maritime territories. The resolution formulated some principles:

> To combine organically economy, defense and security; to mobilize internal resources and simultaneously strengthen multifaceted relations with external partners, especially Pacific and East Sea countries, toward multilateralisation and creation of counterweights to fend off coercive and bullying behavior of big powers, enhance our strength and bargaining position to settle maritime disputes in a peaceful manner.
>
> The top priority is to develop maritime economy, expand economic activities in maritime zones and islands under our sovereignty and jurisdiction to exploit maritime resources, assert sovereignty, and enhance capabilities to defend territorial and maritime integrity.
>
> To build up islands and coastal regions into pivotal economic regions, which serve as springboards to expand seaward and economic locomotives to engine the growth of other regions.
>
> Exploitation of marine resources must go hand in hand with environmental protection, efficient usage of resources, restoration and enrichment of renewable resources.[33]

On 22 September 1997, the Politburo of the Communist Party of Vietnam issued Directive 20-CT/TW on the industrialisation and modernisation of the Vietnamese maritime economy. It was assessed that Vietnam had not successfully controlled its maritime domain, and the increased violations against national security, sovereignty, national interest and navigational safety became more complex. To deal with these problems, the directive proposed the extension of the 'people's security and all people's defense' to the maritime realm. One of the concrete measures proposed in the directive was to develop offshore fisheries.[34] Between 1997 and 2001, the government provided preferential credits worth US$94 million to the offshore fishery programme. Besides, there were other types of subsidies to fishermen, such as investments in fisheries infrastructure, fuel cost support, training programmes, new vessels and engines, insurance and calamity supports.[35] In this regard, the Vietnamese believed that the presence of Vietnamese fishermen at sea was a robust demonstration of the country's sovereignty and jurisdiction.[36]

On 9 February 2007, the Central Committee adopted Resolution 09-NQ/TW on Vietnam's maritime strategy to 2020. General Secretary Nong Duc Manh stated at the end of the plenum that, 'A correct ocean strategy is the foundation and condition for the further exploitation of the role of the ocean in the construction and defense of the Motherland, and the realization of the industrialization and modernization causes'.[37] The details of these documents remain classified, but the key principles were mentioned in the media. The main emphasis was still laid on maritime economy. But the new strategy was said to pursue a more ambitious goal that the marine economy would make up 53–55 per cent of Vietnam's gross domestic product and 55–60 per cent of its exports by 2020.[38] It should be noted that the maritime economy accounted for 48 and 49 per cent of the GDP of the country in 2005 and 2007, respectively.[39] The goal was indicative of a strategic shift in economic development from the rice fields in the deltas of Red River and Mekong River to the sea arena in terms of a preferred avenue for development.

These policies laid the basis for Vietnam to expand vigorously seaward in pursuit of its rights to resources as authorised by international law. Oil and fisheries were no doubt key areas for maritime development. Hanoi paid attention to offshore hydrocarbons right after unification in 1975. However, not until June 1986 was the first commercial barrel of oil extracted from Bach Ho (White Tiger) field. Since then, offshore hydrocarbons became vital to Vietnam's economic development as the major source of hard currency, and one of the most attractive areas for foreign investment. It was estimated that in the period of 1975–2010, Vietnam's oil and gas industry had accumulated revenue of US$110 billion, equivalent to 18–20 per cent of gross domestic product (GDP), and made a contribution of 28–30 per cent of the state income. On average, the sector grew 20 per cent per annum.[40] Obviously, Vietnam's oil and gas industry gained momentum only after the promulgation of the Law on Foreign Investment in 1988, which opened the door for Western energy firms. Between 1988 and 1995, the state-run Oil and Gas Corporation of Vietnam signed 29 Production-Sharing Contracts (PSC) with foreign oil firms from diverse countries granting rights to explore offshore blocks.[41] By 2007, PetroVietnam, an upgrade of Oil and Gas Corporation of Vietnam, had concluded 37 PSC agreements, one Business Cooperation Contract and seven Joint Operating Contracts with more than 50 foreign energy firms.[42] By 2012, PetroVietnam had entered into a total of 60 oil and gas exploration and production undertakings with foreign partners.[43] As a result, Vietnam's oil production rose up by eight times from roughly 50,000 barrels a day in 1990 to 400,000 barrels a day in 2004 (see Figure 5.1).[44] No doubt, the advanced technologies of the Western energy firms helped Vietnam tap into oil and gas reservoirs in its continental shelf.

As an important sector of the economy, the marine fishing industry was also developing quickly in the *Doi Moi* period. No doubt, the industry provided an important source of protein and a livelihood base for many communities inhabiting the 3,260 kilometre coastline, as well as products for export. The total yield of captured fisheries went up from 709,000 tons in 1990, to 1,062,000 in 1997, to 1,876,000 tons in 2007, and 2,520,000 tons in 2011. In the same period, the number of fishing vessels declined from 72,723 in 1990, to 71,500 in 1997, but increased to 85,758 in 2007, and 130,000 in 2011.[45] Though the increase in the number of

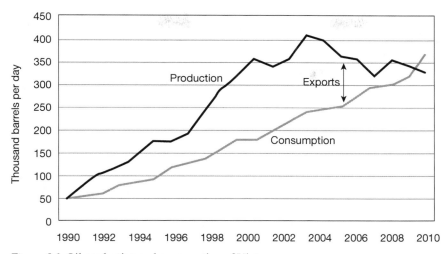

Figure 5.1 Oil production and consumption of Vietnam

Source: *Vietnam: Country Analysis Brief*, US Energy Information Administration, 9 May 2012

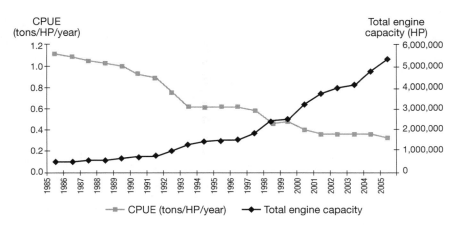

Figure 5.2 Fisheries total capacity and catch per unit effort of Vietnam (1985–2005)

Source: UNEP, VIEP and WWF, *Fisheries Subsidies, Supply Chain and Certification in Vietnam, Summary Report*, Hanoi, September 2009, p. 21

vessels was small, the rise in total engine capacity was much higher, rising roughly twice between 1990 and 1997, and six times between 1990 and 2005 (see Figure 5.2). This was the result of an increase in the number of vessels with capacity of over 90 horsepower, especially after 1997, as an outcome of implementation of the policy on development of offshore fishing and stabilization of coastal exploitation and credit programmes for building offshore vessels.[46] By 2008, there were 17,000 vessels with a capacity over 90 horsepower. As a result, the offshore fishing production significantly increased, making up of 40 per cent of total fishing production.[47] These figures indicated the Vietnamese fishermen sailed further afield and increased their presence in the South China Sea.

Other areas of the maritime economy of Vietnam have also grown significantly over the last two decades. In particular, the size of the Vietnamese fleet for maritime transport expanded quickly. Its tonnage rose by 2,152 per cent between 2000 and 2011, around 10 times higher than the average increase of Southeast Asian countries.[48] The shipping industry recorded high growth rates of over 30 per cent annually in terms of total output in the late 1990s and early 2000s, before being hit by the global financial crisis.[49] In 2010, Vietnam ranked fifth among the world's largest shipbuilders in terms of orders.[50] Vietnam has so far set up three marine economic zones, 30 export-oriented industrial zones and 80 seaports, which have the capacity of handling 100 million tons per year.[51] Obviously, the shipping and shipbuilding industries have been priority sectors in Vietnam's developmental plan. The Vietnamese government has put forth ambitious programmes and made heavy investments through state-owned corporations to develop these industries. However, these efforts have not yielded expected results due to rampant mismanagement and the impact of the global financial crisis in 2009. By 2009, maritime incomes were primarily derived from oil and fisheries, which account for 64 per cent and 14 per cent, respectively, of the total marine-based revenue.[52] However, Vietnam's maritime development did not go unchallenged. Other South China Sea coastal states were also increasingly interested in exploiting oceanic resources and expanded their marine-based activities. Because these countries pushed for maritime development, the number of clashes and incidents, especially over fishing activities, markedly increased. Also, since 1992, Vietnam faced new disputes over maritime regions as China offered concessions in areas much closer to its coastline and coastal islands. Obviously, Vietnam's pressing need for maritime resources and, from Hanoi's point of view, China's unjustifiable claims, as well as its assertive actions, prompted Hanoi to take UNCLOS more seriously.

Adjustments in Vietnam's law of the sea claims

After *Doi Moi*, Vietnam maintained its long-standing claim to the Paracels and Spratlys in their entirety on a historical and legal basis, but without defining the extent of its claim. This claim was restated in all key legal instruments, such as the National Assembly's resolution to ratify UNCLOS in June 1994, the Law on National Border promulgated in 2003 and the Law of the Sea of Vietnam adopted in June 2012. There has been no indication that Hanoi would move to clarify the limits of its claim to the archipelago and specific islands, or would be willing to make any compromise on these offshore territories. Vietnamese leaders resisted any call to reveal their bottom line before China, the biggest claimant, clarified its sovereignty claims and the legal regimes that could be applied to these features are decided. Currently, Vietnam is occupying 33 features in the Spratlys, including 21 islands and 12 low-tide elevations with structures. It was reported that six Vietnamese resident households now live in this area.[53]

Nonetheless, it was observed that Vietnam adopted a more cooperative approach in handling territorial disputes, and has increasingly defined its claims in terms of coastal states' rights as granted by UNCLOS. In June 1994, Vietnam ratified UNCLOS and asserted sovereignty over its internal waters and its territorial sea, and claimed contiguous zones, EEZs and continental shelves as stipulated by UNCLOS. The resolution of the National Assembly of Vietnam that ratified UNCLOS required the Standing Committee of the National Assembly and the administration to review and amend domestic legislation to align it with UNCLOS.[54] This was an indication that the Vietnamese were aware of the gaps between their claims and UNCLOS provisions. In June 2003, the National Assembly of Vietnam adopted the Law on National Borders, which also stipulated that the legal regime, protection and administration of Vietnamese contiguous zones, EEZs and continental shelves must be in conformity with UNCLOS and international treaties to which the country is a party.[55] In June 2012, the National Assembly of Vietnam adopted the Law of the Sea of Vietnam, which was to 'codify the letter and the spirit of the UN Convention on the Law of the Sea'.[56]

Hanoi has made some important adjustments to make its law-of-the-sea claims more consistent with UNCLOS. First, Vietnam dropped its claim to a regime of 'historic waters' in the Gulf of Tonkin. Two rounds of negotiations on the delimitation of the Tonkin Gulf were held in 1974 and 1977–1978 without any concrete progress. The central controversy of the Tonkin Gulf negotiation was the status of the French-Chinese Treaty in 1887. Vietnam insisted that the red line, which is the north-south line with no southern terminus drawn along 108°3′13″ longitude in the Gulf, as defined by the 1887 French-Chinese Treaty, could serve as the boundary line in the Gulf of Tonkin (see Map 8).[57] The application of the 1887 French-Chinese Treaty as a historic demarcation line not only favoured Vietnam proportionately, but also gave it full control of the Song Hong Basin (Yinggehai), the most promising area for oil exploration.[58] That was the main reason that Beijing rejected Vietnam's 'historic demarcation line' proposal and left aside the question of the legal status of the Gulf.[59] The Chinese held that this line was no more than a division of the islands, and not a division of the sea area, or the waters of the islands and seabed.[60] The Chinese also maintained that an extension of the red line in the Treaty would allow China to claim the Paracels and Spratlys.[61] The dispute effectively barred Vietnam, but not China, from prospecting for oil in the Gulf. By the end of 1973, Hanoi asked Beijing to start talks on the delimitation of the Gulf. Beijing accepted the request with the condition that no surveys would be conducted in a 20,000 square kilometre neutral area of the Gulf, pending a final settlement. Vietnam deferred to the Chinese request and refrained from inviting foreign companies to survey the Gulf. Yet, in 1979, China published maps of seismic survey blocks that crossed over both the red line and the line of equidistance, but deliberately spared the 'neutral area'. Some seismic survey blocs were then awarded to Western energy firms. Hanoi perceived Beijing's manoeuvre as a bluff. Vietnam not only protested by statements, but also resorted to forceful actions to prevent Chinese exploration activities. Vietnamese gunboats fired upon Chinese exploratory vessels in 1979 and 1982.[62]

After the normalisation of their bilateral relations in November 1991, Vietnam and China resumed talks over the border disputes, including the division of the Tonkin Gulf. However, negotiations did not mean an end to Chinese action. In August 1992, it was reported that China installed an oil-drilling platform in a disputed area in the Gulf of Tonkin, which the two sides agreed to avoid.[63] Three months before, China's expansion of oil exploration to the area off the southeast coast of Vietnam gave rise to a speculation that China would claim all the waters within the historic nine-dash line (see Map 2).[64] It should be noted that Stein Tønnesson hypothesised that Vietnam's claim to 'historical waters' would legitimise China's historic nine-dash line claim, which encompasses 80 per cent of the South China Sea.[65] The Vietnamese negotiators denied any links between its claim to historic waters in the Gulf of Tonkin and Chinese nine-dash line claim. China had not made the nine-dash line official until May 2009, when it protested the joint submission of Vietnam and Malaysia on extended continental shelves. However, they did not see any prospect for the claim to historic waters in the Gulf of Tonkin. Consequently, Vietnam and China agreed to negotiate on the basis of international law to divide the Gulf. On 19 October 1993, the Vietnamese and Chinese leaders then agreed to 'apply international law and consult international practices, following the principle of equity and accounting for all relevant circumstances in the Gulf, in order to achieve an equitable solution'.[66] Hanoi suggested using UNCLOS as the common legal basis for negotiation. Accordingly, Vietnam adopted the principle of equidistance and attempted to maximise the impact of coastal islands on the median line. Beijing accepted Vietnam's proposal when it ratified the Convention in June 1996. On 25 December 2000, Vietnam and China signed an agreement that mapped out a single line defined by coordinates for both EEZ and continental shelf boundaries in the Gulf of Tonkin. The coordinates defined in the agreement showed that an equidistant line with slight variations, which reflected the impact of the Bach Long Vi and Con Co Islands, was used as a boundary line (see Map 11). The agreement itself was evidence that Hanoi opted out of its previous claim to 'historic waters' and the 'historic demarcation line' in the Gulf of Tonkin. The final agreement showed that Vietnam was awarded 52.23 per cent of the Gulf because of Vietnam's longer coastline and its ownership of Bach Long Vi Island, which lies in the middle of the Gulf.[67]

Second, Vietnam also moved to clarify the outer limits of the maritime zones it claimed. In the mid-1990s, the Vietnamese signalled a change in their position over the legal regime of the Spratly features and their effects on the delimitation of their claims. Vietnam pointed to Article 71 (1) of UNCLOS to claim a 200 nautical mile EEZ from its mainland coast or large island areas, and a continental shelf beyond 200 nautical miles as a natural prolongation of its central and southeast coast. However, in July 1995, a legal adviser to the Foreign Ministry of Vietnam disclosed that Vietnam now viewed the Spratly Islands as not qualified to generate EEZs and continental shelves, but rather territorial seas. It represented a significant departure from Vietnam's previous position in the 1977 statement. This change was probably prompted by China's attempts to prospect for oil and gas in the continental shelf that Vietnam claimed for its mainland coast. In May 1992, China announced a concession contract between China National Offshore Oil Corporation and the US-based Crestone Energy Corporation to explore 25,155 square kilometres of the Vanguard Bank area (Tu Chinh in Vietnamese). The acreage designated in the contract is 600 nautical miles from mainland China, but only 135 nautical miles from the Vietnamese coast, or 84 nautical miles from Vietnam's coastal islands. This area is a natural prolongation of the Vietnamese continental landmass and is separated from the Spratly group by a 2,000 metre trench (see Map 4). Yet, Beijing argued that this area belonged to China because it lay on the Chinese side of a median line between the nearest Vietnamese island to the west and the Prince of Wales Bank of the Spratlys that China claimed. The Chinese vowed to use force to protect Crestone's operations.[68] Vietnam strongly protested China's Crestone contract, and asserted that Tu Chinh lies fully in its continental shelf as defined by UNCLOS and outside the periphery of the Spratly Islands.[69] The tension waned when Chinese Premier Li Peng made a visit to Hanoi in December 1992. Reportedly, Li Peng proposed to shelve the dispute to focus on joint development in disputed maritime areas of the Spratlys, implying its implementation in the Tu Chinh area.[70] Vietnam rejected Li Peng's proposal on the basis that it was a tactic Beijing had used to justify Chinese presence in its EEZs and continental shelves. Vietnam's Foreign Minister Nguyen Manh Cam forcefully argued, 'Tu Chinh is neither a disputed area nor an outstanding problem left by history but a problem arising newly after the normalisation of the relations'.[71]

Tensions around Tu Chinh were renewed in April 1994, when Crestone conducted seismological surveys in the area. In response, Vietnam issued a statement by a spokesman of the Foreign Ministry reiterating its long-standing position that the Tu Chinh area was located 'fully' within Vietnam's exclusive economic zone and continental shelf, and was decidedly not a disputed area. At the same time, Vietnam signed an exploration contract with the American Mobil Oil Company in the Thanh Long (Blue Dragon) oil field that was next to the Tu Chinh area. China protested that Thanh Long was 'part of *adjacent waters* of Nansha islands' (emphasis added). Vietnam quickly refuted China's accusation, and asserted that both the Tu Chinh and Thanh Long areas belonged to its EEZ and continental shelf, where Vietnam was entitled to sovereign rights to explore and exploit its natural resources.[72] The diplomatic exchange of protests then turned into naval harassment and confrontation at sea. Reportedly, Chinese naval vessels drove off a Vietnamese ship, which carried supplies to the Mobil oil rig, and the Vietnamese warships forced a Chinese navy research vessel to leave the Crestone block.[73]

Though the Chinese never bothered to explain the limits of their claims in a formal and detailed manner, China's claims to Tu Chinh and Thanh Long seemingly derived from its claim to sovereignty over the Spratly features or its nine-dash line claim. It meant that China considered these features as fully fledged islands, which were entitled a full suite of maritime zones as stipulated by UNCLOS. Though Vietnam never recognised China's sovereignty over the Spratlys, these developments prompted Hanoi to clarify the bases of its claims to the Tu Chinh and Thanh Long areas, and the legal regime that applied to the Spratly features. In June 1994, the National Assembly of Vietnam ratified UNCLOS. Hanoi reportedly hired the Washington-based Covington and Burling law firm to examine the competitive claims to the Tu Chinh and Thanh Long areas.[74] A book about Covington and Burling's opinion on the issues was published in 1996 in Hanoi.[75] It was argued that the Thanh Long, or nearly the entire Tu Chinh area, must belong to Vietnam for three reasons. First, Thanh Long and a large part of the Tu Chinh is situated in the 200 mile exclusive economic zone Vietnam is entitled under UNCLOS. Second, the entire Tu Chinh and Thanh Long area lay well within Vietnam's legitimate continental shelf because the natural prolongation of Vietnam's mainland allows it to claim more than a 200 nautical mile continental shelf seaward. Third, the delimitation of the continental shelf boundary on the principle of equidistance and proportionality would give Vietnam the whole of the Thanh Long and Tu Chinh areas. A book on the law of the sea published by the Foreign Ministry of Vietnam in 2004 stated:

> The islets in the Spratly archipelago do not sustain human habitations and do not have their own economic lives so they are not entitled to continental shelves of their own. Neither can these features be grouped as 'an archipelagic state' for the purpose of claiming continental shelf.

It also rebuffed the validity of China's nine-dash line as the basis to claim the Tu Chinh and Thanh Long areas.[76]

However, the Vietnamese government did not clarify the limits of its EEZ and continental shelf until 2009. In May 2009, Vietnam and Malaysia sent their joint submission to the Commission on the Limits of the Continental Shelf (CLCS), and Vietnam submitted its partial report for the northern part of its maritime area.[77] In these submissions, Hanoi provided precise coordinates for the limits of the EEZ and extended its continental shelf beyond 200 nautical miles as measured from the baseline of its mainland coastline. It should be noted that no EEZ or continental shelf was delineated for the Spratly and Paracel features. Vietnam implied that the South China Sea offshore islands might be rocks that were not entitled to an EEZ and continental shelf, or may have very limited weight in maritime delimitation. Clearly, if Vietnam was of the view that the Spratly and Paracel features had EEZs and continental shelves of their own, it could negatively influence the CLCS's work.[78] Vietnam's leading legal expert, Nguyen Hong Thao, pointed out that Vietnam, Malaysia and other ASEAN claimants seemed to agree that almost all disputed features are entitled to only a territorial sea.[79] The 2012 Law of the Sea of Vietnam made it clearer that the islands claimed by Vietnam fall under the purview of Article 121 of UNCLOS. The Vietnamese law specifies that insular formations that can sustain human habitation and have an economic life of their own are entitled to an EEZ or continental shelf of their own, while rocks, which do not meet these criteria, are not.[80]

The submissions, together with other maritime boundary delimitation agreements that Vietnam signed with China, Indonesia, Malaysia and Thailand, significantly redrew the map of Vietnam's maritime claims in a more consistent manner with UNCLOS. It was clear that Vietnam delineated the boundaries of its EEZ and extended continental shelf in the central and southern coast in conformity with the rules established by UNCLOS. The only missing patch in the map of Vietnam's claim was the area beyond the Gulf of Tonkin and to west of the Paracels. Currently, Vietnam and China are negotiating to delimit this area. Vietnam also redrew the map of its petroleum activities in a way more consistent with its adjusted claims. In the map published by PetroVietnam in April 2011, all petroleum concession blocks are apparently located within the continental shelves measured from the baseline of its mainland coast. In this context, the single line of Vivian L. Forbes' 2001 map is no longer valid in portraying Vietnam's maritime claim in the South China Sea. Instead, the map produced by Clive Schofield and Andi Arsana in the *American Journal of International Law* titled 'Agora on the South China Sea', published in January 2013, illustrated more precisely the current maritime boundaries of Vietnam's maritime claims (see Map 3).

The Chinese viewed the CLCS submissions as internationalising the South China Sea disputes and a violation of the Declaration on Conduct of the Parties in the South China Sea signed in November 2002. In July 2007, the Chinese sent naval vessels to the southern part of the South China Sea to intercept Vietnam's ships, which were gathering data for defining the limits of the extended continental shelf.[81] Despite Chinese pressure, Vietnam persisted with survey and data collection and submitted the CLCS reports before the deadline of 13 May 2009. The Vietnamese submissions were no doubt political statements rather than legal ones. The Rules of Procedures of the CLCS provided that if there is a land or maritime dispute, 'the Commission shall not consider and qualify a submission made by any of the states concerned in the dispute'.[82] Vietnam's tenacity to assert its rights was perhaps motivated by China's renewed assertive actions at sea since the mid-2000s. It should be noted that China's constructive engagement with ASEAN in the late 1990s and early 2000s stabilised the South China Sea situation. A significant step was the signature of the Declaration on Conduct of the Parties in the South China Sea in November 2002, which served as an important reassurance of peaceful intentions, especially by China, and indicated hopes for progress towards a legally binding code of conduct for the region. However, the process of operationalising the DoC soon met an impasse because of a disagreement among China and ASEAN countries on the consultation formula. Vietnam and other ASEAN countries proposed that ASEAN members should consult among themselves before meeting China, while China insisted on consultations with 'relevant parties'.[83] Besides, the DoC was by no means an assurance of stability, because claimants made use of this ambiguity to undertake calculated measures, one way or another, to bolster their claims.[84] Last but not least, distrust increased when China and the Philippines cut a side deal on a joint survey project in the Spratly area in September 2004, without consulting other claimants.

Vietnam's oil production output peaked in 2004 and was likely to decline if no new oil fields were exploited. In the meantime, energy consumption increased dramatically as industrialisation speeded up. In view of the prospect of becoming a net energy importer, Vietnam intensified its cooperation with foreign oil companies to prospect for offshore oil and gas in the continental shelf that it claimed since the mid-2000s. PetroVietnam tendered for nine blocks in the Phu Khanh Basin in 2004 and for nine blocks in the Song Hong Basin in 2007. However, these efforts were met with quiet but tenacious resistance by China. Between 2006 and 2007, China issued 18 private warnings to international oil companies to withdraw from their offshore oil exploration and development projects with Vietnam.[85] In 2006, China protested the operations of the following oil companies: the Korean National Oil Company (KNOC South Korea) in Block 11-2, Pogo (US) in Block 124, Chevron (US) in Block 122, the Oil and Natural Gas Corporation (ONGC India) in Blocks 127/128, Premier Oil (UK) in Block 12, and BP (UK) in Block 117. In 2007, China voiced objections to the following projects: BP (UK) in Block 05-2, Gazprom (Russia) in Block 112, CGG Veritas (France) in Blocks 04-1/04-3, Idemitsu (Japan) in Block 05-1, Petroleum Geo-Services (PGS Norway) in Block 146, Pearl Energy (UK) in Block 06-94, Chevron (US) in Block 122, and Santos (Australia) in Block 123.[86]

A US diplomatic cable from Hanoi released by Wikileaks confirmed that in 2007, four US and eight international oil firms received Chinese warnings about undefined consequences to their businesses in China if they continued their commercial undertakings with Vietnam. Five projects were cancelled or halted, though the companies' executives believed that Vietnam's maritime claims were more valid.[87] In July 2008, Beijing no longer hid its fist, but went public to demand the ExxonMobil to withdraw from its production-sharing contract with Petro-Vietnam. Chinese officials threatened 'risks' to ExxonMobil energy businesses in China if further activities conducted.[88] Apparently, China only targeted Vietnam for its newfound energy fight. There were no reports on China's objection to other Southeast Asian countries' concession agreements with international oil firms in the South China Sea at the same time.[89] In the meantime, Vietnam's fishing activities in the South China Sea also confronted more harassment and intimidation from Chinese maritime enforcement units. A Vietnamese source revealed that between 2005 and 2010, China arrested 63 Vietnamese fishing boats and 725 fishermen.[90] There were a number of serious incidents involving shooting or ramming to sink Vietnamese boats. Two incidents occurred in January 2005 and July 2007 in the area near the Spratlys, where Chinese naval vessels opened fire on Vietnamese fishing boats, causing several deaths and injuries.[91] While the Vietnamese fishermen were deprived of access to many fishing grounds, Chinese fishing fleets, supported by modern logistic ships and fishery administration vessels, vigorously expanded their activities in the South China Sea.

Hanoi was obviously resentful and frustrated by these Chinese activities, because all the parcels awarded to foreign companies were located within Vietnam's continental shelf as authorised by UNCLOS. Vietnamese officials strongly felt that some blocks were so proximate to the Vietnamese coast that they were not connected to the Spratly Islands, or any part of China under UNCLOS provisions.[92] China's flexing of muscle clearly put Vietnam in a new dilemma. Though Chinese claims to these areas were excessive and legally groundless, Vietnam was unable to persuade these companies to defy Chinese threats. In response, Vietnam carefully calibrated its acts of defiance and counter-measures. First, Vietnam stood firm in face of Chinese pressure and reassured the companies that Hanoi would take all measures to protect their activities. In April 2009, it was revealed that Vietnam sought to enhance its defence capabilities by purchasing six Russia-made Kilo-class submarines.[93] The first submarine, named after the capital city of Hanoi, was delivered in January 2014. Second, Vietnamese officials privately approached US diplomats to discuss Chinese assertive behaviour and urged them to request US companies to resume their collaboration with Vietnam. Third, Vietnam moved to clarify its maritime claims in terms of the Law of the Sea to gain the support of the international community. No doubt, bilateralism did not favour Vietnam, given Chinese superior military and economic power. In this connection, Vietnam's 2009 CLCS submissions were one important component of its strategy of internationalising the dispute to deter Chinese assertiveness.

The reports by Vietnam and Malaysia were not considered by the CLCS because China lodged *notes verbales* to protest these submissions. Vietnam did suffer for its determination to assert its rights, as China retaliated with increased assertiveness at sea. However, the submissions were by no means useless. They were not only a meaningful step forward to the implementation of UNCLOS on the part of Vietnam and Malaysia, but also a necessity to force other claimants to clarify their claims. In the *notes verbales* submitted to the United Nations in 2009, China attached a map of the nine-dash line claim. By attaching this map to an official communication, China had for the first time admitted that the nine-dash line was somehow part of its claim in the South China Sea. However, it was still not clear how China sees the status of the waters within the nine-dash line. In its *note verbale* of 27 May 2009, China stated, 'China has indisputable sovereignty over the islands in the South China Sea and the *adjacent waters*, and enjoys sovereign rights and jurisdiction over the *relevant waters* as well as the seabed and subsoil thereof (see attached map)' (emphasis added).[94] This statement contained many ambiguities that could not be consistently explained by UNCLOS.[95] In other words, China's official publication of the nine-dash line map put it at odds with UNCLOS.

Vietnam also modified its controversial position regarding the right of innocent passage. In its previous legal instruments, Vietnam demanded that military vessels proceeding through its territorial sea and contiguous zone must have its authorisation 30 days before their actual passage. Vietnamese legal experts were well aware that this regulation, which was designed at the time Vietnam was under the US-led embargo, was inconsistent with UNCLOS provisions. It was reported that there was an ongoing debate as to whether the regulations on maritime navigations should be revised.[96] Yet, no amendment to Decree No. 30-CP, dated 29 January 1980, was made until the adoption of the Law of the Sea of Vietnam by the National Assembly of Vietnam in June 2012. The new maritime law recognises the right of innocent passage of foreign military ships. Yet, it also stipulates that for these vessels to traverse its territorial sea, they must provide prior notification to competent authorities in Vietnam (Article 12 (2)). No specific time frame was mentioned. The law was adopted in the context of increased tension resulting from China's illegal seizure of Vietnamese fishing boats and cable-cutting incidents relating to Vietnamese survey ships. The change indicated Vietnam's compliance with international law, particularly UNCLOS, in contrast to China.

The Foreign Ministry of Vietnam was obviously aware that Vietnam's 1982 straight baseline system was not fully in conformity with Article 7 of UNCLOS.[97] It was expected that Vietnam would consider revising its baseline system after its ratification of UNCLOS. However, to the disappointment of many legal experts – and after considerable debate among Vietnamese experts on this issue – the 2012 Law of the Sea of Vietnam did not entail any revisions to the baseline models proposed in the 1982 Declaration. The reason was perhaps that Vietnam's 1982 baseline position was merely a point of departure for negotiation. Vietnam's baseline system, as well as that of Thailand, was apparently disregarded in the negotiation on the delimitation of the Gulf of Thailand between Vietnam and Thailand. It was also inconsequential in the maritime negotiations between Vietnam and Malaysia.[98] Besides, it should be noted that the 2012 Law of the Sea of Vietnam also provided that 'in case of differences between this law and international treaties to which the Socialist Republic of Vietnam is a party, the provisions of these international treaties will be applied' (Article 2 (2)). This provision was obviously designed to leave the door open for changes resulting from negotiated agreements in the future. Ostensibly, this baseline system was only valuable in terms of expanding the scope of internal waters, which served as a buffer zone for Vietnam's important economic and security hubs in the southern part of Vietnam.

Conclusion

After *Doi Moi*, Hanoi carefully redefined its claims to maritime zones and jurisdictions to make them more consistent with international law, particularly UNCLOS. Specifically, the Vietnamese government has clarified the limits of its EEZ and continental shelf claim as measured from the baseline of its land territory, and has implied that the Spratly and Paracel features do not qualify as fully fledged islands. It abandoned its claim to 'historic waters' in relation to the Gulf of Tonkin, paving the way in 2000 to the conclusion of the Vietnam-China agreement on maritime delimitation in the Gulf on the basis of UNCLOS. Vietnam also modified its stance to recognise the right of innocent passage of foreign military vessels in its territorial sea. These cooperative changes on the part of Vietnam have been shaped by two important developments. First, Vietnam has been increasingly interested in exploring and exploiting maritime resources for its own development. Because Vietnam's top priority shifted to economic development, physical control of the remote, barren islets became less pressing, while the access to maritime resources, especially oil, gas and fisheries, became increasingly important. Second, China's expansive claims and its assertive actions to enforce these claims made the Vietnamese leaders aware that the costs of radically bending international law to Vietnam's own advantage were greater than the benefits gained by observing law. Consequently, Hanoi has gradually moved from an approach that seeks to maximise its gains to a strategy that minimises Vietnam's potential loss through a stricter application of UNCLOS. No doubt, these positive shifts in Vietnam's maritime behaviour laid the ground for the settlement of several long-standing territorial and border disputes between Vietnam and its neighbours, particularly China, Thailand, Malaysia and Indonesia. This contributed significantly to enhancing its image as a responsible stakeholder of regional peace and security.

Notes

1 See Ministry of Foreign Affairs, 'Vietnam's Sovereignty over the Hoang Sa and Truong Sa Archipelagos', Hanoi, 1979; Ministry of Foreign Affairs, 'The Hoang Sa and Truong Sa Archipelagos: Vietnamese Territories', Hanoi, 1981; Ministry of Foreign Affairs, 'The Hoang Sa (Paracels) and Truong Sa (Spratlys) Archipelagos and International Law', Hanoi, 1988.

2 See Pao-Min Chang, 'A New Scramble for the South China Sea Islands', *Contemporary Southeast Asia*, 12(1), 1990.

3 Mark J. Valencia, Jon M. Van Dyke and Noel A. Ludwig, *Sharing the Resources of the South China Sea*, M. Nijhoff, Cambridge, MA, 1997, p. 33.

4 Socialist Republic of Vietnam, 'Statement on the Territorial Sea, the Contiguous Zone, the Exclusive Economic Zone, and the Continental Shelf of Vietnam', Hanoi, 12 May 1977.

5 Monique Chemillier-Gendreau, *Sovereignty over the Paracel and Spratly Islands*, Kluwer Law International, The Hague, 2000, p. 16.

6 Socialist Republic of Vietnam, 'Declaration on the Baseline of the Territorial Waters of the Socialist Republic of Vietnam', 12 November 1982.

7 Nguyen Hong Thao, *Nhung dieu can biet ve Luat bien*, People's Police, Hanoi, 1997, p. 114.

8 Luu Van Loi, *Vietnam: Dat, Bien, Troi*, People's Police, Hanoi, 1990, pp. 87–88.

9 Vu Phi Hoang, 'May van de Phap ly trong Tuyen bo cua Chinh phu ta ve Duong Co So ven Luc dia Viet nam', *Luat hoc*, 1(10), 1983, p. 16.

10 UNCLOS, Article 7.

11 Bureau of Intelligence and Research (US Department of State), 'Limits in the Seas: Straight Baselines: Vietnam', *Report No. 99*, Washington, DC, 1983, p. 8.

12 Hai Thanh quoted in Bureau of Intelligence and Research (US Department of State), 'Limits in the Seas: Straight Baselines: Vietnam', p. 12.

13 Hoang, 'May van de Phap ly trong Tuyen bo cua Chinh phu ta ve Duong Co So ven Luc dia Viet nam', p. 12.

14 J. R. V. Prescott, *Limits of National Claims in the South China Sea*, Asean Academic Press, London, 1999, pp. 11–12.

15 Ban Bien Gioi Chinh phu, *Cac Van ban Phap quy ve Bien va Quan ly Bien cua Viet Nam*, National Political Publisher, Hanoi, 1995, pp. 27–39.

16   Valencia, Van Dyke and Ludwig, *Sharing the Resources of the South China Sea*, p. 31.
17   Vivian Louis Forbes, *Conflict and Cooperation in Managing Maritime Space in Semi-Enclosed Seas*, Singapore University Press, Singapore, 2001, p. 137.
18   Henry J. Kenny, *Shadow of the Dragon: Vietnam's Continuing Struggle with China and the Implication for U.S. Foreign Policy*, Brassey's, Washington, DC, 2002, p. 58; Leszek Buszynski and Iskandar Sazlan, 'Maritime Claims and Energy Cooperation in the South China Sea', *Contemporary Southeast Asia: A Journal of International and Strategic Affairs*, 29(1), 2007; International Crisis Group, 'Stirring up the South China Sea (II): Regional Responses', *Asia Report No. 229*, 24 July 2012, p. 35.
19   Bureau of Intelligence and Research (US Department of State), 'Limits in the Seas: Straight Baselines: People's Republic of China', *Report No. 43*.
20   Sam Bateman and Clive Schofield, 'State Practice Regarding Straight Baselines in East Asia: Legal, Technical and Political Issues in a Changing Environment', Paper prepared for International Conference on Difficulties in Implementing the Provisions of UNCLOS, organised by the Advisory Board on the Law of the Sea (ABLOS), Monaco, International Hydrographic Bureau, 16–17 October 2008.
21   Epsey Cooke Farrell, *The Socialist Republic of Vietnam and the Law of the Sea*, Martinus Nijhoff, The Hague, p. 65.
22   Farrell, *The Socialist Republic of Vietnam and the Law of the Sea*, pp. 29–33.
23   Quoted from Farrell, *The Socialist Republic of Vietnam and the Law of the Sea*, p. 4.
24   Carlyle A. Thayer, 'Vietnamese Foreign Policy: Multilateralism and the Threat of Peaceful Evolution', in Carlyle A. Thayer and Ramses Amer (eds), *Vietnamese Foreign Policy in Transition*, Institute of Southeast Asian Studies, Singapore, 1999, pp. 2–6.
25   Lee Lai To, *China and the South China Sea Dialogues*, Praeger, London, 1999, p. 93.
26   See Ramses Amer, 'Sino-Vietnamese Relations: Past, Present and Future', in Carlyle A. Thayer and Ramses Amer (eds), *Vietnamese Foreign Policy in Transition*, Institute of Southeast Asian Studies, Singapore, 1999, pp. 74–87; A. C. Guan, 'Vietnam-China Relations since the End of the Cold War', *Asian Survey*, 38(12), 1998, pp. 1128–1129.
27   See Ramses Amer and Thao Nguyen Hong, 'The Management of Vietnam's Border Disputes: What Impact on its Sovereignty and Regional Integration?', *Contemporary Southeast Asia*, 27(3), 2005.
28   Amer and Hong, 'The Management of Vietnam's Border Disputes'.
29   Leszek Buszynski, 'ASEAN, the Declaration on Conduct, and the South China Sea', *Contemporary Southeast Asia*, 25(3), 2003.
30   Doan Thien Tich, *Dau khi Viet Nam*, Vietnam National University, Ho Chi Minh City, 2001, p. 56.
31   Dang Cong san Viet Nam, *Van kien Dai hoi Dai bieu Toan quoc lan thu VIII*, National Political Publisher, Hanoi, 1996, p. 211.
32   Maritime economy was defined as a combination of offshore oil and gas exploration and exploitation, fisheries and aquaculture in coastal areas, shipping industries, maritime logistics, and transportation and tourism.
33   Politburo of the Communist Party of Vietnam, 'Resolution 03-NQ/TW on Key Tasks to Develop "Maritime Economy"', 6 May 1996, http://123.30.190.43:8080/tieng viet/tulieuvankien/vankiendang/details.asp?topic=191&subtopic=279&leader_topic=688&id=BT180556630 (accessed 17 September 2013).
34   Politburo of the Communist Party of Vietnam, Directive 20-CT/TW on Industrialization and Modernization of the Vietnamese Maritime Economy, 22 September 1997, http://123.30.190.43:8080/tiengviet/tulieuvankien/vankiendang/details.asp?topic=191&subtopic=279&leader_topic=&id=BT1780956204 (accessed 9 September 2013).

35 UNEP, VIEP and WWF, 'Fisheries Subsidies, Supply Chain and Certification in Vietnam', *Summary Report*, Hanoi, September 2009, pp. 24–28.

36 Hong Chuyen, 'Ngu dan Viet Nam chua mot ngay nao de mat Hoang Sa', *Infonet*, 15 January 2014, http://infonet.vn/ngu-dan-viet-nam-chua-mot-ngay-nao-de-mat-hoang-sa-post113207.info (accessed 17 January 2014).

37 Nong Duc Manh, 'Strengthen Guidance, to Realize the Solid, Effective, and Thorough Implementation of the Central Committee's Decisions', *Nhan Dan Newspaper*, 25 January 2007.

38 Ministry of Justice, 'Mot so Van de Co ban cua Chien luoc Bien Viet Nam den nam 2020' [Major Issues of Vietnam's Maritime Strategy toward 2020], 24 May 2010, http://moj.gov.vn/ct/tintuc/Pages/thong-tin-khac.aspx?ItemID=4208 (accessed 16 August 2013).

39 Ngoc Bach, 'Nam 2020, Kinh te Bien dong gop khoang 53–55% GDP', Vietnam Ministry of Natural Resources and Environment, 16 May 2011, www.monre.gov.vn/v35/default.aspx?tabid=428&CateID=53&ID=101068&Code=0YDK101068 (accessed 12 December 2013).

40 'PM Congratulates PetroVietnam on Anniversary', Vietnam News Agency, 30 August 2010, http://en.vietnamplus.vn/Home/PM-congratulates-PetroVietnam-on-anniversary/20108/11808.vnplus (accessed 6 September 2013).

41 'Vietnam Oil Output Sets Quarterly Record', *Asian Wall Street Journal*, 7 April 1995, p. 17.

42 Buszynski and Sazlan, 'Maritime Claims and Energy Cooperation in the South China Sea', p. 157.

43 Leszek Buszynski, 'The South China Sea: Oil, Maritime Claims, and US-China Strategic Rivalry', *The Washington Quarterly*, 35(2), 2012, p. 141.

44 'Vietnam: Country Analysis Brief', US Energy Information Administration, 9 May 2012.

45 Directorate of Fisheries, 'Stages in the Development of Vietnam Fisheries Sector', 17 July 2012, www.fistenet.gov.vn/introduction/about-directorate-of-fisheries/history-of-fisheries-development (accessed 14 September 2013).

46 Ibid.

47 Ibid.

48 Tran Xuan Tinh, 'Van tai bien Viet Nam doi mat voi nhieu Thach thuc', Vietnam News Agency, 18 December 2013, www.vietnamplus.vn/van-tai-bien-viet-nam-doi-mat-voi-nhieu-thach-thuc/235851.vnp (accessed 19 January 2014).

49 'Vietnamese Shipbuilding', Global Security, June 2009, www.globalsecurity.org/military/world/vietnam/shipbuilding.htm (accessed 19 January 2014).

50 Norwegian Agency for Development Cooperation, 'Study of the Vietnamese Shipbuilding/Maritime Sector', Final Report, June 2010.

51 Nguyen Hung Son, 'Vietnam: A Case Study in Naval Modernization', in Geoffrey Till and Jane Chan (eds), *Naval Modernization in South-East Asia: Nature, Causes and Consequences*, Routledge, London and New York, 2014, p. 122.

52 Pham Thi Thanh Binh, 'Thuc trang Phat trien Kinh te bien Viet Nam, Bao Dien tu Dang Cong san Viet Nam', 22 October 2009, www.cpv.org.vn/cpv/Modules/News/NewsDetail.aspx?co_id=0&cn_id=366824 (accessed 20 January 2014).

53 'Vietnam to Recover Sovereignty over the Paracels by Peaceful Means', *Vnexpress*, 25 November 2011, http://vnexpress.net/tin-tuc/thoi-su/viet-nam-doi-chu-quyen-hoang-sa-bang-hoa-binh-2212051.html (accessed 24 January 2014).

54 Resolution of the National Assembly of Vietnam to ratify UNCLOS dated 23 June 1994.

55 Article 2, The Law on National Borders, adopted by the National Assembly of Vietnam, June 2003.

56 Nguyen Hung Son, 'Vietnam: A Case Study in Naval Modernization', p. 124.
57 Article 3 of the French-China Convention on Delimitation of the Frontier between China and Tonkin signed on 26 June 1887 read, 'In Kwangtung, it is understood that the disputed points which are situated to the east and northeast of Monkai, beyond the frontier as fixed by the Delimitation Commission, are located to China. The islands which are east of the Paris meridian of 105°43' east, that is to say the north-south line passing through the eastern point of the islands of Tcha's-Kou ou Ouan-Chan (Tra-co) which forms the boundary are also allocated to China. The island of Gotho [Kao Tao] and other islands west of this meridian belong to Annam'. 'Trung Quoc ep Cong ty Dau lua My' [China Pressurized US Energy Company], *BBC Vietnamese*, 20 July 2008, www.bbc.co.uk/vietnamese/vietnam/story/2008/07/080720_exxonmobil_warning.shtml (accessed 13 August 2013).
58 Chi-kin Lo, *China's Policy towards Territorial Disputes: The Case of South China Sea Islands*, Routledge, New York, 1989, p. 130.
59 Farrell, *The Socialist Republic of Vietnam and the Law of the Sea*, p. 71.
60 Ramses Amer, 'Assessing Sino-Vietnamese Relations through Management of Contentious Issues', *Contemporary Southeast Asia*, 26(2), 2004, pp. 331–332.
61 Nguyen Hong Thao, *Luat Quoc te va Chu quyen tren hai quan dao Hoang Sa va Truong Sa*, People's Police, Hanoi, 2009, pp. 111–112.
62 Lo, *China's Policy towards Territorial Disputes: The Case of South China Sea Islands*, pp. 129–130.
63 Thayer, 'Vietnam: Coping with China', p. 358.
64 Valencia, Van Dyke and Ludwig, *Sharing the Resources of the South China Sea*, p. 91.
65 Stein Tønnesson, 'Vietnam's Objective in the South China Sea: National or Regional Security?', *Contemporary Southeast Asia*, 22(1), 2000, p. 210.
66 General Agreement on the Basic Principles to Settling the Disputes relating to the land border and delimitation of the Tonkin Gulf between Vietnam and China, signed on 19 October 1993.
67 Zou Keyuan, 'The Sino-Vietnamese Agreement on Maritime Boundary Delimitation in the Gulf of Tonkin', *Ocean Development & International Law*, 36, 2005, p. 15.
68 Michael Vatikiotis, 'China Stirs the Pot', *Far Eastern Economic Review*, 155(27), 1992, p. 14.
69 Nguyen Hong Thao, 'Vietnam and the Code of Conduct for the South China Sea', *Ocean Development & International Law*, 32(2), 2001, p. 106.
70 Carlyle A. Thayer, 'Vietnam: Coping with China', *Southeast Asian Affairs*, 21, 1994, p. 360.
71 Thayer, 'Vietnam: Coping with China', p. 360.
72 Thao, 'Vietnam and the Code of Conduct for the South China Sea', p. 106.
73 Craig Snyder, 'The Implication of Hydrocarbon Development in the South China Sea', *International Journal*, 52(1), 1996–1997, p. 146.
74 Barry Wain, 'Sea Battle: Vietnam Fires New Weapons in Oil Dispute: The Law', *Asian Wall Street Journal*, 16 June 1995.
75 Brice M. Claget, *Nhung Yeu sach Doi khang cua Viet Nam va Trung Quoc o khu vuc Bai ngam Tu Chinh va Thanh Long trong Bien Dong*, National Politics, Hanoi, 1996.
76 Ministry of Foreign Affairs, *Gioi thieu mot so van de co ban cua Luat bien Viet Nam*, National Politics, Hanoi, 2004, p. 195.
77 'Joint Submission by Malaysia and the Socialist Republic of Vietnam to the Commission on the Limits of the Continental Shelf', 6 May 2009, www.un.org/Depts/los/clcs_new/submissions_files/submission_mysvnm_33_2009.htm (accessed 2 June 2014); 'Submission by the Socialist Republic of Vietnam to the Commission on the Limits of the Continental Shelf', 7 May 2009, www.un.org/depts/los/clcs_new/submissions_files/submission_vnm_37_2009.htm (accessed 2 June 2014).

78 Robert Beckman, 'South China Sea: Worsening Dispute or Growing Clarity in Claims?', *RSIS Commentaries*, 16 August 2010; Robert Beckman, 'The UN Convention on the Law of the Sea and the Maritime Disputes in the South China Sea', *The American Journal of International Law*, 107, 2013, pp. 152–153.
79 Nguyen Hong Thao, 'Vietnam's Position on the Sovereignty over the Paracels and the Spratlys: Its Maritime Claims', *Journal of East Asia International Law*, 1, 2012, p. 200.
80 Article 20 (2), The Law of the Sea of Vietnam, adopted on 21 June 2012.
81 Tran Truong Thuy, 'Recent Developments in the South China Sea: From Declaration to Code of Conduct', in Tran Truong Thuy (ed.), *The South China Sea: Towards a Region of Peace, Security and Cooperation*, The Gioi, Hanoi, 2011, p. 104.
82 Article 5, Annex I, Rules of Procedure of the Commission on the Limits of the Continental Shelf.
83 Fravel M. Taylor, 'Maritime Security in the South China Sea and the Competition over Maritime Rights', in P. M. Cronin (ed.), *Cooperation from Strength: The United States, China and the South China Sea*, January 2012, p. 44.
84 See Nguyen Hong Thao, 'The Declaration on Conduct of Parties in the South China Sea: A Vietnamese Perspective, 2002–2007', in Sam Bateman and Ralf Emmers (eds), *Security and International Politics in the South China Sea: Toward a Cooperative Management Regime*, Routledge Security in Asia Pacific Series, Routledge, London and New York, 2009.
85 Taylor M. Fravel, 'China's Strategy in the South China Sea', *Contemporary Southeast Asia*, 33(3), 2011, pp. 302–303.
86 Information based on personal communication with Vietnamese officials; Fravel, 'China's Strategy in the South China Sea', pp. 302–303.
87 'Sino-Vietnam Territorial Dispute Entangles Multiple Multinational Energy Firms', *US Diplomatic Cable from Hanoi (released by Wikileaks)*, 7 September 2007, http://wikileaks.org/cable/2007/09/07HANOI1599.html (accessed 14 August 2013).
88 'Trung Quoc ep Cong ty Dau lua My'.
89 'Sino-Vietnam Territorial Dispute Entangles Multiple Multinational Energy Firms'.
90 'Vietnam Demands Unconditional Release of Fishermen Held by China', Thanh Nien News, 8 October 2010.
91 'Chinese Missteps in Vietnam are a U.S. Opportunity', *US Diplomatic Cable from Hanoi (released by Wikileaks)*, 5 January 2005, http://wikileaks.org/cable/2005/01/05HANOI247.html (accessed 12 August 2013). In his article 'Vietnam, China Clash Again over Spratlys', *Strait Times*, 19 July 2007, Roger Mitton informed that the incident took place on 9 July 2007, near the Spratlys. However, according to the US diplomatic cable dated 20 July 2007 from Hanoi, an MOFA official confirmed the occurrence of the incident but corrected that the incident occur at the end of June 2007 in the Paracels and no Vietnamese vessels were sent to the scene.
92 'Foreign Ministry Summons Ambassador to Discuss Sino-Vietnamese South China Sea Dispute', *US Diplomatic Cable from Hanoi (released by Wikileaks)*, 11 September 2007, http://wikileaks.org/cable/2007/12/07HANOI2045.html (accessed 15 August 2013).
93 Greg Torode, 'Vietnam Set to Buy 6 Russian Submarines', *South China Morning Post*, 28 April 2009.
94 Note Verbale CML/17/2009 from the Permanent Mission of the People's Republic of China to the UN Secretary General, 7 May 2009, www.un.org/depts/los/clcs_new/submissions_files/submission_mysvnm_33_2009.htm (accessed 2 June 2014); Note Verbale CML/18/2009 from the Permanent Mission of the People's Republic of China to the UN Secretary General, 7 May 2009, www.un.org/depts/los/clcs_new/submissions_files/submission_vnm_37_2009.htm (accessed 2 June 2014).

95 Beckman, 'The UN Convention on the Law of the Sea and the Maritime Disputes in the South China Sea', pp. 152–153.
96 Thao, *Nhung dieu can biet ve Luat bien*, p. 100.
97 Ministry of Foreign Affairs, *Gioi thieu mot so Van de co ban cua Luat Bien o Viet Nam*, pp. 44–46.
98 Johan Henrik Nossum, 'What Vietnam Could Gain from Redrawing its Baselines', *IBRU Boundary and Security Bulletin*, Winter 2001–2002, p. 103.

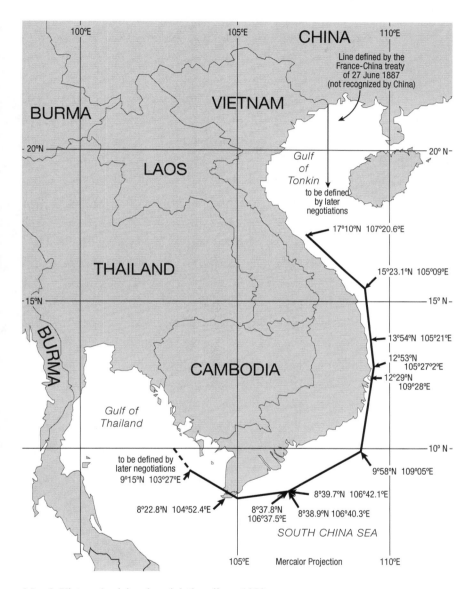

Map 8 Vietnam's claimed straight baselines, 1982

Source: J. Ashley Roach and Robert W. Smith (editors), 'Excessive Maritime Claims, International Law Studies', 66: 59.

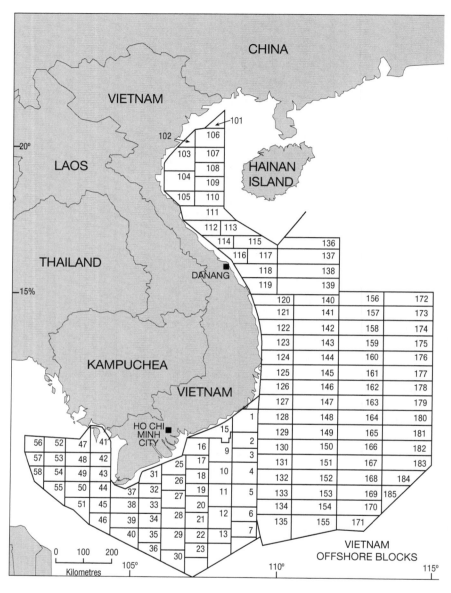

Map 9 Vietnam petroleum concession block map (1980s)

Source: Mark J. Valencia, Jon M. Van Dyke and Noel A. Ludwig, *Sharing the Resources of the South China Sea*, M. Nijhoff, Cambridge, MA, 1997, p. 12.

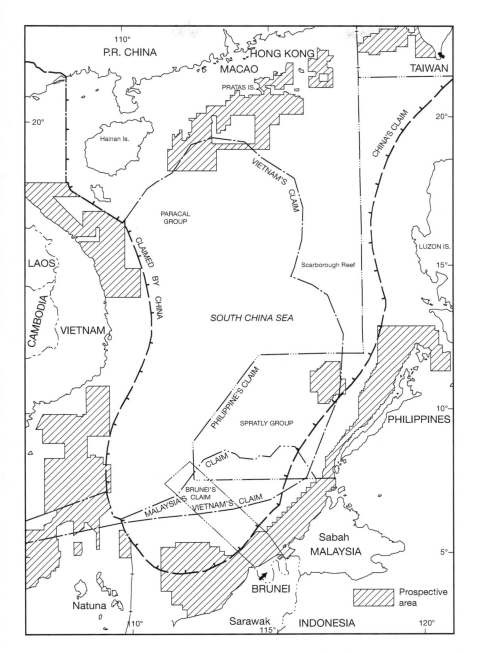

Map 10 Map of South China Sea claims by Vivian L. Forbes (2001)

Source: Vivian L. Forbes, *Conflict and Cooperation in Managing Maritime Space in Semi-Enclosed Seas*, Singapore University Press, Singapore, 2001.

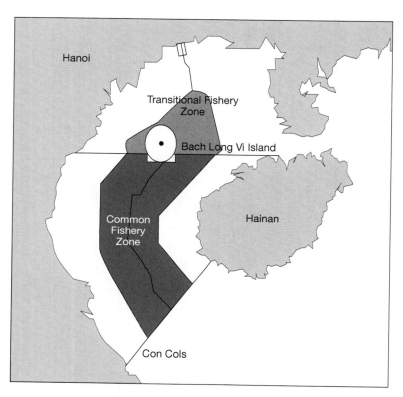

Map 11 Delimitation line and joint fishing zone (Gulf of Tonkin)

Source: Nguyen Hong Thao, 'Maritime Delimitation and Fishery Cooperation in the Tonkin Gulf', *Ocean Development & International Law*, 36, 2005. The map is reproduced with permission by Nguyen Hong Thao.

6 The 2012 Scarborough Shoal stand-off

From stalemate to escalation of the South China Sea dispute?

Renato Cruz De Castro

Introduction

This chapter examines the 2012 Scarborough Shoal stand-off between the Philippines and China as a case study of conflict escalation of the South China Sea dispute. It discusses the legal basis of the Philippines' claim on the Spratly Islands and the Scarborough Shoal, and examines China's coercive strategy against the Philippines that began as early as 1995, when Chinese forces occupied Mischief Reef. In 2010, China aggressively challenged the Philippines by building up its navy, undermining the other claimant states diplomatically and militarily. It engaged the Philippines in a maritime brinkmanship game. This culminated in the 2012 confrontation between a Philippine Coast Guard vessel and four Chinese Maritime Surveillance (CMSU) ships at Scarborough Shoal. This stand-off was a tipping point in China's coercive moves against the Philippines in the disputed area. Lasting for two months, the stand-off has since strained Philippine-China bilateral relations, which have further deteriorated as China intensifies its efforts to consolidate its expansive maritime claim, and the Aquino administration takes countermeasures against an assertive China. This chapter addresses this main question: What events led to the Scarborough Shoal stand-off? This chapter also raises these ancillary questions: (1) What is the legal basis of the Philippines' claim on the Spratlys and the Scarborough Shoal? (2) How has China challenged and undermined the Philippines' claim to these land features? (3) What happened during the two-month-long Scarborough Shoal standoff? (4) What are the underlying causes of the stand-off? (5) How will the stand-off impact upon Philippines-China relations, and China's pursuit of its expansive maritime claim in the West Philippine Sea? (6) What are the consequences of the stand-off that can affect the region?

Legal basis of Philippine claim

The Philippines' claim on the Spratlys was originally staked out by Captain Tomas Cloma, who, in 1956, discovered a group of islands in the South China Sea, which he called Kalayaan ('Freedom') Islands. Contending that these islands were not owned by any state and without a sovereign authority (*terra nullius*), Cloma appropriated the territory for the Philippines.[1] Interestingly, the Philippines' Department of Foreign Affairs (DFA) was at a loss, and did not know how to respond to Cloma's declaration of formal possession of the area. The other littoral states, however, such as France, Vietnam and Taiwan, protested vigorously against Cloma's claim. Despite this opposition, the Philippine government staked out its claim to the area and noted its strategic value to the external defence and security of the nation.[2] By the late 1960s, Manila signified its intention to make a formal claim on the area. In 1971, President Ferdinand Marcos officially declared that this area was obtained by the Philippines through modes of acquisition recognised by international law, such as occupation and effective administration.[3] In the same year, Philippine Marines occupied eight of the islands that comprised Cloma's original claim. In April 1972, these islands were officially designated as part of the province of Palawan, to be administered as a single municipality with its own mayor, who presides over a small population of Filipino civilians and military personnel on these land features.[4]

In 1978, the Philippine government laid formal claim to the area and issued Presidential Decree No. 1599, establishing the Philippines' Exclusive Economic Zone (EEZ), which extends to a distance of 200 miles from the country's baseline.[5] Section II of the decree gives the Philippines the right to exercise sovereign rights over Kalayaan because it is within the country's EEZ. On 10 March 2009, the Philippines strengthened the legal basis of its claim by passing Republic Act 9522, or the 2009 Baseline Law, which defines the country's archipelagic baseline according to the United Nations Convention on the Law of the Seas (UNCLOS) provisions. Likewise, the Philippines aligned its national legal and policy frameworks on maritime territorial borders with the various maritime jurisdictional zones specified in UNCLOS.[6] The Philippines thus defined its maritime borders and its exclusive economic zone (EEZ), as well as claims to portions of the Spratlys and other rocks and shoals in the South China Sea, in conformity with UNCLOS-designated archipelagic baselines. Specifically, R.A. 9522 provides that the Scarborough Shoal and the islands in the South China Sea claimed by the Philippines will be governed by the regime of islands under Article 12 of UNCLOS.[7] This legal act further implies that the Philippines lays an EEZ claim from its archipelagic baselines of its main islands, as well as an extended continental shelf claim into the South China Sea beyond the outer limits of its EEZ.[8] Unfortunately, China has challenged the Philippines' legal claim to these numerous islands, islets, rocks, reefs and banks by using its naval prowess to back up its coercive diplomacy. This challenge began in the early 1990s, intensified in the second decade of the twenty-first century, and culminated in the tense two-month-long stand-off between Philippine and Chinese civilian vessels at the Scarborough Shoal.

'Touch and go' in China's coercive strategy

China bases its sacred and inalienable claim on the South China Sea on alleged historical accounts of Chinese navigators and sailors who had sailed on its waters during the Han, Yuan, Ming and Ching dynasties. This claim is actually predicated on China's geo-strategic exigencies and status as a great power in East Asia. As the biggest among littoral states, China has been historically preoccupied with the control of its 'Southern Seas'. The South China Sea has served as the main corridor of Chinese maritime trade into Southeast Asia and South Asia. China's decline as a great power in the late nineteenth century coincided with its loss of control on this sea to Western powers, especially France.[9] China's attempts to regain its great power status in East Asia have always begun with the modernisation of its navy to stave off the encroaching Western, and later Japanese, power in the South China Sea.[10] In the late 1980s, China competed with Vietnam in a creeping occupation of uninhabited reefs and atolls in the Spratlys, which culminated in the March 1988 naval skirmish between Chinese and Vietnamese forces on Fiery Cross Reef. In February 1992, the National People's Congress passed a territorial law that practically transformed the South China Sea as China's internal waters and allowed the People's Liberation Army Navy (PLA-N) to evict all foreign vessels in the area.[11] In late 1994, Chinese forces occupied Mischief Reef, an underwater atoll 135 miles off the southern coast of the Philippines' western island of Palawan. This was confirmed by the Philippine Air Force's (PAF's) reconnaissance aircraft, which photographed Chinese-built octagonal structures resembling guard towers with a satellite disk.[12] Then, President Fidel Ramos quickly condemned the Chinese move and ordered the reinforcement of the Philippine garrison in the Spratlys. This incident also made Manila realise the importance of American military presence in its territory, which ended when the Philippine Senate did not concur with the Philippine-American Cooperation Treaty (PACT) in 1991, and the US subsequently withdrew its forces from Subic naval base in 1992. The Mischief Reef incident prompted Manila to negotiate and to sign a Visiting Forces Agreement (VFA) with Washington in 1998. The Philippine Senate concurred to the agreement in 1999, and the VFA revived military cooperation between the Philippines and the US. China, however, did not allow its ties with the Philippines to deteriorate, despite the row over the structures on Mischief Reef and the signing of the VFA with the US. In 1995, it agreed to discuss the South China Sea dispute with the ASEAN in the ASEAN Regional Forum (ARF). After three years of negotiations, China and the ASEAN member states signed, in 2002, the Declaration of the Conduct of Parties in the South China Sea, which calls for the claimant states to resolve their territorial and jurisdictional disputes by peaceful means, and to refrain from occupying presently uninhabited atolls and shoals in the area.[13]

Simultaneously, the emergence of China as an economic powerhouse in the early twenty-first century enabled it to reshape a regional order. This development allowed Southeast Asian states to freely side with either of the two powers (China and the US) without making any firm commitment to any of them.[14] With its economic and political clout, China substantially improved its relations (mainly in trade, investment and official development assistance) with the Southeast Asian countries, including the Philippines. During President Gloria Mapacagal Arroyo's term, economic ties between China and the Philippines expanded. Bilateral trade grew dramatically from US$2 billion in 1998 to US$30 billion in 2007. Arroyo facilitated the Chinese-funded North Luzon Railway project to symbolise the 'new and friendly relations and cooperation between the Philippines and China'.[15] Furthermore, she took up President Hu Jintao's challenge for Manila and Beijing to collaborate strategically in pursuit of peace and economic development. This partnership was reflected in the frequent exchange visits of officials, increased level of bilateral trade, concerted efforts in the global campaign against terrorism and transnational crimes, policy coordination and implementation of the ASEAN-China Free Trade Agreement, and, most importantly, the conduct of the Joint Marine Seismic Undertaking (JMSU) (see Maps 5 and 6) to explore and develop the resources in the South China Sea.[16] The JMSU was signed in September 2004 by the Philippine National Oil Corporation (PNOC) and the China National Offshore Oil Corporation (CNOOC) to signify the two governments' commitment to transform the South China Sea into an area of cooperation. In March 2005, when Vietnam complained about the bilateral agreement, the JMSU became a tripartite effort in the South China Sea, with the entry of Vietnam's PetroVietnam. Trade between China and the Philippines expanded. The huge Chinese market became an important outlet for Philippine exports. Later, these bilateral ties broadened to include security and even military matters. Consequent improvements in Philippines-China economic relations led to the Philippine-China entente during President Arroyo's term (2001–2010), which lessened the tensions in the South China Sea. Through economic links and adroit diplomacy in the early years of the twenty-first century, Beijing also succeeded in erasing the perception among Southeast Asian states that China was a regional security threat bent on building up its military capability. China's foreign policy gambit of peaceful emergence enhanced its image as a responsive regional power and ensured its long-term security. Nevertheless, the image of China as a benign and responsive great power in East Asia gradually dissipated as Beijing pursued its expansive claims to the South China Sea and began applying its coercive strategy against the small claimant states in the second decade of the twenty-first century.

China's renewed coercive strategy

With its robust economy, China has incrementally developed a formidable navy. This navy has shifted from pre-empting possible US intervention in the Taiwan Straits crisis to developing the capacity to deny the US Navy access to the East China Sea and South China Sea or inside the 'First Island Chain' that runs from Japan, to Okinawa, to Taiwan, down to the Philippines. China has had an annual double-digit increase in defence spending since 2006. In recent years, the PLA-N has acquired a growing fleet of Russian-made diesel-electric Kilo-class submarines and *Sovremenny*-class destroyers, along with several types of indigenously built destroyers, frigates and nuclear-powered attack submarines. At the advent of the twenty-first century, China has introduced three new classes of destroyers (*Luyang* I, *Luyang* II and *Luzchou*) with sophisticated radar and air defence weapon systems, as well as frigates (*Jiangwei* II, *Jingkai* I and *Jingkai* II) with improved war-fighting capabilities and seaworthiness.[17] The PLA-N has enhanced its operational capabilities across the waters surrounding Taiwan with the deployment of two new classes of ballistic and attack submarines. These capability developments have enabled the PLA-N to extend its operational range from the first-island chain to the second-island chain, which extends from northern Japan to the Northern Marianas Islands, Guam, and further south to Palau.[18] Freed from its strategic focus on Taiwan, China has the naval capabilities to generate regional tension by challenging the claims of small littoral states over parts of the South China Sea, and by changing the strategic pattern in the maritime commons of East Asia and West Pacific where the US Navy is still dominant. Interestingly, Chinese media commentators, academics and analysts have emphasised the significance of naval power and the need to protect China's sovereignty over its surrounding waters. They agree unanimously that the PLA-N should have unlimited operational range, and must possess blue-water capabilities to show a military presence at sea, provide deterrence and conduct military diplomacy missions.[19] China's assertiveness in pushing its claims in the South China Sea and East China Sea has increased in tandem with the expansion of its navy and maritime services.[20] To support its maritime claim, China conducts numerous naval exercises that employ more modern surface combatants, and even submarines.[21] These naval exercises are aimed to show China's determination to unilaterally and militarily resolve the dispute, to flaunt its naval preponderance, and to impress upon the other claimant states its de facto ownership of these contested maritime territories.

In late 2010, not satisfied with applying diplomatic pressures on the ASEAN states prior to the 2nd US-ASEAN Leaders Summit in New York, the PLA-N conducted its fourth major naval exercise in the South China Sea. Taken together, the PLA-N's four naval exercises in 2010 were 'a demonstration' of China's indisputable sovereignty over the South China Sea and its capacity to sustain larger naval deployment deep into this maritime territory.[22] These developments worry China's neighbours, who are still reeling from their confrontations with Chinese patrol vessels in the contested sea. In the short run, Chinese naval analysts project the deployment of future PLA-N aircraft carriers in its coral-island-assault campaign against the other claimant states.[23] In the long run, these carriers will give the PLA-N the offensive air capabilities to attack its enemy navies' rear and to become a regional-blue-water navy operating effectively in what Chinese naval analysts call the 'far seas'.[24] Apparently, the PLA-N believes that superior naval power will resolve China's territorial row with the small claimant states, according to Chinese terms, and force the US Navy to steer clear of the South China Sea and other disputed maritime areas around its periphery. The Chinese Navy backs the official claim of Beijing that the South China Sea is its territorial waters. Hence, Vietnamese and Philippine vessels are harassed, detained or even fired upon by Chinese patrol craft. These incidents demonstrate China's heavy-handed behaviour to pressure these claimant states to back away from the disputed area.[25] Indeed, the pattern of Chinese actions and pronouncements signifies that China has taken the top hierarchical position in the regional pecking order and bears all the requirements (economic and military might, diplomatic prowess and willingness to pull its weight against the smaller powers) of a traditional power determined to change the power game in East Asia.

The littoral/maritime states, both in Northeast and Southeast Asia, are jittery because China might seize some of the disputed islands in the East China Sea and South China Sea considering their importance as potential sites of energy resources and as sea lines of communications (SLOCs).[26] In June 2011, Vietnam, the Philippines and Japan filed formal complaints against China's nautical movements and unilateral actions in the disputed waters that have generated tension in the region.[27] Small claimant states such as Vietnam and the Philippines occasionally dispatch ships or aircraft to the disputed waters individually, but they can neither match nor overcome China's military might, even if they combine their manpower, equipment and defence budgets. In reality, these small powers' militaries do not even contemplate pooling their resources and forming a collective defence force to confront China. Again, the stumbling block is their extensive and mutually beneficial economic and political ties with China, which they do not want to jeopardise. By early 2012, China's fervent nationalism, growing naval prowess and unilateral moves were overtly directed against a militarily weak Philippines. As early as the last quarter of 2010, DFA noted increased Chinese naval presence and activities in the Spratlys and monitored around six or seven major intrusions by Chinese vessels into the waters claimed by the Philippines. On 25 February 2011, Filipino fishermen alleged that they were fired upon by a *Jianghu*-B class missile frigate off Jackson Atoll, 140 miles west of Palawan.[28] On 2 March 2011, two Chinese patrol boats reportedly harassed a survey vessel commissioned by the Philippine Department of Energy (DOE) to conduct oil exploration in the Reed Bank, 150 kilometres east of the Spratly Islands and 250 kilometres west of the Philippine island of Palawan. Then in June 2011, the Philippine Navy discovered a number of Chinese structures in the vicinity of Philippine-claimed Iroquois Reef-Amy Douglas Bank near Palawan and within the country's 200 nautical mile EEZ. Armed forces observers reported that China Marine Surveillance (CMSU) vessels and PLA-N ships unloaded building materials, erected an undetermined number of posts and placed a buoy near the breaker of the Amy Douglas Bank. Again filing a diplomatic protest with the Chinese Embassy in Manila, the DFA argued that any new construction in the vicinity of the uninhabited Amy Douglas Bank is a clear violation of the 2002 ASEAN-China Declaration on the Conduct of Parties in the South China Sea.[29]

In response, the Chinese Foreign Ministry sternly told the Philippines to stop 'harming China's sovereignty and maritime rights and interests, which leads to unilateral actions that can expand and complicate [*sic*] South China Sea dispute'.[30] It was Beijing's reaction when the Philippines protested against China's PLA-N to construct an oil rig deep within the Philippines' EEZ. The Philippines also sought clarification on the recent sightings of China CMS and PLA-N ships near the

Kalayaan group of islands. Beijing went on to demand that Manila seek Chinese permission first before it could conduct oil exploration activities even within the Philippines' EEZ. At the same time, the Chinese Ambassador in Manila justified the actions of the two Chinese patrol boats that harassed a Philippine survey ship at the Reed Bank. He regarded it as an exercise of jurisdiction over an area that is a part of China's territory.[31] He added that the Philippine surveying activity in the area is a 'violation of Chinese sovereignty and that is something that we [China] are against'. Thus, China's aggressive actions against the Philippines and Vietnam in the first half of 2011 heightened the tension in the contested sea. Consequently, the Aquino administration recognised that the Philippines is potentially on a collision course with China relative to the South China Sea imbroglio.[32]

The 2012 Scarborough Shoal stand-off

During the 2012 Philippines-US Bilateral Strategic Dialogue in Washington, DC, Philippine Foreign Secretary Albert del Rosario made this unprecedented but honest remark:

> It is terribly painful to hear the international media accurately describing the poor state of the Philippine armed forces. But more painful is the fact that it is true, and we only have ourselves to blame for it. For the Philippines to be minimally reliant upon a U.S. regional partner . . . it therefore behooves us to resort to all possible means to build at the very least a most minimal credible defense posture.[33]

Candidly, Secretary Del Rosario conveyed the Philippines' vulnerability and utter desperation in its impasse with a militarily powerful China at the Scarborough Shoal, north of the disputed Spratly Islands, 124 nautical miles from Luzon, and well within the country's EEZ. The two-month standoff between the Philippines and China at the Scarborough Shoal epitomised an international incident waiting to happen. Prior to the crisis, the Philippines sought the support of ASEAN for its proposal to create a 'Zone of Peace, Freedom, Friendship and Coopera- tion'. This proposal aims to clarify maritime boundary claims in the South China Sea by all parties, as well as to turn disputed areas into special enclaves where conflicting parties can jointly develop projects.[34] China, however, did not want the issue to be multilateralised, preferring to resolve the dispute bilaterally. Furthermore, in a more serious vein, the delimitation of maritime borders involves clarification of China's ambiguous, questionable and expansive nine-dash line claim. Beijing also took note of Vietnam and the Philippines' proposals for ASEAN to declare an official position on the South China Sea dispute during the ASEAN Summit in Cambodia on 3–4 April 2012. However, China pressured the host country to keep the South China Sea dispute off the summit agenda. Interestingly, the 9 April 2012 issue of the unofficial *Global Times* emphatically warned the Philippines against underestimating 'the strength and will-power of China to defend its territorial integrity'.[35]

The stand-off began on 8 April 2012, when a Phillippine air force reconnaissance aircraft spotted eight Chinese fishing boats around the shoal. Immediately, President Aquino ordered the navy to step up its monitoring activities and enforce the country's fisheries and maritime environmental protections laws. Accordingly, the Philippine navy deployed the *BRP Gregorio Del Pilar*, the recently purchased US Coast Guard cutter that sailed from its homeport in Palawan into the shoal. The ship was tasked with protecting marine environment and resources and asserting the sovereignty of the Philippines as a coastal state. On the morning of 10 April, the *BRP Gregorio Del Pilar* verified the presence of eight Chinese fishing vessels anchored inside the lagoon. Following the established rules of engagement, the Philippine ship dispatched a boarding team to inspect the fishing vessels. Large amounts of illegally collected corals, giant clams and live sharks were found inside the compartments of the first fishing vessel boarded. In the past, Philippine ships had arrested Chinese fishermen in the shoal who were charged with illegal entry, illegal fishing and violation of the International Convention on International Trade in Endangered Species of Wild Fauna and Flora. The Philippine ship also confiscated the Chinese fishing vessels' catch, along with electric blasting caps, time fuses, dynamite sticks and cyanide, allegedly used by the Chinese fishermen. The *BRP Gregorio Del Pilar* tried to apprehend several Chinese fishing boats at the Scarborough Shoal, but before it could do this two Chinese marine surveillance vessels arrived and placed themselves between the arresting Philippine warship and the Chinese fishing boats. The surveillance vessels not only prevented the arrest of the Chinese fishermen, but also informed the captain of the *BRP Gregorio Del Pilar* that he had strayed into Chinese territorial waters. Clearly, China's reaction was a complete turnaround from its previous stance on maritime encroachments. First, the Chinese patrol vessels prevented the PN from arresting the fishermen. Second, China defied Philippine territorial rights over the shoal, which is only 224 kilometres from the province of Zambales in Luzon, and well within the country's EEZ, which extends outwardly up to 200 nautical miles. Fearing that the incident might escalate into a dangerous armed confrontation with the Chinese patrol vessels, the Philippines defused the tension by replacing its surface combatant with a smaller coastguard vessel. Instead of reciprocating, China raised the stakes by deploying the *Yuzheng-310*, the most advanced and largest patrol vessel, equipped with machine guns, light cannons and electronic sensors. When the Philippines filed a diplomatic protest, the Chinese Embassy in Manila contended that the three Chinese surveillance vessels in Scarborough Shoal were 'in the area fulfilling the duties of safeguarding Chinese maritime rights and interests'. It added that the shoal 'is an integral part of the Chinese territory and the waters around the traditional fishing area for Chinese fishermen'.[36]

In the past, Philippine Navy ships had arrested Chinese fishermen in the shoal who were charged with illegal entry, illegal fishing and violation of the International Convention on International Trade in Endangered Species of Wild Fauna and Flora. The Philippine Navy also confiscated the fishing vessels' catch along with electric blasting caps, time fuses, dynamite sticks and cyanide allegedly used by the Chinese fishermen. In response, the Chinese Embassy in Manila protested the apprehension of their fishermen, but did not challenge Philippine jurisdiction over the shoal, which is considered as a traditional fishing ground for Chinese fishermen, but not a Chinese territory.[37] The Chinese Ambassador even apologised that the number of Chinese fishermen in the area had increased considerably and that the Chinese government had difficulty controlling them. In fact, in 2001, after the Philippine Navy arrested 10 Chinese fishing vessels, the Chinese Foreign Ministry disclosed that it had started looking for alternative sources of livelihood for the arrested fishermen. This posture, however, dramatically changed during the 2012 Scarborough Shoal crisis. Clearly, this incident underscored an international reality – Chinese economic and naval power cast a long shadow over the Philippines and Vietnam, which are at the forefront of a maritime dispute with China in the South China Sea.[38]

The following day, Manila saw the possibility of a dangerous face-off with an emergent and assertive China. President Aquino recalled the *BRP Gregorio Del Pilar* and sent a smaller coastguard vessel to defuse the tension. Instead of reciprocating Manila's gesture, Beijing dispatched its most advanced and latest fishery patrol ship, the *Yuzheng*-310, to join the two other civilian patrol vessels already in the shoal. The Xinhua News Agency quoted the Chinese Foreign Ministry as saying that:

> the Philippines' attempt to carry out so-called law enforcement activities in the waters of Huangyan Island has infringed upon China's sovereignty, and runs counter to the consensus reached by both sides on maintaining the peace and stability in the South China Sea.[39]

The ministry, likewise, warned the Philippines 'not to complicate and escalate the situation'. On 15 April, the Chinese Foreign Ministry ordered the Philippines to withdraw its lone coast guard ship from the shoal. A few days later, the Philippines filed a diplomatic protest over the alleged harassment of the MV *Sarangani*, which was commissioned by the Philippine National Museum to conduct an archaeological survey of sunken Chinese junks in the area. Eventually, Manila withdrew the research boat amidst the escalating tension between the two sides. Then, the Philippines dared China to bring the case before the International Tribunal on the Law of the Sea (ITLOS), which the latter readily rejected. Instead, China insisted on a quiet, bilateral diplomatic negotiation to end the deadlock.

At the beginning of the stand-off, China obviously had the upper hand when it used a civilian vessel to force a PN surface combatant to back away. With an armada of armed civilian maritime vessels at its disposal, China put the onus on either escalating or resolving the incident on the Philippines. Afterwards, China sent an additional patrol ship, and consequently three Chinese ships confronted a lone Philippine coastguard vessel in the shoal. This incident proved that China has expanded its operational reach in the South China Sea and is capable of providing Chinese fishing vessels with physical protection. It also demonstrated that this emergent Asian power is adept at handling territorial disputes using naval brinkmanship. The 2012 Scarborough Shoal stand-off reflected the historic pattern of Chinese protracted, low-intensity and incremental moves to gain control of a large portion of the South China Sea. China's maritime strategy involves:

drawing a line in the sea using civilian maritime vessels to challenge these littoral states, and leaving them with the risky option of escalating matters by resorting to military means which will have dire consequences since the People's Liberation Army's Navy (PLA-N) ships are lurking in the background.[40]

This strategy aims to put the onus on the smaller littoral states to respond by driving them to the brink of a naval confrontation to resolve what is essentially a maritime jurisdiction issue.[41] In 2012, China targeted the Philippines in its naval brinkmanship game. The Philippines has the weakest navy in the region, and its air force cannot adequately patrol and monitor its vast maritime territory.

Escalating the coercive strategy against the Philippines

While Chinese and Philippine patrol vessels were at an impasse at the Scarborough Shoal, the Chinese Embassy in Manila confirmed that both countries were engaged in a lengthy and tedious diplomatic negotiation. Again, the Chinese Embassy articulated the official mantra that the Scarborough Shoal is an integral part of Chinese territory. It also warned Manila not to take actions that could irreparably damage Philippines-China relations and affect the stability of the South China Sea.[42] By the end of April 2012, Philippines-China negotiations were getting nowhere. The Chinese Embassy accused Manila of negotiating in bad faith and distorting the facts during the lengthy and tedious discussions. It also 'urged the Philippines to stop illegal activities and leave this area', as it insisted once more that China has sovereign rights over almost the whole of the South China Sea. The embassy spokesperson also said 'that ever since the ancient times, numerous documents on Chinese history have put down definitely in writing that Huangyan Island belongs to Chinese territory'. Manila, in turn, criticised China's aggressive stance against other claimant states such as the Philippines.[43] Tersely, it reminded China that the 'responsibility for resolving the stand-off in the South China Sea rests not just with one party but both parties', and challenged it to let the ITLOS mediate the dispute.

Exasperated by the Philippines' refusal to withdraw its lone coastguard vessel from the shoal, China decided to raise the ante. On 9 May 2012, Vice Foreign Minister Fu Ying summoned and told the Filipino charges d' affaires at the Philippine Embassy in Beijing that 'the Philippine government has repeatedly made erroneous remarks which misled the Philippine public and the international community, thus severely damaging the atmosphere of the bilateral relations between China and the Philippines'.[44] She added that the Philippines should withdraw all its vessels from the waters surrounding the shoal and stop operations against Chinese fishing boats and law enforcement vessels. Cryptically, she said 'that it is hard for us [China] to be optimistic about the situation'.[45] To exert more pressure on the Philippines, China deployed another civilian patrol boat and additional fishing boats at the Scarborough Shoal. By 9 May 2012, exactly a month after the start of the stand-off, four Chinese surveillance ships and ten fishing boats were facing a Philippine coastguard ship and an innocuous Fisheries Bureau vessel. The following day, China's General Administration of Quality Supervision announced that 1,200 containers of fruits from the Philippines were placed under quarantine in various ports.[46] On the same day, the China International Travel Service suspended all scheduled flights to the Philippines on 'safety grounds'.[47] Because of the travel ban, Chinese tour groups cancelled their trips to the Philippines. Then, in May and June 2012, China Southern Airlines cut flights between Guangzhou and Manila due to the relatively small number of passengers. These developments – perceived fallout of the Scarborough Shoal stand-off – made Filipino businessmen apprehensive.[48] The Philippine Banana Growers and Exporters Association warned the Aquino Administration that up to 200,000 banana farmers and ancillary workers could lose their livelihood without the huge and lucrative China market. The President of the Association, Stephen Antig, said, 'With 70 percent of Philippine bananas exported to China, a lengthy ban could affect the livelihood of half a million Filipinos'.[49] Consequently, other prominent Filipino businessmen asked the Philippine government to quickly resolve the impasse and stop the rapid deterioration of Philippine-China economic relations. The president of the Philippine Exporters Confederation (PHILEXPORT), Sergio Ortiz, warned the government that 'We [the Philippines] have more to lose than them [China]'. A Filipino legislator also cautioned the Aquino Administration not to provoke China, since this might lead to a considerable slump in Philippines-China trade. Party-List Representative Teodorico Haresco told the Aquino administration that 'Beijing might decide to send Filipino workers in Macau and Hong Kong back to the Philippines, which would surely devastate the national economy'.[50]

To put more pressure on Manila, the Chinese military floated the idea of using force against the Philippines, and possibly against other claimant states in the South China Sea. The *People's Liberation Army Daily* warned that the regular annual Philippine-US *Balikatan* military exercises increase the risk of an armed confrontation over the contested South China Sea.[51] On 22 April 2012, the *Global Times* editorial urged the Chinese government to engage the Philippines in a small-scale war to end the stalemate once and for all. It stated that 'once war erupts, China must take resolute action and deliver a clear message to the outside world that it does not want a war, but definitely has no fear of it'.[52] It exhorted the Chinese leadership to apply 'cold treatment to Manila that should last for a certain period'.[53] Major General Luo Yuan of the People's Liberation Army Academy of Military Sciences suggested taking a proactive stance against the Philippines by 'strengthening Chinese sovereign presence on Huangyan Island (Scarborough Shoal) by hoisting the national flag, erecting a sovereignty monument, building military bases or at least setting up fisheries bases'.[54] Further, he said that the Scarborough deadlock creates an opportunity for China to formulate 'a model for cracking the South China Sea dilemma'.[55] The volley of threatening rhetoric from the PLA continued way into the month of May. On 9 May, the *People's Liberation Army Daily* ran a toughly-worded editorial saying that China would not tolerate any violation of Chinese sovereignty on Huangyan Island. According to the editorial, 'Not only will the Chinese government not agree, nor will the Chinese people, and the Chinese Army will disagree even more'.[56] This statement is indicative of the PLA's non-compromising position when it comes to territorial disputes. On 14 May, media reports from Japan and Taiwan alleged that China's South Sea Fleet had forward-deployed a landing ship flotilla and a naval task force consisting of destroyers and amphibious assault ships in waters off the Philippines.[57] Two days later, the PLA denied that the Guangzhou Military Region, the South Sea Fleet and other units of the army assumed a state of readiness for possible military action against the Philippines.[58] The PLA's denial underscored the heightened tension between the Philippines and China, and the growing national belligerency against the Philippines, in particular, and other claimant states, in general. This media revelation was a double-edged sword. On the one hand, it disclosed the domestic clamour for a stronger and more confrontational action against the Philippines. On the other hand, it brought to light that some elements in the Chinese government and in the PLA were considering the use of force to resolve the impasse. PLA Major General Luo Yuan scolded the 'nationalist warmongers' in the Philippines, 'and commented China could rein them if Manila could not do it'.[59] The general was referring to a naval battle to teach the Philippines a lesson. Also, condescendingly, he quipped, 'We have repeatedly exercised forbearance and our patience has run its course. There is no more need to take caution'.

The Scarborough Shoal deadlock enabled the hawkish elements in the PLA to articulate their belligerent position against the Philippines (and the US) in the official media. This was unimaginable during Deng Xiaoping and Jiang Zemin's administrations, when military officers were banned from speaking out.[60] Observing the plethora of bashing by the PLA and the Chinese media, two American Sinologists noted:

> The coverage of the China-Philippines stand-off was accompanied by an uptick and broadening in Chinese criticism of others over the South China Sea dispute. Official Chinese media in mid-April averred that the tension was rising in the South China Sea, [and this] underlined Chinese determination to protect its interest against foreign encroachment and interference.[61]

China's diplomatic, verbal and economic pressures against the Philippines, however, generated a 'rally-around effect' in the country. The majority of Filipino legislators backed up the embattled Aquino Administration and allocated more funds for the AFP modernisation programme. At the height of the stand-off, the Philippines' fractious power blocs, as well as the normally apathetic public, became united and solidly swung behind the government as Philippine civilian vessels confronted their Chinese counterparts at the Scarborough Shoal.[62] The Catholic Bishops' Conference of the Philippines (CBCP) stopped its criticism of the pending government-sponsored reproductive health bill, and supported rallies and demonstrations in front of Chinese embassies and consulates around the world. Even the Communist Party of the Philippines, in principle, even goaded the government to assert the nation's sovereignty and territorial integrity against Chinese encroachments on the shoal.

Emboldened by the strong public support, the beleaguered Aquino administration hastened to establish a modest but 'comprehensive border protection program' against Chinese creeping expansionism in the South China Sea. This programme is anchored on the surveillance, deterrence and border patrol capabilities of the Philippine Armed Forces (PAF), the PN and the Philippine Coast Guard that extend from the country's territorial waters to its contiguous and exclusive economic zone.[63] This task involves upgrading the AFP's capabilities, prioritising its needs and gradually restructuring its forces from internal security to territorial defence. The long-term goal, according to the 2011 *AFP's Strategic Intent*, is to develop the force structure and capabilities enabling the Philippine military to maintain a 'credible deterrent posture against foreign intrusion or external aggression, and other illegal activities while allowing free navigation to prosper'.[64] The Philippines appealed for diplomatic and military support from the US, its strategic ally. During the stand-off, the *USS North Carolina* (SSN 777), a Virginia-class fast-attack submarine, arrived at Subic Bay on 13 May 2012. The submarine's visit hinted to China that the US is prepared to honour its defence treaty commitments to the Philippines in case of an armed confrontation at the Scarborough Shoal. It also coincided with the report that the PLA-N had mobilised its Southern Fleet for any eventuality.[65] A month later, another nuclear-powered attack submarine, the *USS Louisville*, made a port call to Subic Bay. These visits were actually routine port calls. However, given the fact that they were made during the stand-off and were much-publicised, they intimidated to China that the US will not stand idly by while a treaty ally (the Philippines) is under the threat of an armed attack.[66] The Philippines also called on its fellow ASEAN member states to take a common position against Chinese assertiveness in the South China Sea.

The end of the stand-off and its aftermath

In mid-June 2012, the tension in the disputed area eased when the two countries withdrew their civilian vessels on the pretext of the onset of the typhoon season. On 16 June, President Aquino ordered all Philippine vessels to leave the shoal because of rough seas and heavy rains brought by a seasonal typhoon.[67] On 18 June, Chinese fishing boats and civilian vessels near the area were heading back to port. A Chinese Foreign Ministry spokesperson announced that with the withdrawal of the civilian ships, 'We [China] hope [that] there will continue to be an easing in the situation and bilateral cooperation will recover and be safeguarded'.[68] The following day, the China Maritime Search and Rescue Center deployed a rescue ship to Scarborough Shoal to assist Chinese fishing boats leaving the shoal due to 'rough sea conditions'.[69] The coordinated withdrawal of Filipino and Chinese civilian vessels from the shoal came amid ongoing consultations between the two countries. However, while the withdrawal of these vessels was aimed to de-escalate the tension, both countries have persisted in claiming sovereignty over the shoal. After the Philippines withdrew its lone coastguard vessel from the Scarborough Shoal, China began consolidating its control over the area. The China Maritime Surveillance vessels, along with the China Fisheries

Law Enforcement Command, constructed a chain barrier across the mouth of the shoal to block Philippine access to it. China has also deployed surveillance vessels to protect the fleet of Chinese fishing boats operating deep into the Philippines' EEZ. In October 2012, Chinese Vice Foreign Minister Fu Ying, seeking a diplomatic solution to the dispute, visited Manila. However, instead of searching for a mutually acceptable solution, the high-ranking official warned Manila not to do the following: (1) appeal to the UN; (2) internationalise the dispute in forums such as the ASEAN; (3) coordinate with other countries such as the US; and (4) issue any press release regarding the negotiations.[70] In effect, she badgered the Philippines to accept in silence China's exercise of de facto occupation of the Scarborough Shoal.

The Philippine's filing of statement of claim

It was not a *fait accompli* for China. Philippine officials ignored China's stern orders on the Philippines. In January 2013, the Philippines legally defended its claims over the Spratlys and other land features in the South China Sea when it filed a statement of claim against China in the Arbitral Tribunal of the United Nations Convention on the Law of the Sea. In its Notification and Statement of Claim to the Tribunal, the Philippines laid claims to some of the islands in occupied Spratlys, Scarborough Shoal, Mischief Reef and other land features within its 200 nautical mile EEZ based on the UNCLOS provisions specifically to its rights to a Territorial Sea and Contiguous Zone under Part II of the Convention, to an Exclusive Economic Zone under Part V, and to a Continental Shelf under Part VI.[71] The Philippines' passage of RA 9522 in 2009 and the filing of its Notification and Statement of Claim to the UNCLOS Arbitral Tribunal show that the Philippines' ownership of the six islands in the Spratys and other land features within its legitimate maritime jurisdiction are firmly grounded on international law – specifically UNCLOS. In its statement of claim, the Philippines also made it clear that it does not seek arbitration over which party has sovereignty over the islands claimed by both the Philippines and China. Rather, it merely requests the Arbitral Tribunal to issue an opinion on the following issues: (1) whether China's maritime claim in the South China Sea based on its 'nine-dash line' claim is valid or contrary to UNCLOS; and (2) whether the Scarborough Shoal, Johnson Reef, Cuarteron Reef and Fiery Cross Reef, which are submerged features that are below sea level at high tide, are islands or rocks under Article 121 (3) of the Convention. It also petitions the Tribunal to declare that the Philippines is entitled to a 12 mile Territorial Sea, a 200 mile EEZ and a Continental Shelf under Parts II, V and VI of UNCLOS, and that China has unlawfully prevented the Philippines from exercising its right to exploit resources in its EEZ and to its rights to navigation within and beyond the 200 mile EEZ of the Philippines' archipelagic baselines.[72]

In this appeal to the Arbitral Tribunal, the Philippines wanted to show that its ownership of the six islands in the Spratlys and other land features within its legitimate maritime jurisdiction is firmly grounded on international law –

specifically UNCLOS. Since both countries are signatories to UNCLOS, the Philippines intends to convince China to limit its claims of entitlement to maritime zones measured from islands as stipulated in this legal convention.[73] The Philippine course of action is designed to restrain China from claiming historic rights to and jurisdiction over the waters, seabed and subsoil of the South China Sea. The Philippines also requested the Tribunal to require China to 'bring its domestic legislation into conformity with its obligations under UNCLOS and for it to stop any activities that violate the rights of the Philippines in its maritime domain in the West Philippine Sea (South China Sea).'[74] As expected, China refused to participate in the international arbitration, and openly opposed the Philippines' filing of the case. On 20 February 2013, the Chinese Ambassador in Manila returned the notice of arbitration to the Philippines Department of Foreign Affairs. At the same time, Mr Hong Lei, a Chinese Foreign Ministry spokesperson in Beijing, branded the filing as 'factually flawed'. Moreover, he accused Manila of violating the non-binding 2002 Declaration of Conduct of the Parties in the South China Sea, which provides for ASEAN and China to settle their maritime disputes among themselves.[75] China's rejection of an arbitration process came a week after the Chinese media announced that three Chinese frigates would patrol and conduct drilling operations in the South China Sea after passing through the East China Sea and the Bashi Strait. On 30 March, four Chinese frigates conducted a live-fire exercise at the farthest point of its nine-dash line claim in the South China Sea, some 50 miles from the coast of Malaysia.

Conclusion

The 2012 Scarborough Shoal stand-off between the Philippine and Chinese civilian vessels exemplifies an international crisis waiting to happen. Three years before the incident, China began its relentless pursuit of its expansive maritime claim in the South China Sea. It has built a powerful and formidable navy to back up its territorial claim. It has also vigorously challenged the littoral states' claim on their respective exclusive economic zones, and through military exercises it has shown off its naval prowess, seeking to impose its will on them. These developments coincided with a major political change in the Philippines – the election of Benigno Aquino III to the presidency. After a few months in office, President Aquino started challenging China's claim in the South China Sea by shifting the AFP's focus from internal security to external defence. This, in turn, fuelled the two-month-long stand-off between Philippine and Chinese civilian vessels at the Scarborough Shoal. The stand-off ended when both the Philippines and China withdrew their civilian vessels at Scarborough Shoal in the middle of June. However, the shoal remains a potential tinderbox. The trigger exists as long as China enforces its control the on islands and waters over which it claims sovereignty, while the other claimant countries, such as the Philippines and Vietnam, insist on their own claims in the South China Sea. The Philippines constantly hounds the ASEAN to come up with a binding code of conduct to govern maritime activities in the South China Sea. More significantly, it has filed a statement of claim against

China in the Arbitral Tribunal of UNCLOS. In the process, it seeks a multilateral and legal solution to the persistent territorial dispute. However, China has refused to participate in the proceedings. Instead, it staged a live-fire exercise in March 2013 to flaunt its naval power whenever other claimant states oppose its supposed sovereignty over the disputed area. This is telling of China's position regarding the dispute – that its sovereignty over the South China Sea is non-negotiable. This stance is unlikely to change, since that would politically compromise to its long-held claim of indivisible territorial sovereignty.[76] Given the volatile situation in the South China Sea, one can only hope that the proverbial 'single spark that can start a prairie fire' does not ignite anytime soon.

Notes

1 Xavier Furtado, 'International Law and the Dispute over the Spratly Islands: Whither UNCLOS?', *Contemporary Southeast Asia*, 21(3), December 1999, p. 5.
2 James A. Gregor, *In the Shadow of the Giants: The Major Powers and the Security of Southeast Asia*, Hoover Press, Stanford, CA, 1989, p. 91.
3 Gregor, *In the Shadow of the Giants*, p. 5.
4 Ross Marlay, 'China, the Philippines, and the Spratly Islands', *Asian Affairs: An American Review*, 23(4), Winter 1997, p. 1.
5 Lowell Bautista, 'International Legal Implications of the Philippine Treaty Limits on Navigational Rights in Philippine Waters', *Australian Journal of Maritime and Ocean Affairs*, 1(3), 2009, p. 7.
6 Bautista, 'International Legal Implications of the Philippine Treaty Limits on Navigational Rights in Philippine Waters', p. 3.
7 Robert Beckman, 'The UN Convention on the Law of the Sea and Maritime Dispute in the South China Sea', *The American Journal of International Law*, 104(142), 2012, p. 148.
8 Beckman, 'The UN Convention on the Law of the Sea and Maritime Dispute in the South China Sea', p. 148.
9 Gregor, *In the Shadow of the Giants*, p. 89.
10 Gregor, *In the Shadow of the Giants*, p. 89.
11 Leszek Buszynski, 'ASEAN, the Declaration on Conduct, and the South China Sea', *Contemporary Southeast Asia*, 25(3), December 2003, p. 2.
12 Marlay, 'China, the Philippines, and the Spratly Islands', p. 4.
13 Michael Yahuda, *The International Politics of the Asia-Pacific*, RoutledgeCurzon, London and New York, 2004, p. 301.
14 See Liselotte Odgaard, The Balance of Power in Asia-Pacific Security: U.S.-China Policies on Regional Order, Routledge, New York, 2007, p. 54.
15 BBC Monitoring Asia Pacific, 'Chinese President Predicts China-Philippine Trade Relations', 28 April 2005, p. 1.
16 Xinhua News Agency, 'Chinese President Calls for Further Expanding and Deepening Cooperation with Philippines', 27 April 2005, p. 1.
17 Ronald O'Rourke, 'PLA-N Force Structure: Submarines, Ships, and Aircraft', in Phillip C. Saunders, Christopher Yung, Michael Swaine and Andrew Nien-Dzu-Yang (eds), *The Chinese Navy: Expanding Capabilities, Evolving Roles*, National Defense University Press, Washington, DC, 2011, pp. 154–155.
18 Nan Li, 'The Evolution of China's Naval Strategy and Capabilities: From "Near Coast" and "Near Sea" to "Far Seas"', in Phillip C. Saunders, Christopher Yung, Michael Swaine and Andrew Nien-Dzu-Yang (eds), *The Chinese Navy: Expanding*

Capabilities, Evolving Roles, National Defense University Press, Washington, DC, 2011, p. 129.

19 Daniel M. Hartnett and Frederic Vellucci, 'Toward a Maritime Security Strategy: An Analysis of Chinese Views since Early 1990s', in Phillip C. Saunders, Christopher Yung, Michael Swaine and Andrew Nien-Dzu-Yang (eds), *The Chinese Navy: Expanding Capabilities, Evolving Roles*, National Defense University Press, Washington, DC, 2011, p. 101.

20 Peter Dutton, 'Three Disputes and Three Objectives: China and the South China Sea', *Naval War College Review*, 54(4), Autumn 2011, p. 47.

21 For details on China's training exercises in its surrounding waters, see National Institute for Defense Studies, *NIDS China Security Reprt 2011*, National Insitute for Defense Studies, Tokyo, 2011, pp. 14–21.

22 Carlyle A. Thayer, 'The United States, China and Southeast Asia', *Southeast Asian Affairs 2011*, Institute of Southeast Asian Affairs, Singapore, 2011, p. 21.

23 Daniel J. Kostecka, 'From the Sea: PLA Doctrine and the Employment of Sea-Based Airpower', *Naval War College Review*, 64(3), Summer 2011, pp. 14–15.

24 Nan Li, 'The Evolution of China's Naval Strategy and Capabilities', p. 134.

25 Robert Sutter and Chin-Hao Huang, 'Managing Rising Tension in the South China Sea', *Comparative Connections: A Triannual E-Journal on East Asian Bilateral Relations*, September 2011, p. 1.

26 Michael A. Glosny 'Getting Beyond Taiwan? Chinese Foreign Policy and PLA Modernization', *Strategic Forum*, 261, 2011, p.4.

27 See Edward Wong, 'China Navy Reaches Far, Unsettling the Region', *New York Times*, 15 June 2011, p. 3.

28 See Carl A. Thayer, 'China's New Wave of Aggressive Assertiveness in the South China Sea', *International Journal of China Studies*, 2(3), December 2011, pp. 561–562.

29 'Philippines Protests against China's PLA-Nned Oil Rig, Constructions in Spratlys', *BBC Monitoring Asia-Pacific*, 2 June 2011, p. 2.

30 'China Says Philippines Harming Sovereignty, Interests in Spratlys', *BBC Monitoring Asia-Pacific*, 9 June 2011, p.1.

31 'China Says Philippines Harming Sovereignty, Interests in Spratlys', p. 3.

32 See Edward Wong, 'China Asserts Role as a Naval Power', *International Herald Tribune*, 23 April 2010, pp. 1, 4.

33 'Philippines Sends SOS to the International Community', *Philippine Star*, 2 May 2012, pp. 1–20.

34 See International Crisis Group, 'Stirring Up the South China Sea II: Regional Responses', *Asia Report*, 229, 24 July 2012, p. 8.

35 Robert Sutter and Chin-huo Huang, 'Hu Visits Cambodia as South China Sea Simmers', *Comparative Connections*, May 2012, p. 5.

36 James Hookway, 'Philippine, China Ships Square Off', *Wall Street Journal Asia*, 12 April 2012, p. 2.

37 'Philippines Eyes Tougher Policy in Disputed Scarborough Shoal', *BBC Monitoring Asia-Pacific-Political*, 27 March 2011, p. 1.

38 William Chong, 'Path to Scarborough Far from Fair: South China Sea Rivals no Match for China's Economic, Military Clout', *The Strait Times*, 21 April 2012, p. 1.

39 Thai News Service Group, 'China/Philippines: China Seeks Preservation of Over-All Friendly Relations with Philippines as Tension over Scarborough Shoal Ebbs Momentarily', *Asia News Monitor*, 12 April 2011, p. 1.

40 Thai News Service Group, 'China/Philippines', p. 1.

41 Thai News Service Group, 'China/Philippines', p. 1.

42 Thai News Service Group, 'China/Philippines', p. 2.

43 'Philippines/China: No Agreement Reached with Chinese Government on Pull-Out of Philippine Vessels from Scarborough Shoal—DFA', *Asia News Monitor*, 26 April 2012.

44 'Beijing Warns Manila over Shoal Stand-Off', *The Strait Times*, 9 May 2012, p. 1.
45 'Beijing Warns Manila over Shoal Stand-Off', p. 1
46 Jane Perlez, 'China-Feud over Shoal Heats Up: Tourist Visits Suspended as Beijing Sharpens its Criticism of Philippines', *International Herald Tribune*, 11 May 2012, p. 9.
47 Raiisa Robles, 'Filipino Business Chiefs Urge Peaceful Solution Industry Leaders in Manila Say Scarborough Shoal Row Could Jeopardise Exports to China', *South China Morning Post*, 15 May 2012, p. 1.
48 Robles, 'Filipino Business Chiefs Urge Peaceful Solution Industry Leaders in Manila Say Scarborough Shoal Row Could Jeopardise Exports to China'.
49 Robles, 'Filipino Business Chiefs Urge Peaceful Solution Industry Leaders in Manila Say Scarborough Shoal Row Could Jeopardise Exports to China', p. 1.
50 Pia Lee-Brago, Christina Mendez, Marvin Sy and Paolo Romero, 'Philippines Willing to Hold Diplomatic Talks with China Over Disputed Reef', *BBC Monitoring Asia Pacific*, 11 May 2012, p. 2.
51 'China Paper Warns of Armed Confrontation over Seas', *Right Vision News*, 24 April 2012, p. 1.
52 'Chinese Daily Calls for Small-Scale War against the Philippines', *The Statesman*, 23 April 2012, p. 1.
53 'Chinese Daily Calls for Small-Scale War against the Philippines', p. 1.
54 'BBC Monitoring Quotes from China, Taiwan Press 26 April 2012', *BBC Monitoring Asia-Pacific*, 26 April 2012, pp. 1–2.
55 'BBC Monitoring Quotes from China, Taiwan Press 26 April 2012', p. 1.
56 Perlez, 'China-Feud over Shoal Heats Up', p. 1
57 Alec Almazan, 'U.S. N-Sub in Subic a Strong Signal to China: Routine Visit Comes amid Reports China is Mobilizing Fleet for Philippines Ops', *The Business Times*, 18 May 2012, p. 1.
58 Brian Spegele, 'China: China Denies War-Preparation Rumors', *Wall Street Journal Asia*, 14 May 2012, p. 4.
59 Willy Lam, 'China's Hawk in Command', *Wall Street Journal Asia*, 2 July 2012, p. 1.
60 Lam, 'China's Hawk in Command', p. 1.
61 Robert Sutter and Chin-hao Huang, 'Hu Visits Cambodia as South China Sea Simmers', *Comparative Connections: A Triannual E-Journal on East Asian Bilateral Relations*, May 2012, p. 6.
62 Alan Robles, 'Filipino United in Shoal Row Power Blocs and the Public Appear behind the Philippine Government in its Stand-Off with Beijing over a Sovereignty Claim in the South China Sea', *South China Morning Post*, 16 May 2012, p. 1.
63 *National Security Policy 2011–2016*, National Security Council, Quezon City, April 2011, p. 39.
64 Office of the Deputy Chief-of-Staff, *Armed Forces of the Philippines: Strategic Intent*, Camp Aguinaldo, Quezon City, 2011, p. 27.
65 Almazan, 'U.S. N-Sub in Subic a Strong Signal to China', p. 1.
66 Almazan, 'U.S. N-Sub in Subic a Strong Signal to China', p. 1.
67 Jane Perlez, 'Stand-Off over South China Sea Shoal Eases: Beijing and Manila Pull their Ships from Area, but the Dispute is Not Settled', *International Herald Tribune*, 19 June 2012, p. 4.
68 Perlez, 'Stand-Off over South China Sea Shoal Eases', p. 2.
69 Teddy Ng, 'Stand-Off Eases as Sides Withdraw Ships from Shoal Beijing Follows Manila in Pulling Vessels out of Disputed Area because of Bad Weather', *South China Morning Post*, 19 June 2012, p. 1.
70 'Manila Takes a Stand', *Wall Street Journal Asia*, 25 January 2013, p. 1.

71 'Notification and Statement of Claim to the United Nations Convention of Law of the Sea (UNCLOS) Arbitral Tribunal', Department of Foreign Affairs, Manila, 22 January 2013, pp. 12–14.
72 'Notification and Statement of Claim to the United Nations Convention of Law of the Sea (UNCLOS) Arbitral Tribunal', pp. 18–19.
73 Beckman, 'The UN Convention on the Law of the Sea and Maritime Dispute in the South China Sea', p. 159.
74 Bernice Camille V. Bauzon, 'PH Sues China', *Tribune Business News*, 23 January 2013, p. 1.
75 Simone Orendain, 'Philippines to Forge ahead with Sea Dispute Arbitration', *Voice of America/FIND*, 21 February 2013, p. 1.
76 Kailash K. Prasad, 'An Assessment of the Goals, Drivers, and Capabilities of China's Modernizing Navy', *Korean Journal of Defense Analysis*, 24(1), March 2012, p. 57.

7 ASEAN

The challenge of unity in diversity

Christopher B. Roberts

Recent diplomacy by the Association of Southeast Asian Nations (ASEAN) over disputes in the South China Sea has been the subject of significant international focus. However, a deeper understanding of the factors informing ASEAN unity and the potential for an effective response also necessitates an analysis of the Association's long-term diplomacy on the subject. Consequently, this chapter contains three sections. The first section examines the historical basis for a relatively unified ASEAN position over the South China Sea during the 1990s. It then examines the various factors that led to a deterioration of ASEAN solidarity by the time of the 2002 Declaration on the Conduct of Parties in the South China Sea. The second section analyses the nature of Beijing's more assertive diplomacy and the sometimes coercive behaviour exhibited by Beijing since 2007, while the third section examines the notable shift (and motives) in Beijing's diplomacy during 2013. The examination of these three periods provides a more nuanced understanding of why significant ASEAN unity will not be feasible for the purpose of a collective bargaining position vis-à-vis aspects of sovereignty in the South China Sea. Nonetheless, ASEAN's institutions for dialogue and any associated negotiations to institutionalise norms of behaviour – such as through an 'ASEAN Code of Conduct' – may at least help to mitigate the risk of conflict in the future.

ASEAN's early role: mutual threats and interest harmonisation

Early ASEAN-China relations were highly turbulent. Since ASEAN's inception in 1967, Beijing perceived the Association to be a capitalist block that was diplomatically, and in some cases militarily, supportive of the United States. Beijing's provision of financial support to some communist insurgencies in Southeast Asia, together with some substantial episodes of violence against various ethnic Chinese communities, further compounded this mutual distrust.[1] In some instances, these ethnic clashes were interdependent with, and reinforced by, ideological clashes (and scapegoating). For example, an alleged 'attempt' to oust President Sukarno by 'communists' in Indonesia led to an 'anti-communist purge' that resulted in the death of approximately 500,000 Indonesians – many of whom were of Chinese descent.[2] The broader history of the Cold War also meant that some of the original

ASEAN members from the 'capitalist' South did not establish diplomatic relations with China until as recently as 1990 (e.g. Singapore and Indonesia).[3] Consequently, Beijing remained highly critical of ASEAN during the first few decades of its existence.[4]

In 1992, China reasserted its claim to exclusive sovereignty over the bulk of the South China Sea by passing its 'Law of the Territorial Sea and Contiguous Zone of the People's Republic of China'. The area claimed by China conflicted with the claims of four of the then six ASEAN members – Brunei, the Philippines, Malaysia and Indonesia.[5] Further, China had authorised the US Crestone Energy Corporation to explore for hydrocarbon reserves within Vietnam's continental shelf.[6] Given the history of the original ASEAN members, the Association was able to quickly respond though its 1992 'Declaration on the South China Sea'. The declaration referred to the Association's core principles, as elaborated in the Treaty of Amity and Cooperation, and urged 'all parties concerned' to resolve all 'sovereignty and jurisdictional issues' over the dispute via 'peaceful means' and 'without resort to force'.[7] The most significant clause concerned a call to establish a binding 'code of international conduct over the South China Sea'.[8] The declaration also called for the concerned parties to explore the possibility of functional cooperation over non-traditional security issues such as piracy, environmental protection, search-and-rescue operations and the safety of maritime navigation. However, the declaration did not go so far as to raise the possibility of joint exploration concerning the vast hydrocarbon resources believed to be present.[9]

While China was unenthusiastic in its initial response, Vietnam's Foreign Minister, Nguyen Manh Cam, almost immediately stated that the document was 'in conformity with the principles and policies that Vietnam has been pursuing', and provided his unreserved support.[10] Given Hanoi's own claims to the South China Sea, the shift from a historically hostile position towards more amicable relations with ASEAN was unsurprising. Hanoi's position was also informed by its own history with China, including being occupied by China for over 1,000 years, the 1979 border war, and a 1988 skirmish where the Chinese People's Liberation Army Navy (PLAN) clashed with Vietnamese forces near Fiery Cross Reef, leading to the loss of three Vietnamese vessels and 77 crew.[11]

Beijing was not only weary of ASEAN's collective diplomacy over the South China Sea, but also of progress in other areas. During the same year, at the 1992 ASEAN Leaders Summit (Singapore), the ASEAN members announced their intention to strengthen their 1971 Zone of Peace, Freedom and Neutrality (ZOPFAN) through the establishment of a Southeast Asia Nuclear Weapons Free Zone (SEANWFZ).[12] China publically opposed SEANWFZ due to the treaty's inclusion of references to continental shelves and a 200 nautical mile exclusive economic zone (EEZ). Thus, when ASEAN invited China to join, Beijing was worried that its accession, in a de facto sense, would also constrain its own territorial claims, and subsequently rejected the offer.[13]

China's occupation of Mischief Reef in 1995 further crystallised ASEAN's collective voice over the South China Sea. Based on the United Nations Convention on the Law of the Sea (UNCLOS), the Philippines appears to have a clear legal claim to the resources around the reef, as it is well within its 200 nautical mile EEZ (i.e. 127 nautical miles from the Philippine territory of Palawan). From Marvin Ott's perspective, the occupation of 'Mischief Reef was significant, not as a military asset, but as a tangible demonstration of China's determination to project its power and presence into the South China Sea'.[14] The timing of this occupation also coincided with the US withdrawal of its forces from the Philippines.[15] In this sense, the end of the Cold War and associated perceptions of an incremental withdrawal from Southeast and East Asia by the US military since the 1970s (i.e. the Nixon Doctrine) may have contributed to a sense of empowerment within both the Chinese Communist Party (CCP) and its People's Liberation Army (PLA).

The Philippine government responded in early 1995 by providing the international press with photos that revealed 'clusters of octagonal-shaped concrete structures on steel pylons' constructed by Beijing at Mischief Reef. Despite these photos, Beijing initially denied that it had constructed anything other than shelters for Chinese fishermen.[16] While the Philippine government first resorted to military action by sending several naval vessels, and, as stated by Colonel Felipe Gaerlan, its 'entire force of F-5s . . . five of them',[17] the weakness of its armed forces soon forced the government to focus on diplomatic means, including its membership in ASEAN. ASEAN quickly responded through a mix of diplomatic sticks and carrots.

In March 1995, the ASEAN foreign ministers displayed their solidarity by censuring China through a joint statement that expressed serious concern over developments in the South China Sea, and ASEAN referred to the spirit of the 1992 'ASEAN Declaration on the South China Sea' in reiterating its call for restraint from destabilising actions.[18] However, the Association simultaneously encouraged China to participate in 'a network of regional organisations' and workshops, or what Michael Leifer termed an 'embryonic structure of good citizenship'.[19] Despite these efforts, Beijing maintained its long-held position that it was willing to enter into bilateral discussions with other claimant states, but that it would not enter into multilateral negotiations with ASEAN. While 'ASEAN unity did not immediately alter China's behaviour',[20] China subsequently viewed the ASEAN states and their institutional modalities in a different light, and devoted more emphasis on its soft power – something Joshua Kurlantzick fashioned as China's 'Charm Offensive'.[21]

The period between 1992 and 1995 represented the height of ASEAN solidarity over the South China Sea disputes. While ASEAN unity did help to deescalate public and official tensions over the dispute, China continued with its 'creeping assertiveness', and by 1999 Beijing had, inter alia, further fortified its structures on Mischief Reef.[22] During the immediate years that followed, ASEAN's capacity to exercise a collective voice weakened considerably – not just regarding the South China Sea, but also in relation to many other emerging challenges that it faced. Two significant events contributed to this: the deterioration of regional relations during the East Asian financial crisis,[23] and the expansion of its membership to embrace all the Indo-China countries and Myanmar. In the case of the latter, all four of the new members had promoted aspects of socialist ideology in their political institutions, and consequently had been subject to very different processes of socialisation.[24]

Fractious membership, compromised positions and rising tensions

At the 1999 ASEAN Regional Forum (ARF), the Philippines once again garnered the support of its ASEAN counterparts to draft a binding 'Code of Conduct' (CoC) that would manage the activities of the South China Sea claimants.[25] However, such intramural unity was not sustainable due to the divisions generated by their own overlapping claims. As the late Barry Wain summarised in interview:

> disunity developed on the ASEAN side between Vietnam and Malaysia . . .
> In the end, you had the sad spectacle of China, which initially rejected the
> ASEAN approach to a Code of Conduct, being more enthusiastic about
> the final declaration than the ASEAN side.[26]

The outcome from this set of negotiations was the non-binding 2002 'Declaration on the Conduct of Parties in the South China Sea'. The parties also failed to reach an agreement on the guidelines for implementing the declaration, and it fell far short of the binding Code of Conduct that the Philippines had initially sought at the time of the 1992 Declaration on the South China Sea.[27]

Within a year, Beijing demonstrated the ineffectiveness of the communiqué when it negotiated an agreement for joint exploration with the Philippines on 1 September 2004. The 'Agreement on Joint Marine Seismic Undertaking in Certain Areas of the South China Sea' (JSMU) (see Maps 5 and 6) shocked the remaining ASEAN members, as the Philippines had been at the lead in pushing for a united stance vis-à-vis Beijing's claims. Hanoi was particularly outspoken in its opposition, but in March 2005 Vietnam joined an enlarged version of the agreement, and President Arroyo (Philippines) declared the outcome to be 'a diplomatic breakthrough for peace and security in the region'.[28] The shift in policy by Vietnam was undertaken reluctantly, but in the face of an assessment that there was little prospect for ASEAN unity, and therefore, 'if you can't beat them, join them'.[29] Problematically, when further details of the trilateral agreement were released in 2008, it was revealed that the areas for exploration included 24,000 square kilometres of Filipino territory that had not previously been claimed by either China or Vietnam. In the midst of a domestic backlash, where the Arroyo government was accused of having sold out the country's sovereignty, the arrangement ended in June 2008 when the Philippines announced that the JMSU would not be extended.[30] Thus, by 2005, ASEAN solidarity had significantly broken down, and within another two to three years not even Beijing was satisfied with the then status quo. From Beijing's perspective, a new set of tactics was increasingly necessary.

Contrary to the dominant view in the literature, a notable shift in China's approach to the South China Sea dispute occurred in 2007 rather than 2009. For example, in July 2007, Chinese paramilitary vessels drove 'away Vietnamese fishing vessels from the Spratly Islands, sinking three in July 2007'. Beijing also 'forced a British-American-Vietnam oil consortium to abandon development of a gas field off southern Vietnam'.[31] However, it was not until 2009 that the South China Sea dispute significantly recaptured the imagination of the international media. During the year, Malaysia and Vietnam provided a joint submission regarding the southern parts of the subregion to the United Nations' Commission on the Limits of the Continental Shelf. This initiative angered Beijing, and it responded with its own submission that included its 'nine-dash map', which once again claimed nearly all of the South China Sea.[32]

Some analysts believe that Hanoi then applied its leverage as the Chair of ASEAN to internationalise the South China Sea issue.[33] If true, and in the face of constant warnings from Chinese officials against any such action, Hanoi sought and received a statement of support from the United States. Thus, at the July 2010 ASEAN Regional Forum meeting, US Secretary of State Hillary Clinton declared that 'the United States has a national interest in freedom of navigation, open access to Asia's maritime commons and respect for international law in the South China Sea'. Clinton further noted that the issue was a 'diplomatic priority' for the US, and offered to help mediate the dispute.[34] China was so incensed that it reportedly declared, behind closed doors, that it had elevated the South China Sea issue to one of its 'core interests'.[35] Beijing was also concerned about any actions designed to contain China's military rise, and these concerns were reinforced when the US announced the much publicised 'pivot' back to Asia in November 2011.

As the then ASEAN Chair, Vietnam also resumed the sessions of the ASEAN-China Joint Working Group to implement the 2002 Declaration on Conduct of Parties in the South China Sea (DoC).[36] In July 2011, these efforts resulted in the conclusion of a vague set of guidelines. However, this was only possible when ASEAN agreed to Beijing's request, supported by Cambodia, to remove a reference that required consultation between the ASEAN states prior to any agreement with Beijing. An additional guideline also required that any activity or project based on the DoC be reported to the ASEAN-China Ministerial Meeting.[37] Thus, even within ASEAN's formal multilateral framework, China had effectively institutionalised a bilateral process of negotiation that would maintain its asymmetrical primacy and capacity to divide and rule.

The Guidelines to Implement the DoC had little impact, as China's relations with both the Philippines and Vietnam continued to deteriorate, and in 2011 Vietnam alleged that on two occasions Chinese ships cut oil exploration cables. Then, in June 2012, more than a dozen Chinese fishing vessels, two Chinese law enforcement vessels and a single Filipino naval vessel were involved in a stand-off over Scarborough Shoal. Moreover, China also invited foreign tenders for oil and gas blocks in disputed waters (July 2012).[38] The Scarborough Shoal development was further complicated by a Chinese frigate that ran aground on a nearby shoal.[39] Contrary to previous reports, this demonstrated that China's paramilitary forces were operating in coordination with the PLA-N in the South China Sea, and that there has been a higher level of coordination between *certain* agencies than some reports had contended.[40]

A further stand-off occurred in May 2013 when Filipino sources announced that 30 Chinese fishing boats, two Chinese Marine Surveillance Vessels and one PLA-N warship had entered the waters surrounding the Second Thomas Shoal. Despite official Chinese statements that these forces had withdrawn, the vessels are reportedly still there,[41] and this demonstration of 'effective control' is intended to strengthen the legality of China's claims under UNCLOS. Such actions can be depicted as a form of creeping sovereignty where, over time, Beijing could significantly alter the current 'status quo'. As one Vietnamese military official stated, 'there will come a time when no one will remember that we not only rightly held sovereignty over the Paracel Islands, but also did control them until their occupation at the end of the Vietnam War'.[42]

The level of assertiveness exercised by Beijing alarmed several of the ASEAN members. Consequently, they reinvigorated their efforts to strengthen the institutional constraints to coercive tactics through the implementation of the DoC guidelines and the conclusion of the CoC. In the case of the former, an agreement was reached in January 2012 concerning the establishment of four expert committees on maritime scientific research, environmental protection, search-and-rescue activities, and cooperation against transnational crime. However, ASEAN and China failed to agree to an expert committee concerning 'safety of navigation and communication at sea as it was deemed too contentious'.[43] In the case of the CoC, Beijing maintained that the DoC guidelines should first be implemented, and only then, with 'appropriate timing' and 'appropriate conditions', would China consider negotiations regarding the DoC.[44]

Despite Beijing's formal objections, the Philippines drafted a preliminary Code of Conduct and circulated it between the ASEAN members. However, ASEAN's intramural negotiations were hindered by some of the non-claimant members, who view Beijing more as a patron than as a potential threat to security or sovereignty. For example, divisions emerged over Articles 1–6, as these covered issues such as 'joint exploration', the application of UNCLOS and the establishment of a regional 'dispute settlement mechanism'. However, at the 20th ASEAN Summit (Phnom Penh, 3–4 April 2012), China adopted a new position and requested a seat at ASEAN's intramural negotiations over the CoC. Cambodia supported this request, but the Philippines and Vietnam strongly objected, and a compromise followed where ASEAN would continue to work on its own in drafting the CoC. Nonetheless, the new Chair of ASEAN – Cambodia – would update Beijing with developments concerning the draft.[45]

Intra-ASEAN deliberations at a Working Group (April 2012), followed by a Senior Officials Meeting (June 2012), resulted in the drafting of several 'principles' to guide the conclusion of a regional CoC. The shift away from an actual draft of a CoC was an outcome of Beijing's lobbying, and the final draft of the Proposed Elements of a Regional Code of Conduct was submitted at the 45th ASEAN Ministerial Meeting (AMM) on 9 July 2013.[46] However, aside from references to two dispute settlement mechanisms under the Treaty of Amity and Cooperation and UNCLOS (both voluntary), the more contentious aspects of the initial Filipino draft had been removed or significantly reduced in their scope and level of enforceability.[47] Further, the focus of the ASEAN foreign ministers soon shifted away from the principles of a CoC to the content of a joint communiqué that has always been issued at the end of each AMM.

In the context of the joint communiqué, the ASEAN foreign ministers became embroiled in a dispute over a request by the Philippines and Vietnam to include a reference to Chinese aggression (e.g. the Scarborough Shoal incident) and Beijing's award of hydrocarbon exploration leases within Vietnam's EEZ.[48] As the Philippines and Vietnam were not willing to withdraw this paragraph, Cambodia refused to issue the joint statement. Reports soon emerged that Cambodia had been simultaneously consulting with Beijing during the negotiations.[49] For ASEAN, the significance of the incident was reflected in the words of Indonesia's Foreign Minister, Marty Natalegawa, when he stated to reporters that 'I think it is utterly irresponsible if we cannot come up with a common statement on the South China Sea'.[50]

China could not have hoped for a better result. as it wishes to negotiate bilaterally with South China Sea claimants rather than having to tackle a unified front from ASEAN. As Michael Wesley states:

> The Philippines and Vietnam demand that the organisation supports them in standing up to Beijing. On the other side are Cambodia, Laos and Myanmar, with no direct stake in the conflict and which refuse to endorse the Philippines' and Vietnam's confrontational stance. Indonesia, Malaysia and Singapore are concerned about the dispute, but believe that avoiding confrontation with China will improve the prospects for productive negotiations.[51]

Indonesia's Foreign Minister, Marty Natalegawa, responded by embarking on an intense round of shuttle diplomacy to Cambodia, Vietnam and the Philippines. Following these discussions, and in order to reduce the level of intramural tension between the ASEAN claimants, he personally drafted a 'six-point plan', which was publically released in late July 2012. According to one analyst, all the ASEAN countries provided their 'approval to the six principles of "ASEAN's Common Position" on the South China Sea', in particular a commitment to the DoC,[52] and an 'early adoption of a Code of Conduct'.[53] However, the ASEAN members still could not agree to a joint communiqué, and the six-point plan did not introduce anything new. At best, the latter may serve to shelve the dispute for the immediate future.[54] For example, the limitations of this diplomacy were evident when the ASEAN members failed to endorse a 'zero draft CoC' by Indonesia in September 2012,[55] and subsequently declined a request by the Philippines to renegotiate a unified position over the South China Sea at the November 2012 ASEAN Summit.[56]

A further complication concerns a belief, by some regional elite, that the South China Sea issue is a 'status quo dispute'. At one level, this is because a number of the claims are indefensible under international law, and this explains the unwillingness of China, for example, to seek recourse to international arbitration. At another level, some military and political elite have assessed that any change to the status quo will not be in their favour, given considerations such as China's military power. For example, one senior official from Vietnam stated that 'if anything changes regarding the dispute, it will not be in Vietnam's favour, the best we can hope for is to maintain the current status'.[57] Given these considerations, the next section analyses China's growing influence with some Southeast Asian states and how any associated geo-strategic ramifications (e.g. strengthened relations with the US) have affected calculations concerning Beijing's policy over the South China Sea.

Reconstituting an ASEAN consensus: Beijing to the rescue?

Back in 2004, Nicholas Khoo stated, 'in ASEAN's case it is clear that intra-ASEAN security relations are subordinate to those with outside powers'.[58] Today, this observation remains particularly pertinent to a number of the ASEAN members and their respective positions over the South China Sea. In addition to Michael Wesley's contentions above, the failure to issue a joint communiqué in July 2012 was symbolic of the continued divergence in the strategic alignments between the ASEAN members. During a rudimentary survey conducted by the author of 100 political and academic elite from all 10 of the ASEAN countries (2005–2007), a notable result was that the respondents from four of the ASEAN countries listed the United States as one of their top three strategic allies, while three other countries listed China as the same.[59] Such strategic diversity renders a common position on a sensitive issue such as territorial disputes particularly infeasible when the extra-mural disputant is a key strategic (and economic) partner for a number of the ASEAN countries.

In the case of Cambodia, it has been willing to sacrifice the collective interests of ASEAN over the South China Sea as China is now Cambodia's principle source of investment and foreign aid.[60] China ostensibly rewarded Cambodia two months later for having acting as a proxy by providing US$500 million in soft loans and a grant of US$24 million. Cambodia's Secretary of State for Finance publically thanked Beijing for its support and declared that China had 'voiced high appreciation for the part played by Cambodia as the chair of ASEAN to maintain good cooperation between China and ASEAN'.[61] Thus, during interviews in Phnom Penh, it was unsurprising that some government officials were unreserved in admitting that Chinese interests came first because 'Cambodia is a poor country' and 'Beijing provides the most support'.[62]

Meanwhile, China has also become Malaysia's primary source of trade, and the two countries share a number of common interests, including their mutual support for the ASEAN Plus Three Framework – rather than the East Asia Summit (EAS) – as it provides for a more exclusive form of regionalism that, inter alia, excludes the US and other non-Asian countries.[63] The relatively warmer relationship enjoyed between the two countries has been reflected in the level of restraint exercised by Kuala Lumpur when Chinese vessels (mainly fishing) regularly stray into its territory. China, in turn, has also been more flexible with Kuala Lumpur vis-à-vis fishing and hydrocarbon activities in waters disputed by the two countries.[64] Further, in the midst of protests against Chinese 'aggression' by Hanoi and Manila, Malaysia's Prime Minister Najib Abdul Razak actually praised Beijing for the 'remarkable restraint' that it had exercised.[65] Then, in 2013, the Prime Minister declared that he was in favour of joint development, and later, in August, his Defence Minister stated that 'just because you have enemies, doesn't mean your enemies are my enemies'.[66] Moreover, at a time when many of Malaysia's ASEAN counterparts are trying to discourage Chinese naval activity in the South China Sea, Malaysia announced that, for the first time, it would hold joint naval exercises with the PLA-N in 2014.[67]

For Brunei, the 2013 Chair of ASEAN, the maintenance of a constructive role that was representative of the diverse interests of ASEAN necessitated a very difficult balancing act, given its own trade and investment interests with China. Following the onset of the China–ASEAN Free Trade Agreement (CAFTA) in January 2010, trade between Brunei and China increased from US$422 million to US$1 billion – a rise of 142 per cent. During 2012, bilateral trade reached US$1.6 billion, and based on current trends two-way trade should exceed this figure in 2013.[68] Given these considerations, Brunei may have entered into a number of agreements with Beijing to mitigate any harm its role as the ASEAN Chair might cause to its relationship. Here, two particularly pertinent examples include the conclusion of a strategic partnership and a 14 October 2013 agreement for joint exploration between Brunei's stated-owned National Petroleum Company Sendirian Berhad and Beijing's state-owned China National Offshore Oil Company.[69] This follows from a Memorandum of Understanding on joint development that the two countries had been very quietly negotiating since 2010.[70] Such actions undermine ASEAN's influence vis-à-vis Beijing and reinforce China's (preferred) policy to negotiate over joint development and questions of sovereignty on a bilateral basis.

Nonetheless, Beijing's success in managing its relations with some key ASEAN members has resulted in two interdependent costs. First, the fragmentation of ASEAN unity has opened the door to a more active role for non-claimant states in ASEAN's fora (e.g. the United States). As noted, some ASEAN members have actually encouraged the US to play a more active diplomatic role. However, regardless of any such petitioning, the US will remain actively engaged due to a concern that ASEAN disunity and/or associated action by Beijing will negatively affect regional stability and its extensive alliance network. Consequently, the US has sought to address the issue in the ASEAN Regional Forum, the ASEAN Defence Ministerial Meeting Plus (ADMM-Plus) and the EAS.[71] Second, the success by which Beijing has driven a wedge between the ASEAN members has compelled Vietnam and the Philippines to strengthen their relations with the US and other countries such as Japan.

In the case of Vietnam, it has pursued closer military relations with the Philippines, South Korea, France, the United Kingdom, Japan, Russia, India and the United States.[72] Developments with the last three countries have been the most strategically significant. Due to a number of strategically informed bilateral agreements with Russia and India, year-on-year exports to each country rose by 236 per cent (US$991.6 million) and 200 per cent (US$829.8 million), respectively.[73] Vietnam has also entered into arrangements for joint development with state-owned enterprises from both Russia and India, which has significantly increased the costs of any coercive actions by Beijing in the waters associated with each lease.[74] Military relations with Russia have also notably improved as marked by several high-level procurement agreements, including the purchase of six Kilo-636 class fast-attack submarines.[75]

The strengthening of relations with India was symbolised through three major bilateral visits by Vietnam between 2011 and 2013. During the third visit (November 2013), several security agreements were finalised, as well as a major Memorandum of Understanding that built on a 2007 'strategic partnership'.[76] In the case of the US, Vietnam has pursued expanded defence collaboration as part of a wider 'comprehensive partnership' including several US naval visits, the training of Vietnamese military medical and technical staff, annual strategic dialogues and non-combat military exercises.[77] In 2013, Vietnam also issued a joint statement with Japan that noted their collective opposition to any attempt by Beijing to change the 'status quo' through force.[78]

Under its new government, the Philippines has become even more active in its opposition to Beijing's creeping sovereignty. On 21 May 2013, President Aquino announced an additional US$1.8 billion to modernise its navy, communications, intelligence and surveillance systems.[79] In 2012, during the peak of the Scarborough Shoal incident, the Filipino military sought to involve the US on the basis of its security treaty, something the US quickly evaded by 'arguing that the treaty does not require the US to intervene on behalf of the Philippines over reefs'.[80] Nonetheless, the US has publically acknowledged that the Philippines will need modernise its armed forces to the point where it has sufficient 'deterrent capability' to reinforce the likelihood of a diplomatic resolution to its disputes with China.[81] In this context, there has been a significant increase in the level of military assistance and aid to the Philippines.[82] The Philippines has also sought to benefit from the US 'pivot' back to Asia by entering into negotiations over a possible basing arrangement for the US armed forces. Thus, in August 2013, the two countries held their first round of discussions over an increased US rotational presence involving 'US ships, aircraft, marines and the use of Philippine military facilities including Subic Bay'.[83]

Moreover, the Philippines has returned to unilateral diplomacy and sought recourse to the Permanent Court of Arbitration in the Hague as provided by the terms of UNCLOS. However, China argued that the arbitral tribunal had no jurisdiction based on a set of exceptions submitted by Beijing in August 2006, and therefore refused to participate. The Philippines counter-argued that it is seeking arbitration over the interpretation of international law under UNCLOS rather than any of areas that may be exempt from a determination by the court (e.g. the delimitation of the territorial sea, exclusive economic zone or continental shelf).[84] As both are signatories to UNCLOS, the Permanent Court of Arbitration has since constituted a panel of judges and already held its preliminary hearings in Beijing's absence. A final determination over the points raised by the Philippines was expected to occur as early as 2014, but was delayed by Chinese objections.[85]

The above challenges notwithstanding, Brunei's year as the Chair of ASEAN (2013) has been depicted by some analysts to be relatively successful in relation to the South China Sea disputes.[86] However, aside from the earlier noted willingness of Brunei to curry favour with Beijing, a distinct shift in the nature of China's diplomacy occurred primarily because of a decision by Beijing to repair its damaged image.[87] Until 2013, Beijing had consistently argued that it would not consult or negotiate over the details of a CoC until the 'time is ripe'. Then, at the 19th ASEAN-China Senior Officials' Consultation, Beijing announced its willingness to commence discussions with ASEAN on a CoC later in the year.[88] The following week, at the 46th ASEAN Ministerial Meeting in Brunei, the joint communiqué confirmed 'formal consultations between ASEAN and China at the SOM level on the CoC . . . [with the aim] to reach an early conclusion of a Code of Conduct in the South China Sea'.[89] Between 14 and 15 September, ASEAN and China subsequently held their first formal 'consultations' (Beijing eschewed the term 'negotiations') at the 6th ASEAN-China SOM and the 9th ASEAN-China Joint Working Group Meeting on the Implementation of the DoC in Suzhou (China), and further consultations were held during the lead-up to the 23rd ASEAN Summit in Brunei (9 October). These discussions reportedly led to agreement over the modalities for future talks and a search-and-rescue hotline.[90]

Despite such minimalist outcomes, a joint statement by the 18 EAS countries welcomed the 'positive progress' that had been achieved.[91] However, on the ground, China's shift in approach has also been recognised, and various Vietnamese elite commented about Beijing's recent restraint during discussions at the sidelines of the regular Hanoi-based workshop on the South China Sea.[92] Beijing was also particularly active at the bilateral level through the continuation of significant aid to Laos and Cambodia, together with a pledge to help Thailand construct a high-speed railway.[93] During 2013, there have also been several high-level visits by Beijing throughout much of Southeast Asia (but not to the Philippines), including two visits by Foreign Minister Wang Yi and one by Premier Li Keqiang.[94] As Keck notes, 'China even agreed with Vietnam – the ASEAN nation it has clashed with most frequently besides the Philippines – to work towards resolving their row in the South China Sea'.[95]

While attempting to re-establish trust with nine of the ten ASEAN members, Beijing has been seeking to isolate the Philippines ever since the latter sought recourse to arbitration. China's new foreign minister, Wang Yi, avoided the Philippines during his regional visits, and when Philippine President Aquino announced he would be attending the Tenth China–ASEAN Expo in Nanning as the 'country of honour', China withdrew its invitation and requested that he visit 'at a more conducive time'.[96] Beijing has also continued to harass Philippines forces and fisherman, and has unilaterally imposed economic sanctions.[97] Beijing's actions are likely motivated by a desire for retribution over a perceived breach of what it deems to be the boundaries of *acceptable* conduct on the matter. Further, Beijing has long utilised divide-and-rule tactics, and it only needs to disenfranchise one ASEAN member to impede ASEAN's consensus-based decision-making system. Meanwhile, China has sought to isolate Japan in response to their escalating dispute over aspects of the East China Sea.[98] However, this has generated a further cost for Beijing, as both Japan and the Philippines now view China through a very similar lens. In the words of Japanese Prime Minister Shinzo Abe: '[f]or Japan, the Philippines is a strategic partner with whom we share fundamental values and many strategic interests'.[99] Consequently, Philippines President Aquino declared that the two countries had committed to a common stand against any future aggression in the South China Sea.[100]

While ASEAN may have become more proactive in early 2013,[101] Beijing appears to have regained the advantage by adapting its regional approach and by exploiting ASEAN's decision-making processes. In the context of the latter and before the Suzhou meeting, Wang responded to ASEAN's call for an 'early conclusion' for the code by stating that Beijing was in 'no rush', and that the process should be undertaken on a 'step-by-step' basis.[102] During the 'consultations' that followed, Beijing effectively stalled the process by insisting that initial discussions on a draft be downgraded to the ASEAN-China 'joint working group' level rather than the 'senior officials' level[103] – an echelon that will have less autonomy to make decisions and manage the process through to an effective and efficient conclusion. ASEAN also had to accept Beijing's proposal to establish an 'eminent persons and experts group' composed of academics and non-governmental officials to address 'technical issues' that might arise during consultations.[104] Here, Ian Storey argues that 'many observers both inside and outside ASEAN see this as yet another stalling tactic'.[105]

Beijing's preferred order for 'consultations' reinforces the idea that it is seeking to appease its ASEAN counterparts, but in reality has no intention to conclude a draft CoC within a reasonable time frame. In order to make progress, ASEAN prefers to hold separate discussions on the implementation of the DoC and the CoC to enable each set of consultations to proceed at its own pace. However, Beijing insists that any consultations concerning a CoC must take place under a concluded framework for the 2002 DoC.[106] Furthermore, one head of a Chinese state-funded institute declared that Beijing is only interested in the EEZs of the ASEAN claimant states, as this is where the accessible oil and gas is, and 'it is far too difficult to access these resources in the deeper parts of the sea'.[107] Here, a senior official from Vietnam's Ministry of Defence highlighted that there can be no discussion of joint development if Beijing's starting point is the EEZ of other countries.[108]

Given these considerations, Beijing will only cooperate at a pace that works to its advantage: it will seek to push forward when ASEAN unity is weak, but stall should ASEAN garner a more unified position. Meanwhile, even if agreement on the CoC were to become feasible, its conclusion will actually consolidate a new status quo, as any newly institutionalised norms of behaviour will only apply from the time of ratification.[109] This new status quo will include Beijing's effective control of the Scarborough Shoal, the Second Thomas Shoal, Reed Bank and Mischief Reef.[110] Therefore, Beijing will likely seek to maximise the extent to which it can demonstrate 'effective control' in other critical locations within the South China Sea before it finally ratifies the terms of the CoC.

Nonetheless, Beijing's shift in approach can be partly attributed to the consolidation of the new leadership under Xi Jingping. Some analysts have also noted that the CCP has been able to rein in its various ministries, departments and agencies, and thereby centralise its decision-making processes.[111] However, the recent declaration by the People's Liberation Army of an 'Air Defence Identification Zone' in the East China Sea brings the extent and nature of such 'centralisation' into question. Already, a notable divide has emerged between the explanations provided by Beijing's Ministry of Defence and attempts by its Foreign Ministry to retrospectively justify its purpose and intent.[112]

Perhaps even more troubling was the manner by which the Ministry of Defence responded to domestic cries of humiliation when it failed to enforce the zone following the flight of two unarmed US B-52 bombers into the area. In the face of domestic criticism, the PLA has since dispatched fighter jets to patrol the area.[113] While beyond the scope of the current chapter, a key challenge for the maintenance of stability and peace in the South China Sea will, in fact, be the domestic fragility of China.[114] Should the CCP face further instability and any associated challenges to regime legitimacy, then the greater threat would be a *reactive* CCP and/or PLA rather than a set of calculated (and rational) actions based on some 'grand strategy'. Under such circumstances, Beijing might seek to divert public opposition from the regime by inciting and/or exploiting hyper-nationalism over the South China Sea.

Retrospect and prospects

The evolution of the situation in the South China Sea is like the hour hand on a clock. If one watches it closely, it is hard to see any change. However, should one look away for a length of time, then it is always surprising how far it has advanced – this is Beijing's *creeping sovereignty*. While it appears that China is seeking to reinvigorate its charm offensive and curtail some of its more assertive actions, this is not only due to the efforts of ASEAN, but also the unilateral brinkmanship of other claimants and a likely reassessment by Beijing concerning the adverse consequences for its soft power in recent years. An associated increase to regional support for the US pivot and military build-ups are also likely to have figured prominently in any strategic reassessment by Beijing. In this context, the Filipino government's recourse to arbitration has actually benefited ASEAN's bargaining position, as an adverse ruling by the Hague against Beijing – regardless of its refusal to participate – has likely been assessed to be more detrimental than some limited collaboration with ASEAN.

'The solution most often discussed is to put aside sovereign claims and to agree to cooperate in exploration and exploitation of resources in disputed areas through joint development mechanisms'.[115] However, Beijing will only entertain this solution on a bilateral basis, and the absence of a multilateral arrangement renders any such solution near impossible when several competing claimants are involved. Thus, the key difficulty concerns the inability of the ASEAN claimants to gather a common position, while, in the case of China, it continues to insist on a bilateral approach to the dispute. Meanwhile, the disunity of ASEAN renders infeasible a collective position on sovereignty so long as the ASEAN claimants continue to abide by consensus-based decision-making. Here, only the relatively more democratic countries such as Indonesia and the Philippines have been open to change in ASEAN's method of decision-making.[116] ASEAN will not be likely to abandon 'consensus based decision making' and 'non-interference' until significant regime change and political reforms have been undertaken across the region – a prospect that is decades rather than years away.

At this point, the best that can be expected from ASEAN is the conclusion of a Code of Conduct. However, China is likely to support the CoC only when a new 'status quo' has sufficiently advanced in its favour. In this context, there are two potential risks regarding any eventual 'negotiations' over a future Code of Conduct. First, China may be willing to agree to a CoC that is barely a code, in that it provides very little by way of tangible constraints to Chinese actions in the South China Sea. Second, it might agree to a Code of Conduct where the provisions primarily benefit China. Consequently, ASEAN should negotiate on the basis that it is better not to finalise a Code of Conduct should Beijing be unwilling to negotiate in good faith or that the draft fail to be sufficiently balanced in the protections and norms of behaviour that it enforces.

Meanwhile, ASEAN also has some significant intramural challenges to address. First, decision-making continues to be undertaken based on 'self-interest' rather than the 'collective interests' of ASEAN. Second, some ASEAN countries are politically and economically reliant on China. One option that may help to reduce ASEAN's dilemmas is the establishment of a sub-ASEAN working group involving only the claimant states (e.g. ASEAN-X). The benefit of this approach is that it minimises the chance of disunity occurring in broader ASEAN forums and, in so doing, protects the credibility of ASEAN's regional centrality. It also ensures that only self-interested states are involved in the working group, which could increase the chances of reaching a consensus. Such an approach would also need to combine a willingness to pursue joint exploration in the areas that are more ambiguous as far as the interpretation of international law is concerned.

Nonetheless, even within an ASEAN-X mechanism, the creation and main-tenance of a collective position will remain very difficult to achieve, given the duality of some ASEAN claimant countries over the issue. Reviving ASEAN's early period of solidarity is now infeasible, as the members no longer share the same threat perceptions and too many of the ASEAN members depend on Beijing strategically, politically and economically. Critically, Beijing is also likely to resist any initiative that it calculates will multilateralise, internationalise and/or weaken its bargaining position over the dispute. Thus, the most realistic approach for both claimant and non-claimant states is to view ASEAN as an important venue to maintain dialogue and, in the process, hopefully mitigate the potential for tensions to rise even further. Beyond this, recourse to any form of protection and/or enforcement provided under international law (e.g. arbitration in the Hague) will be the more reliable option.

Notes

1 Shaun Narine, 'From Conflict to Collaboration: Institution Building in East Asia', *Behind the Headlines*, 65(5), 2008, http://dspace.cigilibrary.org/jspui/handle/123456789/23951 (accessed 2 June 2014).
2 Christopher B. Roberts, *ASEAN Regionalism: Cooperation, Values and Institutionalisation*, Routledge, London, 2012.
3 For other reasons, including its colonial heritage and its relatively newly independent status (1983), Brunei only established diplomatic relations with Beijing in 1991.
4 Sheldon W. Simon, 'China, Vietnam, and ASEAN: The Politics of Polarization', *Asian Survey*, 19(12), 1979, p. 1172.
5 The two other non-claimant ASEAN members at the time were Singapore and Thailand. Roberts, *ASEAN Regionalism*, p. 78.
6 Barry Wain, 'China Nibbles, ASEAN Dithers', *Wall Street Journal*, 10 March 1995.
7 'ASEAN Declaration on the South China Sea (Manila)', ASEAN Secretariat, www.aseansec.org/1196.htm (accessed 2 June 2014).
8 'ASEAN Declaration on the South China Sea (Manila)'.
9 'ASEAN Declaration on the South China Sea (Manila)'.
10 'Southeast Asia: International Code of Conduct Urged for Spratleys', *Inter Press Service*, 22 July 1992.
11 Rosemary Foot, 'Modes of Regional Conflict Management: Comparing Security Cooperation in the Korean Peninsula, China-Taiwan, and the South China Sea', in Amitav Acharya and Evelyn Goh (eds), *Reassessing Security Cooperation in the Asia-Pacific: Competition, Congruence, and Transformation*, MIT Press, Cambridge, MA, 2007, p. 97; Christopher B. Roberts, 'The Future of East and Southeast Asian Regionalism', in Andrew Tan (ed.), *East and Southeast Asia: International Relations and Security Perspectives*, Routledge, London, 2013, p. 79.
12 'Singapore Declaration', ASEAN Secretariat, www.aseansec.org/5120.htm (accessed 2 June 2014).
13 Roberts, *ASEAN Regionalism*, p. 78.
14 Marvin Ott, 'ASEAN and the South China Sea: A Security Framwork under Seige', Center for Strategic and International Studies, http://csis.org/publication/asean-and-south-china-sea-security-framework-under-seige (accessed 2 June 2014).
15 Ott, 'ASEAN and the South China Sea'.
16 Martin Abbugao, 'Philippines Shows Evidence of Chinese Occupation of Spratlys Reef', *Agence France-Presse*, 9 February 1995.
17 Michael Richardson, 'Chinese Gambit: Seizing Spratly Reef without a Fight', *International Herald Tribune*, 17 February 1995.
18 Derwin Pereira, 'ASEAN Ministers Concerned over Developments in Spratlys', *Straits Times*, 19 March 1995.
19 Cited in Wain, 'China Nibbles, ASEAN Dithers'.
20 Roberts, *ASEAN Regionalism*, p. 80.
21 Joshua Kurlantzick, 'China's Charm Offensive in Southeast Asia', Carnegie Endowment for International Peace, http://carnegieendowment.org/2006/09/01/china-s-charm-offensive-in-southeast-asia/979 (accessed 2 June 2014).

22 Further, 'Chinese research vessels and warships [also] continued to intrude into Philippine waters, laying down markers on unmarked reefs'. Anne Barrowclough, 'China and the Philippines in Stand-Off in South China Sea', *The Times*, 11 April 2013, p. 146.

23 Alan Collins, *Building a People-Oriented Security Community the ASEAN Way*, Routledge, London, 2013, p. 26.

24 Roberts, *ASEAN Regionalism*, p. 65.

25 Cathy Rose A. Garcia, 'RP Finally Takes up Spratlys in ASEAN Forum', *Business World*, 9 March 1999, p. 12.

26 Email correspondence with Barry Wain, Institute of Southeast Asian Studies (Singapore), 22 March 2005.

27 Ian Storey, 'The Institutionalisation of ASEAN-China Relations: Managing the South China Sea Dispute', in Ralf Emmers (ed.), *ASEAN and the Institutionalisation of East Asia*, Routledge, London, 2012, p. 152.

28 Donald E. Weatherbee, *International Relations in Southeast Asia: The Struggle for Regional Autonomy*, 2nd edn, Rowman & Littlefield, Plymouth, 2010, p. 147.

29 Christopher B. Roberts, 'China and the South China Sea: What Happened to Asean's Solidarity?', Institute of Defence and Strategic Studies, 2005, www.ntu.edu.sg/idss/ (accessed 2 June 2014).

30 Renato Cruz De Castro, 'The US-Philippine Alliance: An Evolving Hedge against an Emerging China Challenge', *Contemporary Southeast Asia*, 31(3), 2009, p. 414.

31 Barrowclough, 'China and the Philippines in Stand-Off in South China Sea'.

32 Willima M. Esposo, 'All Filipinos Should Now Rally around the Flag', *The Philippine Star*, 27 January 2013.

33 William Choong, 'Vietnam's Sino-US Dilemma', *Straits Times*, 30 August 2012. See also Carlyle A. Thayer, 'The Tyranny of Geography: Vietnamese Strategies to Constrain China in the South China Sea', *Contemporary Southeast Asia*, 33(3), 2011, p. 352.

34 Paul J. Bolt, 'Contemporary Sino-Southeast Asian Relations', *China: An International Journal*, 9(2), 2011, p. 285. See also Leszek Buszynski, 'Chinese Naval Strategy, the United States, ASEAN and the South China Sea', *Security Challenges*, 8(2), 2012, p. 25.

35 'Asia-Pacific', *Strategic Survey*, 111(1), 2011, p. 355.

36 Thayer, 'The Tyranny of Geography', p. 352.

37 Carlyle A. Thayer, 'ASEAN's Code of Conduct in the South China Sea: A Litmus Test for Community Building?', *The Asia-Pacific Journal: Japan Focus*, 10(34), 2012, p. 2.

38 Randi Fabi and Chen Aizhu, 'Analysis: China Unveils Oil Offensive in South China Sea Squabble', *Reuters*, 1 August 2012.

39 Bagus Saragih, 'RI Finds Common ASEAN Ground in Sea Dispute', *The Jakarta Post*, 23 July 2012.

40 For example, contrast the arguments contained in 'Stirring up the South China Sea (I)', International Crisis Group, Brussels, 2012, pp. 8–13.

41 Carlyle A. Thayer, 'South China Sea Developments in 2013: ASEAN Unity Restored, Sino-Philippine Tensions and ASEAN-China Consultations on a Code of Conduct', in the 5th International Workshop on the South China Sea: Cooperation for Regional Security Development, Melia Hotel, Hanoi, Diplomatic Academy of Vietnam and the Vietnam Lawyer's Association, 2013, p. 7.

42 Interview, Ministry of Defence (Hanoi), April 2013.

43 Thayer, 'Asean's Code of Conduct in the South China Sea', p. 3.

44 Thayer, 'Asean's Code of Conduct in the South China Sea', p. 3.

45 Thayer, 'Asean's Code of Conduct in the South China Sea', p. 3.

46 Dario Agnote, 'China "Temporizing" Talks on Code of Conduct in South China Sea', *Kyodo News*, 11 September 2012.

47 Thayer, 'Asean's Code of Conduct in the South China Sea', p. 3.

48 Donald K. Emmerson, 'ASEAN Stumbles in Phnom Penh', East Asia Forum, 23 July 2012, www.eastasiaforum.org/2012/07/23/asean-stumbles-in-phnom-penh-2/ (accessed 2 June 2014).

49 'Cambodia's Foreign Relations; Losing the Limelight', *The Economist*, 17 July 2012.

50 'ASEAN Struggles for Unity over South China Sea', *Agence France-Presse*, 12 July 2012.

51 Michael Wesley, 'What's at Stake in the South China Sea', *Lowy Institute Strategic Snapshots*, July 2012.

52 Thayer, 'The Tyranny of Geography'; Saragih, 'RI Finds Common ASEAN Ground in Sea Dispute'.

53 Donald K Emmerson, 'Beyond the Six Points: How Far Will Indonesia Go?', *East Asia Forum*, 29 July 2012.

54 Truong Thuy Tran, 'Code of Conduct: Possible Content, Who Participates, How to Conclude?', paper presented at the 5th International Workshop on the South China Sea: Cooperation for Regional Security Development, Melia Hotel, Hanoi, 11–12 November 2013, p. 3.

55 Ralf Emmers, 'ASEAN Neutrality and Unity over the South China Sea Disputes', in *5th International Workshop on the South China Sea: Cooperation for Regional Security and Development*, Melia Hotel, Hanoi, Diplomatic Academy of Vietnam and the Vietnam Lawyer's Association, 2013, p. 5; Yohanna Rirhena, 'RI Circulates Draft Code of Conduct on South China Sea', *The Jakarta Post*, 29 September 2012.

56 Donald K. Emmerson, 'Challenging ASEAN: The US Pivot through Southeast Asian Eyes', *Global Asia*, www.ct2014.com/ (accessed 2 June 2014).

57 Interview with Senior Official, Hanoi, January 2012.

58 Nicholas Khoo, 'Deconstructing the ASEAN Security Community: A Review Essay', *International Relations of the Asia-Pacific*, 4, 2004, p. 40.

59 Roberts, *ASEAN Regionalism*, p. 165.

60 Prashanth Parameswaran, 'China and Cambodia: With Friends Like These . . .', *China Brief*, 13(1), 2012.

61 'Brunei Carefully Pursues Binding Code to Settle South China Sea Dispute', *IHS Global Insight Daily Analysis*, 3 April 2013.

62 Interviews with government, Phnom Penh, April 2013.

63 Gilbert Rozman, 'East Asian Regionalism and Sinocentrism', *Japanese Journal of Political Science*, 13(1): 143–153, 2012.

64 Roberts, 'The Future of East and Southeast Asian Regionalism', p. 287.

65 'Stirring up the South China Sea (II): Regional Responses', International Crisis Group, Brussels, 2012, p. 11.

66 Thayer, 'South China Sea Developments in 2013', p. 23.

67 Ankit Panda, 'China and Malaysia to Hold Maritime Exercises: What Gives?', *The Diplomat*, 15 November 2013.

68 'China's Trade with Brunei in September 2013', *Xinhua's China Economic Information Service*, 4 November 2013.

69 Olivier Boyd, 'China Pursues Hydrocarbon Co-Operation in South China Sea with Brunei Joint Venture', *IHS Global Insight Daily Analysis*, 17 October 2013.

70 Christopher B. Roberts, 'Brunei Darussalam: Consolidating the Foundations of its Future?', in Daljit Singh (ed.), *Southeast Asian Affairs 2011*, ISEAS, Singapore, 2011, p. 43.

71 Emmers, 'ASEAN Neutrality and Unity over the South China Sea Disputes', p. 6.

72 'External Affairs, Vietnam', *Jane's Sentinel Security Assessment*, 6 July 2013.

73 'External Affairs, Vietnam'.
74 'China/Vietnam: Disputed Oil Province Still Locked up Tight', *Energy Compass*, 14 December 2012; Amitav Ranjan, 'Countering China: Vietnam Offers Five Blocks to India on Nomination Basis', *The Indian Express*, 21 November 2013; 'Checkmating the Dragon: A Tough Task Ahead', *Power Politics*, 10 June 2013.
75 'Russia to Hand Over First Submarine to Vietnam in November', *Vietnam.net*, 24 October 2013, http://english.vietnamnet.vn/fms/government/87557/russia-to-hand-over-first-submarine-to-vietnam-in-november.htm (accessed 2 June 2014).
76 Examples that are more specific include the provision by India for a $100 million line of credit for defence procurements, 'a high tech crime lab in Hanoi', support and training for Vietnamese submarine crews, and preliminary negotiations over the purchase of India-Russia jointly developed BrahMos supersonic cruise missiles. Ankit Panda, 'India and Vietnam Continue to Make Important Strategic Inroads', *The Diplomat*, 21 November 2013.
77 Carlyle A. Thayer, 'The US-Vietnam Comprehensive Partnership: What's in a Name', *The ASPI Strategist*, 31 July 2013.
78 'Japan, Vietnam Warn China over South China Sea', *Jiji Press*, 16 January 2013.
79 'An Idyllic Bay that Will Make China Sea Red', *Today (Singapore)*, 3 October 2013.
80 'External Affairs, Philippines', *Jane's Sentinel Security Assessment*, 5 January 2013.
81 'Philippines, US Military Mull Territorial Defence Force', *BBC*, 17 April 2013.
82 'External Affairs, Philippines'.
83 Thayer, 'South China Sea Developments in 2013', p. 12.
84 'New Commitment to a Code of Conduct in the South China Sea?', *The National Bureau of Asian Research*, 9 October 2013, p. 3.
85 'Philiippines Eyes Swift Conclusion of South China Sea Arbitration', *Thai News Service*, 29 October 2013.
86 Thayer, 'South China Sea Developments in 2013', p. 2; Luke Hunt, 'Brunei Caps off a Solid Year at Asean's Helm', *The Diplomat*, 12 October 2013.
87 Tran, 'Code of Conduct', p. 3.
88 Thayer, 'New Commitment to a Code of Conduct in the South China Sea?', p. 3.
89 'Joint Communique 46th ASEAN Foreign Ministers' Meeting, Bandar Seri Begawan', ASEAN, www.asean.org/news/asean-statement-communiques/item/joint-communique-46th-asean-foreign-ministers-meeting-bandar-seri-begawan-brunei-darussalam-29-30-june-2013 (accessed 2 June 2014).
90 Ian Storey, 'China Runs Rings around ASEAN; Bejing Has Repeatedly Blocked Meaningful Action in the South China Sea Disputes', *Wall Street Journal*, 2 October 2013.
91 'Code of Conduct for South China Sea', *The Japan Times*, 4 November 2013.
92 Discussions with Vietnamese government and academic interlocutors, Hanoi, 8–13 November 2013.
93 'Code of Conduct for South China Sea'.
94 'Foreign Media, Experts Laud Chinese Premier's Visit to S.E. Asia', *Xinhua*, 15 October 2013.
95 Zachary Keck, 'China Moves to Isolate Phiippines, Japan', *The Diplomat*, 30 August 2013.
96 Carlyle A. Thayer, 'To Isolate the Philippines, China Woos ASEAN', *The Diplomat*, 1 October 2013.
97 Robert Sutter and Chin-Hao Huang, 'Maritime Disputes – Why China's Tough Stance is Unsustainable', *Bangkok Post*, 23 July 2013.
98 Zachary Keck, 'Why is China Isolating Japan and the Philippines', *The Diplomat*, 26 October 2013.
99 'Japan's Abe Vows Sea Help to Philippines Amid China Row', *Agence France-Presse*, 27 July 2013.

100 'Aquino, Abe Vow Common Stand vs China', *The Philippine Daily Inquirer*, 28 July 2013. Japan has also increased its military aid to the Philippines, including the provision of 10 patrol boats to the Philippine coast guard. 'PM Abe Confirms Japan's Support for Phiippine Coast Guard', *Kyodo News*, 9 October 2013. Meanwhile, Beijing's image as a rising and responsible power was significantly dented when it initially offered US$100,000 in aid following the devastation of Typhoon Haiyan in the Philippines. In response to an international outcry, Beijing increased its aid by an additional US$1.5 million. Jane Perlez, 'China Increases Aid to the Philippines', *New York Times*, 14 November 2013.

101 For example, see Thayer, 'Asean's Code of Conduct in the South China Sea', p. 2.

102 'China Warns against Rush to Set Code of Conduct in South China Sea', *Xinhua*, 5 August 2013; Storey, 'China Runs Rings around ASEAN; Bejing Has Repeatedly Blocked Meaningful Action in the South China Sea Disputes'.

103 Zhang Yunbi, 'China, ASEAN to Ignore "Distractions",' *China Daily*, 16 September 2013.

104 'ASEAN, China Set to Speed up Code of Conduct', *Bangkok Post*, 16 September 2013.

105 Storey, 'China Runs Rings around ASEAN; Bejing Has Repeatedly Blocked Meaningful Action in the South China Sea Disputes'.

106 Thayer, 'To Isolate the Philippines, China Woos ASEAN'.

107 Interview, head of government think tank, Beijing, June 2013.

108 Interview, Ministry of Defence, Hanoi, June 2013.

109 James R. Holmes, 'ASEAN Should Reject a Code of Conduct in the South China Sea', *The Diplomat*, 5 September 2013.

110 Thayer, 'South China Sea Developments in 2013', p. 14.

111 Sarah Raine and Christian Le Miere, 'Beijing's Multifaceted Approaches', in Sarah Raine and Christian Le Miere (eds), *Regional Disorder: The South China Sea Dispute*, Adelphi Series, London, 2013, p. 68; Tran, 'Code of Conduct', p. 4.

112 Beijing's Ministry of Defence first announced the zone on 23 November 2013, which covers disputed territory, including the Senkaku/Diaoyu Islands currently controlled by Japan. As part of the announcement, the PLA declared that it would take 'defensive emergency measures' against unidentified aircraft that fly into the area. 'Beijing's Brinkmanship', *Wall Street Journal Asia*, 26 November 2013. Michael Fabey, 'Chinese "Air Defence ID Zone" Prompts Pentagon Response', *Aerospace Daily and Defence Report*, 26 November 2013. According the expansive Factiva News database, the first reported statement by the Foreign Ministry did not occur until the next day (24 November 2013), when it declared it had lodged a complaint against the reaction from the United States to the zone and (incorrectly) reiterated that the waters within the zone were part of Chinese territory. 'FM Spokesman: U.S. Should "Correct its Mistakes" over China's Setup of Air Defence Identification Zone', *Xinhua News Agency*, 24 November 2013. However, it was nearly a week after the initial announcement (29 November) that the Ministry of Foreign Affairs first *attempted* to provide a more reasoned justification of the ADIZ, where it distinguished between the zone and what it claims as its 'own airspace', noting that the ADIZ did not claim to be part of Beijing's 'exclusive' jurisdiction. 'Air Force Patrols of China's ADIZ Legitimate: Spokesperson', *Xinhua News Agency*, 29 November 2013. For a broader and more detailed analysis of the lack of centralised control of Beijing's various ministries, departments and agencies, see 'Stiring up the South China Sea (I)'.

113 Austin Ramzy, 'U.S. B-52 Flights Prompts Indignant Reaction in China', *New York Times*, 26 November 2013.

114 For an early but highly enlightening overview of the many aspects of state fragility faced by China, see Shaoguang Wang, 'The Problem of State Weakness', *Journal of Democracy*, 14(1): 36–42, 2003.

115 Weatherbee, *International Relations in Southeast Asia: The Struggle for Regional Autonomy*, pp. 146–147.
116 Christopher B. Roberts, 'State Weakness and Political Values: Ramifications for the ASEAN Community', in Ralf Emmers (ed.), *ASEAN and the Institutionalization of East Asia*, Routledge, London, 2012, p. 24.

8 The US rebalance to Asia and the South China Sea disputes

Ralf Emmers

Introduction

The United States is the predominant economic and military power in the world. It also calls itself a 'resident Pacific power'. US President Barack Obama has, in recent years, reinvigorated American strategic influence in the region through a pivot, or rebalance, to Asia. Originally named the strategic pivot, the policy move was later rebranded as a rebalancing of forces. In 2010, Secretary of State Hillary Clinton declared in a speech at the East-West Centre in Hawaii that 'America's future is linked to the future of the Asia-Pacific region; and the future of this region depends on America'.[1] The policy announcements emanating from the Obama administration have sought to sustain a long-term strategic presence in Asia, especially through a strong maritime focus. This chapter assesses specifically how and the extent to which the US rebalancing has impacted the South China Sea disputes. The South China Sea is at the centre of competing territorial, economic and strategic interests. The issue is complicated by the number of disputants. While the claimants to the Paracel Islands are the People's Republic of China (PRC), Taiwan and Vietnam, six states assert ownership over the Spratly Islands and/or their surrounding waters, namely Brunei, China, Malaysia, the Philippines, Taiwan and Vietnam. China's traditional claims are defined by an area limited by nine interrupted marks, often referred to in the literature as the U-shaped line or the nine-dash line, that cover most of the South China Sea. The United States is not a party to the sovereignty disputes, but it has declared having a vital interest in the freedom of navigation in the South China Sea and repeated its commitment to a peaceful resolution of the disputes in accordance with the principles of international law.[2] The chapter first examines the origins and main characteristics of the US rebalancing to Asia before describing the traditional American position on the sovereignty disputes in the South China Sea. It argues that the United States has not taken sides in the disputes and has restricted its interest to the preservation of the freedom of navigation. The chapter then discusses whether, and to what extent, Washington has changed its position in recent years in response to renewed Chinese assertiveness in the disputed waters. The chapter also reviews regional responses to the US involvement and concludes by assessing its impact on the peaceful management of the South China Sea disputes.

The US rebalance to Asia

Despite its geographic distance, the United States is central to Asian security. Washington can either mitigate or heighten existing tensions through its presence and network of bilateral alliances and security cooperation in the region. The coming to power of President George W. Bush in January 2001 led to a resurgence of unilateralism in American foreign policy. In Asia, the Bush administration repeatedly indicated its preference for flexibility and mobility over formal and institutionalised arrangements. Significantly, Bush had during his campaign strongly criticised President Bill Clinton's engagement policy with China, stating that he viewed the country as a 'strategic competitor' instead of a 'strategic partner'. Sino-US relations were repeatedly tested during the first few months of the Bush administration, with high-profile visits by then Taiwanese President Chen Shui-bian and the Dalai Lama to the United States in May 2001 angering the Chinese. These visits were preceded by an incident in April 2001 involving the collision of a US EP-3 spy plane with a Chinese fighter, resulting in the latter being lost in the South China Sea.

The 9/11 terror attacks immediately changed American foreign policy priorities. As Washington began to focus on the dangers of terrorism and proliferation, the United States seemed 'less inclined to view China as an actual or potential strategic competitor and more hopeful that, in a post-September 11 world, great powers would be united by common dangers'.[3] However, during Bush's second term, there were rising sources of tension between China and the United States. These resulted from the stalled six-party talks over the North Korean nuclear issue and concern generated over China's military build-up, among other issues.

Initial statements from the newly elected Obama administration suggested a renewed US interest in Asia and an American willingness to move beyond the issue of terrorism.[4] Since the terrorist attacks on 11 September 2001, the United States had been focused on fighting terrorism and the wars in Iraq and Afghanistan. Yet, in his first term, President Barack Obama refocused US diplomacy and military forces towards Asia. At the East Asia Summit (EAS) in 2011, Obama declared that the United States would maintain its presence in the region. Besides deepening its military ties with the Philippines through additional bilateral exercises and other means, Washington announced enhanced military relations with Indonesia, Malaysia, Pakistan, Singapore and Thailand. The United States also announced, in late 2011, the rotational deployment of 2,500 US Marines in Darwin, Australia, and the deployment of up to four of its littoral combat ships (LCS) in Singapore.[5] Finally, in June 2012, US Secretary of Defense Leon Panetta stated that the United States would commit 60 per cent of its naval capabilities to the Pacific Ocean by 2020.

The 2010 Quadrennial Defense Review (QDR), the first to be released by the Obama administration, had already referred to three groups of security partners, namely formal allies, strategic partners and prospective strategic partners.[6] The Philippines and Thailand were defined as US treaty allies. The QDR identified Singapore as a strategic partner, while Indonesia, Malaysia and Vietnam were classified as prospective strategic partners. The US rebalance was further discussed in the *Defense Strategic Guidance* released in January 2012.[7]

Beyond its military component, the US rebalance has also been characterised by a diplomatic and economic dimension. Under the Bush administration, Washington was viewed regionally as mostly disinterested in Asian multilateral cooperation. This was felt most acutely when Secretary of State Condoleezza Rice failed to attend the ministerial meetings of the ASEAN Regional Forum (ARF) in 2005 and 2007. The Obama administration quickly reversed this policy by engaging regional bodies such as the Association of Southeast Asian Nations (ASEAN).[8] Significantly, the administration acceded to ASEAN's Treaty of Amity and Cooperation (TAC) by presidential decree in July 2009, which opened the door for the United States to join the EAS in November 2011. US Secretary of Defense Robert Gates also attended the first ASEAN Defense Ministers' Meeting-Plus (ADMM-Plus) in October 2010. On the economic front, the United States ratified the Korea-US Free Trade Agreement (KORUS) and joined the Trans-Pacific Partnership (TPP) negotiations in November 2009.

It is important to mention that the United States has never neglected Asia, either strategically or economically. The US has historically been committed to the Western Pacific, especially in terms of preventing the rise of a competing naval power, as well as guaranteeing as public goods the freedom of navigation and commerce. These strategic objectives have been at the core of the hub-and-spoke system of alliances based on the San Francisco Peace Treaty of 1951. The Obama administration has nonetheless paid increased attention to the geographical area expected to generate the most economic growth in the next 20 years, and also where the greatest geopolitical challenge to US global predominance is to be found. In an influential *Foreign Policy* article, Hillary Clinton explained that a 'strategic turn to the region fits logically into our overall global effort to secure and sustain America's global leadership'.[9] The United States has repeatedly stressed that the rebalance is not about the containment of China, but rather a recalibration of its diplomacy and military forces. The American decision to pivot to Asia has still been perceived, especially in Beijing, as a response to China's growing regional ambitions.

It is too soon to say, however, whether the United States will be able to afford its long-term ambitions in Asia, especially in light of automatic spending cuts and the constraints they impose on defence budgets. In addition, it is still unclear whether the Obama administration will, in its second term, be equally committed to the rebalance to the region. For example, it is worth noting that Barack Obama and John Kerry, the new Secretary of State, decided to travel, respectively, to Israel and Europe rather than Asia as their first foreign visits in early 2013. Moreover, in contrast to Hillary Clinton, Kerry has become deeply engaged in the Israeli-Palestinian peace process. The Secretary of State addressed these concerns by reaffirming the US commitment to regional peace and stability at the ARF meeting in Brunei in July 2013.

Traditional US position on the South China Sea

There is a growing asymmetry of naval power in the South China Sea to the advantage of China. The country possesses a significant and rising military edge when compared to the Southeast Asian claimants. The only power capable of countering rising Chinese naval capabilities in the South China Sea has been the United States, particularly through its Seventh Fleet.[10] Yet, Washington has traditionally been unwilling to get involved in the territorial disputes over the semi-enclosed sea. The absence of an external source of countervailing power in the disputed waters has thus not resulted from a long-term American strategic retreat from the area. Instead, it has arisen from its unwillingness to get involved in the question of sovereign jurisdiction.

Though following closely the developments in the South China Sea, the United States has consistently limited its interest to the preservation of the freedom of navigation, including commercial shipping, the mobility of its Seventh Fleet and the conduct of military surveillance activities. Blair and Lieberthal remind us that the 'United States has a very long tradition of promoting and protecting the free flow of trade over the world's seas'.[11] The United Nations Convention on the Law of the Sea (UNCLOS) ensures the freedom of navigation, the right of innocent passage and the passage through straits.[12] Still, the issue of military surveillance activities has remained a bone of international contention, as well as a source of tension in Sino-US relations. Graham notes that naval powers such as the United States tend to 'assert maximalist freedoms of navigation and overflight', while many coastal states such as China, India and Malaysia 'prefer to keep the reach of foreign powers at arm's length'.[13] The question of military surveillance is critical in the South China Sea. Indeed, the freedom of navigation principle is in this context mostly associated with the freedoms of navigation and over flight of military ships and aircrafts, as no restriction to commercial shipping is feared in the disputed waters.[14] Due to its own economic interests, China is not expected to interrupt the shipping lanes that cross the South China Sea.

It has remained unclear how far the United States would go to support either Taiwan or the Philippines should conflict occur in the South China Sea. The United States continues to give protection to Taiwan through the Taiwan Relations Act of 1979. This was best evidenced in 1996. China's military exercises in the Taiwan Straits in March 1996 to influence the Taiwanese presidential election led Washington to deploy two carrier squadrons, the largest deployment of US forces in the Pacific since the Vietnam War. If Taipei were to instigate military action for independence on its own, however, the certainty of American backing is less assured. The United States has also continued to sell arms to Taiwan. The Taiwan Relations Act declares the obligation of the US to 'provide Taiwan with arms of a defensive character'.[15] A Chinese-dominated South China Sea would give the People's Liberation Army Navy (PLA-N) a strategic advantage over the United States and its defence of Taiwan. Importantly, one area of tentative agreement between Beijing and Taipei exists on the issue of the Paracel and Spratly

Islands. Both parties acknowledge that the islands are in Chinese territory, putting them in contention with claimants in Southeast Asia.

The Philippines has traditionally relied on the United States to guarantee its security. Washington has, however, repeatedly stated that the Philippine-claimed territories in the South China Sea are not covered by the Mutual Defense Treaty of 30 August 1951, which ties the Philippines to the United States. For instance, on 8 February 1995, the Philippines discovered the Chinese occupation of Mischief Reef located in Philippine-claimed waters. The Mischief Reef incident occurred after a significant development in US-Philippine relations, when American troops were forced to abandon their military bases they had occupied in the Philippines. The Philippine Senate had denied a new base treaty with the United States in September 1991, leading to a complete withdrawal from Subic Bay Naval Base and Clark Air Base by November 1992. By calling for the withdrawal of US forces, the Philippines removed the primary source of deterrence and security protection it had. Chinese military forces were able to capitalise on this power vacuum by establishing structures on Mischief Reef in 1995. The incident did not lead to a strong US diplomatic reaction, except for a statement on the freedom of navigation. Joseph Nye, then US Assistant Secretary of Defense for International Security, declared on 16 June 1995 that the United States would ensure the free passage of ships in the case of a conflict in the Spratlys that would affect the freedom of navigation. The Philippines eventually signed a Visiting Forces Agreement with the United States in February 1998, which was later ratified by the Philippine Senate in May 1999. US-Philippine military relations also further improved after the 9/11 terrorist attacks.

Besides the Philippines, Vietnam is another Southeast Asian state party to the sovereignty disputes. China remains the largest perceived geopolitical threat to Vietnam. This perception derives from its turbulent history with China, as well as geographic proximity. The dispute over the Paracels resulted in armed combat in 1974, when Chinese forces took possession of the island chain from the Vietnamese. The Spratly issue has also seen violence between Vietnam and China. Military conflict between Vietnamese and Chinese naval forces over the islands in 1988 left over 70 Vietnamese dead. Bilateral relations have improved since having been normalised in November 1991, although a clash between Chinese patrol vessels and a Vietnamese boat still led to the death of one Vietnamese sailor in 2007. On the energy front, the Chinese state-owned China National Offshore Oil Corporation (CNOOC) invited, in June 2012, foreign energy companies to tender for exploration rights for nine oil blocks in a southern area of the South China Sea. Vietnam reacted angrily to the CNOOC tender, stating that the area under consideration was located within its 200 nautical mile exclusive economic zone (EEZ), and that it impinged on blocks Hanoi had already awarded to international companies for oil exploration.[16]

The United States has significantly improved its bilateral ties with Vietnam since the establishment of diplomatic relations between the two countries on 11 July 1995. In 2003, a US Navy ship entered Vietnamese waters for the first time since the end of the Vietnam War. Defence ties have continued to strengthen since this symbolic port visit. Still, despite China's assertiveness and its threat to Vietnam's energy security, Hanoi has not reached a formal or tacit alliance with Washington. Hanoi has therefore not gained access to an external source of countervailing power to deter Beijing's actions in the South China Sea. Washington is arguably not keen to forge alliance commitments with Hanoi due to historical reasons, but also in an attempt not to further antagonise Beijing. Moreover, Hanoi has, since the early 1990s, adopted a more diversified foreign policy consisting of avoiding forming new alliances with any of the great powers, developing instead new friendships and promoting economic and trade links.

US response to rising Chinese assertiveness

The US position on the South China Sea has not fundamentally changed in recent years. Washington is still not taking a stand on the sovereignty question, and it continues to limit its core interest to the freedom of navigation in the disputed waters. Still, the United States has become increasingly concerned over the rise of the Chinese naval capabilities and uncertainty over China's commitment to the freedom of navigation principle in East Asian seas. In response, Washington 'has adopted a higher profile policy in support of its allies involved in maritime territorial disputes with China'.[17] The build-up of China's Southern Fleet, even if it is gradual, is a growing concern for the United States. The PLA-N has continued to expand its conventional submarine capabilities (Song, Yuan and Kilo classes), as well as to develop a smaller number of nuclear-powered submarines. China has purchased a large number of destroyers, including from the Russian-built *Sovremenny* class, and frigates. The PLA-N is also in the process of developing an aircraft carrier capability. Finally, it is constructing an underground nuclear submarine base near Sanya on Hainan Island. The base will significantly expand China's strategic presence in the South China Sea by enabling increased Chinese submarine activity in the disputed waters. A Chinese-dominated South China Sea would give China control over the sea lanes that cross the area, and therefore a strategic advantage over the United States.

Despite its growing military power, it is important not to exaggerate the immediate Chinese threat to the American naval primacy in the region. Having acquired new technology, Beijing still requires time for those technologies to be integrated into its existing force structure before they are fully operational. Moreover, China is not yet capable of sustaining naval operations far away from its mainland bases. Discussing the broader Western Pacific, Blumenthal writes that:

> the PLA lacks a sustained power projection capability associated with asserting full control over the area, including sufficient at-sea replenishment and aerial refueling capabilities, modern destroyers with advanced air defense capabilities, and nuclear submarines, as well as regional bases to support logistical requirements.[18]

Finally, the reasons behind the Chinese naval build-up go beyond the sovereignty disputes in the South China Sea. Other factors that drive the build-up include guaranteeing China's economic prosperity and energy supplies, which necessitate protecting sea lanes of communication and the traffic that proceeds through the Strait of Malacca and the South China Sea. Guaranteeing the safety of commercial shipping is an area of maritime security where American and Chinese interests tend to converge, as both their national economies depend on rising trade flows.

Nevertheless, a development occurred in 2009 that deepened American concern over rising Chinese assertiveness. The incident, involving the harassment of the ocean surveillance vessel USNS *Impeccable* by Chinese navy and civilian patrol vessels south of Hainan Island in March 2009, caused alarm in Washington and most Southeast Asian capitals. While Beijing claimed that the *Impeccable* was involved in marine scientific research in its EEZ that requires Chinese consent, Washington argued that the activities of the surveillance vessel were legitimate under the freedom of navigation principle. The United States perceived the *Impeccable* incident as a blatant case of China interfering against military surveillance activities undertaken within its 200 nautical mile EEZ. Referring to the incident, Graham notes that the issue of military surveillance has soured Sino-US relations in the South China Sea, and 'is central to the current American diplomatic concern with upholding freedom of navigation'.[19]

Another significant escalation occurred in April 2012 with Chinese and Philippine vessels involved in a stand-off at Scarborough Shoal in the South China Sea. Philippine naval authorities had discovered several Chinese fishing vessels anchored at the Shoal disputed by both China and the Philippines. A Philippine navy ship attempted to arrest the Chinese fishermen, allegedly accused of poaching and illegal fishing. Two Chinese maritime surveillance ships intervened, however, and prevented the arrest from occurring. These events coincided with the Philippines and the United States holding their annual military exercises on Palawan Island.[20]

The Scarborough Shoal incident led to a tense stand-off between the Philippine navy ship and the Chinese maritime vessels, and eventually resulted in severe tensions between Beijing and Manila that lasted for several weeks.[21] In case of a clash of arms involving the Philippine Navy and Chinese vessels, Washington would have been forced to consult with Manila as a treaty ally and possibly get involved in the dispute. The risks involved with such a scenario were carefully considered in Washington. The United States did not openly side with the Philippines during the Scarborough Shoal stand-off, opting instead to focus its efforts on discreet diplomacy and the de-escalation of the situation. This arguably undermined the credibility of the US defence commitment to the Philippines.

US diplomacy on the South China Sea

At the Shangri-La Dialogue in June 2010, US Secretary of Defense Robert Gates declared that while the United States does not take sides in the sovereignty disputes, it would however oppose any action that could threaten the freedom of navigation in the South China Sea. A statement made by US Secretary of State Hilary Clinton at the ARF in July 2010 declaring that the United States has a national interest in the freedom of navigation in the South China Sea further angered China.[22] Her comments were perceived by Beijing as a form of external interference. Commenting on her intervention at the 2010 ARF meeting, Clinton later wrote in *Foreign Policy* that 'the United States helped shape a region-wide effort to protect unfettered access to and passage through the South China Sea, and to uphold the key international rules for defining territorial claims in the South China Sea's waters'.[23] Clinton again mentioned the South China Sea at the ARF meeting held in Bali in July 2011. President Barack Obama himself raised the South China Sea question at the EAS in Bali in November 2011. He restated that the United States takes no sides in the sovereignty disputes, but that its interests include the freedom of navigation and unimpeded international commerce in the semi-enclosed sea. Chinese Premier Wen Jiabao responded by reaffirming the freedom of navigation principle and calling for a peaceful resolution of the South China Sea disputes.

The United States has, in recent years, openly supported attempts by ASEAN to negotiate a Code of Conduct (CoC) for the South China Sea with China. A first step was taken in this direction with the signing of the Declaration on the Conduct of Parties in the South China Sea (DoC) by China and the ASEAN members in November 2002. The agreement was intended to prevent further tensions over the disputed territories and to reduce the risks of military conflict in the South China Sea. The parties to the declaration stipulated their adherence to the principles of the United Nations Charter, UNCLOS, the TAC, and the Five Principles of Peaceful Coexistence. They agreed to resolve their territorial disputes by peaceful means, 'without resorting to the threat or use of force, through friendly consulta-tions and negotiations by sovereign states directly concerned, in accordance with universally recognized principles of international law'.[24]

Yet, conflict prevention has stalled since 2002, as no real progress has been made towards the implementation of the 2002 DoC.[25] The guidelines for developing a Code of Conduct for the South China Sea signed by China and the ASEAN countries in July 2011 were non-specific and generally perceived as dis-appointing. November 2012, the tenth anniversary of the DoC, was initially set as a provisional deadline for the completion of a code of conduct for the South China Sea in time for the ASEAN Summit to be held in Cambodia. Instead, the parties involved failed to even start the negotiation for a CoC, as China declared that the 'time was not yet ripe' to do so.

Besides China's diplomatic resistance, ASEAN's own disunity on the South China Sea was highlighted in 2012. After the Vietnamese and Indonesian chair-manships of ASEAN in 2010 and 2011, respectively, Cambodia acting as the ASEAN chair and a close economic partner of China sought to appease Beijing by minimising the internationalisation of the South China Sea issue. This first occurred at the ASEAN Ministerial Meeting (AMM) held in Phnom Penh in July 2012, when the Southeast Asian states failed to issue a joint communiqué, a first in the organisation's 45-year history, due to differences over the South China Sea question. The Philippines had insisted on a reference to the stand-off between Manila and Beijing at Scarborough Shoal earlier in 2012, but Cambodia refused on the grounds that the territorial disputes with China are bilateral.

While present at the ARF meeting that followed the 2012 AMM debacle, Hillary Clinton did not interfere in this intra-ASEAN issue. Still, Washington viewed the absence of Southeast Asian unity on the South China Sea as a diplomatic setback and a constraint on its regional diplomacy. ASEAN has traditionally been divided on the South China Sea due to a lack of consensus among the member states on how to address the sovereignty disputes, but also more generally a rising China. The members have differential relationships with China and contrasting views on its potential threat. In addition, some members have conflicting claims in the South China Sea, while others are not concerned about the problem of sovereignty. These sources of disunity have complicated the attainment of a collective stance and undermined the regional impact of American diplomacy, at least in terms of drawing the Southeast Asian states into the US camp and preserving the freedom of navigation principle in the South China Sea.

Beijing eventually proposed, in April 2013, to hasten progress on the COC at a special meeting involving the foreign ministers from the ASEAN countries and China. At their Summit held in Brunei that same month, all the ASEAN leaders favoured working with China on negotiating a CoC for the South China Sea. Consultations on a code finally started in September 2013. Yet, China seems only prepared to support a non-constraining agreement that focuses on dialogue and confidence-building rather than conflict management. China is unwilling to negotiate a document that could be perceived domestically as a concession with regard to its territorial claims. Moreover, the American support for a code of conduct has been considered in Beijing as a form of interference from an external party. At the 2013 ARF meeting, John Kerry reiterated the US position on the South China Sea and indicated his support for the negotiation of a 'substantive Code of Conduct' to preserve regional stability.

Regional responses to the US involvement

The distribution of power between China and the Southeast Asian claimants is rapidly shifting in Beijing's favour. Moreover, since 2010, there has been a significant increase in the number of incidents all over the South China Sea involving the harassment of survey vessels, the cutting of cables and the repeated arrest of fishermen. In response, the Philippines and Vietnam have sought to strengthen their own naval capabilities, as well as the military structures on the reefs and islands they respectively occupy. For example, Hanoi announced the purchase of six Russian Kilo class submarines in April 2009. Still, Vietnam does not have the military capacity to compete with China, as the Vietnamese Navy continues to suffer from ancient platforms and poorly funded programmes. The Philippines fare even worse than Vietnam. The capabilities of the Philippine

Navy and Philippine Air Force are weak, despite a national effort to modernise the military and upgrade its equipment.

The Philippines and Vietnam have therefore sought to gain from American military assistance to contain China in the South China Sea. Vietnam has upgraded its defence relations with the United States and welcomed the rebalancing of its military forces to the region. Ross writes that in 2010:

> Secretary of State Clinton twice visited Hanoi and called for a US-Vietnam 'strategic partnership', Secretary of Defense Robert Gates visited Hanoi, a US aircraft carrier hosted Vietnamese civilian and military leaders, and the United States held its first joint naval exercise with Vietnam.[26]

Since 2010, the United States and Vietnam have conducted annual naval exercises and Hanoi has opened the commercial repair facilities at Cam Ranh Bay to all navies. Secretary of Defense Leon Panetta visited Cam Ranh Bay in June 2012, and the US Navy has sent Military Sealift Command ships for minor repairs. Likewise, Manila has publicly supported the US rebalance.[27] The Philippines has reinforced its defence arrangement with the United States through the holding of more joint naval exercises and asked the United States to deploy spy planes in the South China Sea. The Philippines has offered greater access to its military facilities in exchange for increased US military assistance. In July 2013, Manila also announced plans to relocate air force and navy camps to Subic Bay (a former US base closed in 1992) to gain faster access to the South China Sea.

Hanoi and Manila have responded positively to the US rebalance due to their growing concerns over Beijing's renewed assertiveness in the South China Sea. The United States is keen to preserve the freedom of navigation principle in the disputed waters in light of China's rising naval capabilities. This has provided the Philippines and Vietnam with additional diplomatic leverage in their respective sovereignty disputes with China, boosting their own activities to confront Beijing in the South China Sea.[28] Nonetheless, questions remain in the Philippines and Vietnam over whether the United States can sustain its pivoting of military forces in light of budget cuts at the Pentagon. Moreover, while welcoming the US rebalancing, the two Southeast Asian countries do not want to be forced to choose between Washington and Beijing.

Besides the Philippines and Vietnam, it is important to discuss how the two other Southeast Asian claimants have perceived the US rebalance. Despite its often anti-Western rhetoric, Malaysia has perceived the US presence in Southeast Asia as necessary to preserve regional stability. Yet, in contrast to Hanoi and Manila, Kuala Lumpur has been less supportive of the military component of the US rebalance. Malaysia has traditionally adopted a more neutral foreign policy independent from external assistance or interference. Malaysia has also been less concerned about a rising China, and bilateral ties with Beijing have continued to improve since the early 1990s. On the South China Sea, Malaysia's diplomatic stand has gradually come closer to the Chinese position. Kuala Lumpur has favoured bilateral negotiations with Beijing and preferred to avoid a constraining regional code of conduct or external mediation. Feeling less threatened by a rising China, Malaysia has been more concerned about the pivoting of US military forces and the cycle of mistrust and great power competition it could generate.

The position adopted by Brunei is, to some extent, similar to its immediate neighbour. The Sultanate has established an EEZ of 200 nautical miles that extends to the south of the Spratly Islands and comprises Louisa Reef. Yet, Brunei does not lay territorial claim to the reef, and it is the only party involved in the disputes not to control features. Like Malaysia, Brunei considers the South China Sea question to be predominantly a bilateral rather than a multilateral issue. It has not rejected Beijing's claims to the disputed waters, and 'unlike Vietnam's and the Philippines' relations with China, the South China Sea dispute does not overshadow Sino-Bruneian ties'.[29] While the Sultanate has not officially responded to the US rebalance, it does not support a further militarisation of the South China Sea disputes.

How has Beijing reacted to the US rebalancing to Asia and its focus on the South China Sea? The initiatives adopted by the Obama administration have caused concern in Beijing. In particular, there is a strong perception in China that the United States is enhancing its involvement in the South China Sea and that Washington is thus interfering in what it considers to be a bilateral issue with the four Southeast Asian claimant states. As Beijing and Washington compete for regional influence, there is 'little doubt that the two are engaged in a struggle for the "hearts and minds" of Southeast Asia'.[30]

The United States is likely to remain the hegemon in the Asia-Pacific in the years to come, although its exercise of power is being eroded by the rise of China. Beijing perceives the US rebalance and its focus on the South China Sea as an attempt by the United States to contain its peaceful rise in the region. Related to this issue are the close relations linking Washington to its regional allies and how such ties are perceived in China as an attempt to constrain its power. From a Chinese point of view, the United States is seeking to contain China by strengthening its bilateral alliances and allocating more troops and means to the region. The Chinese Defense Ministry published a defence White Paper in April 2013 that alluded to the United States and its rebalancing to Asia. The report said, '[S]ome country has strengthened its Asia-Pacific military alliances, expanded its military presence in the region, and frequently makes the situation tenser'.[31] Beijing also considers Philippine activities in the disputed waters, for example in Scarborough Shoal, to be orchestrated by Washington. For China, the United States has created an issue over the freedom of navigation in the South China Sea to justify an enhanced military presence in the region to contain its rise. Yet, Beijing also realises that the rebalance, with its limited military troop deployments, does not affect the overall power distribution in Asia.

At the diplomatic level, China and the United States increasingly adopt a confrontational approach towards the South China Sea issue but they seek to prevent a rapid militarisation of the disputes. Beijing and Washington still regard the South China Sea as a problem that requires a diplomatic rather than a military solution, and they are content, for now at least, to let ASEAN lead the conflict management process. They disagree, however, over where the South China Sea disputes should be discussed and how they should be resolved. While the United States wants the question to be highlighted at the ARF, the ADMM-Plus and the EAS, and ultimately to be resolved through international law, all this remains highly problematic for China.[32] Beijing has been concerned over any attempt at internationalising the South China Sea disputes, preferring instead to discuss these matters bilaterally with the smaller Southeast Asian claimants. In that sense, China considers the US rebalance to have had a negative impact on the South China Sea disputes and to have further complicated conflict management in the disputed waters.

Conclusion

The United States has traditionally remained a neutral party in the sovereignty disputes over the South China Sea and limited its interest to the preservation of the freedom of navigation. It officially supports no claims in the area. Yet, as part of its wider rebalance to Asia, the American position on the South China Sea has changed, up to a point, in recent years. While the United States is still not taking sides in the sovereignty disputes, it is concerned over the rise of China's capabilities and uncertain over Beijing's commitment to the freedom of navigation principle in the disputed waters.

The United States has responded by reinforcing its defence relations with the Philippines, a treaty ally, and deepening bilateral ties with Vietnam, a prospective strategic partner. This has provided the two Southeast Asian nations with some external military assistance and additional diplomatic leverage vis-à-vis China. Hanoi and Manila have therefore relied on the US rebalance to advance their sovereignty claims in the South China Sea. In addition to bilateralism, the United States has paid close attention to regional multilateral diplomacy. By relying on the ASEAN-led institutions (ARF, ADMM-Plus and EAS), the Obama administration has acknowledged the centrality of ASEAN in the institutional architecture emerging in the Asia-Pacific. Still, the lack of cohesion and unity among the Southeast Asian states on the South China Sea question has, to some extent, undermined the impact of multilateral diplomacy. While welcomed by the Philippines and Vietnam, the military component of the US rebalance has caused some concern in Malaysia and Brunei. China itself perceives the rebalance and its focus on the South China Sea as a form of interference in what it considers to be a bilateral issue with the Southeast Asian claimant states, and more generally as an attempt by the United States to contain its peaceful rise in Asia.

To conclude, it is important to assess the extent to which the US rebalancing to Asia has impacted the South China Sea disputes. It can be argued that the US rebalance has only had a minimal strategic impact on the South China Sea disputes. With its limited rotational military deployments and bilateral exercises, the United States has not provided the Philippines and Vietnam with a countervailing power to deter Chinese assertiveness in the South China Sea. The two Southeast Asian claimants have therefore not been able to follow a policy of balancing through external association against China. A more immediate impact has been felt in the diplomatic realm, however. The rebalance and its focus on the South China Sea have contributed to the internationalisation of the sovereignty disputes. The United States has repeatedly raised the issue at international forums. It has also called on all the parties involved to negotiate a Code of Conduct for the South China Sea and expressed its commitment to a peaceful resolution of the sovereignty disputes based on the principles of international law. This has provided the Philippines and Vietnam with some diplomatic room for manoeuvre, and to some extent undermined China's negotiation position internationally. Beijing has traditionally called for the South China Sea issue not to be discussed multilaterally, preferring instead to negotiate bilaterally with the other claimants. Still, the United States is partly dependent on ASEAN and its ability to speak with one voice on the South China Sea. Limits to the ASEAN consensus should therefore be expected to restrict US diplomacy on the disputes in the years to come.

Notes

1   Secretary of State of the United States, Hillary Clinton, Speech delivered at the East-West Center, Honolulu, Hawaii, 14 January 2010.
2   Hillary Clinton, 'America's Pacific Century', *Foreign Policy*, November 2011, p. 58.
3   Aaron L. Friedberg, 'The Future of US-China Relations', *International Security*, 30(2), Fall 2005, p. 7.
4   'Hillary Clinton Promises to Attend ASEAN Foreign Minister, ARF Meetings', *China View*, 19 February 2009, http://news.xinhuanet.com/english/2009-02/19/content_10844924.htm (accessed 2 June 2014).
5   The USS *Freedom* was the first LCS to be deployed to Singapore's Changi Naval Base in April 2013 for an eight-month period.
6   United States Department of Defense, 'Quadrennial Defense Review', 1 February 2010, www.defense.gov/QDR (accessed 2 June 2014).
7   United States Department of Defense, 'Sustaining U.S. Global Leadership: Priorities for 21st Century Defense', 3 January 2012, www.defense.gov/news/Defense_Strategic_Guidance.pdf (accessed 2 June 2014).
8   Ralf Emmers, Joseph Chinyong Liow and See Seng Tan, *The East Asia Summit and the Regional Security Architecture*, Maryland Series in Contemporary Asian Studies, University of Maryland School of Law, Baltimore, MD, 2011, pp. 29–34.
9   Clinton, 'America's Pacific Century', p. 58.
10 Lee Lai To, 'China, the USA and the South China Sea Conflicts', *Security Dialogue*, 34(1), 2003, p. 27.
11 Dennis Blair and Kenneth Lieberthal, 'Smooth Sailing: The World's Shipping Lanes Are Safe', *Foreign Affairs*, 86(5), September/October 2007, p. 12.
12 1982 Convention in the Official Text of the United Nations Convention on the Law of the Sea with Annexes and Index, United Nations, New York, 1983.
13 Euan Graham, 'Gazing Down at the Breakers', in Brendan Taylor, Nicholas Farrelly and Sheryn Lee (eds), *Insurgent Intellectual: Essays in Honour of Professor Desmond Ball*, Institute of Southeast Asian Studies, Singapore, 2012, p. 118.
14 Sam Bateman, 'The South China Sea: When the Elephants Dance', *RSIS Commentaries*, S. Rajaratnam School of International Studies, Singapore, 16 August 2010.
15 Taiwan Relations Act, 1 January 1979, www.ait.org.tw/en/taiwan-relations-act.html (accessed 2 June 2014).

16 'China-Vietnam Dispute Deepens', *The Financial Times*, 28 June 2012.
17 Robert Ross, 'The US Pivot to Asia and Implications for Australia', *The Centre of Gravity Series*, paper #5, ANU Strategic and Defence Studies Centre, Canberra, March 2013, p. 3.
18 Dan Blumenthal, 'The Power Projection Balance in Asia', in Thomas G. Mahnken (ed.), *Competitive Strategies for the 21st Century: Theory, History, and Practice*, Stanford University Press, Palo Alto, CA, 2012, p. 179.
19 Graham, 'Gazing Down at the Breakers', p. 119.
20 'Shoal Mates: America's Navy Riles China in its Backyard', *The Economist*, 28 April 2012.
21 Matikas Santos, 'Poaching Triggers Scarborough Stand-Off', *Philippine Daily Inquirer*, 11 April 2012, http://globalnation.inquirer.net/32493/illegal-poaching-activities-of-chinese-vessels-cause-standoff (accessed 2 June 2014); Mark Valencia, 'Current Spat May be a Sign of Future Tensions', *The Straits Times*, 14 May 2012.
22 It is claimed that Chinese officials defined the South China Sea as a core Chinese interest in April 2010. See Edward Wong, 'Chinese Military Seeks to Extend its Naval Power', *New York Times*, 24 April 2010, p. 1. China's position on a 'core interest' is non-negotiable, and its protection may involve the use of military force.
23 Clinton, 'America's Pacific Century', p. 58.
24 Declaration on the Conduct of Parties in the South China Sea, Phnom Penh, Cambodia, 4 November 2002.
25 See Ian Storey, 'The Institutionalization of ASEAN-China Relations: Managing the South China Sea Dispute', in Ralf Emmers (ed.), *ASEAN and the Institutionalization of East Asia*, Routledge, London, 2012, pp. 145–149.
26 Ross, 'The US Pivot to Asia and Implications for Australia', p. 3.
27 Mark Valencia, 'High-Stakes Drama: The South China Sea Disputes', *Global Asia*, 7(3), Fall 2012, p. 62.
28 Valencia, 'High-Stakes Drama', pp. 59–60.
29 Ian Storey, 'Testing Brunei's Resolve over China', *The Straits Times*, 10 December 2012.
30 Mark Valencia, 'Is ASEAN Becoming a Big-Power Battleground?', *The Straits Times*, 24 July 2012.
31 Cited in Jane Perlez and Chris Buckley, 'China Paper Suggests US is Making Asia "tenser"', *International Herald Tribune*, 17 April 2013, p. 1.
32 Valencia, 'High-Stakes Drama', p. 62.

9 Australia's interests in the South China Sea

Michael Wesley

Introduction

The advent of a Coalition government in Australia in September 2013 offers an opportunity for Canberra to forge a new direction on the South China Sea disputes. Pledging to reorient Australian foreign policy to be 'less about Geneva, more about Jakarta', the Abbott government promises to bring a more tightly regional approach, along with a more pragmatic, interests-based philosophy, to its diplomacy. In the early weeks of office, the new government has already signalled its understanding of the seriousness of the South China Sea disputes to Australia's extended interests.

If there is to be a more activist approach to foreign policy, it will present a marked departure from the approach of the outgoing Labor government. Former Foreign Minister Bob Carr told the media in July 2012:

> I don't think it is in Australia's interest to take on for itself a brokering role in territorial disputes in the South China Sea. I don't think that is remotely in our interest, I think we should adhere to the policy we have got of not supporting any one of the nations making competing territorial claims and reminding them all that we want it settled, because we have a stake in it – 60 percent of our trade goes through the South China Sea.[1]

While in subsequent statements Carr seemed to embrace a more involved Australian diplomacy on the disputes, the predominant approach of the Labor government was characterised by emphasising that Australia has no direct interests involved and urging all parties to find a peaceful solution. In trying to remain neutral, the former government chose to support ASEAN's call for a Code of Conduct, an approach opposed by one of the interested parties, China.

It is hard to separate the Labor government's cautious approach to the South China Sea disputes from the rising risk aversion of its political culture as a result of the China boom.[2] This is in marked contrast to past decades, when Australia's creative diplomacy has had a material impact on the resolution of disputes in which it had no direct material interest – but in which, at the time, it discerned broader interests at stake. This chapter presents a case to the new Australian government to change Canberra's approach to the South China Sea disputes. Australia has a great deal more at stake in the unstable dynamics of the South China Sea than the approximately 54 per cent of its trade that traverses that waterway. These larger stakes furnish ample incentives for Canberra to embrace a much more creative, less risk-averse approach in trying to help resolving the disputes.

The many faces of the South China Sea disputes

The beginnings of a new and more creative approach from Canberra to the South China Sea disputes must be a willingness to look at the disputes anew. The conventional view is that the disputes involve and are driven by three factors: overlapping territorial claims, rivalry over what may be significant hydrocarbon resources in the sea bed, and rivalry over the considerable fisheries of the sea. If this is the case, Australia's laid-back attitude would be eminently justified. Each of these three causes of contention is divisible, and therefore should be resolvable in a rational negotiation among the directly concerned parties. Indeed, if these are the three drivers of the dispute it is hard to see why it remains unresolved close to half a century after the disputes were first aired. There is considerable evidence that disputes over divisible commodities are much easier to resolve than those over absolute commodities.

There are at least four broader drivers of the conflict that make it unpredictable and extremely difficult to resolve through rational negotiation among the parties. First, the disputes are a direct manifestation of Asia's changing power topography. The rise of China, a country with the size, wealth and internal unity that make a bid for regional leadership imaginable – and the fear that engenders in its neighbours – has led to a much more dynamic and fluid security environment in Asia than during the last quarter of the twentieth century.[3] Surrounding China is a series of second-tier powers that are either long-term rivals of China, or have current disputes with Beijing, or both: Japan, Vietnam, India and perhaps Russia.[4] Acquiescing to China's regional dominance would be unacceptable in terms of both hard interests and prestige and self-respect. As a result, these powers have been reaching out to each other and to the United States, building economic and security partnerships to offset China's rise.

Asia's pyramidal power topography is intensifying over time. The result is a complex and shifting strategic picture that significantly complicates America's capacity to stabilise the region through 'hegemony-lite'. Asian states' expectations of the United States are rising, while America is becoming more demanding of its Asian allies and partners. China's military build-up has been targeted precisely on the vulnerabilities presented by the American strategic posture in the Western Pacific. As a result, the effort Washington will need to make to simply maintain its strategic predominance in the region will be enormously costly, at a time when the United States faces a huge fiscal challenge. This means that Washington will begin to ask its allies and partners to contribute more towards maintaining the alliance system's predominance in Asia. The problem is that the allies that are most likely to comply – Japan, the Republic of Korea, the Philippines and Australia – lack the heft to seriously help counter the Chinese build-up. And the partners that have the strategic heft – India, Indonesia and Vietnam – are most unlikely to make the necessary commitment, given their long-held non-aligned principles.

There is a normative edge to China's rise as well. China's rapid emergence as the region's largest economy and new industrial heart have given rise to expectations that its smaller neighbours should show it greater deference. To its smaller neighbours, on the other hand, China's behaviour in the South China Sea serves as an unpalatable example of what Beijing's regional hegemony would look like. For this reason, the South China Sea disputes are as much about prestige and national pride as they are about territory, resources or fisheries – and this makes them very difficult to resolve.

The second driver of the disputes is that they reflect the growing anxiety of China about its dependence on external supplies of energy and minerals and the vulnerability of these supplies to manipulation by strategic rivals. Industrialisation and urbanisation have created massive demand for energy, raw materials and consumer markets in China and other rising Asian powers. Between 1990 and 2007, China's oil consumption tripled; and the International Energy Agency estimates that by 2030, China's energy thirst will have doubled again. It is a demand growth that is both insatiable and structural – meaning that if the demand is not met with dependable supplies at sustainable cost, it will threaten social, economic and political cohesion in Asia's largest and most rapidly industrialising society. Particularly for a country with a centuries-long history of self-sufficiency, import-substitution and autarkic policy settings, the sudden and irreversible expansion of economic dependence on the outside world has led to increasing anxiety, particularly as the global economy seems to be gripped by periodic instability with increasing frequency.

The combination of a sense of increasing vulnerability to flows and supplies located outside the country's borders, with the growing strategic rivalries and competition touched off by China's ascent, have led to a growing sense of strategic claustrophobia in Beijing. This strategic claustrophobia manifests itself in the growing anxiety that rivals will play out their strategic designs by manipulating vulnerabilities and dependencies. In many ways, these fears evoke the long-standing Chinese fear of containment by a coalition hostile to its rise.[5] Contemporary discussion among Chinese strategic elites has raised the prospect of a 'mini-NATO' being created in the region, and Washington being behind the greater willingness of China's neighbours to stand up to it. To this school of thought, Beijing can only gain security of its supply routes by asserting a degree of control over them, or at least denying control to its strategic rival, the United States.

The third driver is that the disputes bring the United States and China into direct contention in terms of their deepening rivalry over the regional order. In this sense, they are a manifestation of the broader problem of Washington and Beijing talking past each other. While the United States sees the South China Sea in terms of general principles such as freedom of navigation, Beijing looks at the issue through specifics, such as its particular historical and territorial rights. China has made general statements about supporting freedom of access to the South China Sea, but has refused to be drawn on what it means by this.

On the other hand, the South China Sea tensions stoke Washington's own sense of vulnerability in the Western Pacific: its *strategic* vulnerability in the context of China's maritime weapons systems, as well as its *diplomatic* vulnerability in terms of regional allies' trust in its willingness to support them. The growing territorial frictions in the Western Pacific pose an entrapment danger for the United States. Washington's rhetoric about its 'rebalancing' into the Pacific has bolstered the confidence of Vietnam, the Philippines and Japan in opposing China's claims, both militarily and diplomatically. Repeated low-level confrontations between China and its neighbours pose a never-ending dilemma for the United States about when to show resolve and support for its Asian allies and partners. On the one hand, Washington is keen to demonstrate it can be relied upon, particularly as the memory of America's perceived unreliability during the Asian financial crisis lingers. On the other hand, the US is aware that China may be using territorial disputes to increase frictions between Washington and its allies, while its Asian allies have an incentive to keep the disputes bubbling in order to keep the US engaged in the region.

Finally, the South China Sea dispute can be seen as a case study in the fragility of nomocratic norms – defined as a strong individual and collective commitment by states to liberal domestic and international rules and institutions governing state behaviour – in Asia and the ascendancy of teleocratic norms – the tendency to see rules and institutions as subordinate to the needs and prerogatives of the state.[6] This means that regional institutions, which have played a catalytic role in other regions in resolving disputes, are a particularly weak reed in Asia. The consensus-based approach of Asian institutions means that Beijing has been able to block any from directly addressing the disputes. Furthermore, Beijing, wary of being 'ganged up on' by Southeast Asian states, has refused to deal with ASEAN as a pre-negotiated front on the issue. The teleocratic tendencies of Asian states have also weakened the ability of international law to play a resolution role, notwithstanding Malaysia and Indonesia's agreement to abide by a 2002 International Court of Justice ruling on a bilateral territorial dispute.

Australia's interests

If such a broader view of the South China Sea disputes is taken, Australia's interests are vitally affected – even if it were feasible to reroute the 54 per cent of its trade that currently passes through the waterway. In taking such a low-profile approach to the disputes, the previous Rudd/Gillard Labor government appears to have confused Australia's interests, or the ends of its foreign policy, with the means – and in particular its bilateral and multilateral relationships. This approach to the South China Sea seems to be motivated first and foremost by the desire not to offend key relationships. On the one hand, the protestations that Australia has no role in resolving the disputes appeared to be motivated by a fear of offending China, Australia's largest trading partner and an increasingly important regional actor. On the other hand, Australia's support for ASEAN's Code of Conduct showed a desire to keep the countries of Southeast Asia on side.

In forging a new approach, Canberra must do some first-principles thinking about its interests in relation to the South China Sea disputes. If it does, it will realise that it has vital interests at stake, which are ill served by its former approach. To a first-principles approach, Australia has four *structural* interests and two *relational* interests at play in the South China Sea disputes. Australia's first structural interest is the need to ensure the continued existence of uncontested global commons – be they maritime, aerial, space or cyber. As a small, relatively isolated, heavily trade-dependent country, Australia would be more affected than most by the externalities of rising strategic competition in Asia. As luck would have it, the maritime commons have been controlled since European settlement by its closest allies, but this situation may be coming to an end with the rapid build-up of maritime weapons systems among Asian states. In 2012, SIPRI reported that the period from 2007 to 2011 saw a 200 per cent higher volume of arms transfers into Southeast Asia than there had been between 2002 and 2006. This volume of imports was the highest since the end of the Vietnam War. Naval weapons formed the bulk of these purchases, with ships and maritime weapons accounting for 52 per cent of the total, and another 37 per cent accounting for weapons with a possible maritime role. SIPRI reports that a similar level and profile is evident in weapons acquisition intentions also.[7]

Australia's second structural interest is an international economy oriented towards development and free trade norms – a natural corollary of the structure and trade-dependence of the Australian economy. The crisis and apparent stalling of multilateral trade liberalisation, symbolised by the lack of progress on the Doha trade round, has coincided with the rise of what many have called 'state capitalism' – in the form of state-owned and -controlled enterprises – in the global economy. The proliferation of preferential trade agreements, a rising will to build institutional checks to financial instability, and the growing relative importance of 'behind the border' trade and investment restrictions provide plenty of grounds for pessimism about the future health of an open global trade and investment order.

Third, and perhaps most vital, Australia has a structural interest in the ascendancy, vitality and continuing evolution of a rational, egalitarian, rules-based international order. Some of its earliest independent foreign policy campaigns were oriented towards building checks and balances against great power dominant into post-war global institutions, such as the United Nations. The ascendance of the West for the two centuries following Australia's European settlement has fostered a rules-based egalitarian order, as a reflection of the basic social and cultural values of Western states. The rise of powerful Asian states, however, threatens this order. In social norms, language and cosmology, most Asian societies are strongly hierarchic, and there are signs that with growing wealth and power, they have started to see the region in these terms. At a particularly tense meeting with Southeast Asian foreign ministers in Hanoi in 2010, Chinese Foreign Minister Yang Jiechi fumed, 'China is a big country and other countries are small countries and that's just a fact'.[8] Such attitudes, grounded in a deep conviction of cultural superiority, heighten fears among smaller states of an Asia dominated by rising giants such as China and India, both of which combine a sense of cultural greatness with a conviction of their own moral rectitude. It is Asia's cultural and moral rivalries that make seemingly innocuous disputes intractable and dangerously unpredictable.

Fourth, and more specifically, Australia has a structural interest in a benign strategic order in the Indo-Pacific Peninsula – the archipelago that extends from northern Thailand to northern Australia, along which an armed attack on Australia would most likely come. Peninsular geography interacts with power and the strategic imagination in peculiar ways: it constrains, concentrates, funnels and bundles power. Strategic shifts in one part of a peninsula are likely to cascade through to its other parts. Peninsulas tend to be strategically stable if dominated by a single set of strategic interests; but once a contrary strategic interest gains hold, they become extremely unstable. The Indo-Pacific Peninsula is the land divide between the Indian and Pacific Oceans; it is a vital frontier through which strategically vital Indo-Pacific energy trade must pass – and therefore it is a key asset for any power worried about manipulation of its vulnerabilities by rivals. In an age of rising strategic competition in Asia, it is highly likely that the Indo-Pacific peninsula will become a cockpit of competition.

Australia has two relational interests involved in the South China Sea also. The first is its alliance commitment to the United States. Were Washington to become embroiled in a conflict in the South China Sea, it is highly likely Australia would be expected to fulfil its alliance obligations alongside US forces. An alliance liability of this sort deals Canberra into Washington's policy on the disputes, and behoves Australia to develop its own, well-thought-out approach to these disputes.

Australia's second relational interest is ensuring its acceptance as part of the Asia-Pacific region. Australia is now overwhelmingly dependent on trade with the region, as well as being vitally affected by regional security developments. This has bred a sensible, bipartisan strategy of ensuring Australia is accepted as a full member of the region. However, this status has been contested in the past by countries whose own regionalist designs are best served by keeping Australia, symbolising a Western presence, out. Canberra's energetic diplomacy in the region, including on issues that did not ostensibly involve direct Australian interests, have played a key role in convincing most countries in the region of the sincerity of Australia's regionalist commitments. But Canberra should not rest on its laurels; there are quite imaginable scenarios in which powerful countries may once again seek to exclude Australia from the region as a part of their larger strategic designs.

At least three of Australia's structural interests, and both relational interests, stand threatened by the South China Sea disputes. First, there is the possibility that the global maritime commons will become permanently contested for the first time in Australia's post-European settlement history. There is growing agreement among maritime strategists that the days of American sea control may be numbered, to be replaced by a fluid system of mutual sea deniability among the littoral great powers.[9] What regime will develop in the place of the current high-seas doctrine is hard to predict – but there is little doubt that Australia will be vitally affected. Second, the South China Sea disputes presage a rising tempo of challenges to the nomocratic, rules-based international order by rising powers that do not advance alternative general frameworks, but eat at it with escalating specific claims. Third is the possibility that rising strategic competition in the Indo-Pacific Peninsula among China, the United States and possibly India and Japan could cause instability and conflict in these vital approaches to Australia. For all of these reasons, a new approach is necessary by the Coalition government.

New directions

A new approach to the South China Sea must include a serious analysis of the possible scenarios and outcomes of the disputes. Each scenario needs to be considered not only on its own merits, but in terms of its implications for future disputes in the region. Four possible outcomes suggest themselves. The first is the steady deterioration of the situation, driven by increasing intransigence on the part of all actors as domestic politics and bureaucratic rivalries raise the stakes for each party. Protracted low-level conflict resulting in the functional closure of the waterway for non-military purposes becomes highly likely. This would represent a disastrous outcome, not only for Australia, but for all of the involved parties and the region. The second scenario is a return to the status quo ante, a continuation of the overlapping disputes over which no one wants to push their claims too firmly. This, too, is an undesirable outcome, because it would be vulnerable to flaring into the current situation very quickly. It is also unlikely that there is sufficient trust among the disputants to make this a stable outcome, as the Southeast Asian claimants and China each accuse the other of being motivated by opaque ulterior motives. A third scenario is a Chinese victory, in which Beijing is able to establish hegemony over the waterway and dictate its future adminis-tration. Again, it is hard to see this as a stable solution, given the strong aversion of the United States and Southeast Asian claimants to trusting Beijing's approach to international norms. This leaves the possibility of a moderate solution, in which specific claims are shelved and a joint management regime is developed. This outcome has the advantage of removing specific claims and jealousies from the disputes and replacing them with a joint management system in which all parties are materially invested. This option is also preferable to the others because of the principles it embodies for the evolution of the region in the future: the accommodation of the interests of all affected parties, and the priority of regional stability of particularist claims.

In forging a new approach to the South China Sea disputes, Australian policymakers and diplomats should be guided by four principles. The first is to recognise the fatal weaknesses of current approaches to addressing the disputes.

An ASEAN-developed Code of Conduct is not a likely solution, because in Beijing's eyes it represents the willingness of the countries of Southeast Asia to caucus against China. For China to accede to a Code of Conduct under ASEAN, American and Australian cajoling would, in Beijing's eyes, establish a precedent for China to be forced into positions it objects to by coalitions in other regional settings. On the other hand, Beijing's approach of holding out for joint development negotiated bilaterally with each Southeast Asian claimant is also a non-starter. This plays into many ASEAN states' fears about being played off against each other by Beijing, a concern heightened by Cambodia's non-solidarity with its ASEAN colleagues at the 2012 ASEAN Summit. Furthermore, the image of joint deals with Beijing has been tarnished by the emergence of evidence that the bilateral agreement with Beijing negotiated by the former Arroyo administration in the Philippines was lubricated by substantial corruption of Philippines officials by Chinese money. Finally, the weaknesses of both regional organisations and international law to furnish a solution should be acknowledged. Manila's formal referral of the disputes to UNCLOS adjudication is only likely to harden Beijing's opposition to these forums. The second guiding principle should be to search for a different dynamic, by identifying elements of shared interests among the disputants and building momentum behind these. At the moment, the incentives of all of the disputants work actively against resolution. China believes time is on its side. Some Southeast Asian claimants believe that maintaining tensions will keep an isolationist-inclined America engaged in the region and perhaps even deliver more military aid. Others have become fixated on maintaining ASEAN unity at all costs. As a creative broker, Australia must look for alternative interests that can overcome these obstructive conceptions. One might be to sponsor a broader conversation about the prospects for the regional commons in an era of rising and complex interdependence and rivalries. As an intensive trading region, with heavy commitment to energy imports and global production sharing, every disputant has an overriding interest in maintaining uncontested commons and a free trade and investment order. Such a conversation could have the benefit of nesting the South China Sea in the context of a broader set of more vital interests – and thus changing the momentum towards resolution.

The third principle should be to borrow liberally from past successes. Australia can justifiably look back on a rich history of creative diplomacy towards regional problems, from the Colombo Plan to the Cambodia Peace process, the Antarctica Treaty and the Bali Process on People Smuggling. Each of these offers rich suggestions for the contemporary period: the Colombo Plan's identification of shared development and stability interests among diverse and often mutually suspicious countries; the Cambodian Peace Process's use of informal talks over years to find innovative approaches to a solution; the Antarctica Treaty's shelving of sovereignty claims in favour of joint management; and the Bali Process's use of bilateral and plurilateral partnerships to build momentum towards a common approach. The fourth principle should be to build on current successes. One such example is the recent agreement negotiated between Taiwan and Japan to allow Taiwanese fishermen to fish around the disputed Senkaku/Diaoyutai Islands.

Under the terms of the agreement, Tokyo has not stepped back from its administration of the islands and Taipei has not renounced its claim to them; rather, they have bilaterally agreed to allow joint usage. A similar agreement is currently under negotiation between Taipei and Manila. There are powerful reasons for the new government in Canberra to change its approach to the South China Sea disputes. Australia has in the past risked its immediate relationships with regional countries to advocate solutions in its – and the region's – long-term interests. It should be prepared to again.

Notes

1   Radio Australia Transcript, 30 July 2012, www.radioaustralia.net.au/international/radio/program/connect-asia/australia-should-stay-out-of-south-china-sea-dispute-says-carr/987932 (accessed 2 June 2014).
2   Michael Wesley, 'Australia and the China Boom', in James Reilly and Jingdong Yuan (eds), *Australia and China at Forty*, UNSW Press, Sydney, 2012.
3   Michael Wesley, 'Asia's New Age of Instability', *The National Interest*, November/December 2012.
4   On the complex and ambiguous Sino-Russian relationship, see Bobo Lo, *Axis of Convenience: Moscow, Beijing and the New Geopolitics*, Chatham House, London, 2008.
5   Avery Goldstein, *Rising to the Challenge: China's Grand Strategy and International Security*, Stanford University Press, Palo Alto, CA, 2005.
6   Michael Wesley, 'The New Bipolarity', *The American Interest*, January/February 2013.
7   Siemon T. Wezeman, 'The Maritime Dimension of Arms Transfers to South East Asia, 2007–11', in *SIPRI Yearbook 2012: Armaments, Disarmament and International Security*, Oxford University Press, Oxford, 2012.
8   'The Dragon's New Teeth', *The Economist*, 7 April 2002.
9   Mutual sea deniability refers to a state of affairs in which no one power is able to assert sea control, or the safety of its own and its allies' shipping at all times in a given body of water. In a state of mutual deniability, the maritime powers in any given body of water are able to threaten the shipping of rivals – a situation that, according to the great naval strategist Sir Julian Corbett, is the usual state of affairs in world politics, whereas the last 60 years of maritime control by the US Navy is the anomaly.

10 The South China Sea as a 'crisis'

Brendan Taylor

In recent years, numerous commentators have portrayed the Asian region as one engulfed by a series of strategic crises or 'flashpoints'. Prominent among these, Robert Kaplan has characterised the South China Sea as a body of water that is set to be 'the 21st century's defining battleground'.[1] In a similar vein, former Australian Prime Minister Kevin Rudd has described the South and East China Seas as akin to 'a tinderbox on water', not unlike the situation in the Balkans over a century ago.[2] Rudd's compatriot Hugh White predicted at the end of 2012 that China and Japan would go to war over the disputed Diaoyu/Senkaku Islands during the following 12 months.[3] And the respected observer of Korean Peninsula security matters Victor Cha has written that 'there is a real risk of war on the Korean Peninsula'.[4]

Are Asia's crisis points equally perilous, or are some more dangerous than others? Few, if any, analysts have paused to ask this question through a comparative analysis that disaggregates the South China Sea, the Korean Peninsula and the East China Sea to ascertain which among them is the most combustible and potentially catastrophic. This chapter undertakes such a comparative analysis and contends, contrary to much recent commentary on East Asian security, that the South China Sea is the least dangerous among Asia's present crisis points. Unlike tensions on the Korean Peninsula and in the East China Sea, the chapter argues that crisis in the South China Sea is by no means imminent.

There is a voluminous body of scholarship examining a range of strategic crises and their various elements. Much of this literature was developed during the Cold War period and focused on such areas as crisis dynamics, crisis diplomacy, crisis management and crisis prevention.[5] Interestingly, there was little consensus among authors of this significant body of work regarding what actually constitutes a 'crisis'. Some analysts have suggested, for instance, that an element of surprise is an integral characteristic of any crisis. Others have insisted that any crisis needs to be focused upon a single issue, such as 'a territorial dispute, an economic boycott, a threat to a political regime'. Others distinguish between 'foreign policy' and 'international' crises, wherein the former is a 'crisis' for an individual state resulting from changes in that state's internal or external environment, and the latter involves two or more states and also has broader effects in terms of destabilising the structure of an international system.[6]

This chapter employs a recent and more broad-ranging definition of 'crisis' employed by Michael Swaine in his widely acclaimed co-edited volume addressing Sino-American crises. In this volume, Swaine suggests that a political-military crisis generally has three primary characteristics. First, it must involve key or core interests of the players involved. Second, a sense of urgency ought to surround the crisis. And third, threats or advantage to the interests of all involved players in the crisis are possible, to the point where military conflict could conceivably eventuate. If great powers are involved, such conflict could ultimately threaten the structure and stability of the international system.[7] The chapter will now proceed to apply these three criteria against contemporary tensions in the South China Sea, on the Korean Peninsula and in the East China Sea, with a view to assessing the legitimacy of their respective claims to political-military 'crisis' status.

The South China Sea

The South China Sea has been routinely referred to as one of, if not *the*, most dangerous and flammable crises points in Asia today. Considering the first of Swaine's three criteria, there has certainly been much speculation in recent years that China's leaders increasingly regard the South China Sea as an area of 'core interest'. The use of this terminology is particularly significant in China's case, given the specific connotations associated with it. The term 'core interest' was one that officially first entered the Chinese foreign policy lexicon on a regular basis in 2003–2004, and was used to describe areas or issues that Beijing would be willing to employ armed force to defend.[8] Traditionally, those areas have come to be recognised as being Taiwan, Tibet and Xinjiang. Certainly, China's leaders have exhibited little reluctance in referring to these three areas in such terms. Speculation that China also regards the South China Sea as a core interest was sparked by an April 2010 *New York Times* article, which alleged that Chinese officials had applied similar terminology to this body of water during a meeting – albeit one held 'behind closed doors' – with senior US counterparts.[9] Further fuelling that speculation, US Secretary of State Hillary Clinton went on the record in November 2010 during an interview with the veteran Australian journalist Greg Sheridan, confirming that Chinese officials had again referred to the South China Sea as a 'core interest' during the May 2010 gathering of the US-China Strategic and Economic Dialogue.[10]

Analysts seeking to explain why Beijing might regard the South China Sea as a core interest typically refer to energy security considerations. In particular, the South China Sea is estimated by the authoritative US Energy Information Administration to contain 11 billion barrels of oil and 190 trillion cubic feet of natural gas[11] – quantities that would certainly go a long way towards meeting China's voracious energy requirements, if secured. The geostrategic location of the South China Sea is also regarded as significant from an energy security perspective. Approximately 80 per cent of China's energy imports, for instance, come from Africa and through the Malacca Strait. China's 'Malacca Dilemma' is that this narrow choke point could be cut off by an adversary during a crisis, thereby starving China into submission.

While made increasingly frequently, the above claims that Beijing regards the South China Sea as a core interest are open to question. It is interesting to note, for instance, that Chinese officials have yet to publicly refer to the South China Sea in such terms. A similar degree of reticence is certainly not apparent in their public statements on Taiwan, Tibet or Xinjiang, where references to these areas as 'core interests' remain routine.[12] Just as significant, China continues to employ the use of economic levers and paramilitary coastal patrol vessels – rather than military vessels – in its dealings in the South China Sea. Once again, this more calibrated approach stands in contrast to Beijing's stance on the Taiwan issue, where, for example, relatively large-scale military exercises were conducted in waters adjacent to Taiwan during the 1995–1996 Taiwan Strait crisis.

A strong case can be made that China's energy dependence upon the resources lying beneath the waters of the South China Sea is also overstated. For instance, research published recently by Andrew Erickson and Gabriel Collins suggests that China's 'Malacca Dilemma' is not as acute as many commentators claim. They point out that Beijing's capacity to divert its energy imports via alternative routes – including the Lombok Strait, the Sunda Strait and even South of Australia – is often overlooked. According to their estimates, such diversions could impose additional costs of as little as US$1–2 per barrel of oil shipped.[13] Likewise, while the US Navy remains the only one in the world that genuinely has the capacity to impose a blockade of the Malacca Strait for any prolonged period of time, certainly there is little in the American foreign policy tradition to suggest that it would take such a step in circumstances short of all-out war with China. As two leading authorities on this subject, Dennis Blair and Kenneth Lieberthal, have observed:

> The United States has a very long tradition of promoting and protecting the free flow of trade over the world's seas. When Washington has used its naval dominance to blockade shipping, it has done so judiciously . . . Nothing in the United States' foreign political tradition indicates that the country would abuse its maritime power for its own narrow interests.[14]

A number of commentators have also made the case that the US is increasingly regarding the South China Sea as a 'core' or 'vital' interest.[15] Those making this argument typically attach importance to Secretary of State Hillary Clinton's July 2010 statement that the US has a 'national interest' in the peaceful resolution of the South China Sea disputes. Over the next couple of years, statements of this nature were reiterated by other senior officials. Commentators will often interpret growing American interest in the South China Sea as reflective of a view in Washington that these disputes are a litmus test for China's challenge to America in the broader Asia-Pacific. As Patrick Cronin and Robert Kaplan have observed, 'the South China Sea will be the strategic bellwether for determining the future of U.S. leadership in the Asia-Pacific region'.[16] An alternative, albeit closely related, interpretation suggests that America's commitment to its Southeast Asian allies – particularly the Philippines – will be seen by its other Asian allies as indicative of Washington's commitment to them also.

Once again, such arguments are open to contestation. While it is true that the balance of military power in the South China Sea between China and a number of Southeast Asian countries – especially Vietnam and the Philippines – is shifting decisively in China's favour, it is important not to uncritically extrapolate from these trends a looming Chinese challenge to American power in the Asia-Pacific. While its naval power is certainly on the rise, the limits to Chinese military power still remain significant. As far as the South China Sea is concerned, China remains some way off from being in a position to decisively project power across this body of water. As Dan Blumenthal has observed:

> the PLA lacks a sustained power projection capability associated with asserting full control over the area, including sufficient at-sea replenishment and aerial refueling capabilities, modern destroyers with advanced air defense capabilities, and nuclear submarines, as well as regional bases to support logistical requirements'.[17]

Suggestions that tests to the credibility of the US-led network of Asian alliances will also occur in the South China Sea are also questionable. During the March 2012 stand-off between Chinese and Filipino vessels at the disputed Scarborough Shoal, for example, American backing for its Southeast Asian ally was not particularly robust. Washington did go so far as to confirm that it would meet its obligations to Manila under the terms of the 1951 Mutual Defense Treaty between the US and the Philippines. However, the US also consistently made clear that it does not takes sides in territorial disputes and remained ambiguous on the question of whether the Mutual Defense Treaty actually applies in a disputed area, such as Scarborough Shoal.[18] Yet, that seems to have done little to shake the confidence of other regional allies regarding the reliability of the US security guarantee to them. Australia's inaugural National Security Strategy of January 2013, for instance, described the US-Australia alliance as a 'pillar' of Australia's national security, while a subsequent Australian Defence White Paper in May 2013 described that alliance as 'our most important defence relationship'.[19]

Moving to the second of Swaine's criteria, notwithstanding alarmist assessments of the kind made by commentators such as Rudd and White, a strong case can be made that a sense of urgency does not, as yet, surround the South China Sea disputes. This is partly because the South China Sea's maritime strategic environment also reduces the sense of urgency surrounding these disputes. In his seminal text *The Tragedy of Great Power Politics*, John Mearsheimer suggests that maritime tensions have often historically tended not to escalate with the same rapidity as those on land due to what he terms the 'stopping power' of water. Here, Mearsheimer is referring to the additional time that maritime environments afford diplomats and their search for solutions to crises, in contrast to disputes over more proximate land borders, where crises are prone to escalate more quickly.[20]

This brings us to the third of Swaine's criteria and to the question of whether the South China Sea has the potential to escalate into a conflict that could threaten the structure and stability of the international system more generally. History suggests that a conflict of such proportions is unlikely to develop over the South China Sea. When previous military clashes have occurred in the waters of the South China Sea – such as in 1974, when Chinese and Vietnamese forces clashed over the Paracel Islands, and again in 1988 over the Johnston South Reef – lives have been lost, but these losses have been less than 100 (53 and 70 Vietnamese sailors, respectively), and theses clashes have subsequently been contained.[21]

Added to this, Beijing and Washington have, over the last two or more decades, demonstrated their capacity to manage crises in the US-China relationship, including in the waters of the South China Sea. In April 2001, for instance, a serious crisis in US-China relations erupted when a US Navy EP-3 surveillance aircraft operating over the waters of the South China Sea collided with a Chinese jet fighter and was forced to make an emergency landing on Hainan Island. To be sure, efforts to address this crisis did not initially proceed particularly smoothly, as Chinese officials refused to answer incoming calls from the US Embassy. Ultimately, however, those most intimately involved in this crisis – such as then Commander of the US Pacific Command Admiral Dennis Blair – have written subsequently regarding the efforts that US policymakers made to exercise 'prudence and restraint' in addressing this crisis. They have also acknowledged that their Chinese counterparts 'made a series of grudging concessions that ultimately resulted in success . . . after they decided that it was important to overall Sino-American relations to solve the incident'.[22] More recently, when in 2009 a number of Chinese vessels performed provocative and potentially dangerous manoeuvres in close proximity to a survey ship, the USNS *Impeccable* – again in the waters of the South China Sea – US and Chinese policymakers went to considerable lengths in their public statements to emphasise a desire to work to deepen their bilateral ties and to ensure that episodes such as the *Impeccable* incident did not become the norm in US-China relations.[23]

The Korean Peninsula

While commentators for some time now have referred to the North Korean nuclear 'crisis', in general a much greater sense of complacency has tended to surround tensions in this part of the region than has been the case in recent times in many analyses of the South China Sea disputes. South Korean public opinion polls, for instance, routinely show a populace that fears the North Korean nuclear threat far less than the prospect of a peaceful Korean reunification, given the substantial financial costs that such a scenario would impose on the South. As alluded to at the outset of this chapter, however, in recent years respected commentators such as Cha have referred to the Korean Peninsula as a dangerous crisis point. Most notably, in late December 2010 –and in the aftermath of the March 2010 *Cheonan* sinking and the November 2010 Yeonpyeong Island bombardment – Cha made the following chilling assessment:

> There is a real possibility of war on the Korean Peninsula. The cause is not a second North Korean invasion of the South like in June 1950, which was successfully deterred by U.S. and South Korean forces. The danger stems from two combustible trends. A North Korea which mistakenly believes it is invulnerable to retaliation due to its nascent nuclear capabilities, and a South Korea that feels increasingly compelled to react with military force to the string of ever more brash provocations like the artillery barrage on Yeonpyeong Island.[24]

Applying the first of Swaine's three criteria, there is little question that the Korean Peninsula is an area where the core interests of both China and the US are genuinely engaged. Indeed, the strategic importance of North Korea to China goes back several decades and is reflected in Beijing's long-standing references to that relationship as akin to the intimacy between lips and teeth. The bond is partly historical in nature, and relates to the significant number of Chinese troops – more than a million, according to one respected authority[25] – who fought and died in the Korean War of 1950–1953. China also fears the potential flood of refugees that could come spilling across its shared land border with North Korea in the event of severe economic or political dislocation there.

Arguably even more significant than these considerations, North Korea's geostrategic position as a 'buffer' between China and a number of key American allies – namely Japan and South Korea – render the Korean Peninsula, more generally, and North Korea, in particular, an area of vital interest to Beijing. To be sure, there has been some speculation in recent times that Beijing is growing increasingly frustrated with Pyongyang's nuclear and missile provocations, and that an increasingly vigorous North Korea policy debate within China itself is indicative of the extent to which Beijing can no longer be relied upon to back Pyongyang in the manner it traditionally has. For example, China supported new sanctions imposed against North Korea in January and March 2013 following their latest ballistic missile and nuclear tests. According to South Korean officials, Beijing has instructed local governments to implement these measures.[26] China's three largest banks announced in May 2013 that they were ceasing to deal with North Korea. New Chinese President Xi Jinping has also asserted that 'no one should be allowed to throw a region and even the whole world into chaos for selfish gains' in a statement widely interpreted as being directed at Pyongyang.[27]

An equally strong case can be made, however, that North Korea's significance to China has only increased in recent years against the backdrop of the US 'pivot' or 'rebalancing' strategy. Despite Washington's reassurances to the contrary, Chinese strategic analysts remain convinced that the rebalance has been designed and implemented with a view to 'containing' China's re-emergence. The view that the Obama administration is out to 'contain' China's rise is especially prevalent among the People's Liberation Army (PLA), whose influence on the making of China's North Korea policy is particularly strong. This group sees little value in taking a tougher line against North Korea, particularly if any ensuing collapse of the Kim Jong-Un regime were to lead to a reunification of the two Koreas. As Cha has recently observed:

> such an outcome would only reinforce in Chinese minds an important lesson of history – instability on the Korean peninsula has never redounded to Chinese interests. The last two times this occurred, the result was war with Japan (1895) and the US (1950), which cost China dearly.[28]

A strong case can also be made that US interest in the Korean Peninsula is also significant. The interests of America's two closest, and arguably most important, Asian allies are readily apparent here. For South Korea, the military threat posed by the approximately 30,000 North Korean artillery pieces positioned within striking distance of its capital, Seoul, is of most immediate concern. For Japan, the North Korean missile threat serves to focus strategic minds in Tokyo. Previous North Korea missile tests have, for instance, flown over Japanese territory.

Both alliances are central in the wider US-led network of Asian alliances that has been operative in the region since 1951 – the 'San Francisco System'. Indeed, for much of the period since, Washington has referred to the US-Japan alliance as the 'lynchpin' of that system.[29] In more recent years, US officials have also taken to describing the US-South Korea alliance relationship in such terms.[30] Other American allies seeking to gauge Washington's commitment to its strategic partners at any given point in time are thus likely to pay particularly close attention to the credibility of the US commitment to these two central players, particularly during periods of crisis. This, in part, serves to explain, therefore, why Washington's backing of South Korea in the wake of the aforementioned *Cheonan* sinking and the Yeonpyeong Island bombardment was so robust – even in the face of Beijing's equally strong opposition to US-South Korean military exercises in waters proximate to China at various times during 2010.[31]

A less compelling case can be made regarding the second of Swaine's criteria as far as the sense of urgency surrounding tensions on the Korean Peninsula is concerned. Indeed, a curious feature of developments in recent decades has been the sense of complacency that has surrounded political and security developments here. When the US and North Korea signed what appeared at the time a landmark 'Agreed Framework' in October 1994, for instance, some US officials privately regarded this as a useful stalling mechanism while they awaited the inevitable collapse of North Korea. According to this view, time was on Washington's side and the North Korean 'can' was one that the US could afford to essentially keep 'kicking down the road'.[32] That said, there remain periods when tensions continue to spike on the Korean Peninsula, and where that air of complacency gives way to a greater sense of urgency. The above quote from

Cha regarding what he saw as the prospect for conflict in the aftermath of the *Cheonan* sinking and the Yeonpyeong Island bombardment serves to illustrate this point.

Moving to the third of Swaine's criteria and its applicability to the Korean Peninsula, history suggests that the prospects for system-altering conflict here are also very real. The Korean War of 1950–1953, for example, claimed the lives of an estimated 2 million military personnel.[33] Estimates produced at the height of the 1993–1994 North Korean nuclear crisis suggested that conflict on the Korean Peninsula at that time would likely result in the loss of up to 1 million lives and cost somewhere in the vicinity of US$ 1 trillion during the first 90 days of conflict.[34] It is worth noting here that such estimates were made at a time when North Korea's nuclear and missile programs were significantly less advanced than is the case today.

The East China Sea

Tensions between China and Japan over disputed islands in the East China Sea – that the Japanese refer to as the Senkakus and China the Diaoyu – have been building over recent years. In September 2010, for instance, tensions intensified between Beijing and Tokyo following a collision between a Chinese fishing trawler and a Japanese coastguard vessel. But reference to Sino-Japanese tensions as reaching full-blown 'crisis' proportions began to become much more prevalent following Tokyo's September 2012 announcement of its intention to purchase three of the disputed Senkaku/Diaoyu Islands from their private Japanese owner.

During the period since, both China and Japan have increased their maritime patrols around the disputed islands. Chinese vessels have, on at least four occasions, provocatively locked fire control radar on to their Japanese counterparts. China has also penetrated Japanese airspace for the first time since 1958, leading Tokyo to scramble fighter jets in response. Consistent with this, Japan's 2013 Defence White Paper exhibited a particularly strong anti-China sentiment, making specific reference to the aforementioned locking of fire control radar on to Japanese vessels and observing that 'coupled with the lack of transparency in [China's] military and security affairs these moves are a matter of concern for Japan'.[35] Likewise, Japan's Prime Minister Shinzo Abe has more recently made public statements highlighting Tokyo's willingness to take on a more assertive role in countering the rise of China.[36]

According to the first of Swaine's criteria, it seems fair to conclude that disputes between China and Japan over the East China Sea involve key interests of the players involved. Indeed, in recent times Chinese scholars affiliated with the People's Liberation Army (PLA) have taken to publicly referring to the East China Sea as a Chinese 'core interest'.[37] The waters of the East China Sea are certainly economically significant to both China and South Korea, in particular, in view of the fact that the trans-pacific trade of both countries passes through these waters. Trillions of cubic feet of natural gas and billions of barrels of oil are also thought to lie beneath the waters of the East China Sea – resources that are of particular interest to energy-hungry China and energy-dependent Japan. The East China Sea is equally of growing strategic significance to the region's key players. As China's gateway to the Pacific Ocean, for instance, Japan's Ryukyu Island chain has become an increasing preoccupation of Chinese strategic thinkers, while the Chinese Navy has, in recent years, traversed this patch of the East China Sea on their way to conduct military exercises in the wider Pacific Ocean.[38]

Developments in the East China Sea are also of key or core interest from Washington's perspective, particularly as these relate to regional perceptions regarding America's commitment to its Asian allies. To an even greater extent than the case of the US-South Korea alliance referred to previously, the US-Japan alliance has long been, and remains, a barometer for America's alliance commitment among its other Asian allies. This is arguably why routine enquiries from Tokyo as to whether the US would meet its alliance commitments to Japan in the case of a military clash over the Senkaku/Diaoyu Islands have tended to draw a positive response from Washington.[39] As an analyst from the Australian Strategic Policy Institute (ASPI) has recently observed:

> The costs to America's alliance and partner network in Asia would be huge. Abandoning Japan would mean relinquishing the alliance, and likely also America's whole position in Asia. Talk of an Asian 'pivot' or 'rebalance' – already being challenged in many circles – would clearly be done for.[40]

Moving to the second of Swaine's criteria and its applicability to the East China Sea disputes, for some time commentators have taken refuge in the high level of economic interdependence between China and Japan to make the case that war between East Asia's two historical great powers is virtually unthinkable.[41] Others have described the evolving strategic competition between them as having something of a 'slow motion' character to it, making the case that it thus lacks the sense of urgency required by Swaine's conception of crisis.[42]

For two reasons, however, a case can be made that the East China Sea disputes, and indeed the larger China-Japan relationship, has a growing sense of urgency associated with it. At one level, societal antipathies between the Chinese and Japanese public are at their worst ever levels. Public opinion polling conducted in 2013, for instance, revealed that more than 90 per cent of the Japanese and Chinese publics now view the other negatively.[43] That animosity was certainly on display when crowds took to the streets in more than 100 Chinese cities following Japan's aforementioned 'island grab' of September 2012. Added to this – and unlike the case of the US-China relationship discussed earlier in this chapter – there remains a dearth of crisis management mechanisms and shared experiences between Beijing and Tokyo at present. Indeed, as a recent edition of the *PacNet* publication usefully documents, Beijing and Tokyo have consistently tried, and failed, to implement a series of relatively modest confidence-building and communication mechanisms designed to prevent maritime incidents from spiralling out of control.[44]

Moving to the third of Swaine's criteria, the prospects of a system-altering conflict between China and Japan are also worrying. As Rana Mitter's meticulous new study of the last Sino-Japanese War (1937–1945) reminds us, an estimated 14 million people perished on the Chinese side alone during that conflict.[45] Were such a conflict to occur today, it is important to bear in mind that China and Japan currently possess Asia's two most powerful militaries – meaning that the potential for similar, if not even more significant, damage to be inflicted would be substantial, particularly given the likelihood that neither side would be able to readily gain a decisive advantage in any such conflict. As the respected naval strategist James R. Holmes has recently observed:

> Despite Japan's latter-day image as a military pushover, a naval war would not be a rout for China. While the Japanese postwar 'peace' constitution forever renounces war as a sovereign right of the nation and the threat or use of force as means of settling international disputes, the Japan Maritime Self-Defense Force (JMSDF) has accumulated several pockets of material excellence, such as undersea warfare, since World War II. And Japanese mariners are renowned for their professionalism. If commanders manage their human, material, and geographic advantages artfully, Tokyo could make a maritime war with China a close-run thing – and perhaps even prevail.[46]

This is not to mention the fact that, for reasons outlined above relating to issues of alliance credibility, the US would find it exceedingly difficult not to also become embroiled in any such conflict. Hence, the potential for Sino-Japanese tensions to spiral to the point of major war remain disturbing.

Asia's 'crises' compared

Asia's 'strategic flashpoints' are receiving more attention currently than perhaps at any other time previous. Yet, few, if any, analyses have thus far attempted to disaggregate the various points of tension in the region and to differentiate these from one another in terms of their prospective combustibility and potential consequences. Using a definition of political-security crisis developed by Michael Swaine, this chapter constitutes a 'first cut' at such an exercise in disaggregation – more of which are still needed in the future. Of the three most prominent points of tension in contemporary Asia examined in this chapter – the South China Sea, the Korean Peninsula and the East China Sea – only the last unambiguously meets Swaine's three criteria for qualification as a crisis at present. The Korean Peninsula meets two, while lacking the sense of urgency that Swaine deems necessary. Of particular interest to readers of the current volume, it remains questionable whether the South China Sea meets any of Swaine's three criteria, and hence whether it is genuinely a political-security crisis or has the potential to become one.

In the final analysis, this is not to dismiss altogether the strategic significance of the South China Sea. As studies of international conflict dating back to

Thucydides' famous history of the Peloponnesian Wars have demonstrated, 'a quarrel in a far-away country' that bears little obvious or immediate relevance to the central dramas of the international politics of the day can still provide the spark that ignites wars of epochal proportions.[47] That said, it is equally important to think rigorously, and in a discerning and objective manner, regarding the prospects for conflict emanating over any point of tension in international politics – if only to avoid unduly and indiscriminately overstating the importance of each and every one. For to do so in relation to the South China Sea, this chapter suggests, unnecessarily raises the temperature around a set of disputes that, while protracted and complex, appear imminently manageable and conducive, with time and patience, to creative diplomatic solutions. Beyond this, the analysis undertaken in this chapter highlights two possible avenues for further research. First, while understandings of the term 'crisis' and much of the study of this phenomenon have tended to study 'crises' in isolation, further work looking at various points of tension in comparative perspective might be helpful, both in terms of highlighting the commonalities and differences between Asia's various 'flashpoints'. Little work of this nature has thus far been undertaken. One obvious exception, of course, is Ralf Emmers' excellent study of the influence of geopolitical factors upon the South China and East China Sea disputes.[48] More work of this nature would be helpful in terms of ascertaining whether 'strategic learning' can occur both within and between various crises. It would also assist in highlighting when any degree of interdependence exists between various flashpoints – in other words, whether developments in one point of tension can condition another. It might also reveal something regarding the nature of relations between East Asia's major powers – China, Japan and the US – in terms of whether they are pursuing coherent and consistent strategic approaches, and with what implications for the region's emerging strategic order. Second, and flowing directly from this observation, much more work could usefully be done in terms of drawing from the voluminous body of scholarship on crisis – crisis diplomacy, crisis dynamics, crisis management and crisis prevention, to name just a few areas – that was developed during the Cold War period. Some of this work could certainly be adapted and applied to the contemporary East Asian context. For as Evelyn Goh has recently observed, 'in none of these flashpoints is there widespread political appetite for the difficult process of actually solving the conflicts'.[49] Understanding the dynamics of 'crisis', and having rigorous analytical frameworks through which to illuminate these dynamics, is thus becoming an increasingly important and necessary scholarly endeavour.

Notes

1 R. D. Kaplan, 'The South China Sea is the Future of Conflict', *Foreign Policy*, 188: 76–85, 2011.
2 K. Rudd, 'A Maritime Balkans of the 21st Century', *Foreign Policy*, 30, January 2013, www.foreignpolicy.com/articles/2013/01/30/a_maritime_blkans_of_the_21st_century_ east_asia (accessed 2 June 2014).

3   H. White, 'Caught in a Bind that Threatens an Asian War Nobody Wants', *Sydney Morning Herald*, 26 December 2012.

4   V. Cha, 'What to Do About N. Korean Aggression', *The Chosun Ilbo*, 6 December 2010.

5   For a sampling of this literature, see C. Bell, *The Conventions of Crisis: A Study in Diplomatic Management*, Oxford University Press for the Royal Institute of International Affairs, London, 1971; J. H. Kalicki, *The Pattern of Sino-American Crises*, Cambridge University Press, Cambridge, 1975; J. L. Richardson, *Crisis Diplomacy: The Great Powers since the Mid-Nineteenth Century*, Cambridge University Press, Cambridge, 1994. On crisis management/prevention, see A. L. George (ed.), *Managing U.S.-Soviet Rivalry: Problems of Crisis Prevention*, Westview Press, Boulder, CO, 1983.

6   These definitions are each elaborated in a useful overview of the concept of crisis provided in M. Brecher and J. Wilkenfield, *A Study of Crisis*, University of Michigan Press, Ann Arbor, MI, 1997, pp. 2–10.

7   See M. D. Swaine, 'Understanding the Historical Record', in M. D. Swaine and Z. Tuosheng (eds), *Managing Sino-American Crises*, Carnegie Endowment for International Peace, Washington, DC, 2006, p. 1.

8   Swaine observes that official Chinese media outlets used the term 'core interests' during the 1980s and 1990s, but that they did so only with reference to the 'core interests' of *other* nations, not those of China. As Swaine points out, in 2003–2004 Chinese officials themselves began employing the 'core interests' terminology, explicitly with reference to China. See M. D. Swaine, 'China's Assertive Behavior: On "Core Interests"', *China Leadership Monitor*, 34, 2011.

9   E. Wong, 'Chinese Military Seeks to Extend its Naval Power', *New York Times*, 24 April 2010.

10 G. Sheridan, 'China Actions Meant as Test, Clinton Says', *The Australian*, 9 November 2010.

11 US International Energy Information Administration, 'South China Sea', 7 February 2013, www.eia.gov/countries/regions-topics.cfm?fips=SCS (accessed 31 October 2013).

12 Swaine, 'China's Assertive Behavior'.

13 A. S. Erickson and G. B. Collins, 'China's Oil Security Pipe Dream: The Reality and Strategic Consequences of Seaborne Imports', *Naval war College Review*, 63: 92, 2010.

14 D. Blair and K. Lieberthal, 'Smooth Sailing: The World's Shipping Lanes are Safe', *Foreign Affairs*, 86: 12, 2007.

15 See Z. Keck, 'China and America's Dueling South China Sea Statements', *The Diplomat*, 7 August 2012, www.thediplomat.com/china-power/china-and-americas-dueling-south-china-sea-statements/ (accessed 2 June 2014).

16 P. M. Cronin and R. D. Kaplan, 'Cooperation from Strength: U.S. Strategy and the South China Sea', in P. M. Cronin (ed.), *Cooperation from Strength: The United States, China and the South China Sea*, Center for a New American Security, Washington, DC, 2012, p. 7.

17 D. Blumenthal, 'The Power Projection Balance in Asia', in T. G. Mahnken (ed.), *Competitive Strategies for the 21st Century: Theory, History, and Practice*, Stanford University Press, Palo Alto, CA, 2012, p. 179.

18 F. Whaley, 'U.S. Reaffirms Defense of Philippines in Standoff With China', *New York Times*, 1 May 2012.

19 Australian Government, Department of Prime Minister and Cabinet, *Strong and Secure: A Strategy for Australia's National Security*, Commonwealth of Australia, Canberra, ACT, 2013; Commonwealth of Australia, *Defence White Paper 2013*, Department of Defence, Canberra, ACT, 2013.

20 J. J. Mearsheimer, *The Tragedy of Great Power Politics*, W.W. Norton, New York, 2001, pp. 114–199.

21 R. Emmers, *Geopolitics and Maritime Territorial Disputes in East Asia*, Routledge, London, 2010, pp. 65–86.

22 D. C. Blair and D. V. Bonfili, 'The April 2011 EP-3 Incident: The U.S. Point of View', in M. D. Swaine and Z. Tuosheng (eds), *Managing Sino-American Crises*, Carnegie Endowment for International Peace, Washington, DC, 2006, p. 379.

23 M. Valencia, 'The Impeccable Incident: Truth and Consequences', *China Security*, 5: 25–26, 2009.

24 Cha, 'What to Do About N. Korean Aggression'.

25 S. Snyder, 'Diplomatic and Security Relations between China and North Korea Under Kim Jong-Il', in B. S. Glaser and B. Billingsley (eds), *Reordering Chinese Priorities on the Korean Peninsula*, a report of the CSIS Freeman Chair in China Studies, Center for Strategic and International Studies, November 2012, p. 28.

26 S. Waterman, 'China Doing "Quite Well" Enforcing U.N. Sanctions on North Korea, South Says', *Washington Times*, 15 April 2013.

27 Cited in C. Hatton, 'Is China ready to Abandon North Korea', *BBC News*, 12 April 2013, www.bbc.co.uk/news/world-asia-china-22062589 (accessed 2 June 2014).

28 V. Cha, 'Why China Can't Cut off North Korea', *The Huffington Post*, 6 April 2012, www.huffingtonpost.com/victor-cha/china-north-korea-relations_b_1404178.html (accessed 2 June 2014).

29 See, for example, H. R. Clinton, Secretary of State, speech on 'America's Engagement in the Asia-Pacific', Kahala Hotel, Honolulu, Hawaii, 28 October 2010.

30 See, for example, 'Remarks by President Obama and President Lee Myung-Bak of the Republic of Korea after Bilateral Meeting', Intercontinental Downtown Hotel, Toronto, Canada, 26 June 2010, www.whitehouse.gov/thr-press-office/remarks-president-obama-and-president-lee-myung-bak-republic-korea-after-bilateral- (accessed 2 June 2014).

31 B. Schreer and B. Taylor, 'The Korean Crises and Sino-American Rivalry', *Survival*, 53: 13–19, 2011.

32 For an excellent history of the 1993–1994 North Korean nuclear crisis, see J. S. Wit, D. B. Poneman and R. L. Gallucci, *Going Critical: The First North Korean Nuclear Crisis*, Brookings Institution Press, Washington, DC, 2004.

33 D. Halberstam, *The Coldest Winter*, Pan Books, Basingstoke and Oxford, 2009, p. 4.

34 US Congress, Senate. Hearing before the Committee on Armed Services, *Security Implications of the Nuclear Non-Proliferation Agreement with North Korea*, 104th Cong., 1st sess., 26 January 1995, p. 22.

35 Citied in B. Schreer, 'Feeling Edgy: Japan's New Defence White Paper', *The Strategist*, 11 July 2013. For an excellent summary of recent Sino-Japanese tensions, see also International Crisis Group, 'Dangerous Waters: China-Japan Relations on the Rocks', *Asia Report*, 245, 2013.

36 G. Baker and G. Nishiyama, 'Abe Says Japan Ready to Counter China's Power', *Wall Street Journal*, 26 October 2013.

37 'Senkakus a "Core Interest", Chinese Military Scholar Tells Japan', *The Japan Times*, 20 August 2013.

38 M. Auslin, 'Don't Forget about the East China Sea', *East and South China Seas Bulletin*, 2, 2012.

39 M. J. Green and N. Szechenyi, 'US-Japan Relations: Meet the New Boss/Same as the Old Boss?', *Comparative Connections*, 14, 2013.

40 H. White, 'Stand Firm in the East China Sea', *The National Interest*, 17 September 2013, www.nationalinterest.org/commentary/stand-firm-the-east-china-sea-9080 (accessed 2 June 2014).

41 See, for example, D. Roy, 'The Sources and Limits of Sino-Japanese Tensions', *Survival*, 47: 191–214, 2005.

42 See, for instance, White, 'Stand Firm in the East China Sea'.

43 T. Hiraga, '90 Percent of Japanese, Chinese View Each Other Negatively, Poll Finds', *The Asahi Shimbun*, 6 August 2013.

44 J. J. Przystup, J. Bradford and J. Manicom, 'Japan-China Maritime Confidence Building and Communication Mechanisms', *PacNet*, 67, 2013.

45 R. Mitter, *China's War with Japan, 1937–1945: The Struggle for Survival*, Allen Lane, London, 2013.

46 J. R. Holmes, 'The Sino-Japanese War of 2012', *Foreign Policy*, 20 August 2012, www.foreignpolicy.com/articles/2012/08/20/the_sino_japanese_naval_war_of_2012 (accessed 2 June 2014).

47 See D. Kagan, *The Peloponnesian War*, Harper Perennial, London, 2005, p. 25.

48 R. Emmers, *Geopolitics and Maritime Territorial Disputes in East Asia*, Routledge, London, 2010.

49 E. Goh, 'Ringing in a New Order? Hegemony, Hierarchy, and Transition in East Asia', *Centre of Gravity Series*, Strategic and Defence Studies Centre, Australian National University, October 2013, p. 6. See also E. Goh, *The Struggle for Order: Hegemony, Hierarchy, and Transition in Post-Cold War East Asia*, Oxford University Press, Oxford, 2013.

11 The South China Sea

Stabilisation and resolution

Leszek Buszynski and Christopher B. Roberts

Introduction

Many proposals for a resolution of the dispute have been made in the past. They have sought to tie the claimants to an existing status quo, which, of course, have favoured ASEAN, but not China, and for that reason could not be implemented. Resolution demands the acceptance of the status quo, and while Vietnam and the Philippines would be pleased at the prospect, it would be only be an impediment to Chinese ambitions. It would be fantasy to imagine that such proposals would be accepted at the present time by China against its interests when it has the hope and expectation of obtaining acceptance of its extensive claim. Those proposals, which would, in some way, meet those interests in changed conditions when China may realise the diplomatic and political costs of its efforts to control the South China Sea, would have a greater chance of success. Until that time, these proposals may set a framework that may be applied or invoked when conditions are propitious. One intermediary step is stabilisation of the situation in the South China Sea, which falls short of the resolution of the issue. It entails measures, actions and agreements directed to the maintenance of the status quo, or prevention of activities that may bring about conflict or stimulate clashes between any of the claimants. Stabilisation requires particular constraints on activities to avoid provocation to minimise the risk of escalation that may follow. Such measures may be opposed by those who attempt to change the status quo, or who derive political advantages from raising tensions by challenging it. These measures would only be accepted if the benefits of a more stable environment would outweigh the risks of challenging the status quo, and whatever gains may be obtained by doing so.

Resolution, however, is a further step, and is more than stabilisation, since it addresses the underlying issues, grievances and claims that have given rise to the dispute in a final settlement. It is possible to have stabilisation of a dispute in an uneasy stalemate without resolution, where the disputants are unprepared to deal with others or unwilling to forgo the opportunity of turning the situation to their advantage. An uneasy stalemate of this kind may not last, and there would be the danger of a breakdown and a reoccurrence of hostilities. When the disputants understand that resolution of an issue brings benefits of a kind that cannot be obtained by insisting on the unilateral pursuit of their own claims, they become more amenable to a settlement. Resolution cannot be just an imposition by a superior power, since this would stimulate new grievances and injustices, leading to renewed instabilities that power alone would not be able to contain. A durable resolution is the result of a process of negotiation that would, in some way, accommodate these grievances to the extent possible and give little cause for the renewal of conflict.

Stabilisation of the existing situation

The Code of Conduct

The immediate priority is to stabilise the situation in the South China Sea and to prevent conflict, particularly as Chinese deployment of patrol craft increases, placing greater pressure upon the ASEAN claimants. ASEAN has pursued the idea of a Code of Conduct (CoC) for the disputants as a stabilising measure to prevent the disputants from resorting to force, or threatening its use, or otherwise engaging in provocative activities that could result in conflict. A CoC requires mutual self-restraint based on a common understanding of what activities to avoid, as well as acceptable procedures to be pursued in the event of an incident or event that could get out of hand. It requires conflict-preventive and management procedures that are accepted in the self-interest of the disputants, who understand that the situation would be much more dangerous otherwise. A code does not prohibit a list of activities, as with some legal documents, and its intention would be to evoke voluntary compliance from its signatories, and recognition that adherence to accepted norms of behaviour will reduce the likelihood of conflict. ASEAN's first effort towards a CoC was the Declaration on the South China Sea, which it concluded with China in July 1992. It called on the parties 'to apply the principles contained in the Treaty of Amity and Cooperation in Southeast Asia as the basis for establishing a code of international conduct over the South China Sea'.[1] The Chinese occupation of Mischief Reef in the Philippine claim zone was seen in the Philippines as a violation of this declaration, since it had urged 'restraint with the view to creating a positive climate for the eventual resolution of all disputes'. The Philippines then moved to give more substance to the notion of a code in a way that would be more difficult to ignore. Two rounds of Chinese-Philippine talks were conducted at vice-ministerial level in August 1995, one round in Hangzhou, another in Manila. In Manila, the two sides agreed upon the broad outline of a CoC based on international law and UNCLOS. They also agreed to form committees to discuss CBMs such as cooperation in conservation, meteorology, disaster relief, search and rescue, navigation, and environmental protection.[2] The Philippine side also demanded that China evacuate Mischief Reef, which the Chinese rejected. In the following November, Philippine-Vietnam talks were conducted in Hanoi when the two sides agreed to a nine-point CoC for the Spratly Islands, which included the need to settle disputes by peaceful negotiations, the resolution of disputes on the basis of respect for international law and UNCLOS, the commitment to observe self restraint and to refrain from using force or the threat of force, and to 'desist from any act that would affect the friendship between the two countries and the stability of the region'.[3]

When Vietnamese President Le Duc Anh met his Philippine counterpart President Fidel Ramos later in the same month, they both called for a common CoC to be adopted by all claimants in the Spratlys and a multilateral meeting to deal with the issue.[4] At this stage, the code was to embrace the Spratly Islands, and it was only later that Vietnam advocated its extension to the Paracels as well. The Philippines wanted to prevent China from constructing new structures on features in its claim zone, as it was concerned that China was strengthening and expanding structures on Mischief Reef. The idea of a code was raised at the 29th ASEAN Foreign Ministers Meeting in Jakarta in 1996, and then in the ASEAN Summit in December 1998. ASEAN proposed a CoC to China in April 1999, which continued with negotiations over the issue. Pushed by the Philippines, ASEAN drafted a treaty in July 1999, which was to govern behaviour in disputed areas of the South China Sea. The draft was sent to a working committee for finalisation.[5] ASEAN, however, was divided over the issue, and Malaysia objected to Philippine demands. China drafted its own variant of a code, which included a ban on military patrols in the area, and called upon the parties to refrain from arresting fishermen and seizing fishing boats in disputed waters.[6] Negotiations continued until, finally, China agreed to a declaration on a CoC.[7]

The result of this effort was the Declaration on the Conduct of the Parties (DoC), which was concluded between ASEAN and China in Phnom Penh on 4 November 2002. This was intended to be less than a CoC, but it did include the points that were supposed to be incorporated into a full code. Though it was not legally binding, for all intents and purposes in terms of content it was the code that ASEAN had been seeking. Point 4 enjoined the disputants 'to resolve their territorial and jurisdictional disputes by peaceful means, without resorting to the threat or use of force'. In point 5, the parties agreed 'to exercise self-restraint in the conduct of activities . . . refraining from action of inhabiting on the presently uninhabited islands, reefs, shoals, cays, and other features'. In point 10, the parties reaffirmed that 'the adoption of a CoC in the South China Sea would further promote peace and stability in the region'.[8] How would a full CoC differ from the above? After the Chinese occupation of Mischief Reef, ASEAN wanted firmer reassurance from China in regard to its activities in the South China Sea, and pressed for a legally binding document. If a legally binding document were agreed, it would expose any violation as a transgression against law to the detriment of reputation. However, a legally binding agreement would require a dispute resolution mechanism (DRM) or appeal procedures to a body that would decide upon violations. Moreover, the parties would have to decide the geographic application of the code, as this was absent in the DoC. Initially, the discussions centred on the Spratlys, but Vietnam insisted on the inclusion of the Paracels as well, which China opposed. The inability to resolve this issue left the area of application of the DoC open to the interpretation of the parties. Ambiguity of this kind could be tolerated in a declaration, but in a legally binding code it would create endless difficulties, which could undermine it. The Philippines had to forgo the hope of including a ban on the construction of new structures in the declaration, and had to be content with the restraining effect of point 5.

The DoC was a hailed as a breakthrough in negotiations with China, and ASEAN observers were accordingly elated. While China had declared that it would deal with the claimants bilaterally, its signature to this multilateral document seemed to indicate a welcome change of approach.[9] Why did China sign? One argument was that the DoC was a demonstration of Chinese moderation and its willing acceptance of norms of behaviour in the South China Sea.[10] China's accession to ASEAN's Treaty of Amity and Cooperation (TAC) on 8 October 2003, according to which disputes are to be settled peacefully, was cited within ASEAN as a sign that China would accept such norms in its relations with ASEAN. Article 2 (d) of the TAC enjoined the parties to settle their differences by 'peaceful means', while Article 2 (e) committed the parties to the 'Renunciation of the threat or use of force'.[11] A second argument was that China could use the DoC to constrain the activities of the ASEAN claimants in the South China Sea and prevent them from fortifying islands or features that could weaken the Chinese position there. A third argument was that China wanted to avoid pushing ASEAN towards the US over the issue and could use the DoC to separate ASEAN from the US.[12] After China had expanded structures on features in the Philippine claim zone, President Joseph Estrada sought US support, which induced caution from the Chinese. After having removed the US naval presence from Subic Bay in 1992, the Philippine Senate, in May 1999, ratified a Visiting Forces Agreement with the US, which was signed in the previous year, allowing the US to rotate naval forces though Philippine ports on short visits.[13] Continued pressure on the ASEAN claimants would draw in the US, which the Chinese wanted to prevent. In this sense, the DoC was a diplomatic device to forestall US involvement in the issue.

For ASEAN, however, the DoC was inadequate. It was still a declaration that did not indicate a full commitment from the Chinese side that could be understood as legally binding. Moreover, it did not detail actions to be avoided or procedures to be adopted in relation to clashes over fishing, exploration and survey activities, or means of communication and consultation between the parties that would minimise the danger of conflict. Nonetheless, ASEAN continued along two paths. One was the implementation of the DoC for which ASEAN China senior officials established an ASEAN-China Joint Working Group in 2004. In July 2011, ASEAN and China agreed to guidelines on the implementation of the DoC, which mentioned possible joint cooperative activities, measures and projects such as marine environmental protection, marine scientific research, safety of navigation and communication at sea, and search and rescue operations. The second path was the CoC, which was intended to compensate for the deficiencies of the DoC. In July 2009, at the 16th ARF, the Chairman's statement noted that ASEAN and China 'looked forward to the eventual conclusion of a Regional Code of Conduct'.[14] Vietnam had high hopes of making progress on the CoC when it was ASEAN chair in 2010. The Chairman's statement from the 17th ARF, which was held in

Hanoi in July 2010, noted that members 'encouraged efforts towards the full implementation of the Declaration and the eventual conclusion of a Regional Code of Conduct'.[15] In its position as shaper of an ASEAN consensus, Indonesia has been pushing strongly for a code as an expression of ASEAN agreement over the issue. While the Chinese Ambassador to the Philippines Liu Jianchao claimed that China was willing to negotiate a CoC with ASEAN, there have been conflicting signals from the Chinese side.[16] Indeed, at the 20th ARF, held on 20 July 2013, the issues of the implementation of the DoC and the CoC remained unresolved. Members of the ARF were 'encouraged' by the Senior Officials Meetings (SOMs) and the joint working group on the implementation of the DoC and agreed to work towards the adoption of a CoC. They also noted the move to establish an Eminent Persons and Experts Group (EPEG) and/or other mechanisms to provide support for these consultations, but there was little else to indicate any progress over the issue.[17]

China has resisted the CoC because it would constrain its harassment tactics against the ASEAN claimants and reduce its freedom of action in the South China Sea. As a rising power, it has no incentive to accept ASEAN proposals and manoeuvres to deal with the ASEAN members individually. For this reason, some Vietnamese think the whole idea of a CoC a chimera, despite the fact that their government has promoted it.[18] The CoC proposal does, however, keep ASEAN focused on the South China Sea issue and contributes to some sense of unity in the organisation, however fragile that may be. However, a proposal whose principal value is the maintenance of organisational unity does not augur well for future negotiations with a China that is continually evading it. There are other problems with the proposal, as Vietnam has pressed for its application to the Paracels, which other ASEAN members resist, leaving its geographical scope vague and open. ASEAN has also differed over whether the code should be legally binding, as demanded by the Philippines and Vietnam, and what kind of dispute resolution mechanism should be included. Difficulties have also arisen over the way in which the proposed code should be negotiated. China has demanded that ASEAN negotiate directly with it over the drafting of the code, which would then be a common product. ASEAN claimants fear that this would allow China to play upon ASEAN differences, with the result that an emasculated version of a code would emerge that would not meet their purposes. Philippine President Benigno Aquino has resisted the Chinese demand, and with the support of Vietnam and Thailand has insisted that ASEAN agree on a CoC first, and then present it to China in separate negotiations. China's ally within ASEAN, Cambodia, was more than willing to involve China in the negotiations since the issue did not concern it directly. Indonesia's Foreign Minister Marty Natalegawa smoothed over the differences within ASEAN by proposing a six-point platform and circulating a draft CoC that included conflict prevention and conflict management measures.[19] The code has American support, which was expressed by Hillary Clinton during the 17th ARF in Hanoi in July 2010, and also by Ambassador to the Philippines Harry Thomas, who said that the US was willing to 'help craft a legally binding Code of Conduct'.[20]

Chinese views have differed over the issue. The academic Zhang Yunling thought that a CoC was possible as a stabilisation measure, but not to resolve disputes.[21] Foreign Minister Wang Yi warned ASEAN against 'unrealistic expectations' and that progress on the code depended on the extent to which the claimants followed the DoC, which he accused the Philippines of violating.[22] Later, Wang complained that the DoC was 'disrupted by some parties' and insisted that it be implemented first before the parties would gradually move to the Code of Conduct.[23] China's concern was the Philippines, which had vociferously raised the issue of Chinese harassment over Scarborough Shoal in April 2012 in an effort to galvanise ASEAN into action. The Chinese expected ASEAN to curb the Philippines and its demands before a CoC could be concluded, and played on frustration with Manila within the organisation. The price of a Code of Conduct for ASEAN was a compliant Philippines, which would be tantamount to ASEAN acquiescence in China's activities in the Philippine claim zone. It would turn the code into a meaningless formality, applicable only where there are no disputes. If ASEAN settled for such an outcome for the sake of the relationship with China, it would entail a sacrifice of Philippine interests, which would not help the other claimants, Vietnam or Malaysia, should they come under direct Chinese pressure in the South China Sea. China agreed to continue with 'official consultations' with ASEAN over the code 'within the framework of the implementation of the DoC'.[24] The 20th ARF, which was held in Brunei, noted that steps would be taken to create an 'Eminent Persons and Experts Group (EPEG) and/or other mechanisms to provide support to such consultations'.[25]

What are the prospects for the CoC? It represents a means of stabilising the situation in the South China Sea through mutual restraint of conduct, and demands trust between the parties that is yet to be established. While the Chinese feel they have a superior position in relation to the ASEAN claimants, they have little incentive to agree to the kind of CoC that ASEAN desires. If it is to be legally binding in the sense that the parties regard it as having the force of law, it would freeze the status quo to the detriment of China. If it were to be a declaration based on voluntary compliance, it would be no more than a restatement of the DoC. China, however, has used the negotiations for the code as part of its strategy in dealing with what it regards as an obstructionist Philippines. It uses the incentive of improved relations in its dealings with ASEAN to sideline the South China Sea dispute in a way that would weaken the position of the ASEAN claimants within the organisation. In this respect, China's tactics exacerbate existing divisions within ASEAN, which would ensure that any code that ASEAN may produce would be, at best, an anodyne reiteration of the DoC. Despite the limited prospects for the code at present, it may have a better chance of success in a different situation when fear of conflict or escalation would act as a deterrent to China's provocative activities in the area. The code would then be a means of defending China's position there and securing gains already made. It would be important to put in place the framework of the code, which could be invoked at some future time when necessary.

An Incidents at Sea Agreement

One variant of a CoC that may prove to be of value in this context is an Incidents at Sea Agreement (INCSEA) to avoid clashes in the South China Sea between naval and coastguard vessels, and to prevent accidental escalation if clashes occur. Such an agreement would differ from the code ASEAN has been seeking by involving the navies of external powers, as well as the maritime vessels of the claimant states. It would also be more specific in targeting maritime incidents, though in the South China Sea that would include the most disturbing and provocative. Such an agreement would detail procedures to avoid collisions between patrol vessels by ensuring safe distance from each other, and would require commanders to use caution in approaching other vessels. It would also include procedures for communication between navies and governments in the event of a clash, and the establishment of hotlines between the naval commands or coastguards in the area. The most notable example is the INCSEA between the US and the Soviet Union, concluded on 25 May 1972, after a series of incidents at sea involving harassment, simulated attacks and dangerous manoeuvres. The agreement listed specific actions that commanders were to take, including steps to avoid collision, avoiding manoeuvres in areas of heavy sea traffic, requiring surveillance ships to maintain a safe distance from the object of investigation and not 'simulating attacks at, launching objects toward, or illuminating the bridges of the other party's ships'. A protocol to the agreement signed on 22 May 1973 added that the parties would not make 'simulated attacks by aiming guns, missile launchers, torpedo tubes and other weapons at non-military ships of the other Party'.[26] On 19 January 1998, the US and China concluded an agreement to improve maritime safety by establishing a 'channel for consultation' to 'promote common understanding regarding activities undertaken by their respective maritime and air forces'. That channel would include annual meetings, working groups and special meetings as required to discuss 'measures to promote safe maritime practices and establish mutual trust as search and rescue communications procedures when ships encounter each other'. [27] The US-China agreement was vague and consultative, and lacked the detail found in the earlier agreement with the Soviet Union. It also reflected Chinese reluctance to accept any constraint upon their actions.

China's attitude might change, however, if its harassment tactics resulted in clashes and conflicts that would threaten dangerous escalation. If the Chinese increased the pressure in the South China Sea and ASEAN claimants stood firm to defend their maritime claims with American support, this possibility could not be discounted. China may then face the consequences of an accidental clash or a crisis that would bring home the dangers of escalation and the need for maritime safety procedures of the kind outlined above. The Soviet Union was initially resistant to this proposal for an agreement with the US, but eventually changed after numerous incidents at sea involving harassment and simulated attacks stimulated fears of an unintended clash. That danger exists, as illustrated by the stand-off involving the *USNS Impeccable* in the South China Sea on 5 March

2009 and the USS *Cowpens* on 13 December 2013. Tense moments arose around the Senkaku/Diaoyu Islands as well. On 19 January 2013, a Chinese destroyer locked its fire control radar on a ship-based Japanese helicopter around the islands, while a similar incident occurred on 30 January when a Chinese destroyer locked its fire control radar on a Japanese destroyer, provoking a furore in Japan.[28] Japanese reports claimed that the Chinese commanders were acting on their own without orders from above, seemingly motivated by the nationalism that gripped the country over the issue. Such incidents may indeed become more common in the future in the South China Sea as the Chinese expand their presence there and become impatient with the presence of the ASEAN claimants.

These incidents would be better managed if an INCSEA were in place. Any such agreement for the South China Sea would have to be drafted at two levels. On one level, it would have to deal with the maritime presence of external powers that have an interest in the area, not only the US, but Japan as well, where similar provisions similar to the 1972 agreement could be agreed. On another level, the ASEAN claimants would have to be included without prejudice to the sovereign claims of any of the parties. It would be important to specify that maritime vessels avoid collisions, overt harassment and simulated attacks, and keep a safe distance from each other. Communication and consultation procedures between navies, coastguards and maritime surveillance commands would also be required to defuse incidents that would have the potential to escalate. The very scale and complexity of such an agreement would ensure its initial rejection by the Chinese, who may be interested in negotiating with external powers, but not with ASEAN claimants. An agreement of this kind would be a barrier to China's effort to maintain the pressure on the ASEAN claimants, and China will reject any such multilateral agreement at present. The idea of an INCSEA may become more attractive, however, should a clash or crisis be triggered that would threaten escalation.

Resolution

Second-track diplomacy

The first attempt to seek a resolution of the issue was by means of informal workshops or track-two diplomacy. Such workshops have been used as a means of dispute resolution when formal diplomacy reaches a stalemate and the parties are searching for a way out of their predicament. Often called interactive problem-solving, this approach may be used to stimulate ideas and proposals that may be carried over into formal diplomacy. While this approach cannot resolve an issue on hand that would be well beyond it, it can at least produce ideas and proposals that may circumvent a diplomatic deadlock and facilitate progress towards a resolution. Such was the case when Indonesian Ambassador Hasjim Djalal promoted workshops on the South China Sea that were sponsored by the Indonesian Foreign Ministry, and until 2001 funded by the Canadian International

Development Agency (CIDA). They have since continued with ad hoc funding. Entitled 'Managing Potential Conflicts in the South China Sea', the first was held in Bali in January 1990, continuing on an annual basis subsequently. They involved government officials and technical experts on maritime cooperation and resource development from 11 countries, initially the ASEAN six, Taiwan, Cambodia, Laos and Vietnam; China and Taiwan joined in 1991. Attempts were made to carry the recommendations of the workshop to the first track diplomatic level, but they were resisted by the Chinese. Indonesian Foreign Minister Ali Alatas, in 1994, declared that his intention was not to convert the workshop into a formal forum, but that 'the time may have arrived to formalise some of the proposed activities of the workshop in certain agreed areas in order to engage government agencies or authorities more directly'. [29] Ali Alatas again proposed involving government officials in the implementation of projects at the 1995 workshop.[30] This effort to gradually formalise the workshops was resisted by the Chinese, and since then they have become exercises in repetition.

What did the workshops achieve? Its organisers have claimed that the Chinese were made more aware of the views of the other claimants as a result of participating in these workshops, which were regarded as a 'sounding board' for new ideas.[31] Because of the workshops, the fishing problem was 'more broadly appreciated', and areas of cooperation, such as biodiversity protection, marine scientific research, environment and ecology, living resource management and conservation, were identified, and related projects initiated.[32] The 'Declaration on the South China Sea', which was endorsed by both ASEAN and China in July 1992, was a product of discussions in the second workshop in Bandung in July 1991. In that workshop, it was agreed that parties in the dispute would 'exercise self-restraint in order not to complicate the situation', this phrase was included in the 1992 ASEAN declaration. Hasjim Djalal thought that this was a positive example of how track-two workshops could influence deliberations at the track one level.[33] Similarly, the idea of a CoC as a proposal was a product of the second meeting of the technical working group (TWG) on legal matters, which met in Pattaya in 1995.[34] Nonetheless, whatever its merits, second-track diplomacy has failed to achieve its primary goal, though it may have made the claimants more aware of each other's position. It held out some promise in the 1990s when China wanted to strengthen relations with ASEAN, and responded to ASEAN overtures in terms of participating in institutional dialogue in the ARF or the ASEAN-China SOMs.[35] Subsequently, however, as Hasjim Djalal noted, by 1999 the workshop process had 'stalled', and it had indeed reached its limits.[36] If it could not discuss territorial issues and ways of resolving them, it became a repetitive and frustrating experience for those who had placed their hopes in them. Despite the disappointment, the second-track approach may become more important in the future in another form when the disputants are ready to discuss ways to bring about a legal settlement. When this time comes, however far off it may be, the ASEAN-China Eminent Persons Group (EPG), which was created in 2005, may assume an important role in formulating proposals to resolve the issue.

Legal settlement

A legal resolution means applying the principles of UNCLOS according to an agreed equitable formula that would take into account the claims of the littoral states. Article 279 of Part XV says that the parties have an 'obligation to settle disputes by peaceful means'. A logical approach would be to apportion maritime territory according to contiguous EEZs and continental shelves, where they have been declared, using coastline lengths to determine the maritime zones to which occupied islands may be entitled. Something similar was proposed in 1994 by Indonesian Foreign Minister Ali Alatas, when he called for a 'doughnut' solution that would allow each state to claim a 320 kilometre EEZ, leaving an inner hole like a doughnut (see Map 4). This inner area would then be subject to joint development, and the revenue would be divided according to an agreed formula.[37] The proposal was promoted by Ambassador Hasjim Djalal when he visited the ASEAN countries over May to June 1994, but it was clearly too ambitious to attract support.[38] A related proposal by Ji Guoxing of the Shanghai Institute of International Studies is to allow Vietnam, the Philippines, Malaysia and Brunei to have their declared EEZs and continental shelves, while China would surrender the nine-dash line and its claim to 'historic waters', and would be compensated by the doughnut section. In overlapping areas, an equidistant line would be applied, and if this were not possible bilateral or trilateral development would be adopted.[39] Aside from the practical difficulties of arranging the apportionment, the major problem is that neither China nor Vietnam has defined their claim. China's nine-dash line has not been officially explained, and whether it is a claim to islands or an exclusive claim to sea territory is unclear. Its exact boundaries are still undefined. Vietnam has issued declarations of sovereignty over the islands without specifying exactly what is included in its claim or what the coordinates are. Moreover, these proposals would significantly reduce the maritime area available to China, which would be stripped of its claim to the entire area with little compensation, particularly as the oil and gas fields are located along the coastlines and outside the centre area.

The ASEAN claimants have been clarifying their claims to ensure conformity with UNCLOS. Legality, indeed, is their defence against China, and if they could create a legal regime in the area based on their common agreement China might be obliged to follow. On this basis, it has been argued that if the claimants all complied with UNCLOS, the claims would be clarified and a legal framework established for cooperation between them.[40] The sovereignty issue could then be circumvented and eventual resolution of the issue would be possible in the spirit of mutual cooperation. On 6 May 2009, Malaysia and Vietnam made a joint submission to the UN Commission on the Limits of the Continental Shelf (CLCS) to clarify their continental shelf and EEZ claims. On the following day, Vietnam made a separate submission to the Commission on the continental shelf in the north of the South China Sea.[41] China, however, protested. On 10 March 2009, the Philippines passed the Republic Act 9522, or the Archipelagic Baselines Law, which defines the archipelagic baselines of the Philippines in Kalayaan and

Scarborough Shoal according to UNCLOS provisions.[42] The law created a 'regime of islands' separate from the mainland, but included in the Philippine archipelago. The Philippine Commission on Maritime and Ocean Affairs (CMOA) argued that the status of Kalayaan and Scarborough Shoal as a 'regime of islands' would be similar to the relationship of Hawaii to the mainland United States; Hawaii was not included in the baselines of the US, but is undoubtedly US territory.[43] Once again, China protested the Philippine move.[44]

China, however, has not clarified its claim according to UNCLOS, and has been adopting a very different approach to the issue. China seeks legal validation of its claims in ways that would either stretch the limits of current legal interpretation or depart from the existing legal framework considerably. It is, as yet, unclear whether China would persist in this effort, but if it continues it would demand legal recognition of a claim based on historical grounds, either claiming rights of first discovery or historical contact over the centuries. It may argue, as some Asian scholars do, that the current legal framework is a Western imposition on East Asia, developed by the dominant Western powers, and does not take into account historical claims and rights that were understood in the past.[45] However, any attempt to revise international law in this way would trigger a legal crisis that would divide Asia and create many more problems than could be resolved. China may not challenge the corpus of existing law, but may call for a special exception for the South China Sea, one that would allow it to impose a settlement upon the ASEAN claimants. Using harassment tactics over a prolonged period, during which the ASEAN claimants would be convinced that they would have no choice but to settle with a powerful neighbour, a Chinese-sponsored settlement would be devised that would then be declared legal. It would be understood as a regional solution to the issue, which would extend Chinese rights in the area beyond what would be permitted by UNCLOS, and correspondingly reduce those of the ASEAN claimants. China may also press for legal recognition of the right of states to claim archipelagos as a justification for its claim to the South China Sea, though it has not received legal endorsement. It would argue that the legal principle of an archipelagic state, such as Indonesia or the Philippines, was enshrined in UNCLOS and can be extended to an archipelago belonging to a state.[46] During the negotiations for UNCLOS, the proposal had the support of 10 other states, including India, France and Canada, which had distant islands they wanted to secure under this principle.[47] International law is still evolving, and this proposal may yet attract support.

Legal adjudication

Article 287 of UNCLOS enjoins parties to a maritime dispute to resort to four dispute resolution mechanisms: the International Tribunal for the Law of the Sea (ITLOS) in Hamburg, the International Court of Justice (ICJ) in The Hague, ad hoc arbitration in accordance with Annex VII, or a 'Special Arbitral Tribunal' constituted for certain categories of disputes. Compulsory mediation with binding authority is voluntary, and UNCLOS stipulates that 'a state shall be free to choose' one of these methods of dispute resolution. UNCLOS has no immediate way of dealing with a situation where the claimants have no intention to resort to binding mediation. International lawyers have expressed considerable faith in legal mediation, particularly in the UNCLOS provisions noted above. Should China persist in rebuffing ASEAN claimant attempts to devise a legal resolution, the claimants may collectively or separately invoke the legal process of adjudication. The difficulty is that China is unlikely to accept legal adjudication over what it increasingly regards either as a domestic issue or a matter concerning the claimants only. Some Chinese scholars nonetheless support the idea. Ji Guoxing has argued that a third party, the ICJ, an Arbitral Tribunal or an arbitrator could play a role without internationalising the dispute, which China would oppose.[48] The only attempt to invoke legal adjudication over the issue occurred on 22 January 2013, when Philippine Foreign Secretary Albert del Rosario announced that the Philippines would invoke Annex VII and take the issue to a UN 'Special Arbitral Tribunal'. The Philippines requested the Arbitral Tribunal to rule that: (1) China's rights to the area are based on UNCLOS; (2) China's maritime claims, as based on the nine-dash line, are contrary to UNCLOS and invalid; (3) China should bring its domestic legislation into conformity with its obligations under UNCLOS; and (4) China should desist from activities that violate the rights of the Philippines in its claimed zone.[49] Later, Albert del Rosario explained that arbitration would clarify Philippine fishing rights, rights to resources and 'rights to enforce laws within our Exclusive Economic Zone'.[50] Needless to say, the Chinese opposed the move, and as the *People's Daily* commented, 'China takes the position that it already owns the disputed territories and is therefore exempt from any international jurisdiction and arbitration under international law'.[51] In April 2013, the International Tribunal for the Law of the Sea (ITLOS) appointed five members of the ad hoc UN Tribunal that will hear the case, and on 11 July proceedings began in The Hague.[52] The challenge for the Tribunal is to clarify whether it has jurisdiction in a complicated case such as this, and if it did, how would it proceed.[53] An important issue raised by China's refusal to cooperate was whether the issue could be heard without Chinese representation, and the presentation of Chinese documents, which would throw light on Chinese claims. Huang Huikang, Director-General of the Treaty Department of the Chinese Foreign Ministry, declared that China's refusal to submit to arbitration was strictly in accordance with international law, since the Philippines has no legal rights over the territory in question.[54] The Tribunal may avoid adjudicating the case in view of its complexity, and in the face of Chinese refusal to cooperate it may declare lack of jurisdiction. If it went ahead with the case, it may give an advisory opinion, or alternatively not come to a clear decision of the kind the Philippines has sought. The result may well be indeterminate.

Joint development

For many years, joint development was regarded as a way of overcoming the sovereignty imbroglio. If claimants could be induced to cooperate over oil and gas extraction, perhaps they would learn to overcome their differences over sovereignty in a cooperative solution. The idea was first broached by Chinese Premier Li Peng in Singapore on 13 August 1990, when he called upon claimants to set aside sovereignty to enable joint development to proceed. The Chinese Premier wanted to improve relations with ASEAN after the Tiananmen Square events of June 1989, and the naval clash with Vietnam in the South China Sea in March 1988, which had alarmed ASEAN. The idea of joint development was later raised by various ASEAN leaders and Chinese officials, but without further clarification. Did it mean cooperation over surveillance and exploration, drilling and production? In what areas would joint development take place, and how would the finances be arranged and the benefits be apportioned? Would the Chinese be prepared to shelve sovereignty over areas they claim, or would they insist upon it as a condition for what they would call joint development, but others would call investment in Chinese claimed areas? Zhiguo Gao, in 1994, claimed that only a regional 'cooperative approach in the form of joint development can resolve the situation', and called for regional round-table meetings on joint development and a coordinating body to supervise joint development projects.[55] The idea has been raised by Chinese officials at different times, but with little clarification. After the Mischief Reef incident in 1995, Assistant Foreign Minister Wang Yinfan told Philippine Emissary Alfonso Yuchengco that China National Offshore Oil Corpopration (CNOOC) would be interested in a joint venture with Philippine oil. China, he said, would pursue joint development on a bilateral basis, though other countries, such as the US, could be involved at a later stage.[56] After Chinese Premier Li Keqiang visited Kuala Lumpur, Malaysian Prime Minister Najib Razak called for joint development on 3 June 2013, which was unusual, since his own government had previously rejected the notion. Foreign Minister Wang Yi mentioned 'common exploitation' as one of the three ways in which the South China Sea dispute could be resolved, the other two being direct bilateral negotiations and implementation of the DoC.[57] President Xi Jinping declared that China's approach to maritime issues was to shelve disputes and carry out 'Joint development for areas over which China owns sovereign rights, while expanding common convergent interests with other countries'.[58] How joint development would work in practice while China insists on sovereignty has yet to be explained. Chinese statements have added little to the proposal, leaving the impression of either diplomatic formality or an effort to undermine the positions of the ASEAN claimants. They are concerned that China's understanding of joint development is exploitation of the resources in their claim zones in a way that would compromise their legal claims. Some Chinese scholars have confirmed this view, arguing that joint development would be possible only in the EEZs of the ASEAN claimants, since the oil reserves are located there.[59] For this reason, Vietnam has declared that it would not accept the idea of shelving disputes and engaging in joint development in its own EEZ or continental shelf.[60]

Under the right conditions, joint development may contribute to a resolution of the dispute, but that would demand, among other things, a detailed agreement on the area, the activities to be pursued and the allocation of profits. There are four Asian precedents for joint development that may lend some optimism: Vietnam/Malaysia in the gulf of Thailand, June 1992; Japan/South Korea, February 1974; Malaysia/Thailand, 1979 and 1990; and the Timor Gap agreements between Indonesia and Australia in 1989, and Timor Leste 2002. These agreements illustrated what was required to ensure that joint development would work. First, and most fundamental, was a definition of the area subject to joint development. Second was an institutional framework that would establish the legal basis of the enterprise, providing security for the investments of international oil companies. It would decide which law would apply on taxation, customs, exploration, and drilling and environmental impact.[61] The institutional framework could either be a supranational authority or commission, as in the Timor Gap and Malaysia/ Thailand cases, or it could be created by joint operating agreements, as in the Malaysia/Vietnam agreement.[62] The above agreements are all bilateral, where a particular area in between the claimants could be designated for joint development, but the complications would be multiplied in the multilateral dispute; for example, how the disputants could agree on a suitable area in a situation of overlapping claims in the South China Sea is not clear. While claimants might agree on a limited version of joint development in particular parts of the South China Sea where the problems would be minimised, they are not yet prepared for a multilateral institutional authority to regulate their activities in this way.

The Joint Marine Seismic Undertaking (JMSU)

One example of joint activity that did not reach the developmental stage was the JMSU, which involved the Philippines, Vietnam and China in an agreement for joint exploration (see Maps 5 and 6). In September 2003, on a visit to Manila, Chairman of the National People's Congress Standing Committee Wu Bangguo proposed joint exploration with the Philippines.[63] In November, it was announced that the China National Offshore Oil Corporation (CNOOC) had agreed to work with the Philippine National Oil Company (PNOC) to determine the oil and gas potential of the Spratlys and to examine those areas where joint exploration could be realised.[64] President Macapagal-Arroyo agreed to a joint seismic survey of an area in the South China Sea during her state visit to China in September 2004. It involved the PNOC and CNOOC in oil exploration in a designated area in a western part of the South China Sea, mainly in the Philippine claim zone. At first, it was a bilateral agreement with China. Vietnam, however, objected, as it impinged upon its own claim, and as a result the bilateral agreement was expanded on 14 March 2005 to include PetroVietnam in a tripartite arrange-ment over a three-year period from 1 July 2005 to 30 June 2008.[65] The stipulation was that 'the agreement shall not undermine the basic position held by the govern-ment of each party on the South China Sea issue'. Article 2 of the agreement with China stated that the area covered was 1,420,886 square kilometres, as defined in Annex A, which was mainly in the Philippine claim zone. According to Article 12 (2), data and information obtained under the agreement 'shall be jointly owned by the parties'.[66] The tripartite agreement with Vietnam included the terms and provisions above, but with the additional sentence that the parties 'have expressed their commitment to pursue peaceful efforts to transform the South China Sea into an area of peace, stability, cooperation and development'. Moreover, Article 10 of the tripartite agreement stated that the information obtained 'will be kept confidential for the duration of the agreement, and for 5 years after its expiration'. President Macapagal-Arroyo praised the agreement as 'a break-through in implementing the provisions of the CoC in the South China Sea among ASEAN and China to turn the South China Sea into an area of cooperation rather than an area of conflict'. She also praised its importance for Philippine energy security.[67]

A furore erupted in the Philippines when the terms of the agreement were discovered. The congressional opposition was appalled that 80 per cent of the survey area, as noted in Article 2, was within the Philippine claim zone and the remaining 20 per cent was in contested waters. Six islands occupied by the Philippines were included in the area of the seismic undertaking.[68] The major objection raised by legal experts was that the Philippines had weakened its claim to the area by involving China and Vietnam, which had overlapping claims to much the same territory. Nonetheless, islands claimed by both China and Vietnam were also included, and the legalists did not mention if their claims were also weakened.[69] A second objection was that it violated the national patrimony clause, or Article 12 (2) of the 1987 constitution. This provision called for a 60 per cent share for Filipinos in any co-production agreement or joint venture involving Filipino citizens, and it stipulated that the President was to notify Congress of any such agreement 'within thirty days from its execution'.[70] The Philippine government was understandably very cagey about how revenue would be apportioned if oil were discovered, and there was no mention of this in the document. The President claimed that if the oil exploration project were successful, and if oil were discovered outside Kalayaan in the Spratly Islands, the national government would have exclusive rights to the revenue. However, there was nothing in the agreement to support this claim.[71] The President deflected all discussion of the national patrimony clause and how the country would benefit, which raised the suspicion that this issue simply was not discussed. The government claimed that an agreement for geological research had been concluded, which did not involve oil exploration, so that the national patrimony clause did not apply.[72] Legalists argued that the JMSU should have been covered by a treaty that would have required Senate approval, as in this way transparency would have been assured.[73] The President insisted, however, that 'commercial papers' were involved and public disclosure before the Senate was not required according to regular commercial practice.[74] The Arroyo Administration had intended to extend the agreement after its expiry in July 2008, but desisted following the outburst of criticism that resulted.[75] The outrage that had erupted died with the expiry of the agreement, but the strong feeling that the Administration had compromised the Philippine claim to the South China Sea, and therefore could not be trusted with the country's security, persisted. The JMSU was the first attempt to bring claimants together in common activity, and its failure illustrated the difficulty of implementing the idea. Joint development may yet be possible, but as part of a broader agreement on a cooperative maritime regime.

Cooperative maritime regime

A cooperative maritime regime has often been proposed for the South China as a path towards the resolution of the dispute. A maritime regime is a cooperative effort to regulate behaviour in a given area according to agreed rules and norms that give effect to the notion of the common good. Article 123 of UNCLOS stipulates that states 'bordering an enclosed or semi-enclosed sea should co-operate with each other in the exercise of their rights and in the performance of their duties under this Convention'. The article adds that they should do so 'directly or through an appropriate regional organization'. Mark Valencia has championed this approach, arguing that regional maritime cooperation could proceed progressively from policy consultation to policy harmonisation, coordination and national policy adjustments. A maritime regime could involve the creation of a Spratly Resource Development Authority (SRDA) or a Spratly Management Authority (SMA), which would grant permits for exploration and joint development. It would be an international organisation with a secretary general, a secretariat and a council. It would also create a regional common heritage area, which would allow access only to the claimants, as joint development companies could be established based on areas of overlapping claims. The claimants would contribute to a common fund to promote joint development of the area's oil and gas fields. Shares would be allocated equally between the claimants, but 5 per cent would be reserved for non-claimant states, and another 5 per cent for operating expenses.[76] It would also negotiate agreements for sustainable fisheries management following, for example, the Sino-Vietnamese joint fisheries agreements for the Tonkin Gulf, which were concluded in December 2000.[77] These agreements establish a joint fishery committee (JFC), including representatives from each country who decide on conservation and management, the allocation of fishing quotas, and access to traditional fishing grounds.[78] However, an extension of this bilateral agreement to the whole South China Sea would be a major task in view of the complexity. The idea of a cooperative maritime regime for the South China Sea has appeal as part of a comprehensive resolution of the issue. It would require a legal basis and sufficient agreement between the disputants on their claims to allow the institutional development that a regime of this kind would require. However, it would be a product of a resolution of the issue, but not a means to bring it about. Though the idea may act as an incentive to the claimants to resolve their claims, its acceptance would, in particular, require a political decision by China that, at present, is unlikely.

UN conference on the South China Sea

Proposals for a cooperative maritime regime might be more realistic if the means for their realisation under current circumstances could be explained. One such way of realising a regime of this kind would be a UN-sponsored conference on the South China Sea, which would be convened to give effect to Article 123 of UNCLOS. The problem is that UNCLOS has not provided sufficient guidance in regard to the procedures to be adopted to resolve the legal issues raised by a semi-enclosed sea such as the South China Sea. To deal with this situation and to bring UNCLOS to completion would be the task of a special conference, which would involve China and the ASEAN claimants in the first instance, as well as external stakeholders. It would deal with significant gaps in UNCLOS as they are exposed in this and other maritime disputes. Such a conference would reveal the legal weaknesses of the claims, including the nine-dash line, and would seek their cooperative adjustment according to the notion of joint condominium, or shared sovereignty. A cooperative maritime regime, which would include provisions for joint development, would, one way or another, require a decision on sovereignty, without which they would be unrealisable. As a precedent, the ICJ recognised the concept of joint sovereignty in the El Salvador/Honduras maritime frontier dispute of 1992. In this case, the ICJ noted the precedent created by the Central American Court of Justice in 1917 that the disputed waters of the Gulf of Fonseca were subject to 'a condominium created by joint inheritance of an area'. It agreed that 'the waters of the Gulf have remained undivided and in a state of community which entails a condominium or co-ownership'.[79] This concept of co-ownership could be extended to cover semi-enclosed seas where complex overlapping claims make a legal resolution difficult. Implementation of this concept in the South China Sea would also require the formation of a regional body or cooperative regime that would adopt rules regarding fishing practices and quotas, oil and gas exploration and the passage of naval vessels in the maintenance of freedom of navigation in the area.

An international conference on the Spratlys under UN auspices has been proposed before, and it is not an entirely new idea. Philippine President Fidel Ramos, in 1992, raised it, as did his Foreign Minister Raul Manglapus, at the ASEAN Foreign Ministers meeting in July 1992, but the details were not fleshed out. China has rejected multilateral negotiations of the issue in the past, and may continue to insist that the South China Sea is Chinese territory, and that a conference of this kind is unacceptable. However, the incentive for China to join this process of resolution is to legalise its position in the South China Sea and stabilise the area without the prospect of raising tensions or increasing the risk of conflict with external powers. Clearly, China will not gain legal acceptance of its claim by insisting on historical rights to the area, which it cannot demonstrate, or by resorting to power to intimidate the ASEAN claimants. Furthermore, it would poison its relationship with the region if it rode roughshod over their rights. An international legal resolution of the issue under the UN would offer a way out for the Chinese leadership that has allowed itself to become boxed in by the nationalist forces it has stoked over this and other issues. It would be more acceptable to China than any lesser alternative, which would be rejected downright. China would gain considerable benefits by doing so. It may confirm its position in the Paracels, as well as some occupied features in the Spratlys, and would strengthen its relationship with ASEAN, earning the gratitude of the organisation, which would show up in various ways. It would ease the regional polarisation created by China's attempt to gain unilateral benefits in the sea by resorting to power. China would also avoid pushing the ASEAN claimants to the US and Japan for support, and would give external powers no cause to cooperate against it. It would also remove the main motive for America's pivot strategy, stimulating cooperation rather than rivalry with the US. Indeed, China's regional position would be enhanced and its international credibility elevated.

Conclusion

Neither China nor Vietnam may be ready for a resolution of this kind, which would demand that they surrender their extensive claims. The Chinese leadership has invoked nationalism over this and other issues, which would make it particularly difficult for it to accept a negotiated resolution of the issue. China may have locked itself into an uncompromising position when compromise and adjustment would be in its best interests, and would further its policy aims in the region. In the past, governments have been locked into seemingly unyielding positions but have been compelled to change when faced with the prospect of conflict and escalation in a crisis. The shock effect of a crisis often releases blockages in immobilised decision-making systems, making political leaders aware of the dangers of continuing with familiar behaviour, and demanding of them a major change of policy and attitude. A clash between naval or coastguard vessels caused by error or miscalculation by a local commander, swayed by heady nationalistic spirit, to remove one of the ASEAN claimants from an occupied island there cannot be excluded. At the present moment, it seems that only crisis will trigger the necessary change of attitude over the South China Sea, particularly within China.

Notes

1 '1992 ASEAN Declaration On The South CHINA SEA: Adopted by the Foreign Ministers at the 25th ASEAN Ministerial Meeting in Manila, Philippines on 22 July 1992', www.aseansec.org/1196.htm (accessed 2 June 2014).
2 *Straits Times*, 11 August 1995; Daniel J. Dzurek, 'Maritime Briefing – The Spratly Islands Dispute: Who's on First?', *International Boundaries Research Unit*, 2(1), 1996.
3 'Joint Statement on the Fourth Bilateral Consultations between the Republic of the Philippines and the Socialist Republic of Vietnam', in Theresa C. Cariño (ed.), *China–ASEAN Relations: Regional Security and Cooperation*, Philippine-China Development Resource Centre, Quezon City, 1998.
4 *Straits Times*, 1 December 1995.
5 *Straits Times*, 7 July 1999.
6 The Chinese draft said that the parties should 'refrain from conducting any military exercises directed against other countries in the Nansha Islands and their adjacent

waters, and from carrying out any dangerous and close in military reconnaissance'. *Straits Times*, 21 February 2000.

7   Nguyen Hong Thao, 'The 2002 Declaration on the Conduct of Parties in the South China Sea: A Note', *Ocean Development & International Law*, 34: 279–285, 2003.

8   'Declaration on the Conduct of Parties in the South China Sea', www.asean.org/asean/external-relations/china/item/declaration-on-the-conduct-of-parties-in-the-south-china-sea (accessed 2 June 2014).

9   ASEAN and the DoC.

10   Wu Shicun and Ren Huaifeng, 'More than a Declaration: A Commentary on the Background and the Significance of the Declaration on the Conduct of the Parties in the South China Sea', *Chinese Journal of International Law*, 2(1): 311–319, 2003.

11   'Treaty of Amity and Cooperation in Southeast Asia Indonesia', 24 February 1976, www.asean.org/news/item/treaty-of-amity-and-cooperation-in-southeast-asia-indonesia-24-february-1976- (accessed 2 June 2014).

12   Li Mingjiang, 'China's South China Sea Dilemma: Balancing Sovereignty, Development and Security', in Sam Bateman and Ralf Emmers (eds), *Security and International Politics in the South China Sea: Towards a Cooperative Management Regime*, Routledge, London, 2009, pp. 142, 147.

13   Renato Cruz de Castro, 'The US-Philippine Alliance: An Evolving Hedge against an Emerging China Challenge', *Contemporary Southeast Asia*, 31(3), December 2009.

14   Chairman's Statement, 16th ASEAN Regional Forum, 23 July 2009, Phuket, Thailand, ASEAN Regional Forum, www.aseanregionalforum.org/PublicLibrary/ARFChairmans StatementsandReports/tabid/66/Default.aspx (accessed 2 June 2014).

15   Chairman's Statement, 17th ASEAN Regional Forum, 23 July 2010, Hanoi, Vietnam, ASEAN Regional Forum, www.aseanregionalforum.org/PublicLibrary/ARFChairmans StatementsandReports/tabid/66/Default.aspx (accessed 2 June 2014).

16   'China, ASEAN Working on South China Sea Code-Ambassador', *ABS CBN News*, 1 October 2010.

17   Chairman's Statement, 20th ASEAN Regional Forum, 2 July 2013, Bandar Seri Begawan, Brunei Darussalam, ASEAN Regional Forum, www.aseanregionalforum.asean.org/files/library/ARFChairmansStatementsand Reports/ (accessed 2 June 2014).

18   Interview with Vietnamese Foreign Ministry official, Hanoi, 7 April 2013.

19   Yohanna Ririhena, 'RI Circulates Draft Code of Conduct on South China Sea', *Jakarta Post*, 29 September 2012.

20   'US Willing to Help in South China Sea CoC: Envoy', *Agence France-Presse*, 4 October 2010, www.abs-cbnnews.com/global-filipino/world/10/04/10/us-willing-help-south-china-sea-code-conduct-envoy (accessed 2 June 2014).

21   Director of the Institute for International Studies under the Chinese Academy of Social Sciences, 'Timing not Right for New CoC', *Global Times*, 18 July 2012, www.global times.cn/content/721876.shtml (accessed 2 June 2014).

22   'China Agrees South China Sea Talks amid New Row with Manila', *Reuters*, 30 June 2013; 'China Says in no Hurry to Sign South China Sea Accord', *Reuters*, 5 August 2013.

23   'Chinese FM: South China Sea Disputes Could be Solved with Three Ways Together', *Xinhua*, 2 August 2013.

24   Chen Jipeng, 'News Analysis: Confusion of Bilateral, Multilateral Efforts on South China Sea', 1 July 2013, *English.news.cn*, http://english.people.com.cn/90883/8306 338.html (accessed 2 June 2014).

25   Chairman's Statement, 20th ASEAN Regional Forum, 2 July 2013.

26   'Agreement between the Government of the United States of America and the Government of the Union of Soviet Socialist Republics on the Prevention of Incidents on and over the High Seas', US Department of State, www.state.gov/t/isn/4791.htm (accessed 2 June 2014).

27 'China on Establishing a Consultative Mechanism to Strengthen Military Maritime Safety', *Federation of American Scientists*, 19 January 1998, www.fas.org/nuke/control/sea/text/us-china98.htm (accessed 2 June 2014).

28 Aya Igarashi, 'China Denies Using Fire-Control Radar on MSDF', *Yomiuri shimbun*, 9 February 2013; 'Japan Sees China Radar-Use as Threat of Force under UN Rule', *The Mainichi*, 7 February 2013.

29 Daluo Jia, 'Indonesia Opens Workshop on Troubled South China Sea', *Agence France-Presse*, 26 October 1994.

30 *Straits Times*, 12 October 1995.

31 Ian Townsend-Gault, 'Preventive Diplomacy and Pro-Activity in the South China Sea', *Contemporary South East Asia*, 20(2), August 1998.

32 Ian Townsend-Gault, 'The Contributions of the South China Sea Workshops', in Sam Bateman and Ralf Emmers (eds), *Security and International Politics in the South China Sea: Towards a Cooperative Management Regime*, Routledge, London, 2009, pp. 189, 190.

33 Hasjim Djalal and Ian Townsend-Gault, 'Preventive Diplomacy: Managing Potential Conflicts in the South China Sea', in Chester A. Crocker, Fen Osler Hampson and Pamela Aall (eds), *Herding Cats: Multiparty Mediation in a Complex World*, United States Institute of Peace Press, 1999.

34 Ian Townsend-Gault, 'The Contributions of the South China Sea Workshops', p. 199.

35 Lee Lai to, 'The South China Sea: China and Multilateral Dialogues', *Security Dialogue*, 30(2), June 1999.

36 Hasjim Djalal and Ian Townsend-Gault, 'Preventive Diplomacy: Managing Potential Conflicts In the South China Sea'.

37 Douglas Johnson, 'Drawn into the Fray: Indonesia's Natuna Islands Meet China's Long Gaze South', *Asian Affairs: An American Review*, 24(3), 1997.

38 Nayan Chanda, 'Divide and Rule', *Far Eastern Economic Review*, 11, August 1994.

39 Ji Guoxing, 'Maritime Jurisdiction in the Three China Seas: Options for Equitable Settlement', Policy, Institute of Global Conflict and Cooperation, University of California, Policy Paper 19, 1995, http://igcc.ucsd.edu/publications/igcc-publications/publications_2011032339256.htm (accessed 2 June 2014).

40 Robert Beckman, 'The UN Convention on the Law of the Sea and the Maritime Disputes in the South China Sea', *The American Journal of International Law*, 107(1), January 2013.

41 Robert Beckman, 'The UN Convention on the Law of the Sea and the Maritime Disputes in the South China Sea'.

42 'An Act to Amend Certain Provisions of Republic Act no. 3046, as Amended by Republic Act no. 5446, to Define the Archipelagic Baseline of the Philippines and for Other Purpose', Lawphil Project Online, www.lawphil.net/statutes/repacts/ra2009/ra_9522_2009.html (accessed 2 June 2014).

43 Tessa Jamandre, 'RP to Initiate Talks on Border Row', *GMA News*, 16 March 2009, www.gmanews.tv/story/152933/RP-to-initiate-talks-on-border-row (accessed 2 June 2014).

44 'Envoy Conveys to DFA China's Displeasure with RP Baseline Law', *GMA News*, 14 March 2009, www.gmanetwork.com/news/story/152704/news/nation/envoy-conveys-to-dfa-china-s-displeasure-with-rp-baseline-law (accessed 2 June 2014).

45 Seokwoo Lee, 'Intertemporal Law, Recent Judgments and Territorial Disputes in Asia', in Seoung-Yong Hong and Jon M.Van Dyke (eds), *Maritime Boundary Disputes, Settlement Processes, and the Law of the Sea*, Matinus Nijhoff, Leiden, 2009.

46 Hungdah Chui, 'South China Sea Islands: Implications for Delimiting the Seabed and Future Shipping Routes', *The China Quarterly*, 72, December 1977.

47 Sophia Kopela, *Dependent Archipelagos in the Law of the Sea*, Martinus Nijhoff, Leiden, 2013, p. 31.

48 Ji Guoxing, 'Maritime Jurisdiction in the Three China Seas: Options for Equitable Settlement'.

49 'SFA Statement on the UNCLOS Arbitral Proceedings against China', Department of Foreign Affairs, Republic of the Philippines, 22 January 2013, www.dfa.gov.ph/index.php/2013-06-27-21-50-36/unclos (accessed 2 June 2014).

50 Xianne Arcangel, 'PHL to Submit Pleading on Sea Dispute with China before UN Tribunal in 2014', *GMA News*, 4 December 2013, www.gmanetwork.com/news/story/338282/news/nation/phl-to-submit-pleading-on-sea-dispute-with-china-before-un-tribunal-in-2014 (accessed 2 June 2014).

51 Jia Xiudong, 'What are So-Called Eight Facts of the Philippines', *People's Daily*, 18 July 2013, http://english.peopledaily.com.cn/90883/8332348.html (accessed 2 June 2014).

52 The Arbitral Tribunal is composed of Judge Thomas Mensah from Ghana, Judge Jean-Pierre Cot from France, Judge Alfred Soons from the Netherlands, Judge Stanislaw Palak from Poland representing China, and Judge Rudiger Wolfrum from Germany representing the Philippines. Sara Susanne D. Fabunan, 'UN Tribunal on Sea Row Convened', *Manila Standard*, 17 July 2013, http://manilastandardtoday.com/2013/07/17/un-tribunal-on-sea-row-convened (accessed 2 June 2014).

53 Tarra Quismundo, 'UN Court to Rule Soon on PH Case', *Philippine Daily Inquirer*, 9 August 2013.

54 Zhang Qian and Wang Jinxue, 'China's Refusal of Arbitration Request by Philippines Meets International Law: Senior Diplomat', *Xinhua*, 30 August 2013, http://english.peopledaily.com.cn/90883/83883304.html (accessed 2 June 2014).

55 Zhiguo Gao, 'The South China Sea: From Conflict to Cooperation?', *Ocean Development & International Law*, 25(3), July–September 1994.

56 *Straits Times*, 1 June 1995.

57 'Chinese FM: South China Sea Disputes Could be Solved with Three Ways Together'.

58 'Xi Advocates Efforts to Boost China's Maritime Power', *Xinhua*, 31 July 2013.

59 Interview sources, Beijing, 6 June 2013.

60 *Vietnam and the East Sea*, Vietnam Peace and Development Foundation, Hanoi, 2012.

61 Robert Beckman, Ian Townsend-Gault, Clive Schofield, Tara Davenport and Leonardo Bernard (eds), *Beyond Territorial Disputes in the South China Sea: Legal Frameworks for the Joint Development of Hydrocarbon Resources*, Edward Elgar, Cheltenham, 2013, pp. 291–311.

62 David M. Ong, 'The 1979 and 1990 Malaysia-Thailand Joint Development Agreements: A Model for International Legal Cooperation in Common Offshore Petroleum Deposits?', *The International Journal of Marine and Coastal Law*, 14(2), May 1999.

63 *Business Times* (Singapore), 1 September 2003.

64 'Chinese, Philippines Firms Join Forces to Look for Oil in South China Sea', *Channel News Asia*, 13 November 2003, www.channelnewsasia.com/stores/afp_asiapacific_business/view/57052/1/.html (accessed 2 June 2014).

65 Monica Feria, 'South China Sea Flashpoint', *Philippine Daily Inquirer*, 19 April 2008, www.inquirer.net/specialfeatures/spratlys/view.php?db=1&article=20080419-131474 (accessed 2 June 2014).

66 'An Agreement for Joint Marine Scientific Undertaking in Certain Areas in the South China Sea by and between China National Offshore Oil Corporation and Philippines National Oil Company', 1 September 2004.

67 'PGMAs Speech During the Presentation of the Signed Tripartite Agreement for Joint Marine Seismic', *Office of the President*, 14 March 2005.

68 Those islands were Patag (Flat), Lawak (Nanshan), Parola (Northeast Cay), Panata (Lankiam Cay), Kota (Loaita) and Likas (West York) Islands.

69 Islands claimed by Vietnam included in the survey area were Sonca (Sand Cay), Nam Yit Islands, Collins, Da Nu Thui (Petley) Reefs; islands claimed by China were

Landsowne (Da Len Dao), Nan Xun Jiao (Gaven), Kennan, Subi. Sinh Cow, as well as Yong Shu Jian (Fiery Cross), which was the site of the March 1988 clashes between Chinese and Vietnamese naval forces. Yvonne T. Chua and Ellen Tordesillas, '6 Philippine-Occupied Islands Covered in Spratly Agreements', GMA News, 9 May 2009, www.gmanews.tv/story/84023/6-Philippine-occupied-islands-covered-in-Spratly-agreements (accessed 2 June 2014).

70 See Article XII, The 1987 Constitution of the Philippines.

71 Office of the President, Republic of the Philippines, 13 April 2005, www.op.gov. ph/index.php?option=com_content&task=view&id=19875&itemid=2 (accessed 2 June 2014).

72 '"Its Research, Not Exploration." Says GMA on Accord with China on the Spratlys', Office of the President, Republic of the Philippines, 8 September 2004, www.op.gov. ph/index.php?option=com_content&task=view&id=10203&Itemid=2 (accessed 2 June 2014).

73 Miriam Grace A. Go, 'A Policy of Betrayal (Second of Three Parts)', *Newsbreak*, 15 March 2008, www.abs-cbnnews.com/special-report/03/15/08/policy-betrayal-second-three-parts (accessed 2 June 2014).

74 A Tripartite Agreement for Joint marine Scientific Research in Certain Areas in the South China Sea by and Among China National Offshore Oil Corporation and Vietnam Oil and Gas Corporation and Philippines National Oil Company.

75 Myrna M. Velasco, 'Gov't Drops Bid to Renew Spratly Oil Exploration Pact', *Manila Bulletin* 14 March 2009.

76 Mark J. Valencia, *China and the South China Sea Disputes*, Adelphi Paper 298, 1995, pp. 65–66.

77 'Agreement on Fishery Co-operation in the Tonkin Gulf between the Government of the People's Republic of China and the Government of the Socialist Republic of Vietnam', http://faolex.fao.org/docs/pdf/bi-51872.pdf (accessed 2 June 2014).

78 David Rosenberg, 'Fisheries Management in the South China Sea', in Sam Bateman and Ralf Emmers (eds), *Security and International Politics in the South China Sea: Towards a Cooperative Management Regime*, Routledge, London, 2009, p. 74.

79 Case Concerning Land, Island and Maritime Frontier Dispute (El Salvador/Honduras: Nicaragua intervening) Judgment of 11 September 1992, International Court of Justice, www.icj-cij.org/docket/index.php?sum=390&code=sh&p1=3&p2=3&case=75&k= 0e&p3=5 (accessed 2 June 2014).

Conclusion

The South China Sea maritime dispute has, in recent years, escalated in intensity, unsettling the region and disturbing external powers whose trade and oil lifelines go through it. Brendan Taylor reminds us in his chapter that the dispute is the least dangerous among Asia's present crisis points, and that a crisis in the South China Sea is by no means imminent. Nonetheless, it is a festering issue that troubles the region and the major players. As Clive Schofield observes, the states involved are 'seemingly "adrift" on complex waters' as the South China Sea becomes an 'increasingly complex and contested maritime space'. Chinese maritime surveillance and enforcement agencies, as well as Chinese-flagged fishing vessels, have moved into the area to enforce or demonstrate Chinese claims, as based, officially at least, on the nine-dash line. These interventions have disrupted Malaysian, Philippine and Vietnamese oil and gas survey and exploration activities, and have given rise to a series of disturbing incidents that may, in the future, get out of hand. The ASEAN claimants, Indonesia, Malaysia, the Philippines and Vietnam, have undertaken these survey and exploration activities in their own EEZs, or in areas proximate to their mainland and main island coasts, which have been granted to them by UNCLOS or international law. China, however, has been increasingly prepared to enforce its claim by resorting to assertive action in what it regards as 'Chinese waters', while denouncing the claims of others as 'illegal'. These Chinese actions may have far-reaching consequences for regional stability, as the ASEAN claimants, as well as external powers such as the US and Japan, are affected.

Jian Zhang writes positively in this volume about China's motives, claiming that despite this assertiveness, Beijing does not want to let the South China Sea issue dominate its relationship with ASEAN or the claimant states. He writes that China will act to reduce the damage caused by its increasingly assertive actions by promoting closer economic, political and even military relationships with ASEAN. Accordingly, Chinese actions cannot be interpreted as short-term or reactive, but a long-term, proactive and purposeful approach to bolster Chinese claims. He argues also that this new assertiveness does not mean that China would resort to force, but that it would 'employ legal, diplomatic and administrative measures to augment the basis of its claims to gain leverage in future diplomatic and legal negotiations'. Clearly, China's motives in resorting to this assertiveness must be understood.

One significant problem is that there is a fundamental conflict between the Chinese approach to the issue, which relies on history to justify the claim, and the ASEAN claimants, who rely upon rights granted by contemporary international law, and the Law of the Sea in particular. China has claimed historical rights over the South China Sea in the 11-dash line, which was first promulgated in 1947, and modified to nine dashes in 1953. It has argued that contemporary law cannot displace its historical rights to the area, and that those rights precede the Law of the Sea in time and should have priority in this context. The conflict pits rights supposedly granted by history against rights allowed and enshrined in contemporary international law and the Law of the Sea. Rights over maritime areas have been extended and legalised by developments in contemporary international law and its application in the Law of the Sea. States have been allowed to claim islands, rocks and atolls on the basis of effective occupation, or the demonstration of state authority in some way. Littoral states such as Vietnam, the Philippines and Malaysia were prompted to occupy these features in their claim zones by deploying garrisons or planting markers on them. By occupying islands, which UNCLOS distinguished from rocks and atolls, they hoped they would be allowed to claim full EEZs and continental shelves, which would give them control over hydrocarbon resources, as well as fisheries. Donald Rothwell notes, however, that under the legal principle of 'land dominates the sea', rights to maritime zones in semi-enclosed areas would be determined by coastline length; those with longer coastlines could claim more, those with shorter coastlines would be obliged to settle for less. The maritime claims of the littoral states would be reduced and adjusted in any legal resolution of the dispute, but this has not prevented them from insisting on their claims and asserting them nonetheless.

And what is the validity of the Chinese historical claim? While the South China Sea was China's southern maritime frontier, it was not regarded as part of the dynastic state. In fact, the Chinese border followed the coast in dynastic times when the Chinese had no concept of sovereignty over the ocean. China, however, now insists on rights of first discovery, or rights obtained by the settlement of local fishermen on the islands. Whatever the nature of these rights, they are insufficient to demonstrate title according to contemporary international law. The activities of local fishermen or the discovery of Chinese artefacts may indicate contact with the area, but a claim to administrative jurisdiction by the centre of empire in Beijing is another matter. When the Chinese use historical presence as a justification for their claim, the historical records point to a picture that differs significantly from the official interpretation upon which Beijing now insists. Despite the Chinese insistence on ancient title, China's claim to the area is relatively new and a product of interaction with foreign powers, specifically Japan and France, in the early twentieth century. By the late nineteenth century, China's southern maritime border had shifted to the Paracel Islands, which are now in dispute with Vietnam. As the current occupant, China's claim to the Paracels may be supported by international law if China can satisfactorily demonstrate continuous and effective occupation, but the Spratly Islands are another matter. China only occupied seven to nine features there from 1988, and the rest are in the hands of the ASEAN claimants. Moreover, Chinese interest in the Spratly Islands was comparatively recent, and certainly not ancient. It was only as a result of Japanese and French intrusion into the area that Chinese interest was extended further south from the Paracels to include the Spratly Islands.

Leszek Buszynski writes that China is attempting the national territorialisation of the South China Sea, or the conversion of what was previously a maritime frontier outside the borders of the dynastic state into a recognised and accepted part of the modern state. This conversion has several features that are worth noting. First, there is the absence of convincing historical support for the claim of title over the entire south China area, or the nine-dash line, however it may be interpreted. China may have a case of sorts in regard to the Paracels on the basis of effective occupation and early twentieth-century historical records, but the claim to the Spratly Islands based on history is dubious. In the absence of historical support for their claim, the Chinese have resorted to repeated public assertions of 'indisputable sovereignty', as though these should be sufficient to establish title. Second, the conversion requires the use of incremental degrees of force on the part of Chinese maritime surveillance vessels to harass the ASEAN claimants into accepting the Chinese claim. Continuous pressure in this way is intended to make the ASEAN claimants realise the difficulties they would be compelled to face if they continued to uphold their own claims and to lead them to the point where they would become receptive to a resolution of the dispute on Chinese terms. Third, this conversion has been accompanied by the invocation of public nationalism in China and the creation of the belief in the Chinese public mind that the South China Sea has always been a part of China, as much as Taiwan or any other territory of China. Despite the fact that the South China Sea was never Chinese to begin with, Chinese domestic audiences are told that China somehow 'lost' the area as a result of foreign intrusion, and that the islands there are 'lost territories' to be returned to the motherland. To reinforce this belief, the nine-dash line appeared on new Chinese passports as part of a map of China, and in January 2013 China published maps that included both the South China Sea and Taiwan as indistinguishable features in a 10-dash line with the mainland.

China may be preparing for negotiations with the ASEAN claimants over the issue, but to what purpose? There are two possibilities. The first is that China will continue with a prolonged campaign of harassment against the ASEAN claimants to bring them to point where they would accept China's sovereignty over the South China Sea. This would require that the ASEAN claimants surrender their legal rights under UNCLOS and international law, and recognise China's historical claim. The result would then be declared legal and UNCLOS would be adjusted accordingly to accommodate the idea of a regional solution to competing claims. According to this view, power can shape law. Jian Zhang has observed that many Chinese scholars view international law as dynamic and evolving in accordance with state practice and shifting power relations between the major players. These scholars suggest that China can shape notions of international law to its own advantage, so what was considered illegal and unacceptable can become legal and acceptable. A solution of this nature would have considerable repercussions for

UNCLOS and international law, as China would demand a special exception that would entail the recognition of unsupported historical claims. What would remain of the legal claims raised by the ASEAN claimants under UNCLOS in this solution can only be a matter of guesswork. In the Zhou Enlai era, once Chinese supremacy was recognised, China would reveal a sense of magnanimity towards smaller neighbours and there would be some recognition of the rights of the ASEAN claimants. Today, however, an assertive nationalism has taken hold in China, which, at times, has become vindictive, making it difficult to envisage any respect for the rights of the ASEAN claimants. Despite the attraction of such a solution for Chinese scholars, and Western strategists who think that a rising China should be allowed possession of the South China Sea to remove regional tensions, it would be an unlikely outcome.

The second possibility is more likely. Despite its intentions, China would not be able to harass the ASEAN claimants into accepting its primacy over the area, since the issue does not exist in isolation. External powers, particularly the US and Japan, have become concerned that Chinese dominance of the South China Sea would impact upon freedom of navigation for foreign oil exploration, as well as of maritime surveillance vessels. Chinese control of the area would undermine their own positions, Japan over the Senkaku/Diaoyu Islands and the US in the Western Pacific. They have therefore been encouraging the ASEAN claimants, Vietnam and the Philippines, to resist Chinese pressure, which could create the conditions for escalation of the dispute should the Chinese persist in their pressure tactics. In this scenario, China may avoid stoking a conflict with the ASEAN claimants by keeping its harassment activities at a low and manageable level while continuing with its public denunciations of their positions. Such an outcome depends upon a number of factors, including Beijing's ability and willingness to control the activities of Chinese maritime surveillance agencies and provincial authorities. Once public nationalism has been invoked over the issue, however, it may become much more difficult for the Beijing leadership to exercise that control, particularly if factional conflicts within the leadership emerge, and were this to happen, the appeal to nationalism would be intensified in this dispute and others.

Do Thanh Hai explains the Vietnamese perspective and notes that Vietnam is not about to surrender its own claims to the South China Sea. Vietnam may have lost the Paracels Islands to China, but it has the dominant position in the Spratly Islands, and a long history of resistance to China does not suggest a willingness to concede Chinese sovereignty in exchange for peaceful and untroubled relations with Bejing. As expected, Vietnam will be China's main obstacle in asserting primacy over the South China Sea, one that the Chinese habitually underestimate. Vietnam relies on effective occupation of features in the Spratly Islands and continues to insist on historical title to challenge the Chinese position in the Paracels. Nonetheless, China's expansive claims and its assertive actions in the area have made the Vietnamese leadership aware that international law and UNCLOS may serve as an effective defence. Vietnam has redefined its claims to make them more consistent with international law and UNCLOS by clarifying the limits of its EEZ and continental shelf as measured from its mainland baselines. It has accepted the prevailing view that the Spratly and Paracel Islands may not be able to generate full maritime zones, and has also recognised the right of innocent passage of foreign military vessels in its territorial sea.

The Philippines has borne the brunt of China's harassment tactics, first in regard to Mischief Reef in 1995, and then Scarborough Shoal in 2012, both of which have been lost as a result of Chinese occupation. China had targeted the Philippines for various reasons; one of which was that the Philippines, among the ASEAN claimants, has the weakest capability to defend its claim to part of the South China Sea. Another reason was that Philippine political leaders have vacillated over the issue, and at times have revealed little determination to defend their claim. President Fidel Ramos and his disgraced successor Josef Estrada vigorously supported the claim, but Gloria Arroyo-Macapagal was more interested in securing economic and trade benefits with China. Renato De Cruz Castro notes that Chinese pressure against the Philippines coincided with the election of Benigno Aquino III as President. Aquino differed from Arroyo-Macapagal and resisted Chinese pressure in a way that resulted in a two-month standoff between Philippine and Chinese civilian maritime vessels at Scarborough Shoal, beginning in April 2012. When the stand-off ended in June, the Chinese were left in possession of the Shoal and strung a chain across the entrance to prevent Philippine vessels from entering. In January 2013, the Philippines took the unprecedented step of appealing to an Arbitral Tribunal under UNCLOS to rule over its rights in its own EEZ, but China has refused to participate in the proceedings. De Cruz Castro regards the issue as a 'potential tinderbox'.

The Philippines had appealed to ASEAN to support its case both over the Mischief Reef and Scarborough Shoal issues, but has been disheartened by the lack of ASEAN interest. In many respects, ASEAN has been immobilised by the South China Sea dispute and, as Christopher Roberts has noted, ASEAN decision-making is based more on 'self-interest' than 'collective interest', particularly for those members that are politically and economically reliant on China. ASEAN disunity prevents a collective position on sovereignty so long as the ASEAN claimants continue to abide by consensus-based decision-making. ASEAN's non-claimants, Thailand, Singapore and Cambodia, have no interest in the dispute and resent Philippine efforts to obtain the collective support of the grouping. Malaysia, which is also a claimant in the South China Sea, disassociates itself from both Vietnam and the Philippines and pursues its own bandwagoning policy towards China, hoping, it seems, that protestations of friendship would offer protection against it. As Roberts observes, ASEAN can only agree on a Code of Conduct (CoC), which some members want legally binding, as the best that can be expected in managing relations with China over this issue. China has resisted the idea and continues to procrastinate, as a CoC would act as a constraint upon its actions and pressure tactics against the ASEAN claimants. China may agree to an emasculated CoC that would be a restatement of the earlier Declaration of Conduct of the Parties (DoC), providing few tangible constraints on its actions in the area. A CoC is unlikely in the way ASEAN expects, leading Roberts to propose the formation of a sub-ASEAN working group, or ASEAN-Xm, involving only the claimant states to discuss the issue. This may minimise the chance of disunity and increase the prospects of reaching a consensus.

Should ASEAN continue to struggle over this issue, it faces the very real prospect of division and fragmentation between those members that will gravitate towards China for political and economic reasons and those such as the Philippines that would reach out to the US. Would the US get involved should the stakes be raised? Ralf Emmers examines the Obama administration's 'pivot' strategy, or its effort at 'rebalancing' towards Asia, but he doubts that it has had much impact upon the South China Sea dispute. The US, he argues, has not provided the Philippines and Vietnam with the countervailing power to deter Chinese assertiveness, and cannot act as a balance against China in the way these claimants expect. Nonetheless, Ralf Emmers claims that the US rebalance and its focus on the South China Sea have contributed to the internationalisation of the issue, something that China wanted to avoid. The US has repeatedly raised the South China Sea issue at international forums, defending what it regards as the right of its naval and maritime surveillance vessels to use the area. The US has supported the CoC proposal, and has supported the resolution of the dispute based on the principles of international law. Ralf Emmers opines that in this way, the US has supported both the Philippines and Vietnam, and has, to some extent, undermined China's negotiation position internationally. How will the US react as China increases the pressure on the ASEAN claimants? The Americans will no doubt avoid any direct confrontation with China, and will support the ASEAN claimants in other ways. However, any perceived failure to support these claimants may hasten the tendency for ASEAN to accommodate China, Vietnam notwithstanding. From an Australian perspective, Michael Wesley considers the implications for Australia as a middle power on the sidelines of the dispute, and argues a case for greater Australian interest and involvement in the dispute. In any case, should the US become more directly involved, as a close ally Australia would most likely follow.

How can the dispute be resolved? Leszek Buszynski and Chris Roberts distinguish between stabilisation, which calls for measures to maintain the status quo and to prevent conflict, and resolution, which addresses the underlying cause of the dispute. Incidents involving maritime and naval vessels have occurred with greater frequency in recent years, and have stimulated fears of conflict and escalation. Stabilizing measures that could prevent conflict include the CoC or an agreement to avoid incidents at sea (INCSEA) that would involve China, the ASEAN claimants and the US. China, however, has shown little interest in such proposals. Its attitude may change, however, should it actually face a conflict that could threaten to escalate. Donald Rothwell stresses the importance of UNCLOS and international law for a resolution of the dispute or the ASEAN states in defending their maritime claims. He argues that there are three ways of examining the application of the Law of the Sea to the situation in the South China Sea. The first is through UNCLOS itself and how it can be interpreted consistently with treaty law. The second is through state practice and how that practice may have evolved since UNCLOS was concluded. The third way is through the jurisprudence of international courts and tribunals in interpreting UNCLOS and related provisions, particularly in the light of the 2012 ICJ decision in *Nicaragua v. Colombia*. In terms of legal adjudication, the Philippines' appeal to an arbitral tribunal under UNCLOS highlights the significance of the Law of the Sea as a means towards a resolution of the issue. In terms of the interpretation of UNCLOS provisions, it is becoming accepted that some South China Sea maritime features have a limited capacity to generate either an EEZ or a continental shelf. Even if those features could generate a maritime entitlement, their capacity to influence maritime boundaries between continental or mainland states may be limited. Rothwell argues that an understanding of the limited entitlement of these maritime features may bring the claimants to the realisation that there is little to be gained by insisting on their own claims. Much more could be obtained through a legal resolution of the issue, including a negotiated political agreement on maritime claims.

The volume concludes with a proposal for a resolution of the dispute. At some point in time, there should be a UN conference on the South China Sea to deal with the legality of the claims, as well as providing a basis for the cooperative management of the area in a maritime regime. A conference of this kind is required to bring UNCLOS to completion, particularly in relation to semi-enclosed seas where claims to islands are in dispute and where maritime zones overlap. It would give effect to Article 123 of UNCLOS, which enjoins states bordering an enclosed or semi-enclosed sea to 'co-operate with each other in the exercise of their rights and in the performance of their duties under this Convention'. The Article also calls upon these states to cooperate 'directly or through an appropriate regional organization'. China is likely to reject any such notion at the present time, and will insist on its 'indisputable sovereignty' over the area. However, there is an incentive for China to join this process of resolution in order to legalise its position in the South China Sea and stabilise the area without the prospect of raising tensions or increasing the risk of conflict with external powers. Repeated and mechanical assertions of 'indisputable sovereignty' will not provide China with a legal basis for its claim, nor compensate for the lack of persuasive evidence to support its historical claim. Nor can it legalise its position by resorting to harassment tactics or displays of military power to intimidate the ASEAN claimants. Through an international legal resolution of the issue under UN auspices, China would gain legal endorsement of a position in the South China Sea, which it would have to share with the ASEAN claimants in a cooperative maritime regime. China could gain considerable benefits in this way. It would strengthen its relationship with ASEAN, thus earning the gratitude of the organisation, while eliminating the possibility of conflict and escalation, which could involve external powers, and the US in particular.

Index